Interests and Power in Language Management

PRAGUE PAPERS ON LANGUAGE, SOCIETY AND INTERACTION

Edited by Jiří Nekvapil, Tamah Sherman and Petr Kaderka

VOLUME 6

PETER LANG

Marek Nekula / Tamah Sherman / Halina Zawiszová (eds.)

Interests and Power in Language Management

PETER LANG

Bibliographic Information published by the Deutsche Nationalbibliothek

The Deutsche Nationalbibliothek lists this publication in the Deutsche Nationalbibliografie; detailed bibliographic data is available online at http://dnb.d-nb.de.

Library of Congress Cataloging-in-Publication Data

A CIP catalog record for this book has been applied for at the Library of Congress.

The preparation of this book was partially financed within the statutory activity of the Czech Language Institute of the Czech Academy of Sciences (RVO No. 6837809). The print is covered by the University of Regensburg.

ISSN 1866-878X
ISBN 978-3-631-86061-8 (Print)
E-ISBN 978-3-631-86467-8 (E-Book)
E-ISBN 978-3-631-87081-5 (EPub)
DOI 10.3726/b19351

PETER LANG Open

Peter Lang – Berlin · Bern · Bruxelles · New York · Oxford · Warszawa · Wien

This publication has been peer reviewed.

www.peterlang.com

Contents

Contributors

Solvita Burr (née Pošeiko) is a senior researcher at the Latvian Language Institute of the University of Latvia and lecturer at the University of Washington (USA). Her research interests focus on the comprehensive study of cityscapes (linguistic, semiotic, cultural landscapes) in terms of multilingualism, language policy and language management, glocalization, and edusemiotics.

Email: solvita.burr@gmail.com

Vít Dovalil is an assistant professor at the Department of Germanic Studies, Charles University, Prague. He obtained his MA in German and Political Sciences at the Faculty of Arts, and in law at the Faculty of Law, Charles University, Prague. He earned his PhD in 2004. His research interests include language policy, language planning and management of multilingualism in the European Union. He also studies German as a foreign language in the Czech Republic as well as German grammar both from the structural and sociolinguistic perspective (processes of language standardization and destandardization).

E-mail: vit.dovalil@ff.cuni.cz

Lisa Fairbrother is a professor in the Department of English Studies at Sophia University, Tokyo, where she teaches sociolinguistics, intercultural interaction, TESOL and English. Her main research interests focus on language management in intercultural contact situations, particularly in the multilingual workplace, and during study abroad. She has also conducted research on native-speakerism and Japanese language education policy. Her research has been published in the *International Journal of the Sociology of Language*, the *Journal of Asian Pacific Communication* and the *Japanese Journal of Language and Society* and she is co-editor of *A Language Management Approach to Language Problems: Integrating Micro and Macro Dimensions* (John Benjamins) and *The Language Management Approach: A Focus on Research Methodology* (Peter Lang).

Email: l-fairbr@sophia.ac.jp

Björn Jernudd continues his search for solutions to describing and explaining language problems in the framework of Language Management Theory. He also works on describing the For language used among the For people in Darfur (the Land of the For in Sudan) and on organizing data once collected in 1968 in Papua New Guinea on the early organized development of Tok Pisin.

E-mail: jernudd@gmail.com

Chikako Ketcham is an adjunct lecturer at Sophia University and Musashino University Graduate School of Language and Culture, Tokyo, Japan, where she teaches Japanese in academic and business fields. Her research interests include Business

Japanese language education and evaluation of Oral Proficiency Interviews in Japanese.

E-mail: chikakoketcham@gmail.com

Goro Christoph Kimura, PhD, is professor at the Faculty of Foreign Studies, Sophia University, Tokyo. He specializes in sociolinguistics, especially focusing on the social functions of second and foreign languages, interlingual communication as well as the revival and revitalization of minority languages (in Europe and Japan). Recently he published the book *Igengokan komyunikesyon no hoho: baikaigengo o meguru giron to zissen* [Interlingual communication strategies: arguments and reality], Tokyo: Taishukan 2021.

E-mail: g-kimura@sophia.ac.jp

Nadiya Kiss is a postdoctoral researcher in Giessen Center for East European Studies (GiZO) in Justus Liebig University of Giessen, Germany. She received her Master of Arts in Comparative Literature at National University of Kyiv-Mohyla Academy, Ukraine and defended her PhD dissertation on Ukrainian juridicial terminology in Yurii Fed'kovych National Chernivtsi University, Ukraine. She is also the author of a book about rhetoric of Ukrainian Euromaidan protest. The main fields of her research interests are sociolinguistics, language policies in Ukraine and post-Soviet countries, protest rhetorics and the language biography method.

E-mail: Nadiya.Kiss@slavistik.uni-giessen.de

Jakub Kopecký is a researcher at the Czech Language Institute, Czech Academy of Sciences. He earned his M.A. and Ph.D. in Czech Language from Charles University, Prague. His research focuses on language management in the Czech Republic, argumentation in interaction, online communication and interdiscursivity in multimodal discourse.

E-mail: kopecky@ujc.cas.cz

Roland Marti is professor emeritus of Slavonic philology at Saarland University, Germany. He studied in Basel, where he obtained his academic degrees, and in Moscow. He has taught in Switzerland, Germany, France, and Ukraine. His areas of interest include historical philology (especially Old Church Slavonic), problems of written languages, minority languages (especially Lower and Upper Sorbian) and problems of their language management.

E-mail: rwmslav@mx.uni-saarland.de

Marek Nekula is professor of Czech and West Slavic Studies at University of Regensburg, Germany. He studied in Brno (CZ) and Berlin, where he obtained his academic degrees respectively. His linguistic areas of interest include Czech grammar, comparative linguistics and typology, (Czech-German) bilingualism and (historical) sociolinguistics including language policy, language planning and language management.

E-mail: marek.nekula@ur.de

Hiroyuki Nemoto is professor of Sociolinguistics at Ritsumeikan University, Japan. He received his Ph.D. from Monash University, Australia. His research interests lie in the area of sociolinguistics, including sociocultural approaches to SLA, intercultural interactions, identity transformation, translingual literacy, and language management.

E-mail: hnemoto@fc.ritsumei.ac.jp

Ben Ó Ceallaigh is a lecturer in Celtic Studies in Aberystwyth University in Wales. He has a degree in Politics, Sociology and Philosophy and a MA in Language Planning from the National University of Ireland, Galway, and a PhD from the University of Edinburgh. He has worked in a professional and voluntary capacity on language revitalization in Ireland and Scotland.

E-mail: benoceallaigh89@gmail.com

Stephanie Rudwick is a linguistic anthropologist employed in the Department of African Studies/Political Science at the University of Hradec Králové, Czech Republic. She is also an honorary researcher at the University of KwaZulu-Natal, South Africa where she also conducts most of her fieldwork. Her research focuses primarily on the sociocultural politics of language, race, ethnicity, and gender and she has published widely on these topics.

E-mail: stephanie.rudwick@uhk.cz

Tamah Sherman is a researcher at the Czech Language Institute, Czech Academy of Sciences, and an assistant professor at the Institute of General Linguistics, Charles University, Prague. Her research focuses on interaction and meta-linguistic behavior, using the framework of Language Management Theory, Ethnomethodology, and Conversation Analysis. The particular focus of her investigation is on situations of multiple language use in the Czech Republic after 1989.

E-mail: tamah.sherman@ff.cuni.cz

Petar Vuković is a professor at the Department of West Slavic Languages and Literatures, University of Zagreb, where he teaches Czech linguistics. His research focuses on sociolinguistics and language standardization.

E-mail: petar.vukovic@ffzg.hr

Halina Zawiszová is an assistant professor at the Department of Asian Studies at Palacký University Olomouc. Her main research foci revolve around topics related to emotion, language, and social interaction. She is also interested in management of foreign languages and social identities at different levels of organization.

E-mail: halina.zawiszova@upol.cz

Acknowledgments

The creation of any book is a long process. This was also the case with our volume. Along the way, we have experienced a wide range of assistance. For this, we would like to thank those who have contributed to and supported the creation of this book.

The road to this book began with the symposium of the same name, *Interests and Power in Language Management*, the fifth in the series of international language management symposia. This symposium took place in September 2017 at the University of Regensburg. The realization of the symposium would not have been possible without the work of the scientific committee and local organizing committee. At minimum, we would like to thank Jiří Nekvapil and Marián Sloboda, whose experience and ideas helped the symposium to succeed. However, we would also like to thank all of the numerous participants who, in the discussion, further developed the questions raised by this symposium. Their lively engagement served as encouragement for us to tackle the volume as well.

On the main road to the actual realization of the volume, we were able to rely on many helpers who, however, cannot be named, as is required in an anonymous peer-review process. The gratitude due to them for their unselfish help, without which such a publication could not be produced, is not diminished by this—rather the opposite. We would also like to thank the student assistants who supported us in the formal review of the accepted contributions. Tabea Knüppe is mentioned here as a representative. Above all, we would like to thank the authors for their active cooperation in the creation of the volume, as well as for their understanding that the creation process lasted somewhat longer than we thought at the beginning.

Last but not least, we would like to thank Jiří Nekvapil as one of the editors of the series in which this volume appears who accompanied and encouraged us along the way and who also did the final reading of the book. We would also like to thank Björn Hansen and Paul Rössler from the University of Regensburg, who supported us in finding funding for the volume and its open access publication.

The editors

Introduction

Marek Nekula / Tamah Sherman / Halina Zawiszová

Exploring interests and power in language management

1 Introductory remarks

This volume continues in the tradition of volumes and special journal issues exploring the language management (LM) framework with a focus on one of its specific aspects or broader themes. In the first of these, a special issue of the *Journal of Asian Pacific Communication* (Marriott & Nekvapil 2012), the emphasis was placed on the first phase of the LM process, noting. Most recently, volumes have been published devoted to methodology in LM research (Fairbrother, Nekvapil & Sloboda 2018) and the interaction of micro and macro perspectives in LM (Kimura & Fairbrother 2020). As can be observed, multiple steps have been taken toward a comprehensive picture of LM, but the future leads in many more thus far insufficiently explored directions. Interestingly, moving along these paths involves going back to the beginnings of both Language Management Theory (LMT) and Language Planning and Policy (LPP) and examining the degree to which individual aims, topics and perspectives in selected original programs have been fulfilled.

Interests and power, the themes selected for the present volume, have been long acknowledged as important factors in various approaches in LPP. Despite this fact, it is not an exaggeration to claim that very little focused attention has been devoted to them compared to other factors such as motivation or goals of LPP. In LM, with its focus on noted deviations from norms, the evaluations of those deviations, and the design and implementation of adjustments, it can be, however, argued that interests and power are in fact the driving forces, observable and describable at every step of the process. The interests can be seen as a background for established norms and norms that emerge through simple and especially organized LM, and power may determine their reach in the process in LM. In fact, the seminal LM text from Björn H. Jernudd and Jiří V. Neustupný (1987) discusses this point extensively.

In order to show the importance of interests and power for LM, we first must have a look at how these concepts have thus far been understood. As the texts in this volume reveal, both are seen as something somehow possessed (or lacked) by social actors, power is acquired (or lost), someone may be in a "position of power," or we can talk about "power dynamics," "power balances" and "imbalances" or "hierarchies," while interests are "declared," "negotiated," "pursued," or "achieved." On the other hand, languages or other non-human entities or concepts can also have or give power, but not interests and intentions.

2 Interests

Interests can be viewed as dispositions perceived as positive or beneficial for individuals, groups, institutions, and the like. They can take the form of internal psychological entities such as desires or needs, or be more explicit, aware, or declared, such as ambitions, aims, ends, or goals. They may be personal, political, ideological, material, or otherwise. We can illustrate this with the example of an act of LM: learning a specific language. It may serve one's personal interests if the language is used in a (mixed) family, one's political interests if the acquisition of majority and minority language is legally regulated, one's ideological interests if the ethnic identity is respected, or one's material interests if it is instrumental in finding employment.

Jiří V. Neustupný has defined interests as "aspirations for a certain state of affairs that is favourable to the subject" (Neustupný 2002: 3). And in their seminal 1987 text, a reaction to Brian Weinstein's (1987) exposition on the role of interests in language planning, Jernudd and Neustupný discuss how varied this "subject" can be, pointing out that there is often no set of universal interests that can be associated with an individual society or community. Individual interests may vary within a single community, and the collective interests of different communities may vary greatly or even stand in opposition or conflict to one another.

There are many examples of such language conflicts between linguistic communities within a society (for example between Walloons and Flemish in Belgium, Catalonians and Spaniards in Spain or Czechs and Germans in the Czech Lands) in which linguistic and non-linguistic interests are combined. In language conflicts, the suppression of linguistic interests of a minority or dominated community to communicate in their language may stem from the linguistic, social, and economic interests of a majority or ruling community which are also realized through the control of communicative domains. On the one hand, the communicative norms based on the differing status of respective languages seem to have to do with interests and power of the linguistic majority or dominant community and with powerlessness of linguistic minority or dominated community, as described in classical theories of nation building and LPP (Hroch 2015; Haugen 1966). On the other hand, we have to deal with the enforcement of non-linguistic (social and economic) interests of a social group within a minority or dominated community by combining them argumentatively with the linguistic interests of the whole linguistic minority or dominated linguistic community. This is one way of mobilizing the members of such communities in order to gain power in the fight against the imagined linguistic (and social) suppression, as constructivist theories of nation building and "imagined communities" suggest (Gellner 1983; Anderson 1991). They even contest the "imagined non-communities" to save the interests of children educated outside of their linguistic community (Zahra 2010). These "monolingual" linguistic communities and their interests are the result of the narration of "many as one" (Bhabha 2008 [1990]: 202).

Interests can be observed at various stages of the LM process. Foreign accents and learner varieties in the public domain, on the one hand, or the absence of a foreign variety understood as a necessary part of the repertoire of elites (in Central Europe Latin, later German, and now English), on the other hand, can be *noted* (and *evaluated*) by the members of the majority or by elites (Jernudd & Neustupný 1987: 78 f.) to promote their non-linguistic (social, economic) interests—to delimit and to control public and elite domains linguistically. At the stage of *adjustment design* and its *implementation*, the interests behind the norms mentioned above ("native" standard of majority language; knowledge of selected foreign language(s)), are implemented by the school that qualifies for the public sphere (standard needed in the legal system, authorities, education, media) and specific elite domains (English needed in international trade, economy, diplomacy, research) as well as by (language) certificates needed for job or residency applications. It is quite similar to the process of standardization of a language that can be seen as a result of a language planning process with respect to the educated variety whereas territorial and uncultivated social dialects were excluded. This enables the educated (bourgeois) middle classes of a linguistic community to use their cultivated code unfamiliar to other classes and, in this way, to realize their material and social interests—to delimit and control social resources as well as the transfer of knowledge within a linguistic community (Linke 1996).

In his paper on desegregation of the American education system by the act from 1954, Derrick Bell (1980) shows, however, that the interests of social groups need not be only in conflict but can also go together. The change in the American education system started with desegregation, of course, can be interpreted in different ways. On the one hand, the interests of black Americans in obtaining (more) equality in education seem to be enforced against the interests of the white middle classes. With respect to changing social settings inside and outside of America, Bell on the other hand sees the desegregation of the education system as the result of a "convergence" of interests. This change in the American education system then made America more credible, both internally for (black) veterans fighting in World War II for freedom and equality and externally, for the people of the third world where the US was in competition with the Soviet Union. Bell also interprets this change as a chance for industrialization of the southern states. In this sense, the act from 1954 was passed in the interest of white middle classes. There are social, political, and economic interests behind the act that opened the door for the implementation of norms of social equality in the American education system.

Of course, we can view the concept of interest convergence more generally and apply it also to language issues and LPP. The *European Charter for Regional or Minority Languages*, adopted as a convention on June 25, 1992 by the Committee of Ministers of the Council of Europe and entered into force on March 1, 1998, can then be interpreted in a similar way. The *Charter* helps to satisfy the linguistic interests of autochthonous minorities within the European nation-states. At the same time, it also legally solidifies the hierarchy of majority and minority languages and supports the social, political, and economic interests of majorities within the European nation-states by stabilizing them internally as democratic and giving them (and the EU, which adopts these principles) democratic authority externally—in the international context. Against the background of linguistic and non-linguistic conflicts in the post-Yugoslav and post-Soviet territories in the early 1990s, the EU seems to be a haven of stability also from the linguistic point of view although some states—like Greece, Bulgaria, Lithuania, and Latvia—have not signed it to avoid commitments to their minorities. The *Charter* is, however, without sanctions and is intended to protect only the autochthonous minority languages (cf. Raos 2015). The interests of allochthonous minorities (i.e., new migrant groups), which may be similar to the linguistic and social interests of autochthonous minorities, are not involved in the *Charter*. This is because the satisfaction of the interests of the allochthonous minorities would probably be economically more expensive and socially more complex and likely connected with a loss of full control over the communication in the public space, which the majority in the nation-states is interested in and why the majority language is presented as more important than the minority one. Both types of minorities seem to accept these language ideologies and the majority language as necessary social capital and learn it to satisfy their material interests. To promote and to realize such linguistic and social interests, linguistic communities seem to need power.

3 Power

There are many concepts of power discussed with respect to and applied in the analysis of LPP as well as interaction and discourse. Antonio Gramsci and Louis Althusser, for example, investigated the mechanism of "cultural hegemony" moderated by institutions such as churches or schools that appeal to individuals who voluntarily submit themselves—linguistically to the standard or to the majority language—in hope for social advancement (see Busch 2017: 92 f.). Michel Foucault discussed the "dispositive of power" based on institutional mechanisms and knowledge structures established in and controlled by (public) discourse (Foucault 1984: 109) which has to do not only with its categories but also with varieties and language choice. Norman Fairclough (1989) analyzed the power behind a (public) discourse and exercised in and performed through it. In this sense, the public discourse on allochthonous and autochthonous minorities enables or now allows the (limited) public use of the autochthonous minority language but not of the allochthonous minority language. This, of course, reflects the power distribution in a society. Pierre Bourdieu (1991) explained the relationship between language and power through the concept of "social capital," accumulated by a language within a "social field," that differs from the social capital of other languages in the "language market." In the linguistic exchange, "the power relations between speakers [of these languages] or their respective groups are actualized" symbolically (Bourdieu 1991: 37). Florian Coulmas (2005) discussed language(s) and (their differing) power with respect to a "language regime" based on legal acts and language ideologies that limit speakers in their language use with respect to space established socially and/or territorially. This concept seems to apply to both monolingual and multilingual regimes.

In research on LM, reference is made most frequently to Neustupný's definition of power as "the capacity to realize one's interests" (Neustupný 2002: 4), which more or less corresponds to the understanding of social and economic power of individuals and groups typical for many fields. The power then can be exercised, for example, by a teacher controlling the interaction and giving permission to a specific student to speak on the micro level as well as by institutions authorized by the majority that decide which language will be used as language of instruction and taught as subject on the macro level. In a later text, Neustupný talks about power as the object of management and uses the term "behavior-toward-power" (Neustupný 2004: 3). The power that he sees behind the establishment and dissolution of (linguistic and communicative) norms can be then noted and evaluated with respect to these norms and adjustments can be designed and implemented in this way as well. The linguistic and communicative norms can thus be strengthened or weakened based on the ways in which they are used to realize individual or group interests. Within LM, the power is established and questioned through choice and use, the image and proficiency of varieties and languages as well as images of language communities or territories. In this sense, the "behavior-toward-power" is realized as "behavior-toward-language."

In one case study, Neustupný (2004) specifically explores the process of assimilation of university students from abroad in Japan. Here, language acquisition is connected with power. On the one hand with the empowerment of the students learning Japanese, in which the "competence to communicate to fulfil [...] personal interests" is achieved, and on the other hand with disempowerment of these very same students, when individuals and groups subordinate linguistically (Neustupný 2004: 5). This subordination satisfies the interests of the majority or dominant group within a given context. These two phenomena then come together. In another example, wives of Japanese employees recruited in East Asian countries are, on the one hand, disempowered by having to learn the language of their Japanese husbands, but on the other hand they are empowered by successfully satisfying their needs and interests by learning Japanese.

In extension to Steven Lukes's distinction of "five types of power: coercion, influence, authority, force and manipulation" (Neustupný 2004: 6), Neustupný further suggests other types of power, such as status, prestige, and domination. He imagines "domination based on the norm that participants who are coerced to assimilate; the same is true of those who are influenced, possess lower authority, are affected by force, or are manipulated" (Neustupný 2004: 6). This applies not only for minority languages but also for the language of social groups like non-experts, children, etc.

There have been a number of studies in which power has been discussed in relation to LM as well as to LMT. Within this theoretical frame, Tamah Sherman (2009) discusses the choice of language as the struggle for power in intercultural situations, whereas Jiří Nekvapil and Sherman (2013) show the impact of power on language ideologies supporting the non-acquisition of local language by actors with power on the one hand and the acquisition of dominant—glocal or global languages like German or English—by actors that are interested in achieving greater power in the diglossic settings of multilingual companies in Central Europe on the other hand. The first group is empowered in this way to control the communication on the level of top management but disempowered with respect to communication on the production level. The second group is disempowered in the communication on the level of top management but empowered with respect to communication with the production level. The enforcement of interests may also block other interests.

Likewise, Lisa Fairbrother (2015) analyzes the role of power established and resisted in LM activities at the micro level. In her study, she views the power based in linguistic and ethnic identity on the one hand, and on the other hand, she quotes Foucault and Sara Mills and emphasizes the "fluid" character of power "negotiated through interaction," in which "everyone can be both powerful and powerless" (Fairbrother 2015: 60). Based on "language management summaries" in semi-structured interviews with plurilingual residents in Japan, the author analyzes specific situations in which the choice of and proficiency in Japanese "reinforce social hierarchy, transmit ideology and maintain the authority of institutions" or individuals (Fairbrother 2015: 59), whereas the declared ignorance of Japanese—at least by actors with a Caucasian, not Asian appearance who are not expected to master Japanese—helps to resist the power of Japanese communicative norms by switching to contact norms. This strategy helps to realize individual actors' interests.

Junko Saruhashi (2018), however, shows long-term perspectives relevant for personal empowerment of various actors. Marián Sloboda (2020: 19) explores empowerment within the Vietnamese minority in the Czech Republic. He shows that the "communication in Vietnamese enabled the Vietnamese entrepreneurs to continue their businesses," but this practice at the same time does not encourage them "to acquire Czech or other language skills which would pay off in the long run." The consequence is their disempowerment: they remain dependent on providers of products and services available in Vietnamese. In this case, there is a conflict between the interests of different actors as well as between the interests within the same (group of) actor (s). Stephanie Rudwick (2018) focuses on the power of languages that are connected with specific actors. Afrikaans seems to be disempowered by the use limited to South Africa and specifically by the legacy of apartheid implicating problematic constellations between actors with and without power, whereas English is empowered by the expectations of actors to satisfy the interests of their social elevation and global action. English also profits from not being bound to an ethnic identity like Afrikaans.

All these papers demonstrate the impact of agencies in LM activities in different directions and on different levels. This impact has also been observed in the general LPP literature. Richard B. Baldauf (2006) presented an overview of shifting tendencies in the study of language planning (in which he also included LM), moving from the exclusive macro focus on the activities of polities or large organizations to the meso and micro levels, or even to the interaction between these levels. Within this shift, contexts, actors, and agency in language planning activities were posited as a new nexus from which to view these activities. There have been many applications of Baldauf's conception, including that of Ben Fenton-Smith and Laura Gurney (2016), who examine language policy in regard to academic language and learning at Australian universities. They also empirically elaborate the classification of four types of power related to actors with power, with expertise, with influence, and with interest introduced by Shouhui Zhao (2011) and applied in this volume by Vít Dovalil. Fenton-Smith and Gurney (2016: 74) work with these agencies in relation to "the various levels and forms of power invested in the range of actors involved in policy and planning." They conclude that "people with expertise" and "people with interests" do not have the same position in academic language planning as "people with power" and "people with influence" (Fenton-Smith and Gurney 2016: 74). However, it should be pointed out that these authors, citing Zhao and Baldauf (2012), view people with interests (in this case, primarily students) as people who have *only* interests, that is, who do not have power, influence, or expertise.

There are, of course, also other possibilities for the examination of the interrelations between power and agency. For the specific purpose of negotiation of the standard variety, Ulrich Ammon (2005: 33) models a social power field in which four instances are involved in the negotiation of the standard variety: norm authorities, language experts, codifiers, and their manuals as well as exemplary texts produced by exemplary authors and speakers. This can be applied not only for the elaboration of the standard variety within the organized LM but also for the production of a specific standard text within the simple LM. Robert L. Cooper (1989) distinguished in general between formal elites, influentials, and authorities and mentioned the possibility of overlap between these categories. He traditionally connected the power with the top-down direction. He did not categorize the actors authorized by interests and expertise, who can unfold the power in the bottom-up direction, within the power frame. However, they can also be successful, as illustrated by the examples discussed in the various texts in this volume.

4 Interests and power in LM

As mentioned above, it cannot be stated that interests and power have never been important for LMT. Its foundational paper, published by Jernudd and Neustupný in 1987, entitled "Language planning: For whom?," was devoted predominantly to the issue of interests. Even the question "for whom?" in the title indicates the primary position of interests in interventions into language. The authors stress the need to examine the interests involved in each phase of the LM process, and distinguish between linguistic interests (based on perceived communicative needs) and non-linguistic (social and economic) interests. In one of the first volumes organized to combine the work of the Japanese, Australian, and Central European schools of LM (Nekvapil & Sherman 2009), the position of power in LM was stressed in the texts coming out of the Central European School (see in particular Sloboda 2009; Sherman 2009; Lanstyák & Szabómihály 2009). Our aim in this volume, then, is to focus on both interests and power in their interplay as well as to discuss their role and use within the process of the simple and organized LM on both the micro and the macro level.

At first glance, we can observe that both interests and power are present in and guide or underlie the character of all phases of the LM procedure (i.e., noting, evaluation, adjustment design, implementation, and feedback). First of all, it is clearly observable that interests and power influence *what is noted*. This is related to the question of norm creation, expansion, and maintenance, for example, in the management of standard language varieties. Noting deviations from the standard variety in the classroom, for example, may be part of the job description of the teachers in public schools, who identify colloquial, dialect, and "non-native" variants and varieties that deviate from the standard. The teachers are authorized for this job by both their institutionally approved education and expertise as well as their role in the school system. The school is responsible for the acquisition of standard by the linguistic academy. The academy is responsible for standardization established for the standardization of public communication in whose effectivity the institutional authorities are interested in. This also has a social and economic effect. To guarantee the implementation of these interests of a linguistic community, both give them the power to influence pupils' grades, and ultimately, their future paths in public life that has to do with their material interests. In order to realize their individual interests, the pupils submit to the teachers and acquisition of the (foreign) standard. They later become empowered by their previous disempowerment. That is why they and their parents also accept further steps of the LM oriented to the acquisition of the standard variety on the micro level of a school and an interaction as well as on the macro level of the school system and authorities responsible for standardization (on standard variety as process and product of LM cf. Dovalil 2013).

Evaluation is not only closely connected with noting in LM, but a positive or negative evaluation genuinely has to do with interests as explained above. The positive or negative evaluation implies a specific perspective: some linguistic phenomena or language choices are denied, while others are considered welcome, suitable, appropriate, or even desirable. In some institutional situations, such as in the classroom or among professional language managers (editors, consultants, etc.), the noting and evaluation of style or non-standard are guided by the interests of the given institution such as public schools or media that authorize schools and other actors with expertise for evaluation as well, whereas actors whose activities are the objects of this evaluation rather note and evaluate this institutional noting and evaluation without the power to defend themselves against it. There are of course also other examples of the interplay between interests and power. For example, Czech used in a memorandum addressed from Czech representatives of a Bohemian corporation to the ministry in Vienna before 1918 (see Nekula 2003: 169) not only was noted but also was evaluated negatively by the addressees.

The switch from German to Czech was a clear deviation from the norm of standardized communication between center and periphery based on and perpetuating the linguistic interest of a simple, reliable, and effective communication within a multilingual society. These interests went hand in hand with the non-linguistic interest of a unified state represented by central institutions in Vienna. In this case, the negative evaluation of this deviation is undertaken from the "power side" but there is of course also a positive evaluation of this deviation by the Czech representatives of the Bohemian corporation, albeit without the power to establish a new communicative norm before 1918 which would correspond with their interests for more autonomy and participation. The deliberate deviation from the existing norm, however, can be seen as a negative evaluation of the existing norm by replacing it with an alternative (subversive) language practice.

Adjustment design in LM follows along the line of the interests and power mentioned above. Adjustments are adhered to and taken as legitimate depending on who designs and refers to them. This applies for standard and non- or substandard in general, as implied already in terminology, as well as for orthography reforms specifically, that both are designed by and refer to language experts and language institutions as actors with expertise and power. These can argue for and legitimate orthography reform linguistically by declared modernization of spoken language or rationality of language system, based in and acceptable with respect to linguistic interests of language experts as actors with expertise, whereas non-linguistic opponents of orthographic reforms do not need to listen to these arguments and can argue and legitimate their opposition non-linguistically, based on cultural tradition and identity, the need for democratic participation in language issues as well as economic issues. Such opposing arguments, based on non-linguistic interests, can even weaken an orthographic reform designed by actors with expertise before this can be implemented, if actors with influence such as editors of media are involved and support other actors with (non-linguistic) interests and convince the actors with power. This happened, for example, as amendments of the Czech orthography reform from 1993 were adopted by the Czech Minister of Education. The minister, interested in support by the media and public in the next election, then suspended parts of the Czech orthography reform from 1993 (see Bermel 2007 for more details).

The actors with power can even deny an orthography reform, as exemplified by rejection of the Slovak orthography from 1931 designed by actors with expertise, who were close to the ideology of Czechoslovakism bridging the differences between Czech and Slovak, because their linguistic and other interests differed from the interests of Slovak actors with interests and/or power, who could not identify with the Czechoslovak ideology. However, there also was a remarkable difference between actors with expertise with respect to their linguistic and non-linguistic interests. As Roland Marti (1993) shows, whereas "unionists," interested in the linguistic unity of the emerging Czechoslovak state, preferred to see Czech and Slovak as variants of the "Czechoslovak" state language and were open for convergence in orthography of both languages to enable communication within the state common to Czechs and Slovaks, "separatists" were interested in maintaining the difference of Czech and Slovak orthography. In the orthography commission organized by Matica slovenská (Slovak Foundation) that prepared the 1931 Slovak orthography reform supervised by the young Czech linguist Václav Vážný (1892–1966), the "unionist" actors with expertise could push through. However, the reform could not be fully implemented during the 1930s, as discussed below.

Similar "unionist" and "separatist" arguments were also discussed with respect to adjustments of local standard variants of British vs. American English or of "Binnendeutsch" (Core German) vs. Austrian German. This "unification" also plays a role in the simple LM. Preparing his books for publication in Leipzig in the German Empire, Franz Kafka (1883–1924) tried to support the reception of his book by a broad German public by avoiding Prague and Austrian variants of German and by preferring variants used in the German Empire with respect to codification in German manuals of codification as well as with respect to his norm authorities (see Blahak 2015; Nekula 2016 for more details). This individual disempowerment, a kind of pre-interaction management, was intended as empowerment of his texts in the public sphere.

Coming back to the example of minority languages, we can see that the adjustments depend on context and that experts' adjustments are not listened to and taken as legitimate in the same way in different contexts. With respect to linguistic and non-linguistic interests of speakers of autochthonous minority languages, the *European Charter for Regional or Minority Languages* (1992) argues for education and participation in the minority language not only as a way to maintain language, culture and identity of a minority, but also to guarantee the healthy development of the next generation and the fair democratic participation of minorities and their members in societal issues. These adjustments are not made by experts or rather not listened to by political representations if allochthonous minorities are addressed because of political, economic, and cultural interests of majorities that provide and control political and cultural institutions and economic resources. Because the implementation of these adjustments probably would be too expensive and could lead to the disintegration of communication, the actors with power representing the majority as actors with interests take advantage of their capacity to realize their interests and to prevent other interests.

The *implementation* of an adjustment within LM is closely connected with its design. Adjustments designed by actors with interest but without power, expertise and influence (cf. Zhao 2011: 910) will be hardly considered, let alone implemented. This can change when the adjustment is adopted by actors with influence (or power), such as in the LM for more gender equality or the identity politics expressed by choosing gender and identity sensitive language categories. They can have capacity to realize their interests in spite of the position of actors with expertise arguing, for example, based on the neutrality of generic masculinum, limits of gender-sensitive language use inherent to flexive languages, and uneconomic character of gender-sensitive language use.

Coming back to Bell's example for the concept of "convergence" of interests, the adjustments for maintenance of minority languages designed by activists of autochthonous minorities, that is, actors with interests, will be implemented on the national level if the actors with power are interested in doing so, to legitimize themselves inside and outside as democratic. This symbolic capital makes them able to prevent the implementation of the same adjustments for allochthonous minorities. With respect to the *European Charter for Regional or Minority Languages* (1992), however, the authorities of participating nation-states decide themselves which autochthonous minority language(s) will be protected and how. Supported by actors with expertise, they also decide what is a language and what is a dialect and which adjustments will be implemented. They can also restrict the adjustments territorially according to their political and economic capacities and interests. Then, the *Charter* does not contain any possibility of enforcing the rights of minority languages at the European level. The implementation of the *Charter*, of course, also can be expanded by actors with power in reaction to critique of actors with influence or expertise, as explored in this volume by Dovalil, as well as restricted by actors with power, as discussed in this volume by Ben Ó Ceallaigh. They also were not implemented in nation-states that deliberately did not sign the *Charter*.

The questions of who has the capacity to realize one's interests in this phase of LM process, that is, who decides whether an adjustment is implemented, who chooses the implementation actors and who decides which adjustments are implemented for whom and how, can of course be seen in other areas of language use as well. With respect to the Czech orthography reform of the 1990s, for example, we can see that its opponents, who were the actors with interests in this case, had—supported by actors with influence and some actors with expertise—the capacity to influence the responsible ministry as the most prominent actor with power and in this way to restrict the proposed adjustments to some extent and protect their linguistic and non-linguistic interests by using the old doublets (connected with rejection of acquisition of new orthographic norms argued as preservation of cultural identity). They nevertheless did not have the capacity to prevent the implementation of the orthography reform by actors of power through the school system educating the next generation of users of Czech that prefer to acquire the progressive doublet forms.

Similar questions also apply to a proposed fifth phase of LM process, that is, the feedback or post-implementation stage, that Kimura (2014, 2020) suggests in general: Who evaluates the implementation as successful or not? And who is authorized to do so, that is, to decide about the finish or restart of the LM process? This is what happened with the Slovak orthography reform of 1931. The Slovak public (actors with interests), the actors with influence as well as the "separatists" with expertise around the Slovak journal *Slovenská reč* (Slovak Language) noted and evaluated the results of this reform negatively. This is why a new Slovak orthography reform was expected and undertaken later. This reform was meant to be based both in the linguistic interests (communicative needs based in continuity with the previously used orthography) and in non-linguistic ones (ethnic identity). The Czech linguists were disqualified from this endeavor by actors with power: Vážný was suspended as professor of the university in Bratislava at the end of 1938 and repatriated back to Prague. The later reforms of Slovak orthography and LM activities with respect to Slovak vocabulary enlarged rather than only maintained the linguistic distance between Czech and Slovak by invoking the interests of an imagined Slovak language community constructed in the public discourse as one. Similar processes can be seen, for example, in connection with the elaboration of national languages as a part of the nation building in the post-Yugoslavian territories discussed in this volume by Petar Vuković.

5 The contents of this volume

This volume consists of thirteen chapters divided into three parts and an epilogue. The three parts are entitled: *Language ideologies*, *Minority languages and minoritized languages*, and *Foreign language policies, teaching and learning, and use*. The topics of these three parts emerged organically in the process of preparing this volume but also represent the key issues that are repeatedly addressed when interests and power in LM become the foci of scholarly investigation. The majority of the chapters were presented at the symposium *Interests and Power in Language Management* hosted by the University of Regensburg in 2017. They make use of LMT, but other analytical tools, models, and methods are also adopted. The individual chapters work with highly diverse types of data and concern a variety of languages, areas, institutions, and polities. They approach the theme of this volume from a range of different angles and perspectives, thereby collectively developing our understanding of the role of interests and power in LM.

Language ideologies form an essential, albeit often ignored or backgrounded component of LM, which is in more or less explicit ways present in all the chapters of this volume. Four chapters that deal with the questions related to language ideologies most overtly are included in the first part of the volume, entitled *Language ideologies*.

The first chapter is of a more general and theoretical nature and, as such, contributes to the general discussion presented above. Penned by *Goro Kimura*, it offers an overview of the ways in which interests and power have been approached in LMT thus far and advocates for the notion of language ideology to be fully incorporated into the theory, arguing that it forms a vital part of LM processes both at the macro and micro level. Kimura suggests that language ideology reflects interests and constitutes a resource for power negotiation, and hence, may serve as a conceptual framework that allows us to study the metalinguistic environment of LM processes. So far, language ideology has typically been associated with the macro level. Therefore, in order to illustrate how language ideology operates at the micro level in relation to interests and power, the chapter presents a case study of the language maintenance of Sorbian in Lusatia, a region in Eastern Germany.

The remaining three chapters that constitute the first part of this book represent case studies of LM taking place at specific institutions. *Petar Vuković* draws on LMT in his analysis of the work of the Council for the Standard Croatian Language Norm. Established in 2005, the Council was disbanded only seven years later, following strong criticism coming from both experts and the general public alike. The author explains the Council's lack of power to influence the actual language use by pointing out its disregard for simple LM and narrow focus on the organized LM, without taking into account the ideological stances of its members or interests of the language users.

The chapter by *Jakub Kopecký* presents the results of an analysis of the argumentation used in language consulting telephone interactions between language users and language experts from the Language Consulting Center of the Czech Language Institute of the Czech Academy of Sciences. Drawing on LMT, Kopecký focuses on the cases of disagreement and conflict, uncovering the underlying language ideologies and divergent interests of the parties involved in the interactions as well as the methods in which they resolve their disputes, all the while negotiating their power relations, especially the Center's authority.

The first part concludes with the chapter by *Stephanie Rudwick* in which the author applies LMT to investigate the interplay of interests and power in language policy discussions and changes at Stellenbosch University in South Africa. Rudwick analyzes the University's highly polarizing and conflict-riddled language politics, concentrating on the discourses and the underlying language ideologies related to the role of English, a widely desired academic lingua franca, as opposed to Afrikaans, which used to serve as the primary language of teaching and learning at the University. The case is particularly worthy of consideration because, as the author points out, it represents a successful example of bottom-up LM.

Focusing on diverse interests and power relations of various actors involved primarily in different stages of organized LM, the four chapters comprising the second part of this volume, entitled *Minority languages and minoritized languages*, deal with complex issues concerning minority languages or minoritized languages in different language polities in Central, Western, and Eastern Europe.

The chapter by *Roland Marti* complements the chapter by Kimura, as it details the history and discusses the present state of LM of Lower Sorbian, a severely endangered minority language in Eastern Germany, vis-à-vis Upper Sorbian, and German, the majority language. In particular, Marti focuses on organized LM of Lower Sorbian, initiated by the Upper Sorbian institutions, as well as on the impact of this top-down LM on the LM of Lower Sorbian on part of its speakers, explaining that Lower Sorbian has gone through the same stages of development as numerous other minority languages.

In the next chapter, *Ben Ó Ceallaigh* considers the impact of macro-level economic developments on Irish language policy between the years 2008 (marked by the international economic crash and the beginning of the Great Recession) and 2018. Based on policy analyses and ethnographic research in Gaeltacht (primarily Irish-speaking) communities, the author discusses the influence of economic forces on Irish language vitality, demonstrating the detrimental impact that recent disruptions have had on these areas, including increased unemployment and out-migration. Also examined are the effects of post-2008 austerity measures on organized LM in Ireland and the substantial decrease in state support for the language. It is argued that neoliberalism, the economic hegemony of the last several decades, inherently conflicts with language revitalization.

Nadiya Kiss's chapter introduces the key actors in organized LM in contemporary Ukraine, the power relations that hold between them, and the varied interests that motivate them. Making use of a range of materials, Kiss provides an overview of language policy discussions and changes with regard to the use of Ukrainian and Russian in different domains of public life from the Euromaidan period up till the most recent developments. The ongoing trend towards Ukrainization is shown as closely connected to the socio-political situation in the country and the related changes in language attitudes and language use. Concurrently, it is also linked to the emergence of new problems related to the linguistic rights and needs of the national minorities in Ukraine.

In the closing chapter of the second part of this volume, *Solvita Burr* allows the reader to gain an insight into the language ideologies as well as interests and power relations of individual actors who have played a role in an unresolved dispute over language use on house number signs in Latvia. Framing the issue in terms of LMT, Burr examines the multi-level LM cycles involved in the case of a trilingual house number sign and the related discussions on language use in Latvian linguistic landscape, pointing out that it is possible to distinguish two main interest groups participating in these metalinguistic activities, namely, those that are guided by nationalistic language ideology and those that advocate for the rights of language minority groups.

The third part of the volume, entitled *Foreign language policies, teaching and learning, and use*, considers the management of languages which, in the context of their examination, are regarded as foreign. The four chapters that make up this part bring together the general theme of this volume and such topics as language policies, language teaching, language learning, and language use.

Lisa Fairbrother makes use of LMT in order to explore the intricate web of variously overlapping and intersecting LM processes occurring at different stages of development of the 'Teaching/Learning English in English' policy for high schools in Japan. Fairbrother uncovers the complex interplay of a variety of pedagogical, political, and economic interests as well as power relations between different agents and actors, as they manifest themselves at each stage of the policy-making process from the initial conceptualization of the policy all the way to the post-implementation evaluation. The author points out that the formulation of the policy offers substantial leeway regarding its interpretation, which, in turn, allows the variegated interests of the multiple agents and actors concerned to be met all the while slowly changing the English language high school education in Japan in the intended direction.

The study by *Hiroyuki Nemoto* adopts a mixed methods approach to find out about Japanese university students' investment in the management of their interests and power relations with a view to developing literacy and negotiating identities throughout the translingual processes of their (re-)socialization into academic and social contexts during and after study abroad. Nemoto applies LMT to explicate the correlations between the students' transcultural and translingual development of literacy and identities; their negotiations of both linguistic and non-linguistic interests and social positionings in their individual networks of practice and communities of practice; and their engagement in multidirectional and contextually situated practices through their socialization into the study abroad and the post-study abroad contexts.

The ensuing chapter is closely related to the chapters included in the second part of the volume, dealing with minority languages and minoritized languages. *Vít Dovalil* examines the interests and power relations of institutional social actors that partake in the metalinguistic discourses regarding the position of German in the Czech Republic at the macro level. Dovalil presents both quantitative data that illustrate the situation of German in the country and the results from an LMT-based analysis of organized management activities carried out by different institutions that mostly feel dissatisfied with the current situation and strive to strengthen the position of German in the country, both as a foreign and as a minority language with respect to its tutored acquisition. Based on the analysis of the metalinguistic behavior of the individual actors, the author categorizes them in terms of power, positions them within social networks, identifies the interests that motivate their behavior, and explains the failure of their heretofore efforts by the disparity between the macro and micro levels.

Authored by *Chikako Ketcham*, the final chapter of the third part of the book investigates how and why foreigners employed as white-collar workers in Japan use the Japanese language at their workplace. Ketcham argues that the non-Japanese business people use Japanese instead of English and use Japanese in a particular way with a view to further their own interests, irrespective of the language policy of the company that they work for or the Japanese sociocultural norms, generating thereby new power relations. Making use of LMT, the author distinguishes three domains of interests that seem to govern the non-Japanese business people's choice of Japanese language and specific Japanese language use in their workplace: (1) time efficiency and other work-related goals, (2) development of open communication with Japanese colleagues, and (3) fostering of in-group solidarity.

In lieu of an *Epilogue*, the volume concludes with a paper by *Björn Jernudd*, one of the founders of the LMT. Referring to sociolinguistic and communication theories, Jernudd offers his observations and questions with regard to the topic of power in both simple and organized LM.

6 Concluding remarks and future directions

As we can see in this volume, the study of interests and power constitutes an essential component of LM research and has always been present within it. We see the innovation of this volume in the fact that both areas—interests and power—are not analyzed separately, but are decidedly related to each other and—also considering the phases of the LM process—discussed in relation to their interplay. As far as (linguistic) interests are concerned, we show that these are rationalized by language ideologies, argued as seemingly objective, and thus also legitimized and enforced or delegitimized and prevented. In this way, we also establish the link between interests and power, which serves to mobilize in the pursuit of an agenda. This mobilization gives power to its protagonists, whereby general social norms are transferred to or negotiated through language norms and their underlying language ideologies. The volume shows—albeit in different elaborations in the contributions—the role of actors in the assertion of linguistic interests and relates this to an actor typology that typifies the derivation of their power. However, interests and power are always understood as processual variables of discursive and non-discursive actions. By staking out and spelling out these connections and interplays, we believe we have brought the discussion forward through this volume.

Yet much more remains to be done. We can conclude here that focusing on interests and power in all examinations of LM is desirable, but we should also call for more work, particularly of the theoretical sort, which makes explicit to a greater degree the benefits of using the LM approach for studying the relationships between language issues, power, and interests in general. In this volume, we have traced the linkage of interests and power established by language ideologies, with recourse to LMT, through a series of case studies located both in different language and cultural spaces in Europe, Asia, and Africa, and in different domains of organized LM. In doing so, we have demonstrated the relevance of both linking these categories and LMT to LPP, which deals, for example, with minority languages, foreign language acquisition, or language consulting.

Finally, it should be pointed out that there have been many disciplinary paths to the study of LM, and the exploration and integration of these remains an important goal. Power management is elucidated in this volume as a type of LM which integrates power into the interpretation of LM processes, but the question of how it is linked to the conventional theories of discourse and power is only touched upon. We do name them in this introduction, and they are also recalled in some of the contributions, but they are not discussed in more detail theoretically or consistently related to each other. We are, however, on the way to doing so by addressing the distinction between linguistic and non-linguistic interests as well as their linkage to language ideologies and thus also the linkage of linguistic and social norms, by focusing on organized LM, and by typologizing the power of actors, thus moving into the realm of language politics and language conflict, which is open to multidisciplinary study. Thus, in addition to linguistics, discourse analysis, and philosophy, sociology, political science, or social history are also involved. The next steps thus seem to be clear: the integration of the broader context into the analysis of the (linguistic, communicative, and socio-economic) levels of LM processes connected with gender-equal, simplified, or minority language, as well as the adoption of findings and theoretical approaches used within the disciplines mentioned above to the LMT and vice versa. In this broader context, it is necessary to discuss not only how organized LM proceeds from the simple LM and its generalization, but also how organized LM is carried out through simple LM and adapts itself within it. Thus, a closer focus on simple LM with regard to interests and power that are linked to language ideology and thereby legitimized and enforced or delegitimized and prevented is to be made. Furthermore, the discussion about the relationship between interests and motivation and goals is still pending.

The embedding of interests and power in a broader context, which is dealt with in a multidisciplinary way, as well as the connection of LMT to it has already been mentioned above. In closing, it is thus important to recall the relationship between research and real-life LM, also in consideration of our general disciplinary aims. In the field of sociolinguistics, where issues such as inequality and discrimination have always been central, we find power in particular to be integrated into the analysis. In studies of language acquisition and acculturation or of historical language change, this may be less the case, though it is not entirely absent. We therefore face similar questions here that we face in any type of study: In drawing attention to power and interests, whose interests are we in fact representing or promoting? Can we be neutral as researchers and analysts? Do we even want to be? To what degree can we aim to have the results of our research translated into management by the relevant actors in real life? These are questions which should continue to provoke our inquiries.

References

Ammon, U. (2005) Standard und Variation: Norm, Autorität, Legitimation [Standard and variation: Norm, authority, legitimation]. In L. Eichinger & W. Kallmeyer (eds) *Standardvariation. Wie viel Variation verträgt die deutsche Sprache?* [Variation of Standard: How much Variation is Possible in German?]. Berlin, New York: De Gruyter, 28–40.

Anderson, B. (1991 [1988]) *Imagined Communities: Reflections on the Origin and Spread of Nationalism.* 2nd edition. London, New York: Verso Books.

Baldauf, R. B. (2006) Rearticulating the case for micro language planning in a language ecology context. *Current Issues in Language Planning* 7 (2–3), 147–170.

Bell, D. A. (1980) Brown v. board of education and the interest-convergence dilemma. *Harvard Law Review* 93 (3), 518–533.

Bermel, N. (2007) *Linguistic Authority, Language Ideology, and Metaphor: The Czech Orthography Wars.* Berlin, New York: De Gruyter.

Bhabha, H. K. (ed) (2008 [1990]) *Nation and Narration.* London, New York: Routledge.

Blahak, B. (2015) *Franz Kafkas Literatursprache: Deutsch im Kontext des Prager Multilingualismus* [Franz Kafka's Literary Language: German in Context of Prague Multilingualism]. Cologne, Weimar, Vienna: Böhlau.

Bourdieu, P. (1991) *Language and Symbolic Power.* Translated by G. Raymond and M. Adamson. Cambridge: Polity Press.

Busch, B. (2017) *Mehrsprachigkeit* [Multilingualism]. 2nd edition. Vienna: Facultas.

Cooper, R. L. (1989) *Language Planning and Social Change.* Cambridge: Cambridge University Press.

Coulmas, F. (2005) Changing language regimes in globalizing environments. *International Journal of Sociology of Language* 175/176, 3–15.

Dovalil, V. (2013) Zur Auffassung der Standardvarietät als Prozess und Produkt von Sprachmanagement [On standard variety as process and product of language management]. In J. Hagemann, W. P. Klein & S. Staffeldt (eds) *Pragmatischer Standard* [Pragmatic Standard]. Tübingen: Stauffenburg Verlag, 163–176.

Fairbrother, L. (2015) The management of language and power in intercultural contact situations in Japan. *International Journal of the Sociology of Language* 232, 59–78.

Fairbrother, L., Nekvapil, J. & Sloboda, M. (eds) (2018) *The Language Management Approach: A Focus on Research Methodology.* Berlin: Peter Lang.

Fairclough, N. (1989) *Language and Power.* London: Longman.

Fenton-Smith, B. & Gurney, L. (2016) Actors and agency in academic language policy and planning. *Current Issues in Language Planning* 17 (1), 72–87.

Foucault, M. (1984) The order of discourse. In M. J. Shapiro (ed) *Language and Politics.* Oxford: Blackwell, 108–138.

Gellner, E. (2006 [1983]) *Nations and Nationalism.* Introduced by J. Breuilly. Ithaca: Cornell University Press.

Haugen, E. (2013 [1966]) *Language Conflict and Language Planning: The Case of Modern Norwegian.* Cambridge: Harvard University Press.

Hroch, M. (2015) *European Nations: Explaining Their Formation.* Translated by K. Graham. New York: Verso Books.

Jernudd, B. H. & Neustupný, J. V. (1987) Language planning: For whom? In L. Laforge (ed) *Actes du Colloque international sur l'aménagement linguistique / Proceedings of the International Colloquium on Language Planning.* Québec: Les Presses de l'Université Laval, 69–84.

Kimura, G. C. (2014) Language management as a cyclical process: A case study on prohibiting Sorbian in the workplace. *Slovo a slovesnost* 75 (4), 255–270.

Kimura, G. C. (2020) The bridging role of the researcher between different levels of language management: The case of a research project at the German-Polish border. In G. C. Kimura & L. Fairbrother (eds) *A Language Management Approach to Language Problems: Integrating Macro and Micro Dimensions.* Amsterdam: John Benjamins, 237–253.

Kimura, G. C. & Fairbrother, L. (eds) (2020) *A Language Management Approach to Language Problems: Integrating Macro and Micro Dimensions.* Amsterdam: John Benjamins.

Lanstyák, I. & Szabómihály, G. (2009) Hungarian in Slovakia: Language management in a bilingual minority community. In J. Nekvapil & T. Sherman (eds) *Language Management in Contact Situations: Perspectives from Three Continents.* Frankfurt on the Main: Peter Lang, 49–73.

Linke, A. (1996) *Sprachkultur und Bürgertum* [Language Culture and Bourgeoisie]. Stuttgart: Metzler.

Marriott, H. & Nekvapil, J. (eds) (2012) *Language Management Approach: Probing the Concept of "Noting".* Special issue of *Journal of Asian Pacific Communication* 22 (2), 155–317.

Marti, R. (1993) Slovakisch und Čechisch vs. Čechoslovakisch, Serbokroatisch vs. Serbisch und Kroatisch [Slovak and Czech vs. Czechoslovak, Serbocroatian vs. Serbian and Croatian]. In K. Gutschmidt, H. Keipert & H. Rothe (eds) *Slavistische Studien zum XI. Slavistenkongress in Pressburg/Bratislava* [Slavic Studies at the 9th Slavic Congress in Bratislava]. Cologne, Vienna: Böhlau, 289–315.

Nekula, M. (2003) *Franz Kafkas Sprachen: „...in einem Stockwerk des innern babylonischen Turmes..."* [Franz Kafka's Languages: "...in one Floor of the Babylonian Tower..."]. Tübingen: Niemeyer.

Nekula, M. (2016) *Franz Kafka and His Prague Contexts: Studies in Language and Literature.* Prague: Karolinum.

Nekvapil, J. & Sherman, T. (eds) (2009) *Language Management in Contact Situations: Perspectives from Three Continents.* Frankfurt on the Main: Peter Lang.

Nekvapil, J. & Sherman, T. (2013) Language ideologies and linguistic practices: The case of multinational companies in Central Europe. In E. Barát, P. Studer & J. Nekvapil (eds) *Ideological Conceptualizations of Language: Discourses of Linguistic Diversity.* Frankfurt on the Main: Peter Lang, 85–117.

Neustupný, J. V. (2002) Language and power into the 21st century. *International Conference on Language and Empowerment*, Malaysian Association of Modern Languages, Kuala Lumpur, Malaysia, April 11–13, 2002. On WWW at http://languagemanagement.ff.cuni.cz/bibliography.

Neustupný, J. V. (2004) *Power of Language across National Boundaries: The Case of Tertiary Education.* Essen: University of Duisburg-Essen, LAUD Linguistic Agency.

Raos, V. (2015) Linguistic landscapes in EU member states: Politics of visibility and presence. In S. Seubert & F. van Waarden (eds) *Being a Citizen in Europe: Insights and Lessons from the Open Conference.* Zagreb: EU, 245–268.

Rudwick, S. (2018) The struggle to promote an African language at a South African university: A language management perspective. In L. Fairbrother, J. Nekvapil & M. Sloboda (eds) *The Language Management Approach: A Focus on Research Methodology.* Berlin: Peter Lang, 157–184.

Saruhashi, J. (2018) Personal empowerment through language management. In L. Fairbrother, J. Nekvapil & M. Sloboda (eds) *The Language Management Approach: A Focus on Research Methodology.* Berlin: Peter Lang, 231–258.

Sherman, T. (2009) Managing hegemony: Native English speakers in the Czech Republic. In J. Nekvapil & T. Sherman (eds) *Language Management in Contact Situations: Perspectives from Three Continents.* Frankfurt on the Main: Peter Lang, 75–96.

Sloboda, M. (2009) A language management approach to language maintenance and shift: A study from post-Soviet Belarus. In J. Nekvapil & T. Sherman (eds) *Language Management in Contact Situations: Perspectives from Three Continents.* Frankfurt on the Main: Peter Lang, 15–47.

Sloboda, M. (2020) Demarcating the space for multilingualism: On the workings of ethnic interests in a 'civic nation'. *Working Papers in Language Management.* On WWW at http://languagemanagement.ff.cuni.cz/bibliography.

Weinstein, B. (1987) Language planning and interests. In L. Laforge (ed) *Actes du Colloque international sur l'aménagement linguistique / Proceedings of the International Colloquium on Language Planning.* Québec: Les Presses de l'Université Laval, 33–58.

Zahra, T. (2010) Imagined noncommunities: National indifference as a category of analysis. *Slavic Review* 69 (1), 93–119.

Zhao, S. (2011) Actors in language planning. In E. Hinkel (ed) *Handbook of Research in Second Language Teaching and Learning.* Vol. 2. New York, London: Routledge, 905–923.

Zhao, S. & Baldauf, R. B. (2012) Individual agency in language planning: Chinese script reform as a case study. *Language Problems & Language Planning* 36 (1), 1–24.

Part I
Language ideologies

Goro Christoph Kimura

Why and how ideology matters for Language Management Theory

Abstract Interests and power have been issues for Language Management Theory (LMT) as important, even unavoidable factors that motivate and influence language management, but it is not clear how deeply these concepts are integrated in the theory. Recent promising attempts to link language ideology (LI) with LMT seem to pay due attention to the social context in which management processes occur. So far, however, LI has been associated more with the macro level. In this chapter, LI is presented theoretically and empirically as a concept relevant at the micro level as well. The case demonstrating the micro-level operation of LI is drawn from the Sorbian region in Eastern Germany, where the author has conducted fieldwork. The chapter concludes that, in order for the analysis of interests and power to take the place it deserves in LMT, LI has to be considered as a key ingredient in the LMT process, relevant both to macro and micro processes.

Keywords interests, power, language ideology, Sorbian

1 How interests and power relate to language and language management

This chapter is intended as a review of the current state of research combining Language Management Theory (LMT) and language ideology (LI), aiming to serve as a basis for further developing and deepening this connection. First, the relationship of interests and power to language and their consideration in LMT is discussed. Then, the concept of LI is presented, and the connection between LI and LMT is examined. After discussing the theoretical side, a case study of the micro-level operation of LI is presented in which the function of LI in relation to interests and power is analyzed.

Language is sometimes regarded as a tool that can be used freely by each speaker; however, it is not merely a tool in the hands of individuals, but a social construct in the sense that it becomes a social reality through the accumulation of its use between people. At least two aspects must be considered when language is understood this way: the first is the impossibility of neutrality regarding language, and the second is the intersubjectivity of language. Wee (2011) illustrates the first aspect clearly as follows:

> Language differs from practices pertaining to religion, diet, or dress in that it is *unavoidable*. Unlike other cultural practices, it is simply impossible in most, if not all, situations to avoid the use of a specific language, since some form of communication

> is necessary if the participating individuals or communities are to successfully coordinate their actions. [...] [Hence, rather than attempting to realize an unlikely state of linguistic neutrality, the goal is to acknowledge and foreground the many different interests that are at stake and which need to be negotiated. This alternative would have the advantage of foregrounding the fact that language is always inextricably intertwined with potentially conflicting interests, and that compromises are often necessary in a plural society. (Wee 2011: 15, 17; italics in the original, underline by GCK)

The important point here is the mention of interests. Even if the choice of a language or language variety is perceived as natural in certain contexts, there are interests behind this choice. For example, the use of a standard variety was fostered to serve the unity of a nation, and now the promotion of English is serving, among others, the globalizing economy. Sometimes, the interests are shared by the vast majority and are therefore not overtly contested, but this does not mean that there are no interests involved.

The second aspect is described as follows:

> [L]anguage is ultimately a semiotic resource whose properties in the context of any localized situation are intersubjectively negotiated. [...] [T]he fact that they are intersubjectively negotiated means that any control over them is beyond the reach of any single individual or community, however powerful. (Wee 2011: 163)

Here we deal with the matter of power. In contrast to physical power, which is to a considerable degree based on the physical conditions of individuals or armed forces, language and linguistic power function in the relations between people. Power is not a static attribute of certain speakers by which they control others independently of the context, but an aspect of interaction and results from negotiation between participants in concrete situations.

These two aspects, therefore, are basic characteristics of all language usage. Due to this relevance of interests and power to language and their negotiated character, these concepts have a special affinity with and significance for LMT, which is concerned with metalinguistic processes.

Indeed, LMT has dealt with interests ever since its inception. Jernudd and Neustupný (1987: 72) argued that a neutral language system free from interests is impossible, connecting interests to the management process:

> Each language management process is connected with multiple interests of particular social groups or individuals. A full analysis of different interests is necessary. (Jernudd & Neustupný 1987: 82)

The concern with power was added to LMT later (see the introduction to this volume). The most detailed account on power in LMT is given by Neustupný (2002), who stresses the importance of thinking about power in relation to language, and points out the possibility of analyzing power management at the micro level through the process model of LMT: deviation from norms, noting, evaluation, adjustment design, and implementation.[1] He defines interests and power in the following way:

> Interests are aspirations for a certain state of affairs that is favourable to the subject. Power operates on interests. Power is the capacity to implement one's interests. (Neustupný 2002: 4)

Further explanations of LMT have included this issue, as the following example shows:

> A fourth feature [of LMT] is the insistence on the recognition of the multiplicity of interests within a community. [...] Also, the capacity to implement one's interests, in other words power, are subject to variation, and no language management system can overlook this fact. (Neustupný & Nekvapil 2003: 186)

In concrete research, the matter of interests and power has been taken up in micro-level (e.g., Fairbrother 2015) as well as macro-level studies (e.g., Dovalil 2015). On the other hand, it must be noted that interests and power are invisible in the process models of LMT, so these aspects can be easily overlooked. There seems to be a lack of a clear concept and methodology to deal with interests and power in the LMT process. It is fair, then, to raise the question of how deeply these concepts are really integrated in the theory.

2 Language ideology as an approach to interests and power[2]

This question was previously formulated by Yamada (1999 [2006]), who discussed the relation of LMT to interests and power. According to Yamada, there is a problem with the process model of LMT beginning with deviation from norms, which seems to presuppose that the involved parties share norms that existed prior to the specific situation. Yamada prompts us to focus our attention on the politicized, specific interactions from the perspective of ethnomethodology, which focuses on the jointly constructed "objective reality" within individual situations:

> The problem with the "management process" is that it does not actively theorize that "norms" themselves are a political device that reproduce common knowledge deemed to be self-evident, and that the adjustment of language problems within specific

1 A post-implementation stage (feedback/verification) was proposed later (see Kimura 2014, 2020). See also the explanation of the management process on the LMT website at http://languagemanagement.ff.cuni.cz/en/process. Kimura and Fairbrother (2020) argue for explicitly showing the pre-management stage of "(deviation from) norms" in the process model.

2 This and the following section incorporate the description of LI in relation to LMT presented in Kimura (2011, 2017).

interactions is itself the political stage where power struggles occur. (Yamada 1999: 67; 2006: 38, translation by GCK).

As Yamada points out, it is valid to analyze the negotiation of power or power management within specific situations, given that power within language activity actually operates in micro-level interactions. However, when we talk about norm negotiations, we must be aware that norms are not negotiated from scratch in each and every interaction. Yamada seems to presuppose that only contexts traceable on the surface are relevant for each situation, but the premise of LMT, unlike strict ethnomethodology, is that it also considers mental factors beneath the surface. Jernudd has pointed out that "language management is inevitably constrained by the socioeconomic and political state of affairs in a speech community. It is important to be very clear about this constraint" (Jernudd 2001: 5). As such, it is essential to keep such constraints in mind when examining the negotiation of norms. But how should one go about this?

A valid concept for considering these constraints is LI, which mainly developed in linguistic anthropology but is becoming influential in sociolinguistics and related fields as well. In a classical definition, Silverstein (1979: 193) defines LI as "sets of beliefs about language articulated by the users as a rationalization or justification of perceived structure and use." In a later definition, LI is conceived to be "a mediating link between social forms and forms of talk" (Woolard 1998: 3).

LI starts from the basic insight that we all have value judgments about language, but LI as used in linguistic anthropology is not just another name for "language attitude" or "view of language." First, it assumes that evaluations of language are not completely different from situation to situation, but that there are recurrent patterns shared within a definite range of people. It is difficult to envisage that knowledge and beliefs would be entirely different between individuals; therefore, if similar patterns are observed in different individuals in different scenarios, we can hypothesize that a LI is at work. A second characteristic of LI is its link to social structure, interests, and power, which is particularly relevant to this chapter. This does not mean that LI attempts to explain language use directly from social structures and the like; rather, LI is critical towards trying to explain language use as a mere "reflection" of social factors. LI aims to point out that social forms do not directly produce forms of talk. As such, LI can be regarded as an interpretative filter with its own dynamism, mediating between society (in general) and concrete language usage. It operates in two directions, as shown in Figure 1.

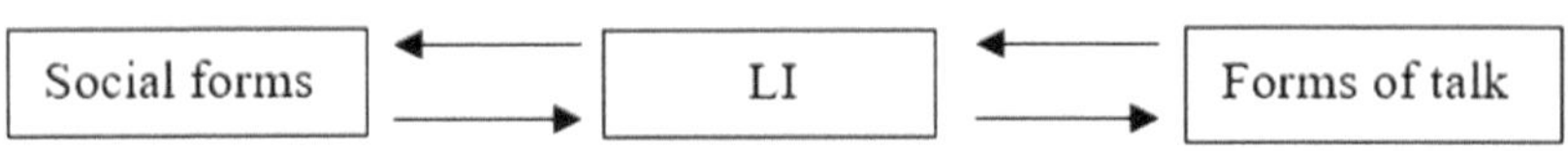

Figure 1: The operation of language ideology (LI)

De Bres (2013) outlines the key features of LI, and three out of the twelve points she lists concern interests and power. First, LIs are "normative with a purpose" (de Bres 2013: 59), as they are tied to the interests of a particular social position. Second, "given their normative nature and relationship to interests, language ideologies always relate to *power relations* within society" (de Bres 2013: 59; italics in the original). Third, "language ideologies are viewed here not as a static system of normative beliefs, but rather as a *strategic resource* that individuals can employ to position and reinforce their own interests" (de Bres 2013: 60). These features suggest that LI can be useful in understanding how interests and power operate in language management.

3 Integrating LI into LMT

Let us now consider the connection of LI to LMT. Neustupný (e.g., 1993, 2002) used the term "ideology" repeatedly in his papers. In one relatively early example, he dedicates an entire paragraph to it. In a paper on language purism, he distinguishes three types of purism (Neustupný 1989: 211–212, italics in the original):

1. linguistic interaction: "what speakers actually do in discourse"
2. metalinguistic idiom: "*ways of communicating* about certain linguistic processes"
3. ideology: "a relatively independent system of thought about language with particular political objectives to be achieved." Ideologies are thought to "accompany the correction processes," e.g., nationalist ideology.

This understanding of ideology is more specific and limited in scope than LI as described above, as the addition of "with particular political objectives to be achieved" indicates. In linguistic anthropology, LI is conceived as a more essential, omnipresent aspect of human language activities, or to use Neustupný's words, "a relatively independent system of thought about language" that can be deduced from "linguistic interactions" as well as "metalinguistic idioms" that serve as strategic resources (Neustupný 1989: 212).

Later, Kimura (2001) was the first to transfer the concept of LI from linguistic anthropology to LMT, proposing that the analysis of situations in which language management occurs should pay attention to the ideological circumstances. Kimura (2001: 27) summarized the discussion as follows:

> Ideologies can be abstracted from texts as well as concrete situations. In my opinion it is most important to distinguish ideology as a structured and to a certain degree durable dimension in its own right from concrete language usage. In other words, to seek factors that can be reduced neither to individual situations nor to social structures.[3]

3 Original: So können Ideologien sowohl von Texten als auch von konkreten Situationen abstrahiert werden. M.E. kommt es vor allem darauf an, die Ideologie als strukturierte und einigermaßen dauerhafte eigene Dimension von den einzelnen Sprachhandlungen zu trennen, mit anderen Worten, nach Faktoren zu suchen,

Recently, the term has come to be used in LMT-based research, especially among Central European researchers (Sherman 2020), but usually without defining or discussing the term itself. The term "norm system" (Sloboda 2009) has also been used to denote normative orientations in a similar sense to LI. Though it cannot be stressed enough that the notion of language management by Spolsky (2004, 2009) is different from LMT (Fairbrother & Kimura 2020: 2, 8–10), it is important to note that Spolsky (2004) also included ideology as a basic concept in his model:

> The members of a speech community share also a general set of beliefs about appropriate language practices, sometimes forming a consensual ideology, assigning values and prestige to various aspects of the language varieties used in it. These beliefs both derive from and influence practices. They can be a basis for language management or a management policy can be intended to confirm or modify them. (Spolsky 2004: 14)

A more focused discussion on the role of LI in LMT was provided by Kimura (2011) (for the main points see Kimura 2017), who examined the controversy over "prohibiting" Sorbian in a workplace in the Sorbian region.[4] His findings showed how shared language ideologies can act as constraints, but also as resources in the process of negotiating norms. According to him, norms would not work without reference to LIs accepted by the participants. He concluded that it can be assumed that LI can essentially help clarify *why* such management processes arise, while investigating language management can help to explore *how* LIs operate.

Similarly, Nekvapil and Sherman (2013: 86) argued:

> that language ideologies represent a normative orientation for the speakers, and in serving as the basis for norms or expectations for communicative behavior, the ideologies guide, influence or underlie what can be noticed as a deviation from the norm, what can be evaluated (negatively, positively or otherwise) and so forth, that is, they guide management processes.

In accordance with Kimura (2011, 2017), they state that LIs "serve as the basis for particular norms" (Nekvapil & Sherman 2013: 90). Lanstyák (2016) summarizes the main characteristics of the concept of LI and provides a comprehensive list of as many as 237 types of ideologies, which can help with orientation in research concerning LI.

Establishing LI, a concept linking the social background to the specific site of language management, as an item for investigation no doubt facilitates "more positive theorization" (to use Yamada's phrase) regarding the discussion surrounding norms and power relations. LIs undoubtedly show potential as a way to understand *what* becomes a norm, *what* is deemed a deviation in a specific situation, and *in what ways* the management process is performed.

---

die weder auf die einzelnen Situationen noch auf die sozialen Strukturen zu reduzieren sind.

4 For the details and processes of the case discussed here, see Kimura (2014).

Recent developments in linking LI and LMT have led to an acknowledgment of a deeper influence of LI in language management processes than previously suggested. While previous mentions of LI in LMT have included "ideology" as a concept in institutional or organized management (Nekvapil 2009: 6; Barát, Studer & Nekvapil 2013: 3), Nekvapil and Sherman (2013: 86) argued that "*any given setting* contains a constellation of language ideologies which then influence *observable practices of language management*," including the fact that LIs underlie/guide not only organized management but also simple management (Nekvapil & Sherman 2013: 92; see also Lanstyák 2016: 5). Lanstyák (2014: 332) also points out that "even minor corrections may be motivated by these factors, e.g., the mere fact that the speaker corrects a language form which does not cause misunderstanding or is not more difficult to understand than the correct one, may be influenced by his/her ideologies." The first example of simple correction from the LMT website below,[5] which shows a correction from common Czech to standard Czech form (underlined by GCK), can be interpreted in terms of ideology in the sense that standard LI connecting standard language and formal public speech is involved here.

Example 1

MODERÁTOR: témata, o kterých bude dnes řeč, možná poznáte už podle jmen pánů, <u>který- kteří</u> přijali dnešní pozvání.

[ANCHOR: the topics which will be discussed today you may recognize just from the names of the gentlemen who- [non-standard form] who [standard form] accepted today's invitation.]

This broader awareness of LI in LMT is in line with the concept in linguistic anthropology, which is thought of as significant in terms of the link between the micro and macro levels. In his consideration of the concept of LI, Woolard (1998: 27) posits that LIs are expected to be helpful in this sense:

> [I]t allows us to relate the microculture of communicative action to political economic considerations of power and social inequality, to confront macrosocial constraints on language behavior, and to connect discourse with lived experiences.

Gal (1998: 319) also perceives LI as allowing for integrative consideration of the circumstances conventionally regarded as a different level of social phenomena:

> Because social organizations and institutions that differ significantly in size, spatial dispersion, and duration (consider, for instance, the differences between states, NGOs, schools, political movements, professional societies, town meetings, friendships, and market interactions) can all nevertheless be constituted around cultural principles about the relation of language to social life, while also enacting implicit understandings

5 http://languagemanagement.ff.cuni.cz/en/complexity. Accessed March 21, 2020.

> of such a relation, a focus on language ideologies can enable analyses to range across social arrangements of different extent and temporality. By starting with linguistic ideologies, one can highlight unexpected links, contestations, and contradictions among such organizations, thereby bringing them within a single theoretical purview.

Acknowledging the omnipresence of LI in language management processes also has consequences for the understanding of simple and organized management. LI was sometimes perceived to be more relevant in organized management than simple management, as the following example shows:

> organized management can be characterized by the following features: [...]
>
> d. Theorizing and ideologies are at play to a greater degree and more explicitly
> (Nekvapil 2012: 167; Nekvapil & Sherman 2015: 8; Nekvapil 2016: 15)

It is understandable that ideologies would usually be more explicit in organized management, but the degree of overtness does not necessarily correspond to the degree at which LIs are actually operating. As mentioned above, LI has been understood as manifested not only by direct verbalization but also through interactions. Indeed, it can be argued that the ideologies that are not overtly discussed are the truly dominant ones (Lanstyák 2016: 6). The general description of LMT in relation to LI should therefore be modified to:

> LMT includes "ideology" as a concept in the institutional or organized as well as simple management of linguistic practice.

This kind of deep concern with LI urges the analyzer to view various management processes in its wider social context, involving interests and power.

4 A case of the micro-level operation of language ideology: Maintenance of Sorbian

Thus far, this chapter has dealt with LI as a conceptual framework to analyze the metalinguistic environment of language management processes. Before closing the chapter, there is still the question of how LI relates to interests and power in concrete cases. This can be divided in two questions. First, how are LIs sustained by and serve interests? Second, how does LI function to support or challenge power relations? In search of the answer to these questions, I would like to present an example of how LI, operating covertly at the micro level, can be linked to interests and power. The example discussed here comes from Lusatia, a region in Eastern Germany, where I conducted fieldwork on the language maintenance of Sorbian, a small Slavic language spoken there (on Sorbian in Germany see also Marti, this volume).

Sorbian has been particularly well preserved among Catholic Sorbs, although following the Reformation more than 90% of Sorbs converted to Protestantism. My research concerned the role of the Catholic Church in maintaining the Sorbian language (Kimura 2015), revealing the continuous efforts of Catholic priests to promote the Sorbian language. One such example is the following excerpt from a preparation class for the Holy Communion, held in the Sorbian language by a Sorbian priest, including among the Sorbian natives some pupils with German as their first language (other examples are in Kimura 2015).

Example 2

PRIEST: A Anne?
ANNE: Moja mać spinka, weil sie Nachtschicht hat.
PRIEST: Aha, ta je spała. To ja wěrju. [...]

[PRIEST: And Anne?
ANNE: My mother sleeps, weil sie Nachtschicht hat [because she has to work at night].
PRIEST: Aha, she was sleeping. I believe that.]

Anne is a pupil of Sorbian ancestry who speaks German at home. Here, she begins to speak in Sorbian but then switches to German (underlined part). The priest repeats the information and adds a comment in Sorbian. There seems to be nothing special in this reaction by the priest, but it is actually an extraordinary act of management, unlikely to happen in social situations outside the church context. The general communicative norm in the society in this region is that German is the dominant language, and when one speaks German, the other(s) has (have) to switch to German as well. However, the priest here tries to switch back to Sorbian.

The language management process by the priest can be described as follows. First, the use of German by the pupil is noted as a deviation from the specific norm that, in this class, Sorbian is the language to be used. The adjustment took the form of switching back to Sorbian, implemented by repeating what was said in German and continuing in Sorbian. After the class, the priest reviewed the occasion with the following words directed at the author, implying the need to promote Anne's Sorbian skills in the class to compensate for the attitudes of her parents, who do not speak Sorbian with her.

Example 3

PRIEST: Anne pěnknje čita, ale dokelz staršej nje... to staj staršej wina. Wona je mudra.

[Anne can read well, but the parents don't... the parents are guilty. She is clever.]

It would be misleading to understand the insisting on Sorbian as the language to be used in the class as an individual act caused by the personal preference of the priest. Instead, this is related to the ideology of the local Catholic Church, which elevates Sorbian. The analysis of recurrent narratives and discourse patterns in journals, documents, and interviews (Kimura 2005) has detected an ideology that appears in the list by Lanstyák (2016: 38) as "jazykový sakralizmus" (language as something holy). This ideology holds that the use of a certain language has a special religious value.

This ideology is related to and supported by different interests. For the clergy and church leaders, Sorbian is a distinctive identity marker that distinguishes Catholic Sorbs from the secularized or Protestant Germans. The Sorbian language is perceived as guarding the maintenance of the faith and perpetuating the influence of the Church. On the other hand, the ideology is supported by many laypeople as well, for whom maintaining the community network is part of their safety net (Kimura 2004). They even actively help to integrate linguistically peripheral members of the community, such as Anne in the example, by including them in popular events held in Sorbian and related to the Church (Kimura 2015).

With regard to power, it is obvious that the priest, as the teacher in this situation, can control the language to be used, and this role is accepted by Anne and her parents because of the above mentioned "holiness" of Sorbian, manifested in the extensive use of Sorbian in the Church (Kimura 2015).

In sum, with regard to the management process, LI as a mutually understood and approved metalinguistic presupposition reflects interests and constitutes a resource of power negotiations surrounding norms within linguistic interaction, and it can be thought of as a prerequisite that participates in the creation of advantage (and disadvantage) for specific people and positions. Therefore, consideration of the LIs that are shared and recreated by the parties in an interaction can be said to be a method to prevent us from overlooking the interest and power constellations involved in seemingly self-evident norms within the analysis of language management.

5 Conclusions

In this chapter, we have first confirmed that interests and power are profoundly related to language, and that LMT has good preconditions to tackle these issues. As interests and power, however, are not sufficiently integrated in LMT conceptually, a full integration of LI into it would be useful. In order to grant the analysis of interests and power the place it deserves in LMT, LI must be conceived as relevant to macro as well as micro processes. Finally, the case study showed how ideology reflects interests and constitutes a resource of power negotiations.

Figure 2 illustrates the potential of ideologies operating in the process of language management. While this chapter only discussed ideologies directly related to language, language management is in fact embedded in wider communicative, sociocultural and sociopolitical/economic behavior. Thus, ideologies on these issues and its relation with language management should be considered as well. This will be a task for further research.

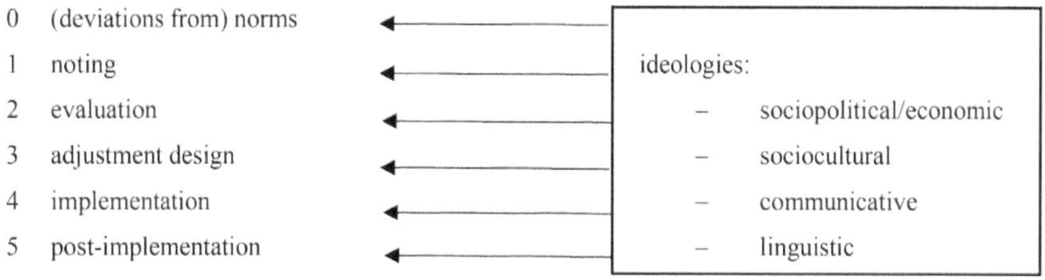

Figure 2: Potentials of ideologies in the management process

References

Barát, E., Studer, P. & Nekvapil, J. (2013) Approaching the study of language use and ideology: An introduction. In E. Barát, P. Studer & J. Nekvapil (eds) *Ideological Conceptualizations of Language*. Frankfurt on the Main: Peter Lang, 1–8.

de Bres, J. (2013) Language ideologies for constructing inclusion and exclusion. In E. Barát, P. Studer & J. Nekvapil (eds) *Ideological Conceptualizations of Language*. Frankfurt on the Main: Peter Lang, 57–83.

Dovalil, V. (2015) Language management theory as a basis for the dynamic concept of EU language law. *Current Issues in Language Planning* 16 (4), 360–377.

Fairbrother, L. (2015) The management of language and power in intercultural contact situations in Japan. *International Journal of the Sociology of Language* 232, 59–78.

Fairbrother, L. & Kimura, G. C. (2020) What is a language management approach to language problems and why do we need it? In G. C. Kimura & L. Fairbrother (eds) *A Language Management Approach to Language Problems: Integrating Macro and Micro Dimensions*. Amsterdam: John Benjamins, 1–28.

Gal, S. (1998) Multiplicity and contention among language ideologies: A commentary. In B. B. Schieffelin, K. A. Woolard & P. V. Kroskrity (eds) *Language Ideologies. Practice and Theory.* Oxford: Oxford University Press, 317–331.

Jernudd, B. H. (2001) Language management and language problems: Part 2. *Journal of Asian Pacific Communication* 11 (1), 1–8.

Jernudd, B. H. & Neustupný, J. V. (1987) Language planning: For whom? In L. Laforge (ed) *Actes du Colloque international sur l'aménagement linguistique / Proceedings of the International Colloquium on Language Planning*. Québec: Les Presses de L'Université Laval, 69–84.

Kimura, G. C. (2001) Intentionale Eingriffe in den Sprachgebrauch: Perspektiven und Probleme einer umfassenden Theoriebildung [Conscious interventions in language use: Perspectives and problems in forming a comprehensive theory]. In S. Fiedler & Liu H. (eds) *Studien zur Interlinguistik* [Studies about

Interlinguistics]. Praha: KAVA–PECH, 19–29. On WWW athttp://www.lingviko.net/db/01_KIMURA.htm#P85_19869. Accessed December 6, 2020.

Kimura, G. C. (2004) Junnō to jikoshuchō no aida de – Sorubujin no seikatsusenryaku e no shiten [Sorbian survival strategies between accommodation and resistance]. In *Tōōshikenkyū* [Journal of Eastern European Studies] 26, 107–115.

Kimura, G. C. (2005) *Gengo ni totte 'jin'isei' towa nanika: gengokōchiku to gengoideorogī, Kerunōgo to Sorubugo o jirei toshite* [What does 'Artificiality' Mean to Language? Case Studies of Cornish and Sorbian as Exemplars of Language Construction and Language Ideology]. Tokyo: Sangensha.

Kimura, G. C. (2011) Watashitachi wa donoyōni gengo o kanri suru noka [How do we manage languages?] In H. Yamashita, M. Watanabe & H. Takada (eds) *Gengoishiki to shakai* [Language Awareness and Society]. Tokyo: Sangensha, 61–89.

Kimura G. C. (2014) Language management as a cyclical process: A case study on prohibiting Sorbian in the workplace. *Slovo a slovesnost* 75, 255–270.

Kimura, G. C. (2015) Spracherhalt als Prozess: Elemente des kirchlichen Sprachmanagements bei den katholischen Sorben [Language maintenance as a process: Elements of Sorbian language management in the Catholic church]. *International Journal of the Sociology of Language* 232, 13–32. English version on WWW at http://languagemanagement.ff.cuni.cz/system/files/documents/Kimura%282015%29Languag_maintenance_as_process.pdf. Accessed December 6, 2020.

Kimura, G. C. (2017) The role of language ideology in norm negotiation. *Working Papers in Language Management* 2. On WWW at http://languagemanagement.ff.cuni.cz/system/files/documents/wplm-02_kimura.pdf. Accessed December 6, 2020.

Kimura, G. C. (2020) The bridging role of the researcher between different levels of language management: The case of a research project at the German-Polish border. In G. C. Kimura & L. Fairbrother (eds) *A Language Management Approach to Language Problems: Integrating Macro and Micro Dimensions.* Amsterdam: John Benjamins, 237–253.

Kimura, G. C. & Fairbrother, L. (2020) Reconsidering the language management approach in light of the micro-macro continuum. In G. C. Kimura & L. Fairbrother (eds) *A Language Management Approach to Language Problems: Integrating Macro and Micro Dimensions.* Amsterdam: John Benjamins, 255–267.

Lanstyák, I. (2014) On the process of language problem management. *Slovo a slovesnost* 75 (4), 325–351.

Lanstyák, I. (2016) Jazykové ideológie (všeobecné otázky a glosár) [Language ideologies (general issues and a glossary)]. *Working Papers in Language Management* 1 (revised in 2017). On WWW at: http://languagemanagement.ff.cuni.cz/system/files/documents/wplm-01_lanstyak.pdf.

Nekvapil, J. (2009) The integrative potential of language management theory. In J. Nekvapil & T. Sherman (eds) *Language Management in Contact Situations: Perspectives from Three Continents*. Frankfurt on the Main: Peter Lang, 1–11.

Nekvapil, J. (2012) Some thoughts on "noting" in Language Management Theory and beyond. *Journal of Asian Pacific Communication* 22 (2), 160–173.

Nekvapil, J. (2016) Language Management Theory as one approach in Language Policy and Planning. *Current Issues in Language Planning* 17 (1), 11–22.

Nekvapil, J. & Sherman, T. (2013) Language ideologies and linguistic practice: The case of multinational companies in Central Europe. In E. Barát, P. Studer & J. Nekvapil (eds) *Ideological Conceptualizations of Language: Discourses of Linguistic Diversity*. Frankfurt on the Main: Peter Lang, 85–117.

Nekvapil, J. & Sherman, T. (2015) An introduction: Language Management: Theory in Language Policy and Planning. *International Journal of the Sociology of Language* 232, 1–12.

Neustupný, J. (1989) Language purism as a type of language correction. In B. H. Jernudd & M. J. Shapiro (eds) *The Politics of Language Purism*. Berlin & New York: Mouton de Gruyter, 211–223.

Neustupný, J. V. (1993) Language management for Romani in Central and Eastern Europe. *New Language Planning Newsletter* 7 (4), 1–6.

Neustupný, J. V. (2002) Language and power into the 21st century. A paper for the *International Conference on Language and Empowerment*, Malaysian Association of Modern Languages, Kuala Lumpur, Malaysia, April 11–13, 2002. On WWW at http://languagemanagement.ff.cuni.cz/bibliography.

Neustupný, J. V. & Nekvapil, J. (2003) Language management in the Czech Republic. *Current Issues in Language Planning* 4 (3–4), 181–366.

Sherman, T. (2020) Researching language management in Central Europe: Cultivation, social change and power. In G. C. Kimura & L. Fairbrother (eds) *A Language Management Approach to Language Problems: Integrating Macro and Micro Dimensions*. Amsterdam: John Benjamins, 69–88.

Silverstein, M. (1979) Language structure and linguistic ideology. In P. R. Clyne, W. F. Hanks & C. L. Hofbauer (eds) *The Elements: A Parasession on Linguistic Units and Levels*. Chicago: Chicago Linguistic Society, 193–247.

Sloboda, M. (2009) A language management approach to language maintenance and language shift: A study from post-Soviet Belarus. In J. Nekvapil & T. Sherman (eds) *Language Management in Contact Situations: Perspectives from Three Continents*. Frankfurt on the Main: Peter Lang, 15–47.

Spolsky, B. (2004) *Language Policy*. Cambridge: Cambridge University Press.

Spolsky, B. (2009) *Language Management*. Cambridge: Cambridge University Press.

Wee, L. (2011) *Language without Rights*. Oxford: Oxford University Press.

Woolard, K. (1998) Introduction. Language ideology as a field of inquiry. In B. B. Schieffelin, K. A. Woolard & P. V. Kroskrity (eds) *Language Ideologies: Practice and Theory.* Oxford: Oxford University Press, 3–47.

Yamada, T. (1999) Esunomesodoroji kara mita 'gengomondai' ['Language problems' seen from the viewpoint of ethnomethodology]. *The Japan Journal of Language and Society* 2 (1), 59–69. Reprinted in: H. Masiko (ed) (2006) *Kotoba, kenryoku, sabetsu: gengoken kara mita jōhōjakusha no kaihō* [Language, Power and Discrimination: The Contribution of Language Rights to the Liberation of Information-Handicapped]. Tokyo: Sangensha, 23–42.

Petar Vuković

Council for the Standard Croatian Language Norm: The failure of 'hard power'

Abstract The Council for the Standard Croatian Language Norm was founded in 2005 by the right-wing conservative government as the highest body responsible for providing "systematic and professional care for the Croatian standard language." Seven years later, it was abolished as "unnecessary" by the left-wing liberal government. In this chapter, the work of the Council is analyzed through the prism of Language Management Theory. The analysis demonstrates that the Council neglected simple language management on the micro level, which is recommended as point of departure of the organized language management, in favor of the organized language management on the macro level to change the praxis (and the accepted norms) on the micro level and refused to acknowledge both ideological stances and the particular interests of its most prominent members. This resulted in the Council's failure to exert any real influence on language use.

Keywords Council for the Standard Croatian Language Norm, organized language management, language ideology, language norm, language use

1 Introduction

The Council for the Standard Croatian Language Norm worked as an advisory expert group at the Ministry of Science, Education and Sports of the Republic of Croatia from April 2005 to May 2012. It was composed of representatives of all academic institutions in Croatia specializing in research of contemporary Standard Croatian, with Radoslav Katičić serving as its president. The Council was founded to deal with what can be broadly defined as the corpus and status planning of contemporary Standard Croatian,[1] but on many occasions, as will be demonstrated

1 In the Decision on the Establishment and Appointment of Members of the Council for the Standard Croatian Language Norm, adopted by Minister Dragan Primorac, the Council was assigned the following tasks: "voditi sustavnu stručnu skrb za hrvatski standardni jezik, raspraviti aktualne nedoumice i otvorena pitanja hrvatskoga standardnog jezika, upozoravati na primjere nepoštovanja ustavne odredbe o hrvatskom kao službenom jeziku u Republici Hrvatskoj, promicati kulturu hrvatskoga standardnog jezika u pisanoj i govornoj komunikaciji, voditi skrb o mjestu i ulozi hrvatskoga standardnog jezika s obzirom na proces integracije Republike Hrvatske u Europsku uniju, donijeti rješenja u svezi s daljnjim normiranjem hrvatskoga standardnog jezika, pratiti jezičnu problematiku i utvrditi načela u pravopisnoj normi." [to conduct systematic professional care for the

later in the chapter, it transgressed the boundaries within which it was supposed to work. Due to controversial recommendations and attitudes toward contemporary language use that some of its prominent members advocated, the Council was exposed to the criticism of both professional linguists and the general educated public (see, e.g., Langston & Peti Stantić 2011; Peti Stantić & Langston 2013: 142–149; Vuković 2016). The most important materials on the work of the Council were published in a special edition of the journal *Jezik* [Language] 60 (2013), No. 2–4.

In this chapter, the work of the Council will be analyzed through the prism of Language Management Theory (LMT), primarily with regard to what Jiří V. Neustupný claimed about the role of power and interests in organized language management. Neustupný recommended that all organized language management be anchored in a simple one in order to limit the power of language policymakers and empower the wider community of language users. In accordance with this, the analysis in this chapter will focus on the way the Council approached the interaction between organized and simple language management. Neustupný also believed that there is no disinterested and value-free language management, so he thought it important that language policy makers openly acknowledge their ideological stances and particular interests. The analysis will therefore seek to answer the question of how the Council acted with regard to this issue. It will be argued that negligence in simple language management and unwillingness to see its own biases substantially contributed to the failure of the Council to exert any real influence on contemporary language use in Croatia. The chapter ends with an attempt to determine the place of the organized language management practiced by the Council in the diachronic typology of organized language management proposed by Neustupný (2006).

2 Power and interests in LMT

As is well known, the notion of "language problem" has a central place in LMT. The term has already been used within the theory of language planning, but in that

---

Croatian standard language, to discuss current issues and open questions about the Croatian standard language, to warn of failures to comply with the constitutional provision on Croatian as the official language of the Republic of Croatia, to promote the cultivation of the Croatian standard language in written and spoken communication, to take care of the place and role of the Croatian standard language with regard to the process of integration of the Republic of Croatia into the European Union, to adopt solutions regarding further standardization of the Croatian standard language, to follow current linguistic issues and to establish principles of the orthographic norm.] Source: Odluka o osnivanju i imenovanju članova Vijeća za normu hrvatskoga standardnoga jezika [Decision on the Establishment and Appointment of Members of the Council for the Standard Croatian Language Norm], *Jezik* 60: 58. (All translations are mine.)

context, it was interpreted primarily as a problem at the level of language code. In LMT, it acquired a wider meaning. Neustupný (1978: 245), for example, suggest that "'language problems' can be reformulated as occurrences of the marker 'inadequate,' which can be attached to certain features of communicative acts or features of communicative systems." In other words, the notion of a language problem also covers the problems of speech, as well as communication and pragmatic problems. Moreover, in LMT, language problems are also perceived as firmly integrated into the socioeconomic structures within which language communication flows. Accordingly, establishing the connections between language problems and conflicting social and economic interests from which they grow is crucial in the analysis. Finally, LMT is based on the assumption that language problems cannot be solved by focusing solely on the dimension of communication. The socioeconomic problems associated with them must also be taken into consideration:

> Hence the requirement of identification of socioeconomic determinants and consequences of language problems by language planners and their active contribution to the solution of such problems. There is also the emerging requirement of language planning, not merely through attempts to reform linguistic inventories, but through the process of varying the socioeconomic determinants of language situations. (Neustupný 1983: 2)

An important innovation of LMT has also been its emphasis on microanalysis, which is related to the insight that language management can be conducted individually, i.e., at the level of discourse, and in an organized way, i.e., with the participation of formalized social networks that strive to influence the language use of the wider community. The sources of all language problems, however, are in the microsphere, at the level of discourse or meta-discourse, if language problems are produced discursively. They do not necessarily have to be classical communication misunderstandings, since perceived "inadequacies" can also be linked to symbolic, socioeconomic or other functions of language.[2] Faced with such "micro problems," communication participants seek solutions and engage in spontaneous interventions, which normally proceed through the same stages as organized language management does. As Neustupný points out: "It is obvious that global language reform and the process of the solution of communication problems of a

2 In connection with this, Neustupný (2002: 435) writes: "Tak se stává, že mluvčí například pociťují v interakci (promluvě) nejen to, že nemohou vyjádřit určitý obsah, nýbrž i to, že jazykem nedostatečně komunikují svou loajálnost k národu nebo že jazyk vytváří sítě, které jsou pro mluvčího nepříznivé (např. v určité konkrétní situaci angličtina socioekonomicky zvýhodňuje rodilé mluvčí angličtiny a státy anglofonního typu)." [For example, it is possible for speakers to feel that in an interaction (discourse) they are not only unable to express certain content, but they also insufficiently communicate by the language their loyalty to the nation, or that the language creates networks unfavorable for the speaker (e.g., in a specific situation, English socioeconomically privileges native speakers and Anglophone countries).]

single individual are processes of the same character. The differences are to a large extent of a quantitative nature" (Neustupný 1983: 1). He therefore insists that every instance of organized language management be linked to a simple one: "It is only logical to require that all language planning must commence with the mapping of language problems in actual discourse, not with their reflections in attitudes or statements of the personnel concerned. Conversely, it is clear that the ultimate removal of a language problem hinges on its removal from actual discourse, a fact of primary importance for the implementation of language planning" (Neustupný 1983: 2).[3]

However, even that is not enough to achieve "objectivity" in language management. In this regard, Neustupný writes: "I fully agree with G. Myrdal's remark that recommendations cannot be made without commitment to value judgments. Principles applied in language treatment are accepted differently by different social groups and as long as social stratification exists no 'objectivity' in language treatment is possible" (Neustupný 1970: 89). This is why Neustupný claims that every form of organized language management should fulfill a very specific requirement: "It has become obvious today that any theory of language planning must provide a full account of all political values involved in language planning processes. The public must be made aware of what political aims are either intentionally or unintentionally supported [...]. This should be not an optional addition but one of the primary objectives of the discipline" (Neustupný 1983: 3).

It is precisely for this reason that LMT gives up the belief that language problems necessarily concern the whole language community and that they can be solved in a neutral way. Instead, Neustupný and Jernudd are convinced that it is always necessary to ask for whose benefit language management is performed:

> In other words, at what costs to what groups in society is a community-wide language planning possible? To whose benefit? When, how and why do groups within a society assume different or even antagonistic positions vis-à-vis the processes of language management? Since different groups normally possess different interests, it would seem that a 'neutral,' 'interest'-free (or 'value'-less) system of language planning and of any language management also is impossible. (Jernudd & Neustupný 1987: 72)

3 Another of Neustupný's succinct formulations of this problem can be cited: "Pokud se týká organizovaného managementu, zdrojem povšimnutí jsou výzkumy jazykové situace. Velmi často však k systematickým výzkumům nedochází a jazyková politika se pak zakládá na neformálních povšimnutích personálu, který je s jazykovou politikou nejúžeji spjat. Takovou situaci teorie jazykového managementu kritizuje." [When it comes to organized management, the source of noting is the research of the language situation. However, systematic research is often not conducted, so language policy is based on informal noting of staff most closely related to language policy. The theory of language management criticizes such a situation"] (Neustupný 2002: 437).

As a result, the question of the solubility of language problems is answered somewhat more realistically: while within language planning it was often believed that all language problems can be solved in a neutral way, LMT is based on the conviction that some problems cannot be solved satisfactorily for all stakeholders, and that some of them cannot be solved at all (see Neustupný 2002: 436).

3 The Council for the Standard Croatian Language Norm

As mentioned in the introduction, the Council for the Standard Croatian Language Norm was a group of experts working as an advisory body at the Ministry of Science, Education and Sports of the Republic of Croatia from April 2005 to May 2012. It was founded by Minister Dragan Primorac, appointed by the right-wing conservative party Croatian Democratic Union (HDZ), and abolished by Minister Željko Jovanović from the left-wing liberal Social Democratic Party (SDP).[4] The president of the Council was Radoslav Katičić, probably the most influential contemporary Croatian linguist, and its members were representatives of all academic institutions in Croatia specializing in the research of contemporary Standard Croatian.[5]

---

4 This was not a coincidence, since right-wing and left-wing politicians (as well as their voters) in Croatia have different attitudes toward centralized language regulation. Minister Primorac, for example, had an exceptionally high opinion of the Council: "Znajte da u Hrvatskoj nema nikoga tko bi u pitanjima hrvatskog standardnog jezika bio iznad Vijeća." [You should know that the Council is the paramount authority in Croatia on questions of the Croatian standard language.] (*Jezik* 60: 56), while Minister Jovanović, on the other hand, insisted there was no need for the Council to continue the mission for which it was founded: "[N]ormom hrvatskoga standardnog jezika [se] trebaju baviti institucije kojima je to zadatak." [The norm of the Croatian standard language should be dealt with by the already existing institutions whose mission is to do so.], *Jezik* 60: 42. Such a polarization of both politicians and society over the Council triggered its use in the Croatian version of the "cultural war." For example, in an interview published in the daily newspaper *Slobodna Dalmacija* on May 27, 2012, the former president of the Council Radoslav Katičić accused the left-liberal government of having abolished the Council because "the spirit of the Croatian language" bothers them. See "Ugasili su nas jer im smeta duh hrvatskog jezika" [They have abolished us because the spirit of the Croatian language bothers them] http://slobodnadalmacija.hr/novosti/hrvatska/clanak/id/168499/akademik-katicic-ugasili-su-nas-jer-im-smeta-duh-hrvatskog-jezika <June 15, 2016>. In contemporary Croatia, it is very common for right-wing politicians and their supporters to accuse the left-wing part of society of not being patriotic enough.

5 Members of the Council were: Joško Božanić (University of Split), Dunja Brozović Rončević (the Institute of Croatian Language and Linguistics), Mislav Ježić (Croatian Academy of Sciences and Arts), Ljiljana Kolenić (Faculty of Humanities and Social Sciences, Osijek), Tomislav Ladan (the Miroslav Krleža Institute of Lexicography, who was later replaced by Marko Samardžija), Mile Mamić (University of Zadar), Dunja Pavličević-Franić (Faculty of Teacher Education, Zagreb), Mirko Peti

The composition of the Council reflected a belief–popular among many ordinary users of Croatian, but partly also among Croatian linguists–that the main difficulty faced by contemporary Standard Croatian is the lack of consensus among linguists on how current language problems should be solved, or even on what the current language problems actually are. By gathering representatives of all relevant linguistic institutions in Croatia, the Council was intended to become a body that would lead to such a consensus. In addition, by relying on both political and expert authority, it sought to be perceived as the supreme language arbiter in Croatia.

Members of the Council met once a month (at least at the beginning, while in the later period of the Council's work, meetings were held less frequently) to discuss a topic chosen by the president of the Council. As a rule, the president prepared an elaborated introduction to the topic, after which a discussion followed. In the discussions, dissonant voices were heard from time to time, but they never influenced the decisions of the Council, since all the proposals of the president were eventually accepted. Minutes from the sessions of the Council, as well as other documents related to its work, were published in the journal *Jezik* [Language] 60 (2013), No. 2–4.

In the remaining part of the chapter, the work of the Council will be analyzed from the perspective of LMT, with a focus on the Council's approach to simple language management, ideology and particular interests. However, before proceeding to the analysis, it should be noted that, in many details, the work of the Council was inspired by the paper "Načela standardnosti hrvatskoga jezika" [Principles of standardness of the Croatian language], written by the Council's president, Radoslav Katičić,[6] and published in 1996.

4 The "principles of standardness of Croatian"

Several fundamental topics are addressed in Katičić's paper. To start with, he points out that the dialect basis of the Croatian standard language is the Neo-Štokavian Jekavian dialect.[7] Its choice was determined by the development of the language

---

(Matica hrvatska), Ivo Pranjković (Faculty of Humanities and Social Sciences, Zagreb), Branka Tafra (Croatian Studies, Zagreb), Marija Turk (Faculty of Humanities and Social Sciences, Rijeka) and Ivan Zoričić (Faculty of Humanities and Social Sciences, Pula).

6 As has already been mentioned, Radoslav Katičić is the most influential among living Croatian linguists. His research covers classical philology, ancient Balkan languages, and Indian and Slavic philology. In the field of Croatian philology, his main contributions were theoretical geno-linguistic and sociolinguistic works, as well as empirical research into medieval and early modern written Croatian. Since 1977, he has been professor of Slavic philology at the University of Vienna.

7 In the central South Slavic area, stretching from Slovenia in the northwest to Bulgaria and Macedonia in the southeast, Slavic dialects are traditionally divided into four major groups. In the northwest of Croatia, Kajkavian dialects are spoken, while

situation and literacy in Croatian lands from the fifteenth until the nineteenth century, during which time the Neo-Štokavian dialects gradually spread both territorially and as a medium of literacy. The final acceptance of the Neo-Štokavian Jekavian dialect as the basis for modern Standard Croatian in the nineteenth century was thus determined primarily by the inherent development of the Croatian language situation, not by the desire for language unification with Serbs.[8]

However, although Standard Croatian is based on the Neo-Štokavian Jekavian dialect, it was also traditionally open to elements—both lexical and grammatical—from other Croatian dialects. This openness to other dialects was radically limited after the language reform in the 1890s, with which coordinated Serbo-Croatian language planning had begun. The reform was marked by the so-called "dialect purism," a view holding that all linguistic features that are not Neo-Štokavian should be eradicated from the standard language. In accordance with that view, all non-Neo-Štokavian elements of Standard Croatian were proscribed, but as many of them nevertheless survived, they became an object of the continuous criticism of Serbian linguists throughout the twentieth century.[9] Katičić believes contemporary Standard Croatian should be open to reviving lexical items that were

---

Čakavian dialects are spoken in Istria and along the Dalmatian coast. Dialects from both of these groups are spoken primarily by Croats. On the other hand, in the southeast of Serbia, Torlakian dialects are spoken, mostly by Serbs. In the central area, covering most of Croatia, the whole of Bosnia-Herzegovina, the whole of Montenegro and most of Serbia, Štokavian dialects are spoken by Bosniaks, Croats, Montenegrins, and Serbs. Within Štokavian, archaic Paleo-Štokavian dialects are distinguished from the more innovative (primarily in accentuation and morphology) Neo-Štokavian dialects, which are further divided into Ikavian (spoken by Bosniaks and Croats), Ekavian (spoken by Serbs) and Jekavian (spoken by Bosniaks, Croats, Montenegrins, and Serbs). While contemporary Standard Serbian is based on Neo-Štokavian Ekavian, contemporary Standard Croatian, Bosnian and Montenegrin are based on the Neo-Štokavian Jekavian dialect.

8 By emphasizing this, Katičić actually responds to the claim that Croats have abandoned their own tradition of literacy in order to accept the "Serbian" Neo-Štokavian dialect. This view is best formulated in the paper "Srbi svi i svuda" [Serbs All and Everywhere] by Serbian language reformer Vuk Karadžić, published in his book *Kovčežić za istoriju, jezik i običaje Srba sva tri zakona* [Treasure box for the history, language and customs of Serbs of all three faiths] in 1849. According to Karadžić, all speakers of Štokavian dialects should be treated as Serbs, including Roman Catholics and Muslims. Speakers of Kajkavian dialects should be included as Slovenes, while Croats are to be limited to speakers of Čakavian dialects only. During the twentieth century, Karadžić's views were often repeated by many Serbian linguists and politicians.

9 Ivo Pranjković (1997) demonstrated that the most important Serbian linguistic journal *Naš jezik* [Our language] labeled such features of Standard Croatian as "regional" or "provincial," and insisted that the further standardization of Serbo-Croatian ensure they be replaced by their "neutral" equivalents used in Serbia.

eradicated at that time, and that even grammatical features of the nineteenth century Standard Croatian should be taught in schools.

In addition to his claim that the revival of eradicated non-Neo-Štokavian lexical elements in contemporary Standard Croatian should be supported, Katičić points out that it is also necessary to encourage the formation of neologisms with domestic Slavic morphemes to pair with already established Europeanisms. According to Katičić, the parallel existence of Europeanisms and domestically coined words has characterized Croatian literacy since its beginnings in the Middle Ages. Although this tradition has been weakened and depreciated during the period of Serbo-Croatian coordinated language policy and planning, Katičić believes that in new circumstances it should be revived.

Finally, Katičić writes about orthography. Nineteenth-century Croatian orthography was morphonological, which means it reflected the phonemic composition of morphemes regardless of the phonetic processes that sometimes happen on the border of morphemes within words. For example, the noun meaning 'signature,' composed of the prefix *pod-* and radix *pis*, was written *podpis* despite the fact that it was pronounced [potpis] due to assimilation in the voice. Similarly, adjective meaning 'oral,' composed of the radix *ust-* and suffix *-ni*, was written *ustni* despite the fact that it was pronounced [usni] due to consonant cluster reduction. However, in the 1890s, Croatian orthography became—from his point of view—predominantly "phonological," meaning that such phonetic processes are reflected in writing, so the two mentioned words are written *potpis* and *usni* today. Katičić claims that it would be too radical to return to morphonological orthography, but that the morphonological principle is nevertheless alive in some details of contemporary Croatian orthography. In these cases, it competes with the dominant phonological principle, and contemporary written use should be monitored to determine which is more convenient for language users and should therefore be followed in codification.

In short, Katičić explains in the paper the basic principles on which, in his opinion, the standardization of Croatian language has been based for centuries. During the existence of Yugoslavia, characterized by a coordinated Serbo-Croatian language policy and planning, these principles were often violated and even openly denied, but the tradition of Croatian language standardization predated it and many specific elements of this tradition survived despite continuous efforts to eradicate them. The article was based on the conviction that, in future, language policy and planning for Croatian should be organized independently of other closely related central South Slavic languages, as hundred years of joint efforts were rather unsuccessful and left too many grievances on the Croatian side. Katičić called on contemporary language planners of Croatian to remain sensitive to the values on which Croatian language standardization was based in the past. Indeed, in the years that followed the break-up of both Yugoslavia and Serbo-Croatian joint language policy and planning, Katičić's paper became rather influential and widely cited among Croatian linguists. The language ideology of the article resonated well in the context of the newly gained political independence of Croatia, so most of

Katičić's ideas were accepted by Croatian linguists as moderate and uncontroversial. However, it turned out that putting them into practice in language management was much more difficult, as the example of the Council clearly demonstrates.

5 The approach to simple language management

When it comes to the Council's approach to simple language management, i.e., to the noting of language problems by users and to the solutions of these problems that they spontaneously arrive at, the best indicator is probably the introductory talk on the reasons for the establishment of the Council given by the Council's president at the first meeting. The minutes of this meeting state: "Another reason is that, despite the fact that we have a well-constructed and elaborated standard language, the relation of the Croatian language community to it is deeply distorted."[10] In other words, Standard Croatian does exist in language manuals, but language users rarely practice it. In the president's talk in the Council's second meeting, a solution to this problem is also offered:

> To traži energičan duhovni zaokret u odnosu prema normi, a ne zaokret u samoj normi, zaokret u prosvjetnoj politici i osobito u nastavi hrvatskoga jezika i književnosti.[11]
>
> [What is needed is an energetic spiritual turn in relation to the language norm, not a turn in the language norm itself; what is needed is a turn in the educational policy, especially in the teaching of Croatian language and literature.]

Since the relation of the users of Croatian to their own standard language is "deeply distorted," the Council's main aim is to coerce them into a "spiritual turn" that would result in their undue respect for the prescribed norms of the standard language.[12] With such a starting point, it is no surprise that the Council demonstrated little understanding of simple (micro) language management as a point of departure of the organized (macro) language management.

The lack of interest of the Council in simple language management is visible at two levels. At the first level, the Council deals with problems that had not existed

---

10 Rasprava o zadaćama Vijeća za normu hrvatskoga standardnog jezika [Discussion about the aims of the Council for the Standard Croatian Language Norm], *Jezik* 60: 62.

11 Temeljna pitanja odnosa hrvatske jezične zajednice prema svojemu standardnom jeziku [Basic questions about the relation of the Croatian language community to their standard language], *Jezik* 60: 67.

12 While in the Decision on the Establishment and Appointment of Members of the Council issued by Minister Primorac, the main task of the Council was set in terms that can be connected primarily to corpus and status planning, these introductory talks of the Council's president demonstrate that the focus was in fact shifted to image and prestige planning. In this way, the Council actually overstepped the boundaries within which it was supposed to work.

for language users until they were created by linguists themselves. Such cases directly contradict the requirement that LMT sets before any form of organized language regulation:

> Jinými slovy, jazykový management se musí odpoutat od situace, kdy lingvisté či jiný personál určovali na základě velmi omezené zkušenosti z jazykové praxe, co je, či není problém. (Neustupný 2002: 435)
>
> [In other words, language management must move away from the situation in which linguists or other staff, on the basis of very limited experience from language practice, determine what is and what not a problem is.]

The three most important problems of that kind which have attracted much attention in the discussions on Croatian orthography since the beginnings of the 1990s are whether prescribed spelling should be *podatci* or *podaci* ('data'), *ne ću* or *neću* ('I will not') and *strjelica* or *strelica* ('arrow').[13] In the first two examples, the Council prescribes, and in the third example strongly recommends the first of the two possible solutions, despite the fact that all of them are extremely rare in contemporary written Croatian.

With regard to the first problem (*podatci / podaci*), the Council's president acknowledges he is aware that his recommendation goes against majority use and the absence of the simple language management in this point:

> Na takav smo se pravopisni propis više manje naviknuli, to smo učili i mnogi su to dobro naučili. Ipak se protiv takva pisanja javlja i spontan otpor.[14]
>
> [We have all got used to that rule [i.e., to writing *podaci* 'data'], we learned it at school, and many learned it well. Yet there is spontaneous resistance against such writing.]

However, he does not provide either data on what social groups of users of Croatian feel such "spontaneous resistance" and on what occasions, or on the methodology used to reach such a conclusion.[15] In connection to the second problem,

---

13 Without going into too much detail, it should be pointed out that the first of the two possible orthographic solutions were common in Croatian standard language until the 1950s, when they were replaced by the second ones, typical of Serbian standard language. In the second half of the twentieth century, the newly prescribed solutions became gradually accepted, so that by the 1990s they were the only ones used in written Croatian. However, in the 1990s, after several influential linguists insisted "original" Croatian forms be revived, many language users became uncertain as to what orthographic solutions to use. Today, most media and publishing houses still use the second solutions, while children are mostly taught the first ones in schools.

14 Prijeporna pitanja hrvatskoga pravopisa: dentalni okluzivi ispred afrikata [Controversial questions of Croatian orthography: dental stops in front of affricates], *Jezik* 60: 72–73.

15 This is one of the cases in which the morphonological principle (*podatci*) competes with the phonological one (*podaci*) and should, in the opinion of the Council, be given priority.

i.e., *ne ću / neću* 'I will not,' the minutes of meetings contain the following sentence: "Profesorica Kolenić je rekla da je u razgovoru s ljudima čula kako se rastavljeno pisanje lako prihvaća." [Professor Kolenić said that in conversation with people she heard that writing ne ću was easily accepted.][16] Although this is not a key argument in the discussion of this problem, in the context of the Council's approach to simple language management this statement is symptomatic. The Council neither feels there is a need to monitor real language use to establish what users of Croatian feel as language problems, nor does it consider it necessary to examine how the solutions that it recommends are accepted by users—in both cases, surface impressions seem to be sufficient.

At the second level, the Council's lack of interest in simple language management is manifested by denying the importance of the language problems with which language users are really faced, as well as of the solutions that they spontaneously arrive at. For example, in connection to the problem of writing derivatives from foreign proper names, which often appears in contemporary written practice, the Council asserts the following:

> Etnici i ktetici od tuđih imena mjesta pišu se glasovno prilagođeno. Tako *Njujorčanin* i *njujorški* od New York, *Lajpcižanin* i *lajpciški* od Leipzig.[17]
>
> [Demonyms and adjectives derived from place names are written in a transphonemized way. So *Njujorčanin* and *njujorški* from New York, *Lajpcižanin* and *lajpciški* from Leipzig.]

This approach was dominant in the codification of Croatian orthography from the 1890s, but written practice, especially contemporary practice, is often different. Moreover, corpus-based empirical research of contemporary written Croatian suggests that derivatives from foreign proper names—nouns, adjectives, and even verbs—are written mostly by keeping the original orthography in the stem, i.e., *Newyorčanin* instead of *Njujorčanin*, *newyorški* instead of *njujurški*, *shakespeareovski* instead of *šekspirovski* (see Vuković 2002). Despite this, the Council sanctions the solutions that are rarely used in written language.

With regard to some other important issues identified by individual Council members as potentially problematic for users of contemporary Standard Croatian, the Council as a whole has refused to even address them. A member of the Council, Joško Božanić, warns for example of the need to conduct systematic research of accentuation, which in contemporary Standard Croatian is certainly no longer classical Neo-Štokavian:

16 Sastavljeno i rastavljeno pisanje niječnice i enklitičkih oblika glagola *htjeti* [Writing negative particle and enclitic forms of the verb *htjeti* together or separately], *Jezik* 60: 77.

17 Pisanje stranih imena i od njih izvedenih pridjeva [Writing foreign names and adjectives derived from them], *Jezik* 60: 54.

> Potrebno je doseći neutralni stupanj u izražavanju standardnim jezikom. To se najviše tiče fonološke slike jezika, akcentuacije. Mimo jezične politike stvorila se jedna norma, urbani govor, koja je u ponečemu udaljena od izvornoga novoštokavskog sustava. I to postaje znakom urbanoga idioma. Tu bi činjenicu trebalo osvijestiti i teoretski valjano opisati.[18]
>
> [It is necessary to attain a neutral level in standard language use. This concerns mostly the phonological image of language, accentuation. Independently of language policy, a norm, urban speech, has been created, which is somewhat different from the original Neo-Štokavian system. Moreover, it becomes a sign of urban speech. We should be aware of this fact and describe it theoretically.]

However, the majority in the Council took a position fully in accordance with the mission of the Council set in the introductory talk by the Council's president:

> Profesor Ježić je rekao da tu treba aktivirati škole i službe u medijima. Treba početi doista učiti ortoepsku normu.[19]
>
> [Professor Ježić said that schools and language services in the media should become more active. Language users should really start learning the orthoepic norm.]

Another member of the Council, Branka Tafra, attempted to open the question of too strict language codification:

> [U] kroatistici prevladava pristup previše restriktivan. Prevelike su razlike između uporabne i kodifikacijske norme. Potrebno je nešto promijeniti u pristupu standardu te smatra da bi trebalo 'olabaviti' normu.[20]
>
> [The approach to language codification of Croatian is too restrictive. There are too many differences between the norms in real language use and codified norms. There is a need to change the approach to the standard language and to make language codification less strict.]

However, the dominant approach in the Council was that it is not language codification, but language users that need to be changed:

> Dunja Brozović Rončević rekla je da je problem u poremećenom odnosu prema standardnomu jeziku. [...] Tijekom školovanja nema prigode uspostaviti primjeren

---

18 Jezična mijena i jezični razvoj; Ortoepska norma u elektroničkim medijima [Language change and language development: The orthoepic norm in electronic media], *Jezik* 60: 132.

19 Jezična mijena i jezični razvoj: Ortoepska norma u elektroničkim medijima [Language change and language development: The orthoepic norm in electronic media], *Jezik* 60: 133. Mislav Ježić served as the vice-president of the Council, and his reply closed discussion on this problem.

20 Standardni jezik i govorni jezik: Izvješće o projektu "Struna" [Standard language and spoken language: Report on the project "Struna"], *Jezik* 60: 139.

> odnos prema hrvatskomu standardnom jeziku. U srednjoj školi uopće nema jezične izobrazbe. A za sve državne službenike bio bi potreban test iz kulture hrvatskoga jezika.[21]
>
> [Dunja Brozović Rončević said the problem was in disturbed relations to the standard language. [...] During schooling, there is no opportunity to establish an appropriate attitude towards the Croatian standard language. There is practically no language education in secondary school at all. Moreover, for all civil servants it should be obligatory to pass an exam in the Croatian standard language.]

A specific problem amongst those addressed by the Council was the use of gender-sensitive language. Though many speakers of Croatian aim at language use that would be more inclusive towards different disadvantaged social groups, with the largest of them being women, the Council rejects such aspirations:

> Stoga se u hrvatskome i većini jezika imenicom muškoga roda često označuju osobe i muškoga i ženskoga spola. [...] Tu nema pomoći nego treba poštovati ustroj jezika ili razumijevanje postaje nemoguće. A to nema veze s neravnopravnošću spolova.[22]
>
> [In Croatian and in most other languages, masculine nouns often denote both men and women. [...] This cannot be changed; the structure of the language should be respected if one does not want communication to become impossible. This has nothing to do with gender inequality.]

However, many users of Croatian see this problem differently, for example, a blogger on a news website wrote (Gruenfelder 2015):

> Tipična muška logika! I to logika onoga koji se nalazi u poziciji moćnika, jer određuje jezične norme. [...] Jezikom, tim najznačajnijim sredstvom ljudske komunikacije, žene se dosljednom uporabom muškog roda čine 'nečujnima' i 'nevidljivima,' briše im se trag. A jezik—i hrvatski jezik—omogućava da se žene 'pojavljuju' kao samosvojne egzistencije.
>
> [This is typical male logic! Moreover, this is the logic of a man who is in a position of power, because he determines the language norms. [...] In language, the most important means of human communication, women are made 'inaudible' and 'invisible' by the consistent use of masculine forms. On the other hand, language—the Croatian language as well—allows women to 'appear' as an autonomous existence.]

---

21 Standardni jezik i govorni jezik: Izvješće o projektu „Struna" [Standard language and spoken language: Report on the project "Struna"], *Jezik* 60: 139. Dunja Brozović-Rončević was the secretary of the Council and this reply of hers closed discussion on the subject.

22 Mišljenje Vijeća za normu hrvatskoga standardnog jezika o uporabi oblika ženskoga roda za zvanja kao izraza poštovanja ravnopravnosti spolova [Opinion of the Council on the use of forms of the feminine gender for profession names as an expression of respect for gender equality], *Jezik* 60: 155.

In accordance with such an understanding, it could be claimed that masculine nouns have generic meaning only if there is consensus among speakers about this. It seems that this consensus in Croatian (and not only in Croatian) is at least in some cases significantly weakened, so many speakers turn to gender-sensitive use. The Council shows no understanding for this problem—in fact, it argues that gender neutral use can only be achieved at the expense of radically reduced language economy, and even then not completely, so it should not be striven for at all.[23] The problem of gender-neutral language use is one of the most serious language problems that users of Croatian face in everyday communication, designing for it numerous different (and sometimes indeed clumsy) solutions. It would be useful if those spontaneously devised solutions were systematically described, since this would be a starting point for recommendations on which of them to use in formal language. However, the Council dismisses this problem altogether.

6 The approach to ideology and particular interests

Ideologies generally play an important role in organized language management, among other things due to the motivational power they can have (for more about language ideologies, see, e.g., Schieffelin, Woolard & Kroskrity 1998; Blommaert 1999, 2006). The Council's approach to language management is also distinctively marked by a specific ideology, which is connected to how the most prominent members of the Council perceive and understand the Croatian language. In their opinion, the Croatian language developed favorably during the nineteenth century within the so-called Philological School of Zagreb. This school worked along the "principles of standardness" that Katičić writes about; however, it did not have the final word on the standardization of modern Croatian. The concluding step towards modern Standard Croatian was made by the language reform of the 1890s, with its morphological and lexical Neo-Štokavization: it resulted in a stable standard language that gradually became more and more accepted, but, at the same time, represented a significant break with earlier language traditions. In connection with this, the president of the Council, Radoslav Katičić, points out:

> Tu je zadaću samouvjereno bezobzirno, ali i funkcionalno uspješno izvršila škola hrvatskih vukovaca.[24]
>
> [That task was accomplished self-confidently and recklessly, but in a functionally successful manner by the Croatian followers of Vuk Karadžić.]

---

23 In Croatian, gender is marked on all nouns, as well as on all other words in a sentence agreeing with nouns, i.e., on adjectives, pronouns, and even some verbal forms. This makes it rather complicated to attain gender-neutral language use.

24 Bivše Vijeće za normu hrvatskoga standardnog jezika [The former Council for the Standard Croatian Language Norm], *Jezik* 60: 45. Vuk Karadžić, the already mentioned Serbian language reformer from the nineteenth century, published numerous books of Neo-Štokavian oral literature, which became quite famous throughout

The language reform of the 1890s was later followed by the imposed orthography by Serbian linguist Aleksandar Belić in the 1920s and the so-called Novi Sad agreement in the 1950s, which both contributed to the further eradication of specific Croatian language features. The Council therefore claimed that its most fundamental role is to bring the Croatian language back to its essence by promoting the "spiritual turn." The language ideology of the Council is visible primarily in the topics that it discussed. On the other hand, the way the Council approaches ideology can be best seen in the arguments it uses to support its proposal.

When it comes to the topics, two of them are particularly indicative. The first concerns the old plural forms for dative, locative and instrumental. In nineteenth century Croatian, each of the three cases had its own form, for example the noun with the meaning 'woman' had the form *ženam* in the dative plural, *ženah* in the locative plural, and *ženami* in the instrumental plural. In contemporary standard Croatian, there is only one form common for all three cases: *ženama.* This new syncretic form, characteristic for the Neo-Štokavian dialect, was codified within the language reform of the 1890s. Moreover, after the language reform had been implemented, Croatian literary classics from the nineteenth century were consistently published in revised editions that followed new grammatical (as well as lexical and orthographical) codification. Katičić urges that they have to be published and read in their original language, which would make it possible for the old plural forms to return to the school curriculum. In Katičić's words, this would heal

> teško narušena cjelovitost hrvatskoga književnog jezika i živ odnos prema njegovoj prošlosti [...]. Time se hrvatska jezična kultura ozdravljuje od bolesnoga stanja zatirana sjećanja, prave *damnatio memoriae*, kojom je bila udarena uz bezobzirno 'osuvremenjivanje' književnih tekstova.[25]

> [the seriously disrupted integrity of the Croatian literary language and live relationship with its past [...]. This would help Croatian linguistic culture to recover from the unhealthy condition, a genuine *damnatio memoriae*, which hit it with the reckless 'modernization' of literary texts.]

The second topic is also connected to Neo-Štokavian "dialectal purism," but it concerns the lexical layer. As has already been mentioned, the language reform of the 1890s insisted that only Neo-Štokavian lexical elements be kept in Standard Croatian, while those from other dialects should be eradicated. The Council rejects this attitude and insists on a more inclusive approach. In connection with this, the Council's president emphasizes:

Europe. This contributed to the fact that many of his followers in Croatia started believing that the Neo-Štokavian dialect best represents the spirit of "our people."

25 Stari množinski padeži u hrvatskoj jezičnoj naobrazbi [Old plural endings in Croatian language education], *Jezik* 60: 92.

> Trebat će pri tome napustiti isključivu orijentaciju prema rječniku kulturne sfere obilježene planinskim stočarstvom, orijentaciju koja sve do danas prepoznatljivo oblikuje strukovne predodžbe o našoj leksičkoj normi, i prihvatiti leksičko bogatstvo drugih hrvatskih kulturnih ambijenata, kao što su jadranski, panonski i podalpski.[26]
>
> [An exclusive orientation toward the vocabulary of the cultural sphere marked by mountain cattle-breeding, which until today recognizably defines the approach of many experts to our lexical norm, will have to be abandoned, and the lexical wealth of other Croatian cultural milieus, such as the Adriatic, Pannonian and Subalpine, will have to be accepted.]

In this quotation, the Neo-Štokavian vocabulary is connected to "the cultural sphere marked by mountain cattle-breeding," which replicates the nineteenth-century stereotype popular in northwestern Croatian towns that the speakers of the Neo-Štokavian dialect are illiterate highland shepherds. According to Katičić, many Croatian linguists still believe it is exclusively the Neo-Štokavian lexical layer that should be represented in Standard Croatian. He, on the other hand, claims that Standard Croatian should be enriched with rejected lexical items typical of urban Croatia: Adriatic (Čakavian dialect), Pannonian (Paleo-Štokavian dialect) and Subalpine (Kajkavian dialect).

It has to be pointed out that neither of these two topics causes contemporary users of Standard Croatian much pain. In fact, the existence of the old plural forms,[27] as well as the alleged oversaturation of Standard Croatian vocabulary with the culture of "mountain cattle breeding," are not common public knowledge. Moreover, it is not clear what the Council thinks should be done with contemporary Standard Croatian to make it more open towards old plural forms and vocabulary from other dialects. The fact that the Council addresses these topics obviously has more to do with the proclaimed "spiritual turn" than with organized language management conducted with the intention of solving language problems faced by users in their interactions.

When it comes to the arguments used to support the proposed solutions, two of them are particularly striking. In the first one, the Council introduced a new theoretical conception, according to which Croatian standard language does not have a Neo-Štokavian base, but is only "stylized" as Neo-Štokavian.[28] The conception is at least questionable, and, at best, it could be discussed in the pages of linguistic journals. However, when one has in mind that the phonological and morphological system of contemporary Standard Croatian is practically completely

26 Temeljna pitanja leksičke norme [Basic questions of the lexical norm], *Jezik* 60: 96.

27 These forms were abandoned by the codification in the 1890s because they were hardly used even at that time.

28 See Dijalekatska osnovica hrvatskoga standardnog jezika; Prilozi o strukovnome nazivlju [Dialect base of Croatian standard language: Contributions to terminology], *Jezik* 60: 115–117.

Neo-Štokavian, as is most of its lexical and syntactic system, it is difficult to conceive what evidence would be used to support such a claim. Interestingly, it also contradicts what Katičić argued in his article of 1996, i.e., that the dialect basis of contemporary Standard Croatian is the Neo-Štokavian Jekavian dialect. Given that this new conception is far from being even marginally accepted, it can hardly serve as a non-controversial theoretical starting point for the organized management of the Croatian standard language.

The second argument that I want to refer to is connected to the problem of whether the plural form of the word meaning 'data' should be written *podatci* or *podaci*, which was already mentioned above. This problem has traditionally been described as one of the orthographic issues where morphonological and phonological principles are in conflict: while the former would require users to write *podatci* (so that the radix *dat* is better represented in writing), the latter would prescribe *podaci* (because the consonant cluster /tc/ on the border between radix and suffix is reduced to /c/, corresponding to pronunciation). Contrary to that, the Council attempts to prove that the phonological principle, if consistently applied, would actually require users to write *dodatci*, not *dodaci*:

> Eksperimentalno je fonetsko istraživanje, međutim, pokazalo egzaktnim mjerenjem da se tu ne izgovara obična afrikata, nego nešto produljena. Ono što se po tome pravopisu pisalo *dodaci* ne izgovara se jednako kao *junaci*. Po fonološkome načelu trebalo bi tu pisati *dodacci*. No udvajanje suglasnika kako bi se označilo da su produljeni nije uobičajeno u hrvatskoj grafiji. Primjerenije je onda pisati *dodatci*.[29]

> [Experimental phonetic research with the help of exact measuring demonstrated that what is pronounced in those positions is not a simple affricate, but a prolonged one. What, according to those [i.e., phonological] rules, is written *dodaci* is not pronounced in the same way as *junaci*. The phonological principle would require us to write *dodacci*. However, in Croatian orthography, double consonants are not a common signal of their lengthening. It is therefore more adequate to write *dodatci*.]

This argument has several weak points. First, the Council does not say who conducted this experimental research and where the results have been published. Second, even if these results were credible, they could only prove how the word is pronounced, not its phonemic composition. Finally, even if the word *podaci* indeed contained the doubling of the phoneme /c/, i.e., /dodacci/, it remains unclear how to come from the phonetic evidence to morphological orthography and why it would be phonologically "more adequate" to write it *dodatci*. In short, the argument remains deeply unconvincing, but it is symptomatic of the way the Council approaches language management.

29 Bivše Vijeće za normu hrvatskoga standardnog jezika [Former Council for the Standard Croatian Language Norm], *Jezik* 60: 48.

The recommendation to write *podatci* is then rather motivated by the Council's language ideology: this way of writing was typical of Croatian until 1960, when it was replaced by another orthographical solution, more typical for Serbian; now the original Croatian solution should be restored. Something similar can be said about the Council's approach to the dialect base of Croatian: during the nineteenth century, Croatian was much more open to different dialects, and only in the 1890s did it become predominantly Neo-Štokavian; the aim should be to restore the original situation. However, instead of acknowledging openly that their aims are motivated by language ideology, the Council attempts to prove that what they favor is better for purely linguistic, exact and scientific reasons, although this interpretation of language development is not a consensus in Croatian linguistics.

To achieve a change, the language ideology has to be shared by the language community. The fact that neither of the Council's recommendations was accepted points to the fact that in this particular situation that was not the case: most active users of Standard Croatian seem to think neither that their relation to language is "distorted" nor that they need the "spiritual turn" that the Council proposes. For them, the most relevant starting point for the discussion of the contemporary Croatian language seems to be the functionality of its present-day use, which actually corresponds to the basic postulates of LMT. In accordance with these postulates, organized language management should look for solutions to real problems that users face in their communication, not for invented ones. Moreover, the proposed solutions should be formulated reasonably to be acceptable for them. These recommendations should not be based on controversial ideologies and "theories," because that automatically decreases their acceptability.

In the Council, such an approach is best represented by its member Ivo Pranjković. In one of the Council's meetings, Pranjković discussed the problem of whether enclitic forms of the verb *htjeti* 'will' should be written separately from the negative particle, i.e., *ne ću* 'I will not' (which was typical of Croatian until 1960), or together with it, i.e., *neću* (which was originally typical of Serbian and in 1960 was also accepted in Croatian). Pranjković claims:

> Ako uvođenje sastavljenog pisanja *neću* i jest bilo rezultat nasilja 1960. godine, nisam za to da se jedno nasilje ispravlja novim, a uvođenje pisanja *ne ću* nasilje je već i zato što oni koji su uvođenje pisanja *neću* eventualno doživjeli kao nasilje imaju danas najmanje 55 godina, a i oni su u međuvremenu stekli novu naviku.[30]
>
> [Even if the introduction of writing *neću* was indeed a result of violence in 1960, I cannot support one act of violence being replaced with another. The introduction of writing *ne ću* today is also violence, because those who experienced the introduction

30 Sastavljeno i rastavljeno pisanje niječnice i enklitičkih oblika glagola htjeti [Writing negative particle and enclitic forms of the verb *htjeti* together or separately], *Jezik* 60: 76.

of ne ću as violence are at least 55 years old now, and, in the meantime even they have developed the new habit [of writing *neću*].]

In short, Pranjković insists that there is no need to intervene into a use that is completely accepted by users, even if we know it is of foreign (Serbian) origin. However, a different approach to this problem prevailed in the Council. Commenting on the fact that most media and publishing houses continue to use *neću*—i.e., the solution to which they are accustomed, regardless of its Serbian origin—one of the most prominent members of the Council, Mislav Ježić, warned that

> da je odbijanje rastavljenoga pisanja u znatnom dijelu visokotiražnih medija rezultat jezične politike i na njoj zasnovane lekture koja se provodi u njima.[31]
>
> [the fact that most of the media reject writing *ne ću* is the result of language politics and of their editing practices based on that politics.]

In other words, Ježić does not accept that the media continue to write *neću* simply because users of Croatian use it and do not believe it is necessary to change it. He claims it is "language politics" that prevents the media from accepting the solution that the Council attempts to reintroduce.

The work of the Council was an important part of the right-wing conservative and nationalist cultural agenda, for which it is central to promote Croatian linguistic identity, especially as opposed to Serbian. However, members of the Council never explicitly reflected how and why the Council was established and claimed that their proposals were motivated by purely linguistic reasons. It is, however, interesting that the way they wanted to promote Croatian linguistic identity was not accepted even by the right-wing part of society. The Council primarily focused on restoring elements eradicated from Croatian during the period of Serbo-Croatian coordinated language policy and planning, but at the same time neglected the contemporary tendencies that are typically Croatian. Two such tendencies have been mentioned above: writing derivatives from foreign proper names and the systematic derivation of feminine nouns. It is precisely these two examples that demonstrate the degree to which the Council neglects the predominant language use as a result of simple language management. Members of the Council also dismiss new developmental tendencies that are typically Croatian and could be used to emphasize a distinct Croatian linguistic identity. The work of the Council was almost entirely focused on language history.

This may be the reason why the propositions of the Council were rejected even by the right-wing part of society. For example, Ivo Sanader, prime minister of the right-wing government that founded the Council, publicly refused to accept orthography solutions proposed by the Council, as did most of the media

31 Sastavljeno i rastavljeno pisanje niječnice i enklitičkih oblika glagola htjeti [Writing the negative particle and enclitic forms of the verb *htjeti* together or separately], *Jezik* 60: 77.

and publishing houses, including the most important right-wing newspapers. It seems that, instead of simply promoting ideology typical of the right-wing part of Croatian society, members of the Council promoted their own—much narrower—interests: to impose their own interpretation of what Croatian should look like and to maintain their social positions as supreme language arbiters, whereby the narrative of the need for a "spiritual turn" in relation to Standard Croatian served as a means to mobilize followers. Recommendations of the Council were eventually rejected by the majority of society, so based on that it can be claimed that the organized language management practiced by the Council was unsuccessful. More than that, it was harmful because it destabilized language use (new school generations vs. users educated before the suggested solution were introduced) and provoked heated discussions by radicalized participants.

7 Conclusion

Analyzing the diachronic development of modern organized language management, Neustupný (2006) distinguished three basic types. The early modern type, which dominated from the beginning of the nineteenth century until the end of the First World War, is characterized by emphasizing the independence of a particular language from other languages and its instrumentalization in strengthening the cohesion of the community of its speakers. Standard language was considered an important symbol of ethnic connectedness, and its dissemination into wider social strata was encouraged. In this type of organized language management, widely conceived reforms were conducted, with linguistic purism often being an important component. The second type of organized language management is characteristic of the period from the end of the First World War until the 1960s. At that time, most language communities in the West already had elaborated and stabilized standard languages, with linguistic communities being relatively isolated from each other. Organized language management was therefore oriented towards functional differentiation of the standard language, i.e., to its adaptation to new communication needs. Only moderate intervention and less emotional engagement were typical of this type of organized language management, with the Prague Linguistic School being one of its prominent representatives. In the 1960s, the late modern (or postmodern) period began in organized language management. Due to globalization, the isolation of nations and language communities decreased, and the development of standard languages was strongly influenced by new media. Class, gender, regional and ethnic variations in language became more visible, but they were no longer perceived as problems—on the contrary, they were often glorified. Accordingly, all types of discrimination were to be removed from language use. The late-modern type of organized language management aims at providing everyone with the opportunity to use their own language variety in public space, without being labeled. At the same time, however, consensus is still strong that, for the sake of communication efficiency, the common language remains important.

In Vuković (2009), these three types of organized language management are called delimitative, functional and inclusive.

The Council for the Standard Croatian Language Norm conducted essentially delimitative organized language management. On the one hand, it neglected the importance of the questions of linguistic functionality and social inclusiveness, which are crucial from the perspective of ordinary language users. On the other hand, it proposed interventions that directly opposed stabilized language use of the majority of language users, which were motivated primarily by an identity narrative. As can be seen from Neustupný's diachronic typology of organized language management, this type of language regulation is more characteristic of the nineteenth than of the twenty-first century. Prominent members of the Council were apparently convinced they had both the authority and power to impose on the whole language community not only language standards, but also the image of what Croatian language actually is. It turned out they were wrong: the majority in Croatian society, including many of its right-wing supporters, accepted neither the ideology of the Council nor the solutions they proposed. Although the recent history of the Croatian language may explain why this type of language ideology has survived until today in parts of Croatian society and among some Croatian linguists, in the present circumstances it is hardly anything but a historical relic which cannot contribute to successful organized language management. If the organized language management of contemporary Standard Croatian is to be successful, it will have to be more attentive to usage and simple language management and based on a much less controversial language ideology. This will ensure that it is not pursuing only the narrow interest of those who are conducting it.

References

Blommaert, J. (ed) (1999) *Language Ideological Debates*. Berlin: Mouton de Gruyter.

Blommaert, J. (2006) Language ideology. In K. Brown (ed) *Encyclopedia of Language & Linguistics* 6. Oxford: Elsevier, 510–522.

Gruenfelder, A. M. (2015) Predsjednik ili Predsjednica? [President or female president?] On WWW at http://www.autograf.hr/predsjednik-ili-predsjednica/. Accessed May 15, 2019.

Jernudd, B. H. & Neustupný, J. V. (1987) Language planning: For whom? In L. Laforge (ed) *Actes du Colloque international sur l'aménagemant linguistique / Proceedings of the International Colloquium on Language Planning*. Québec: Les Presses de l'Université Laval, 69–84.

Katičić, R. (1996) Načela standardnosti hrvatskoga jezika [Principles of standardness of the Croatian language]. *Jezik: Časopis za kulturu hrvatskoga književnoga jezika* 43 (5), 175–182.

Langston, K. & Peti-Stantić, A. (2011) A language academy by any other name(s): The case of Croatia. *Language Policy* 10 (4), 343–360.

Neustupný, J. V. (1970) Basic types of treatment of language problems. *Linguistic Communications* 1, 77–98. (Reprint in J. A. Fishman (ed) (1974) *Advances in Language Planning*. The Hague & Paris: Mouton, 37–48.)

Neustupný, J. V. (1978) Outline of a theory of language problems. In J. V. Neustupný (ed) *Post-Structural Approaches to Language: Language Theory in a Japanese Context*. Tokyo: University of Tokyo Press, 243–257.

Neustupný, J. V. (1983) Towards a paradigm for language planning. *Language Planning Newsletter* 9 (4), 1–4.

Neustupný, J. V. (2002) Sociolingvistika a jazykový management [Sociolinguistics and language management]. *Sociologický časopis* 38 (4), 429–442.

Neustupný, J. V. (2006) Sociolinguistic aspects of social modernization. In U. Ammon, N. Dittmar & K. J. Mattheier (eds) *Sociolinguistics: An International Handbook of the Science of Language and Society*. Berlin & New York: Walter de Gruyter, 2209–2223.

Peti-Stantić, A. & Langston, K. (2013) *Hrvatsko jezično pitanje danas: Identiteti i ideologije* [The Croatian Language Question Today: Identities and Ideologies]. Zagreb: Srednja Europa.

Pranjković, I. (1997) Hrvatski standardni jezik u staroj Jugoslaviji: Na primjeru časopisa Naš jezik [Croatian standard language in old Yugoslavia: On the example of the journal Naš jezik]. *Croatica: prinosi proučavanju hrvatske književnosti* 27 (45/46), 147–155.

Schieffelin, B. B., Woolard, K. A. & Kroskrity, P. V. (eds) (1998) *Language Ideologies: Practice and Theory*. New York: Oxford University Press.

Vuković, P. (2002) O pisanju izvedenica od stranih vlastitih imena u hrvatskome [On writing of derivatives from foreign proper names in Croatian]. *Fluminensia* 14 (2), 85–104.

Vuković, P. (2009) Typologie moderního jazykového managementu [Typology of modern language management]. In E. Rusinová (ed) *Přednášky a besedy z XLII. běhu LŠSS* [Lectures and Talks from the Forty-Second Course of Summer School of Slavonic Studies]. Brno: Masarykova univerzita, 208–214.

Vuković, P. (2016) Vijeće za normu i teorija upravljanja jezikom [Council for the Standard Croatian Language Norm and Language Management Theory]. *Suvremena lingvistika* 42 (82), 219–235.

Jakub Kopecký

Divergent interests and argumentation in Czech Language Consulting Center interactions

Abstract This chapter examines phone interactions between language users and the Language Consulting Center (LCC) of the Czech Language Institute of the Czech Academy of Sciences within the framework of Language Management Theory. Language consulting interactions are considered to be part of a complex process of language management, consisting both of micro and macro management. I focus on cases of diverging interests in LCC interactions, i.e., on instances of disagreement, opposing standpoints or even conflicts between the inquirer and the LCC linguist. The chapter investigates and describes different interests of the interactants, causes and forms of their divergence, ways of solving subsequent disputes and their various outcomes. In these conflicting exchanges, argumentation plays a very important role due to its problem-solving capacity. In connection with the persuasion process, I devote attention to the language ideologies advocated by linguists and inquirers, particularly with regard to the extent to which they coincide or differ. These ideologies have a significant influence on the content of argumentation as well as on the overall course of these conversations. I also discuss the type and degree of authority the inquirers ascribe to the LCC. This authority is continually negotiated during the consulting process and the acceptability of LCC's arguments plays a decisive role in it.

Keywords language management, Language Consulting Center, language cultivation, interest, argumentation, language ideology, linguistic authority

1 Introduction

Language consultancy interactions are an interesting case of contact and cooperation between actors in simple and organized language management (or various types of organized management). Language users, mostly laypeople, from various social groups and environments, contact a language institution to ask for assistance in solving their language and communication problems. Clients of a consulting center enter into these interactions with different assumptions and expectations: they may prefer a specific solution to the problem and ask only for the confirmation that their adjustment is correct, or they may not tend toward a particular solution; they may attribute different language management roles and different degrees of authority to the language institution. In relation to this, they also construct their own roles as language users and language management actors in different ways.

The aim of this chapter is to analyze phone interactions between language users and the Language Consulting Center (*jazyková poradna* in Czech; hereafter LCC), run by the Czech Language Institute of the Czech Academy of Sciences (hereafter CLI), from the point of view of Language Management Theory (hereafter LMT; see Jernudd & Neustupný 1987; Nekvapil 2012). Continuing in the direction taken in studies about LCC interactions by Beneš, Prošek, Smejkalová & Štěpánová (2018) and Prošek (2020),[1] this chapter focuses on cases of disagreement, opposing standpoints or even conflicts between the inquirer and the LCC linguist. In these cases, the interests of both parties diverge and these are the very interactions that can provide extensive information about the language ideologies advocated by their participants, whether they concern solutions to specific language problems, or general issues of organized language management. Contradictory interactions also reveal many valuable insights into the power relationships between the actors involved.

I analyze the sources of these situations and the development of these interactions. How do the participants try to resolve their dispute? How do they use argumentation to convince the other party and how do they react to their opponent's arguments? I also devote attention to the language ideologies advocated by linguists and inquirers, particularly with regard to the extent to which they coincide or differ, since these ideologies have a significant influence on the manner of argumentation as well as on the overall course of these conversations. I also try to find out if these interactions' development reveals anything about the character of the power or authority the inquirers ascribe to the CLI.

2 Language Consulting Center

The LCC assists the general public in dealing with issues related to the Czech language (or regarding language problems in general) (cf. Beneš, Prošek, Smejkalová & Štěpánová 2018; Uhlířová 2002; Nekvapil 2008). Currently the inquiries are received mainly by telephone. The LCC phone line is in service for 2 hours each working day (as of September 2021). The members of the Department of Language Cultivation take turns answering the queries from the public. This phone consultancy is free of charge, the inquirers pay only the regular phone charges. In addition, the LCC provides written statements upon request, which is a paid service and will not be analyzed here.

As for the thematic structure of the queries, most of them concern Czech orthography, lexicon, morphology, word-formation and syntax (cf. Uhlířová 2002). Only a few queries concern pragmatic or sociolinguistic issues. From the point of view of language planning, which distinguishes between status, corpus and

1 Cf. also Jernudd (2018) on language cultivation agencies in Sweden.

acquisition planning (Cooper 1989: 31 f.), the absolute majority of queries concern issues related to the corpus planning of Czech.

Here I term the participants in the LCC interactions *inquirer* and *LCC linguist*. While the role of a linguist is given institutionally, by his/her affiliation and working position in the CLI, the inquirer's role is primarily a construct created by the LCC: the expected action of the LCC clients is to present a language query, as evidenced by both the name of the institution—clients of a consulting center turn to it prototypically for advice[2]—and the text on its website.[3] Most callers meet this expectation and ask the LCC a language question, requesting help with solving a language problem. However, some clients' calls exceed this framework; their actions do not always have a clear and predominantly questioning nature. They do not (just) want to receive "language advice," but, for example, to tell the LCC their opinion about a particular language problem, to criticize the language of the media, to evaluate the activities of the CLI or to make suggestions for changing its activities etc. (cf. examples 11 and 12). Therefore, the term *inquirer* cannot be understood as a precise description of the activity of all callers, but is an institutionally assigned role that not all callers fulfill exactly.

It should be stated at the outset that the activities of the LCC (and the whole CLI) are not supported by any form of legal authority and it is supposed that the general respect for its statements is maintained due to tradition and social reputation with respect to linguistic expertise[4] (Beneš, Prošek, Smejkalová & Štěpánová 2018: 137; Prošek & Smejkalová 2011). One of my aims is to find out whether the course of the analyzed interactions confirms the existence of this general respect and how stable this respect is.

Since 2013, LCC phone interactions have been recorded for further linguistic research. With the support of a grant from the Czech Ministry of Culture, the recorded inquiries have been analyzed, classified and used to create a linguistically structured database[5] (Prošek 2020). Thanks to this project, I could also use the recordings of LCC interactions for the analysis of language management processes.

---

2 In Czech, the word *poradna* ('consulting center') is derived from the verb *poradit* ('advise').

3 For example, right in the first sentence of one of the texts on the LCC website, clients are categorized as inquirers who address language queries to the LCC: "Vzhledem k narůstajícímu počtu zájemců o jazykovou radu doporučujeme tazatelům a dalším zájemcům o češtinu, aby se nejdříve pokusili vyhledat odpověď na svůj dotaz samostatně [...]." [Given the growing number of people interested in language advice, we recommend to inquirers and other people interested in Czech to first try to find the answer to their question themselves [...].]" (http://www.ujc.cas.cz/jazykova-poradna/jak-jazykova-poradna-funguje.html; translated by JK). Accessed June 23, 2019.

4 The only exception is the school edition of *Pravidla českého pravopisu* [The Rules of Czech Orthography] that is binding in the school setting (Beneš, Prošek, Smejkalová & Štěpánová 2018: 137).

5 The database is available online at https://dotazy.ujc.cas.cz/.

For the purposes of this study, I examined more than 320 audio recordings of telephone interactions from 2016 to 2018 (of which about fifty recordings, containing phenomena examined in this study, were analyzed in more detail), using the method of the ethnomethodological conversation analysis (Sidnell & Stivers 2013), which provides a sophisticated apparatus for the study of spoken interactions. I also draw some information in this text from my experience gained through working in the CLI, several years of which took place in the LCC (until 2015).

3 Language management processes in the LCC

The Language Management Framework emphasizes different levels of social processes and the interrelationships between them. It focuses on micro level of everyday interactions (simple, discourse-based management) as well as macro level of institutions and other social networks (organized, institutional management) and it explores the extent to which the activities of actors at different levels are linked (Nekvapil 2012, 2016).

I argue that a language management act (including simple language management) is very often a collective and an interactive activity of which the communication (negotiation) between its participants is an integral part (cf. Kopecký 2014; Miyazaki 2001). This is also the case of interactions between the LCC and inquirers. When an inquirer asks the LCC for advice, he/she is usually the initiator of the language management act (alternatively, another person can have been the initiator, e.g., in the case of a dispute between the inquirer and this person). The LCC then becomes an invited co-actor of this management, and both actors are jointly looking for a solution to a given language problem. These are usually problems based on simple management of speakers (the inquirer, for example, tries to find out how to correctly inflect a noun that he/she wants to use in a text). However, the representatives of various institutions also frequently turn to the LCC addressing various language issues beyond specific interactions, their inquiries are thus part of the organized management of the institution.[6] At the same time, the LCC involvement is a part of the organized language management, which is trans-interactional and consists of the long-term provision of language consultancy. This activity is governed by certain general principles, resulting from the institution's language ideology and forming part of its language policy (see below) (cf. Nekvapil & Sherman 2015). This leads to the confrontation and intertwining of the acts of simple management, performed in the co-operation of the inquirers with the LCC, and the organized management of the LCC. In the case of institutional inquiries, different types of organized management are confronted.

6 E.g., when a municipal official asks for the correct spelling of the phrase *hodnoticí* vs. *hodnotící komise* ('evaluation committee'), which he repeatedly uses in official documents.

Within LMT, the following basic stages of the language management process are distinguished: a speaker's noting of a specific language phenomenon (often a deviation from the norm), positive or negative evaluation of it, planning of an adjustment and implementation of it. At any of these stages, this process can come to an end (cf. Nekvapil 2012). An LCC interaction can contain traces of or reports about some of these stages that occurred before the interaction itself. This applies mainly to the inquirer's noting and evaluation: the speaker can inform the linguist about them during the phone call. Other stages of language management are then conducted directly during the LCC interaction. Typical activities performed by the LCC are the evaluation of the language phenomenon that is the subject of the query, i.e., forming and expressing an opinion on the language problem, and presenting an adjustment proposal. The evaluation and adjustment plan are often accompanied by arguments in favor of these opinions, or, if the inquirer disagrees with the opinion, he/she may argue against it. In some interactions, the inquirer signals the acceptance or non-acceptance of the submitted plan and its future (non-)implementation (cf. Beneš, Prošek, Smejkalová & Štěpánová 2018). The LCC interaction recordings therefore contain a large amount of valuable data on the course of language management and a detailed analysis of these data allows for its description, or partial reconstruction.

4 Language ideologies

Language ideologies held by the inquirers and LCC linguists have a major influence on the course of their interactions. According to Silverstein's classic definition, language ideologies are "sets of beliefs about language articulated by users as a rationalization or justification of perceived language structure and use" (Silverstein 1979: 193). Blommaert defines them as "socially and culturally embedded metalinguistic conceptualizations of language and its forms of usage" (Blommaert 2006: 241). Julia de Bres (2013), continuing in the direction of Kroskrity (2004), Woolard (1998) and others, presents among the key features of language ideologies their normative nature (cf. also Nekvapil & Sherman 2013), their relationship to interests ("language ideologies are used as a means of promoting individual and group interests" de Bres 2013: 57), and a link between language ideologies and power relations within society (cf. also Kimura 2017). I use ideology (in accordance with the above definitions) as a neutral term, without negative (critical) connotations (cf. Woolard 1998: 7–8).

In this section, I will focus primarily on language ideologies expressed by LCC linguists. According to Woolard (1998), Kroskrity (2004) and others, linguistic theories may contain ideological elements or may be directly based on language ideologies. Scientific theories of language cannot be placed in opposition to ideological conceptualizations of language. The main theoretical basis of the language consultancy provided by the LCC is the Prague School theory of language cultivation and the theory of standard language (Havránek 1932; Daneš 1987; cf. Neustupný & Nekvapil 2003: 332 f.). According to Beneš, Prošek, Smejkalová & Štěpánová

(2018: 121), the main aim of the LCC is to "maintain and further develop (cultivate) the Standard Czech language." The aforementioned theories conceive (standard) language as the subject of regulation and cultivation by language institutions (through codification, language education etc.). In opposition to purism, codification should be based on (standard) language use and the standard language norm. The standard language norm is defined as a set of standard language resources and the rules for combining them that are perceived as binding for selected communicative functions by the language community (Nebeská 2016a). Despite its positive attitude towards language regulation, it is obvious that the theory of language cultivation does not represent a pure "top-down" approach to language planning, but rather, it declares the intention to consider the language attitudes of ordinary speakers (especially in its concept of norm).

I see ideological elements of the theory of language cultivation and standard language especially in its antipurism, prescriptivism and the effort to cultivate the standard language, which is understood as its improvement (Havránek 1932), as well as in the concept of Standard Czech as a register with higher social prestige used in situations with higher communicative function and connected with the concept of linguistic correctness (Nebeská 2016b, 2016c; cf. Homoláč & Mrázková 2014); this gives the standard a higher value than the other registers (cf. diversely defined standard language ideology in Milroy 1999; Kroskrity 2004: 502 f.; de Bres 2013: 66; Lanstyák 2017: 305). Therefore, this language cultivation program is referred to hereafter as the ideology of language cultivation.

In line with their orientation on the language cultivation ideology the LCC linguists strive to promote the solution to communication problems in accordance with the language norm. However, as it can be difficult to investigate a norm under time pressure during a phone interaction, the LCC advisers gain their findings about the norm mainly indirectly, from existing codification and from various language data, such as the frequency of language items in different communicative genres. The influence of the ideology of language cultivation in LCC interactions manifests itself in the use of its basic terms by linguists, such as standard language, codification, language norm, functionality, systemicity, etc., and in the application of its principles, such as the rejection of purism, the reference to codification and the language norm and others (see, e.g., example 6 below). In various interactions, these elements are found to varying degrees, depending on the elaboration of expert opinion that is primarily related to the complexity of the query: simple, repetitive questions are often answered without (longer) explication, while in the case of new, not yet described language problems, the explication is longer, it contains more sophisticated argumentation, in which the language ideology of the LCC linguist can become more visible. Within the ideology of language cultivation, various subideologies can be identified in evaluating particular language items, e.g., ideology of normativity or systemicity.

In addition to the language cultivation ideology, other conceptualizations of language are also occasionally manifested in the LCC discourse, e.g., the ideology of the need of representation of gender equality in language (Nekvapil & Sherman 2013: 86), the ideology of (politically) correct language[7] and others. In general, the ideologies related to language regulation (language norm) or evaluation of specific language items are the most common in LCC statements, because compliance with the standard is the subject of most queries.

On the side of the inquirers, the spectrum of language ideologies is considerably wider: from sharing the language cultivation ideology to the widely held ideology of language decline (cf. Lanstyák 2017: 282), ideology of beautiful (Czech) language (cf. Nekvapil & Sherman 2013: 112) to linguistic purism (see example 12), etc.

5 Interests

Interests can be defined as "aspirations for a certain state of affairs that is favorable to the subject" (Neustupný 2002: 3). According to Jernudd and Neustupný, a full analysis of different interests of social actors participating in the language management proces is necessary (Jernudd & Neustupný 1987: 82). For this reason, I will try to describe the typical interests of the LCC interaction participants.

5.1 Inquirer's interests

The inquirers calling the LCC usually ask for advice concerning the use of a language item or some aspect of the Czech language: e.g., the spelling of a word, stylistic marker of a grammatical element, the semantic difference between two words, etc. The inquirers evaluate their own lack of knowledge of respective language norms negatively. This can be a case of pre-interaction management as well as post-interaction management: either the inquirers anticipate a future language problem, i.e., their own deviation from a norm and its negative evaluation by recipients, and try to prevent it, or they are not sure whether a linguistic item in a past interaction was used correctly, which is why they are asking the LCC for advice (cf. Beneš, Prošek, Smejkalová & Štěpánová 2018). However, even in cases of post-management the speaker can consider some future action, such as the correction of the mistake or an apology, hence the post-management becomes entwined with the pre-management and the boundary between them appears to be fluid. Both types of language management also appear in the following example:

7 For the ideology of the need of representation of gender equality in language see, e.g., the recommendation to use the gender-neutral address *Vážení členové, vážené členky předsednictva* ('Dear members /masc./ and members /fem./ of the governing board') instead of generic masculine address *Vážení členové předsednictva* ('Dear Members /masc./ of the governing board') (interaction 5414). For the ideology of (politically) correct language see, e.g., the recommendation to use the term *Rom* ('Romany') instead of *Cikán* ('Gypsy') (interaction 7722).

Example 1 (interaction 6570)[8]

(INQ = inquirer)

INQ: [...] teďka dělám [...] dabing dokumentárního filmu, o Montriolu. jak vyslovovat Montriol.
[...]
INQ: [...] tak poslouchá ček i zprávy třeba. [...] eh i Česká televize má kolikrát hrozný lapsusy. takže jako to ček nemůže brát za bernou minci. ale (.) když de vo sport, tak je vždycky Montriól, a když de vo město, tak je to takový jako (.) eh eh to tam střídaj no.

[INQ: [...] I'm doing [...] the dubbing of a documentary, about Montreal now. how should I pronounce Montreal?
[...]
INQ: [...] for example, one listens to news. [...] eh even Czech Television sometimes has terrible lapses, so it can't be taken at face value. but (.) when it comes to sports, so it is always [montrio:l] and when it comes to the city, so it is like (.) eh eh, it alternates well.]

The inquirer's question about how to pronounce the toponym *Montreal* in the dubbing of a documentary film is a typical case of pre-interaction management. Later, the speaker refers to her knowledge (noting) of the usual pronunciation of the name in various Czech television programs, that is, the interaction also includes elements of post-management of the problematic item.

Despite the interrogative character of his/her utterance, the inquirer often has some knowledge of the item he/she is asking about (see the example 1 above) and can have a hypothesis about the problem, e.g., considers one option to be correct or evaluates a language item in a certain way. Since the inquirer wants to avoid deviating from a norm, he/she intends to verify his/her knowledge with the help of the LCC (see, e.g., examples 2, 3 or 10 below). In the case of post-interaction management, for example, the speaker has used a language item in discourse and is checking whether it was correct. Obviously, the inquirer hopes that he/she hasn't deviated from a norm.

A frequent motivation for calling the LCC is also an ongoing argument between the inquirer and someone else (e.g., a co-worker, a relative; see examples 3 and 10 below). The inquirer's knowledge has been questioned by his/her opponent, so the inquirer asks the LCC to mediate in the dispute.[9]

In all of these cases, it is in the interest of the inquirer to solve his/her language problem in his/her favor. Obtaining the LCC's expert opinion on the problem can be a means of achieving this goal: the linguist's counsel may help the inquirer to

---

8 The transcription conventions are provided at the end of the article.

9 For the analogical cases in the queries sent to The Language Council of Sweden see Jernudd (2018: 113 f.).

select the appropriate language item to reach his/her communication goal most easily, it can help him/her convince the opponent in a language dispute etc. (for other specific goals the inquirers are pursuing, see the examples below). If the inquirer has a hypothesis or opinion about the language item in question, it is in his/her interest for the LCC to confirm his/her standpoint. Therefore, in this case, his/her aim is twofold: (1) to remove his/her doubts, (2) to have his/her standpoint confirmed.

As for the non-linguistic interests of LCC clients related to the linguistic ones, LCC interactions usually do not provide enough information, and we can only learn about them from certain clues. For example, if the inquirer verifies the norm for the use of a particular language item he/she needs to use in official communication, it can be assumed that his/her attempt to be in accordance with the norm is related to the interest in not threatening his/her face in front of the intended recipients or not harming the institution that the speaker represents. A language mistake in an official situation can undoubtedly pose such a face-threatening act.

The LCC is often contacted by the inquirers in professions that require intensive dealing with both written and spoken texts, such as clerks, copywriters, lawyers, scientists and many others. Some of them even work in professions with a certain degree of linguistic expertise, such as proofreaders, translators or Czech teachers. People in these occupations face a multitude of language problems they need to solve. Their linguistic interests are closely linked to their various work-related interests, such as the effort to satisfactorily accomplish a given task or order; these interests may in some cases also be of an economic nature (e.g., financial penalties in case of poor work). However, as noted, the details of these non-linguistic issues and interests are usually not mentioned in the interactions investigated, their existence and nature can therefore usually only be assumed.

The following example is one of the less frequent cases in which the linguist learns basic information about the inquirer's non-linguistic interests which are very closely linked to the language problem discussed here. This is a case of a dispute between a company that the inquirer probably represents and the customs administration:

Example 2 (interaction 4082)

INQ: ono se totiž jedná o: o:. (.) úřední jednání, jedná se o celní delikt, je to (.) ve spojení s problematikou celní sazební zařazování zboží, a mně de o to jestli je totiž správně přeloženo drinking glasses, jako nápojové sklo. mně prostě to spojení nápojový sklo příde moc široký, já si myslím, že by tam mělo bejt pouze skleničky. [...]

[...]

INQ: [...] my sme narazili na celní na celní delikt, kdy celní správa nám přeřadila zboží, (..) a byly to karafy na víno, a právě je dávaj (.) sem pod to nápojové sklo. ale ono je to na sto procent špatně. ale nevíme, jak (se) v tom celním deliktu obhájit, (...) a ja:k to celní správě vymluvit.

[INQ: it i:s it i:s (.) an official act, it is a customs offense, it concerns (.) the issue of the customs tariff classification of goods, and the point is whether the phrase drinking glasses is correctly translated as *nápojové sklo.* the phrase *nápojový sklo* just seems too broad to me, I think there should be only *skleničky.* [...]
[...]
INQ: [...] we came across a customs offense, where the customs administration reclassified our goods, (..) they were wine decanters, and they're just putting them (.) here under the *nápojové sklo,* but it is a hundred percent wrong. but we do not know, how to defend ourselves against the customs offense, (...) and ho:w to convince the customs administration.]

The linguistic interest of this inquirer can be defined as confirming her version of the translation of the phrase *drinking glasses.* This interest crosses over into the legal and economic spheres fundamentally: Confirming the inquirer's linguistic opinion should help the company she represents defend themselves against accusation of a customs offense and possibly reverse it. This is undoubtedly also linked to the economic interests of the company: Although the inquirer does not mention them, in general, customs offenses result in financial penalties, so this is probably also the case here. The interaction therefore illustrates the close connection between language and socio-economic management performed by the inquirer (cf. Neustupný & Nekvapil 2003: 186).

5.2 LCC's interests

I consider the following most important interests of the LCC or, more broadly, the CLI of which the LCC is part:

1. To satisfy public demand for language consultancy. In particular LCC interactions, this is manifested by the linguist's attempt to answer the inquiry—to provide the inquirer with the requested language information. The LCC aims to give professional, well-founded answers, based on scientific findings. Providing this public service (as well as other language cultivation activities—cf. note 10) helps the CLI legitimize its existence and strengthen its position in society. Thanks to this, the CLI can also conduct linguistic research that is primarily intended for the scientific community.
2. To control the discourse on language and thus to maintain and strengthen the expert role of the CLI. This is also reflected in the division of roles of inquirer and LCC linguist (see above in Section 2), implying on one hand a lay speaker in need of advice and, on the other hand, an expert who is able to provide such advice. Also, the effort to strengthen the CLI's expert role undoubtedly helps (as in the previous point) to legitimize its existence and strengthen its social position. One of the means of controlling discourse on language is the ideology of language cultivation described above, which attributes a significant role to linguistic institutions in the process of language cultivation. They

perform it through codification and other language cultivation activities.[10] In this context, a certain harmonizing nature of this ideology should be pointed out. It partially satisfies the needs of both speakers and CLI linguists: on the one hand, it responds to a social demand for language regulation,[11] on the other hand, as mentioned, it helps linguists to control the discourse on language. Moreover, it is based on sophisticated linguistic theory (unlike other regulatory ideologies such as purism or various primarily politically motivated ideologies) that has retained, despite its considerable age, a substantial degree of scientific recognition and influence (cf. Neustupný & Nekvapil 2003: 340), and thus it is still acceptable for a significant portion of linguists (cf. Nebeská 2016c on controversy). It therefore appears that this ideology does not unilaterally satisfy the interests of the linguistic institution, but rather, seeks to harmonize the interests of linguists and the public.

3. The LCC also aims to gain research data through the provision of language consultancy (see the page *LCC Mission* on the CLI website). All phone interactions are recorded so that they can later be analyzed. Unlike the previous two interests, I have not found any evidence of the influence of this interest on the course of the LCC interactions.

5.3 Divergent interests

As is clear from the previous section, the interests of the participants of the LCC interactions are not identical, they can diverge or even become incompatible under certain circumstances. The interests of the inquirer and the LCC correspond primarily in their goals to gain some information about language and to provide this information (which is in line with the CLI language policy). Of course, in some cases the linguist is unable to provide the required information, e.g., when the inquiry is beyond his/her competence (the problem does not lie in the area of

---

10 In addition to providing language consultancy, these include, in the case of the CLI, various popularization and educational activities and providing expert opinions regarding proper names (see http://ujc.cas.cz/expertni-cinnost/index.html). Codification takes the form of publishing language handbooks that are perceived by the public as binding such as *Pravidla českého pravopisu* [The Rules of Czech Orthography], *Internetová jazyková příručka* [Internet Language Reference Book], *Akademická příručka českého jazyka* [Academic Vade Mecum of the Czech Language] (Pravdová & Svobodová 2019) and others.

11 We do not have accurate data on how great this demand is in Czech society, however, indirect indications suggest that it is relatively strong. This is evidenced in particular by the considerable public interest in the mentioned codification and popularization handbooks produced by the CLI as well as in its language consultancy. For example, *Internetová jazyková příručka* (see note 10) recorded over 2,000,000 hits from over 142,500 unique IP addresses in March 2019 (see http://prirucka.ujc.cas.cz/?id=_stat). Accessed June 23, 2019.

linguistics), or when there is no available data about the disputed language item. Nevertheless, the general interest of the LCC is to answer as many queries as possible (to satisfy public demand for language guidance).

There is a danger of potential conflict of interests: If the inquirer prefers one particular answer, it can happen that the LCC considers another solution to be correct. The interest of the speaker to be in harmony with his/her own idiolect can thus conflict with LCC's interest to be in line with the principles of language cultivation. See, for example, the following excerpt:

Example 3 (interaction 4190)

INQ: s někým se přu, o: významu slova ochočit [...] domnívám se že (.) význam slova ochočit se používá eh víceméně pouze se zvířetem. nikoli s člověkem.

[INQ: I've been arguing with somebody abou:t the meaning of the word *ochočit* ('domesticate') [...]. I think that (.) the meaning of the word *ochočit* is used eh only in connection with an animal. not with a human.]

In her answer, the LCC linguist then quotes dictionaries of Czech (created by the CLI), saying that a human can also be figuratively "domesticated," adding that the verb *ochočit* can then be used in this meaning. She thus does not confirm the inquirer's intuition about the meaning (which is based on the inquirer's language experience), but she acknowledges that the opposing party is right. It is not the interest of the LCC to satisfy one or the other party, but to provide information about the language item in accordance with the language norm captured in codification handbooks.

The disagreement between the LCC interactants is usually caused by differing evaluations or explications of language items. These different standpoints can be brought about by different language ideologies (for examples, see below). As stated by de Bres (2013: 61), language ideologies are "always subject to contestation and challenge" and the development of many LCC interactions confirms this statement.

6 Ways of solving disputes – using argumentation

If the LCC linguist reacts polemically to the inquirer's stance, he/she usually tries to convince the inquirer by means of argumentation. Similarly, some inquirers argue in favor of their stances. There is a close link between argumentation and language ideologies to which Silverstein's definition quoted above also refers: language ideologies are "articulated by users as a rationalization or justification of perceived language structure and use" (Silverstein 1979: 193). The actions of rationalization or justification are part of, or equivalents of argumentation. Language ideologies are revealed in interactions through argumentation in particular.

I view argumentation as a linguistic action based on accounting for a controversial position with the purpose of convincing listeners of its acceptability or in order to defend it when it is challenged (cf. Eemeren & Grootendorst 2004: 1; Kopperschmidt 2000: 59). This definition implies that the argumentation can have two functions: (1) persuasive or (2) defensive (Kopecký 2018). It is obvious that both functions often coincide in interaction, but in LCC interactions the persuasive function usually prevails (the LCC typically tries to convince the inquirer), while the defensive function is typical for more competitive types of interaction, such as TV interviews.

Moreover, the argumentation of the LCC can also serve as a proof of the linguist's expert competence and credibility, because the capacity to argue for an expert standpoint presupposes well-founded knowledge of the issue.

The following example of argumentation as a part of the language management process in LCC interaction also reveals the role of language ideologies:

Example 4 (interaction 3725)

INQ: já sem se dočetl v v propagačním letáku, že v Kauflandu prodávají, (.) prodávají paštikovou bonbonieru. mně to připadá jako jazykový aušus. zmetek. protože jesi je to bomboniera, tak tam musí být bombony, a ne: paštiky.

LCC: [...] to máte stejné, jako když se říká kulatá špička. (.) to je taky ((laughing)) jazykový aušus. [...] to slovo (.) mm získalo další další význam. [...] mně by to zas TOlik nevadilo. se přiznám.

[INQ: I have read in an advertising circular that a *paštiková bonboniera* ((literally "paté candy box"))[12] is being sold, (.) is being sold at Kaufland store. ((= <u>NOTING</u>)) it appears to me to be junk language. ((= <u>NEGATIVE EVALUATION</u>)) because if there is *bomboniera* (('box of candies')), then there must be *bombony* (('candies')) in it, no:t pâtés. ((= <u>ARGUMENTATION</u>))

LCC: [...] it is the same case as "round tip/point." (.) it is also ((laughing)) junk language. [...] the word (.) mm has gained another meaning. ((= <u>COUNTER-ARGUMENTATION</u>)) [...] I have to say that it wouldn't bother me SO much. ((= <u>POSITIVE EVALUATION</u>))]

According to this inquirer, the form of a word, or rather, its word-formation structure is decisive for its meaning. We can assume that his argumentation "Because if there is *bomboniera* ('box of candies'), then there must be *bombony* ('candies') in it, not pâtés" is based on the belief: "the original meaning (of this word) should be respected." This opinion could be part of the ideology of language purism, however, solely on the basis of this belief, it cannot be unequivocally concluded whether the inquirer reproduces this ideology.

The LCC linguist counter argues with the analogy (cf. Kienpointner 1992: 384 f.) when she points to the phrase *kulatá špička* 'round tip/point' (of scissors or shoes). The *tertium comparationis* is here the logical incompatibility of a collocation (*špička* 'tip' is defined as a pointed end of something which is incompatible with the attribute *kulatá* 'round') which does not hinder its communicative functionality. Thereafter the linguist describes the item as gaining a new meaning. In this way, she tacitly refers to the concept of semantic shift and to the belief that the

12 Probably with the meaning 'box of pâtés'; *paštiková* = 'pâté' (adj.), *bonboniéra* = 'box of candies/chocolates.'

meanings of words are not untouchable, but can change when necessary, as long as the shift is functional and systemic (regardless of whether the phrase *paštiková bonboniera* can really be considered functional and systemic—this may be questionable, but it is not the subject of this study; what is essential here is the linguist's reference to the phenomenon of semantic shift). This belief is an integral part of the language cultivation ideology. However, the inquirer is probably not in line with this ideology, as his argumentation suggests, and therefore the linguist's counter-argument is not convincing for him, as the following course of interaction shows.

7 The outcome of the dispute

In many cases of initial disagreement between the LCC and the inquirer, we cannot determine with absolute certainty whether the inquirer is finally convinced by the LCC argumentation and changes his/her original opinion, or if it is not a sufficient impulse to change his/her mind. In such ambiguous cases, the inquirer usually responds in some way to the statement of the LCC, for example, by thanking the linguist or producing a receipt token (e.g., *aha*, cf. Heritage 1984), but the inquirer does not unequivocally express his/her consent or disagreement.

Reactions of some inquirers, however, reflect the change in position or the absence of this change with varying degrees of clarity. Not surprisingly, agreement is more often signaled, as it represents a preferred response according to conversation analysis (Pomerantz & Heritage 2013). In the case of disagreement with an opinion of the LCC, it seems that the inquirers tend not to express their position explicitly. This can be explained by both the speakers' respect for LCC's social authority based on its accumulated expertise and by their politeness towards the representative of the institution. In the following part of the study, I try to define different types of development of the LCC disputes.

7.1 The inquirer does not change his/her original opinion

In some disputes, the inquirer is not convinced by the LCC argumentation or by its authority, thus the standpoints of both parties continue to be in opposition. This development is illustrated by the following example:

Example 5 (interaction 2387)

INQ: proč se v současné češtině, (.) koncovka ismus, přepisuje: jako izmus.
[...]
INQ: [...] na jakym základě to vzniklo? protože (.) ta koncovka má svůj význam. a ještě by se to možná dalo pochopit u slov (.) jako je třeba kapitalismus, socialismus, ale úplně nejhorší je to u slova (.) filoSOfie, (.) což znamená, když se to napíše se z, tak to neznamená NIC. protože základem je slovo sofistika, a tam prostě nemůže být z.
LCC: no ten (.) ten obecný důvod proč to je, je: aby se pravopis přizpůsobil výslovnosti.
INQ: no jo ale (.) když se napíše filoZOFIE, takch je to nesmysl.

[…]
INQ: […] prostě jakmile se to začne přepisovat, tak (.) vznikají (.) nesmyslná slova.
LCC: (..) mm (toe) eh jako [mmm]
INQ: [((laughing))]
LCC: ňáký [( )]
INQ: [no nevím] no tak dobře no. takže vy jako myslíte že: je to v pořádku všecko.
LCC: no samozřejmě. na tom [není na tom není nic špatného.]
INQ: [( ) dě]kuju nashle[danou.]
LCC: [nashle] danou.

[INQ: why is, (.) the ending *-ismus*, re-spelled as *-izmus* in contemporary Czech?
[…]
INQ: […] what was it based on? because (.) that ending has its meaning. and it could still be understood by words (.) like *kapitalismus*, *socialismus*, but the worst is the word (.) *filoSOfie*, (.) it means, when it's written with the letter *z*, it doesn't mean anything. because it is based on the word *sofistika* and there simply can't be *z*.
LCC: well (.) the general reason for this is, i:s to adjust spelling to pronunciation.
INQ: but (.) when you write *filoZOFIE*, it is nonsense.
[…]
INQ: […] when people start to write it differently, (.) senseless words are (.) created.
LCC: (..) mm (it's) eh like [mmm]
INQ: [((laughing))]
LCC: some [( )]
INQ: [well I don't know] well ok. so you think eh: it's all right, all of that.
LCC: of course. there's nothing [there's nothing wrong with that.]
INQ: [( ) thank] you. good[bye.]
LCC: [good]bye.]

The inquirer questions the official orthography of some words originating from Latin and Greek. The contemporary rules of orthography allow the forms *-izmus* and *filozofie* (written with the letter *z* instead of *s*) which is based on Standard Czech pronunciation of these items. The inquirer objects that the affected words "lose their meaning"—*filoZofie* "means nothing." The LCC linguist justifies the current orthography with the need to adapt orthography to pronunciation. Through this argumentation, he claims allegiance to the ideology of phonological orthography, according to which the spelling of the words like *filozofie* should follow the phonological principle. This ideology is a part of the language policy of the CLI. However, the inquirer is not convinced by this argument and repeats his objections: *filoZofie* is nonsense and other similarly "re-spelled" words are the same. It is obvious that this "senselessness" has historical or etymological character: orthographically adapted words and their components "lose" their original meanings which were preserved in their original orthographic forms. The inquirer evaluates this etymological meaninglessness as a bigger problem than a synchronic discrepancy between orthography and pronunciation. Thus, we can categorize him as an advocate of the ideology of lexical orthography, according to which the spelling of the words like *filozofie* should follow the lexical principle (cf. Uličný 2013: 120). After the LCC linguist presents no new arguments, the inquirer checks whether his opponent has not changed his mind through the question "Takže vy jako myslíte, že je to v pořádku všecko." [So you think it's all right, all of that.] When the linguist confirms that he has not, the inquirer quickly (though politely) terminates the conversation. This interactional development shows that the inquirer was not convinced about the opposite of his initial standpoint during the phone interaction.

Failure to reach consensus was caused by the incompatible language ideologies of both sides, specifically by different ideas about how Czech orthography should be conceived and what functions it should fulfill. Since neither party withdrew from its ideological position, it was not possible to reach agreement on the spelling of the particular word *filos/zofie.*

7.2 The inquirer is convinced by the argumentation of the LCC

In the following interaction, a proofreader of a technical text from the field of agriculture negatively evaluates the term *hnojařský pokus* ('fertilization experiment') which she encountered in a text, but the LCC linguist approves the word:

Example 6 (interaction 6249)

INQ: [...] tam mně vadí to citový zabarvení, a takovej ten hanlivej nádech, a do odbornýho textu, jo po- podle mě nepatří. je to takový moc expre<sivní> na můj vkus. [...]

LCC: [...] z čistě slovotvorného hlediska (.) je to eh (..) přídavné jméno utvořeno náležitě, eh systémově, [...] je také eh doloženo ve slovnících, eh výkladových slovnících češtiny, [...]

[INQ: [...] the emotional coloring of the term bothers me, and such a pejorative tinge, and (it) doesn't belong in a specialized text, in- in my opinion. it's too expres<sive> for my taste. [...]

LCC: [...] from a purely word-forming point of view (.) this eh (..) adjective is well, eh systemically formed, [...] it is also eh in the explanatory dictionaries of Czech, [...]]

The LCC linguist evaluates the terminological usage of the word positively, because the adjective *hnojařský* is well formed (criterion of systemicity), it is codified in the dictionaries of Standard Czech as a term and it has a long tradition (the word is already in the dictionary *Příruční slovník jazyka českého*, vol. 1 from 1935 to 1937).[13]

13 The adjective *hnojařský* (and in particular the related word *hnojárna*) is used as an expressive and pejorative word (with a slightly different meaning) in nonstandard Czech. The inquirer transfers these connotations also to its terminological usage.

The inquirer is convinced by these arguments and she re-evaluates the word. There are clear signals of the acceptance of LCC argumentation in her turns:

Example 7 (interaction 6249)

INQ: [...] vono se to opravdu asi v odbornym textu snese. [...] ten uživatel toho odbornýho textu primárně nemá tyhlety asociace, který mám jako laik. [...]

[INQ: [...] it can really be tolerated in a technical text. [...] the user of a technical text doesn't primarily have the associations, that I have as a layperson. [...]]

And she is even gratified by the proposed solution because she does not need to correct the term in the text:

Example 8 (interaction 6249)

INQ: [...] to sem ráda, eh to ste mě teda ( ) hrozně potěšil, protože nemusim doporučovat, nic doporučovat jako. [...]

[INQ: [...] I am glad, eh you made me then ( ) very happy, because I don't have to recommend, recommend anything. [...]]

The inquirer has thus revised her adjustment plan: instead of wanting to correct the supposed deviation from a norm, she now wants to cease her activity concerning the word in question.

It is essential that, in contrast to the previous example, there was no ideological difference between the interlocutors in this interaction (as in the case of conflict between ideology of phonological and lexical orthography etc.). The inquirer did not agree with the LCC only in the stylistic characteristics of one particular word, because she lacked knowledge of it as a technical term. Most likely for this reason, and given the convincing argumentation by the LCC, it was possible to achieve consensus.

7.3 The inquirer is convinced more by the LCC's authority than by its plausible argumentation

In the previous example there were signs of the acceptance of the LCC argumentation in the inquirer's utterances. In the following interaction (example 9) these signs are not present. In this interaction, the inquirer asks whether there is a semantic difference between the words *pyšný* ('proud, haughty') and *hrdý* ('proud'). She considers the word *pyšný* to be negatively colored, while *hrdý* is in her opinion positive or neutral. She has a dispute with a woman who finds the phrase *být pyšný na dítě* [to be proud of one's child] correct, while the inquirer does not.

The LCC linguist does not confirm her standpoint: *pyšný* has two meanings according to the dictionary: the first is negative ('haughty'), the second is synonymous to *hrdý*, and so it is positive. The inquirer reacts as follows:

Example 9 (interaction 5776)

INQ: [...] takže: jako nakonec pravdu měla. [...] ale (.) já prostě to pořád tak cítím jako že už (.) už jenom od toho pyšná princezna. pýcha předchází pád. prostě: eh eh tak jako: to cítím že: mně to slovo se prostě nikdy nelíbilo. abych ho jako použila třeba: [...]

[INQ: [...] we:ll she ((= her opponent)) was right in the end. [...] but (.) I still feel that like that even just (.) even just from pyšná princezna ((‘the proud princess’)). pride comes before a fall. in sho:rt eh eh so the:n I still feel tha:t I have never liked the word enough to use it or so: [...]]

Thus, she accepts the LCC verdict (she admits her opponent “was right”), nevertheless she feels the need to express her own, different view, which she argues for by using examples of negative use of that term (which is not inconsistent with the opinion of the LCC, which does not exclude the negative use). At the end of the interaction the inquirer makes sure that she has understood the LCC statement properly: “takže: vlastně v tom kladném se to jako může použít, jo?” [so, it actually can be used positively, right?]. My interpretation of these utterances is that the inquirer accepts the standpoint of the LCC, although it is incompatible with her own understanding of the word, which excludes the use of its positive meaning ‘proud.’ It is not clear which part the argumentation plays in this process (change of her standpoint), because she does not react to it explicitly. It is therefore possible that the authority of the LCC has a decisive influence here.

The following example illustrates the role of LCC authority more clearly. As in the previous case, the starting point here is the dispute between the inquirer and her interaction partner that the LCC should decide:

Example 10 (interaction 6296)

INQ: [...] eh: my sme s manželem měli takove:j dneska menší rozkol, a: eh: já sem říkala, že (.) jesi tedy můžu, eh tak předvčírem, a předevčírem, že to je (..) eh každý jiný. je to pravda? nebo neni.
LCC: [...] obě ty slova: znamenají totéž, (.) eh m [ten den]
INQ: [mhm,]
LCC: před včerejškem, (.) a:
INQ: mhm,
LCC: (..) a: obě: podoby se hodnotí jako: spisovné. jen tedy s tím rozdílem, že: eh podoba předvčírem, eh se užívá výrazně řidčeji: než ta podoba předevčírem. ta je mnohem obvyklejší.
INQ: [...] dobrý. tak to sem chtěla vědět, takže sem <prohrála> (.) sá[zku, já vám]
LCC: [((laughing))]
INQ: mockrát děkuju, ((laughing)) [že ste mi to objas]nila.
LCC: [nemáte zač.]

[INQ: [...] eh: we had a so:rt of minor argument with my husband today, a:nd eh: I said that (.) if I can, eh so *předvčírem*, and *předevčírem*, that there is (..) eh a difference between them. is it true? or is not.

LCC: [...] both wo:rds mean the same, (.) eh m [the day]
INQ: [mhm,]
LCC: before yesterday, (.) a:nd
INQ: mhm,
LCC: (..) a:nd bo:th forms are considered li:ke standard. only with the difference, tha:t eh the form *předvčírem*, eh is used much less often than the form *předevčírem*. that one is much more common.
INQ: [...] ok, that's what I wanted to know, so I <lost> (.) the [bet, I thank]
LCC: [((laughing))]
INQ: you so much, ((laughing)) [for explaining it] to me.
LCC: .. [you're welcome.]]

The very fact that the inquirer turns to the LCC to decide a language dispute with her husband indicates that she probably attributes a certain degree of authority to it. The outcome of this interaction shows that this authority is relatively strong: as in the previous example, the LCC linguist acknowledges that the opposing party is right and she does not confirm the inquirer's assumption that there is an (unspecified) difference between the two variants of the word. The inquirer accepts this verdict without objection, simply noting that she lost the bet. Unlike the previous example, the linguist does not argue for her opinion in this interaction, she merely states that there is allegedly no stylistic or semantic difference between the two words. Her statement is probably based on codification handbooks, as is usual in the LCC, but she does not explicitly cite them. Since the inquirer signals the acceptance of the LCC opinion, it can be concluded that she was convinced by the authority of the linguistic institution.

8 Authority ascribed to the LCC by inquirers

As mentioned above, the influence of the LCC is not based on any legal regulation that would make the LCC verdicts enforceable. In other words, this institution has no "power" in the sense defined by Max Weber (1978: 53): "the probability that one actor within a social relationship will be in a position to carry out his own will despite resistance [...]." If an LCC linguist wants to push the implementation of a specific adjustment through, he/she must convince the inquirer in a non-violent manner.

However, if we define power more generally, as a "capacity to implement one's interests" (Neustupný 2002: 3), then the LCC cannot be denied a certain degree of power. Compared to ordinary speakers, the LCC is definitely in a better position to influence the language practices of other speakers and to promote its language ideologies, because it is endowed with an authority given by its expertise. The type of authority some inquirers ascribe to the LCC (or rather to the CLI), as becomes evident in certain parts of the analyzed interactions, can be specified as the *authority by expertise* (knowledge) or *expert authority*. As Michel Foucault points out, knowledge-production is a process that is closely linked to power relations:

> We should admit that [...] power and knowledge directly imply one another; that there is no power relation without the correlative constitution of a field of knowledge, nor any knowledge that does not presuppose and constitute at the same time power relations. (Foucault 1995: 27)

Many inquirers voluntarily accept the standpoints of the LCC on the grounds of its presupposed expert competence (expertise) and/or on the grounds of the argumentation presented, by which the LCC proves its competence (expertise). In some cases, the inquirers accept the standpoints of the LCC, even though they are inconsistent with their own language intuition (see examples 9 and 10). Other proof of this authority includes interactions where the inquirers ask the LCC to intervene in the language practice of some speakers or (more often) some organizations, especially the media, whose language usage they criticize. These inquirers are usually aware of the fact that the CLI has no coercive power, since there is no language law in the Czech Republic, nevertheless they ask the LCC to intervene on the grounds of its social authority based on its expertise, particularly in the form of educating the public about language.

In the following example the speaker complains of misuse of grammatical endings by different speakers in the public space. After the description of the criticized phenomenon, the inquirer asks a question about the possibility of the CLI performing a specific adjustment:

Example 11 (interaction 3781)

INQ: [...] já bych se chtěl teda zeptat (.) obecně, jestli (.) jako jazyk jako Ústav pro jazyk český, já vim že nemáte kompetence. ale jesi se aspoň nesnažíte a nemáte nějaké (.) možnosti, jak ( ) prostě šířit trošku osvětu. [...]

[INQ: [...] so I would like to ask (.) in general, whether (.) as the Czech Language Institute, I know you have no competencies. but whether you at least try and have some (.) options, to ( ) spread a little education for the public. [...]]

In the following example, the inquirer makes an even stronger appeal to the CLI to use its authority to "protect the Czech language." This purism-oriented speaker criticizes the use of the originally German word *kurzarbeit* in Czech and he advocates the following form of institutional management of loanwords:

Example 12 (interaction 295)

INQ: [...] můj názor jako občana, eh mysim si že tydlety slova by měl Ústav pro jazyk český (.) eh hledat, nebo: prostě: (.) registrovat, což se tedy děje, [ale měl]
LCC: [děje]
INQ: by je měl by je řešit. měl by (.) dát občanům doporučení jaký slovo (.) eh používat. nutit se to nedá, ale měl by oficielně napsat vážení občané, místo tadydletoho slova kurcarbajt, prostě: doporučujeme používat to a to slovo. [...]

[INQ: [...] my opinion as a citizen, eh I think the Czech Language Institute should (.) eh search for, o:r simply: (.) register these words, which is what happens, [but it should]
LCC: [this is happening]
INQ: it should deal with them. it should (.) give people a recommendation of which word (.) eh to use. they can't be forced, but it should issue an official written statement dear citizens, instead of this word *kurzarbeit*, we just recomme:nd that you use such-and-such a word.]

As mentioned, the distribution of knowledge is closely connected with power, according to Foucault (1980, 1995). This also implies a relationship of interdependence between authority and argumentation. The linguist's arguing in individual interactions helps build and maintain the LCC authority, since the use of plausible arguments is proof of the expertise and scientific character of the submitted language statements. On the other hand, authority helps the LCC to promote its language ideologies, to influence the inquirer in their acceptance, consequently increasing the persuasiveness of its argument. This is possible because argumentation lies in the transfer of acceptability from the indisputable argument to the problematic position (cf. Kopperschmidt 2000: 80 f.), so a prerequisite for successful argumentation is the sharing of some basic beliefs and attitudes by the interactants. In the case of discussion on language or language management, these basic beliefs are language ideologies. Thus, although Habermas (1981: 52 f.) speaks of "zwangloser Zwang des besseren Arguments" (non-violent force of the better argument), this does not mean that argumentation is possible only if all power relations between the interaction partners are suspended. On the contrary, a certain type of speaker's non-violent power (authority of knowledge/expertise) can support the persuasiveness of his/her argument.

As stated earlier, there are also cases in LCC interactions in which the inquirer does not accept the LCC standpoint (see example 5). It is obvious that these inquirers do not ascribe that kind of authority to the CLI, at least as far as the given questions are concerned (cf. Beneš, Prošek, Smejkalová & Štěpánová 2018: 136). These speakers regard their own language competence and evaluating standpoints (or maybe other experts or model speakers and their texts) to be a more reliable criterion of linguistic correctness.[14]

Thus, the power of the LCC is not absolute and the legitimacy of its authority is unstable. It is an authority limited by the different attitudes of different speakers. The linguist has no guarantee in any interaction that his/her position will be accepted. At the beginning of the conversation, the linguist usually does not know what language ideology the inquirer holds and what degree of authority he/she

14 The model of power field in which the language correctness is elaborated cf. in Ammon (2005), specifically to the role of LCC and its function within this model cf. Šichová (2017).

attributes to the CLI. Therefore, the LCC authority is re/negotiated in some way in each interaction, and the linguists often have to persuade the inquirers.

It is obvious, therefore, that different speakers attribute different roles to the CLI, and in connection with this, they also have a different perception of how the Czech language as a whole should be managed in terms of corpus planning. The first group, the representatives of which are the inquirers from examples 9 and 10, considers the CLI to be an authoritative body whose statements should be respected and followed by speakers. In case of a discrepancy between their linguistic intuition and the LCC verdict, these speakers incline toward the LCC opinion. As they see it, standard language is an entity, the use of which should be controlled from above (ideology of interventionism; Lanstyák 2017). Organized language management is therefore, in their view, superior to simple language management.

The second group of speakers, represented here by the inquirer from example 5, does not consider the CLI to be an expert authority whose language statements should be respected under all circumstances. In case of a discrepancy between their language intuition and the LCC verdict, these speakers rely on their own judgment of language items. These speakers do not accept the language ideologies of the CLI, but rather, maintain their own ideologies (such as widespread language purism).

Typically, the recorded interactions do not contain unambiguous indicators of whether this rejection of the CLI's authority is based on the ideology of language liberalism/democratism according to which evaluations and adjustments of individual speakers are superior to institutional management, or on the ideology of language interventionism (cf. Lanstyák 2017). In the latter case, the inquirers would prefer authoritative organized management of Czech, but they would not agree with language attitudes and policy of the CLI (for many of them, they may be too liberal) and therefore the institution would lack legitimacy as a language authority for them.

We can summarize that the strength of the LCC authority is primarily decided by the inquirers, depending, among other things, on what language ideologies they hold and the role they attribute to the LCC. Whether authority is assigned to the LCC can also be influenced by the degree to which the LCC argumentation is convincing.

9 Conclusion

In this study, I have analyzed one type of interaction in which simple and organized management are often intertwined: institutional phone interactions between the LCC and its clients that are motivated by speakers' language problems arising in everyday interactions; in some cases, the inquirers are also actors of institutional management that deals with more complex language issues (see Section 3).

The basic interest of inquirers is to solve their language problem in a satisfactory manner, and they involve the LCC in attempting to achieve this goal. This linguistic interest may be closely linked to their non-linguistic interests, e.g., economic, however, inquirers usually do not provide enough information about these. The basic interest of the LCC is to provide language consultancy in accordance with the language policy and ideologies (esp. the language cultivation ideology) of the CLI, thereby controlling the discourse on language and strengthening the expert role and social position of the CLI. Thus, the objectives of both parties of LCC interactions are not identical. Rather, they only overlap partially, and as a result the LCC may in some cases suggest a solution to the presented language problem which is not in accordance with the inquirer's interests.

Focusing on interactions in which there is a conflict of opinions and interests, I examined whether the linguist was able to convince the inquirer of the proposed adjustment plan and the role that argumentation as well as differences or agreement between the language ideologies of the interactants played in this process. The success of this linguist's effort depended mainly on two factors: the degree of authority attributed by the inquirer to the LCC (its type can be specified as the authority of knowledge or expertise) and the degree to which the LCC argumentation was convincing. At the same time, a relationship of interdependence was identified between authority and argumentation.

As for the strength of LCC authority, the analysis has shown that it is unstable and dependent on different inquirers' language ideologies and their attitudes to the role of linguistic institutions. Statements about the social reputation of the CLI and general respect for its linguistic opinions should therefore be taken with caution. The language ideologies of Czech speakers, including opinions on the organized language management of Standard Czech, cannot be considered a homogeneous whole, but rather, must be viewed in light of their diversity.

Appendix: Transcription conventions

[xx]	overlapping speech
?	rising intonation
.	falling intonation
,	continuing intonation
:	prolongation of the previous sound
(.)	a short pause
(..)	a longer pause
(...)	long pause
()	no words could be distinguished in the talk within single parenthesis
(xx)	items enclosed within single parenthesis are in doubt
((xx))	notes of the author
[...]	a part of the transcript omitted
<xx>	laughter during the utterance
filoZOFIE	capital letters indicate emphasis

Acknowledgments

The research for this chapter was supported by the NAKI II grant of the Czech Ministry of Culture No. DG16P02B009 (Access to a Linguistically Structured Database of Inquiries from the Language Consulting Center).

References

Ammon, U. (2005) Standard und Variation: Norm, Autorität, Legitimation [Standard and variation: Norm, authority, legitimation]. In L. Eichinger & W. Kallmeyer (eds) *Standardvariation: Wie viel Variation verträgt die deutsche Sprache?* [Standard Variation: How much Variation does German Tolerate?]. Berlin & New York: De Gruyter, 28–40.

Beneš, M., Prošek, M., Smejkalová, K. & Štěpánová, V. (2018) Interaction between language users and a language consulting centre: Challenges for language management theory and research. In L. Fairbrother, J. Nekvapil & M. Sloboda (eds) *The Language Management Approach: A Focus on Research Methodology.* Berlin: Peter Lang, 119–140.

Blommaert, J. (2006) Language policy and national identity. In T. Ricento (ed) *An Introduction to Language Policy: Theory and Method.* Malden, Oxford & Carlton: Blackwell, 238–254.

Cooper, R. L. (1989) *Language Planning and Social Change.* Cambridge: Cambridge University Press.

Daneš, F. (1987) Values and attitudes in language standardization. In J. Chloupek & J. Nekvapil (eds) *Reader in Czech Sociolinguistics.* Amsterdam: John Benjamins, 206–245.

de Bres, J. (2013) Language ideologies for constructing inclusion and exclusion: Identity and interest in the metalinguistic discourse of cross-border workers in Luxembourg. In E. Barát, P. Studer & J. Nekvapil (eds) *Ideological Conceptualizations of Language: Discourses of Linguistic Diversity.* Frankfurt on the Main: Peter Lang, 57–83.

Eemeren, F. H. van & Grootendorst, R. (2004) *Systematic Theory of Argumentation: The Pragma-Dialectical Approach.* Cambridge: Cambridge University Press.

Foucault, M. (1980) *Power/Knowledge: Selected Interviews and Other Writings 1972–1977.* New York: Pantheon Books.

Foucault, M. (1995) *Discipline & Punish: The Birth of the Prison.* New York: Vintage Books.

Habermas, J. (1981) *Theorie des kommunikativen Handelns* [Theory of Communicative Action]. Vol. 1. Frankfurt on the Main: Suhrkamp.

Havránek, B. (1932) Úkoly spisovného jazyka a jeho kultura [Tasks of the standard language and its culture]. In B. Havránek & M. Weingart (eds) *Spisovná čeština a jazyková kultura* [Standard Czech and Language Cultivation]. Praha: Melantrich, 32–84.

Heritage, J. (1984) A change-of-state token and aspects of its sequential placement. In J. M. Atkinson & J. Heritage (eds) *Structures of Social Action: Studies in Conversation Analysis.* Cambridge: Cambridge University Press, 299–345.

Homoláč, J. & Mrázková, K. (2014) K stylistickému hodnocení jazykových prostředků, zvláště lexikálních [On the stylistic classification of linguistic (particularly lexical) items]. *Slovo a slovesnost* 75 (1), 3–38.

Internetová jazyková příručka [Internet Language Reference Book]. On WWW at http://prirucka.ujc.cas.cz/. Maintained by the Czech Language Institute, Czech Academy of Sciences. Accessed June 23, 2019.

Jernudd, B. (2018) Questions submitted to two language cultivation agencies in Sweden. In L. Fairbrother, J. Nekvapil & M. Sloboda (eds) *The Language Management Approach: A Focus on Research Methodology.* Berlin: Peter Lang, 101–117.

Jernudd, B. H. & Neustupný, J. V. (1987) Language planning: For whom? In L. Laforge (ed) *Actes du Colloque international sur l'aménagement linguistique / Proceedings of the International Colloquium on Language Planning.* Québec: Les Presses de L'Université Laval, 69–84.

Kienpointner, M. (1992) *Alltagslogik: Struktur und Funktion von Argumentationsmustern* [Everyday Logic: Structure and Function of Argument Patterns]. Stuttgart & Bad Cannstatt: frommann-holzboog.

Kimura, G. Ch. (2017) The role of language ideology in norm negotiation. *Working Papers in Language Management* 2. On WWW at http://languagemanagement.ff.cuni.cz/system/files/documents/wplm-02_kimura.pdf. Accessed July 30, 2018.

Kopecký, J. (2014) Přechylování příjmení v češtině jako případ jazykového managementu [Derivation of feminine surnames in Czech as a case of language management]. *Slovo a slovesnost* 75 (4), 271–293.

Kopecký, J. (2018) Argumentace v jazykové interakci [Argumentation in linguistic interaction]. *Slovo a slovesnost* 79 (4), 322–344.

Kopperschmidt, J. (2000) *Argumentationstheorie zur Einführung* [Argumentation Theory for Introduction]. Hamburg: Junius.

Kroskrity, P. V. (2004) Language ideologies. In A. Duranti (ed) *A Companion to Linguistic Anthropology.* Malden, Oxford & Carlton: Blackwell, 498–517.

Lanstyák, I. (2017) Jazykové ideológie (všeobecné otázky a glosár) [Language ideologies (general questions and glossary)]. In I. Lanstyák, G. Múcsková & J. Tancer (eds) *Jazyky a jazykové ideológie v kontexte viacjazyčnosti na Slovensku* [Languages and Language Ideologies in the Context of Multilingualism in Slovakia]. Bratislava: Univerzita Komenského v Bratislave, 251–307.

LCC Mission. On WWW at http://ujc.cas.cz/jazykova-poradna/co-je-jazykova-poradna.html. Maintained by the Czech Language Institute, Czech Academy of Sciences. Accessed June 23, 2019.

Milroy, L. (1999) Standard English and language ideology in Britain and the United States. In T. Bex & R. J. Watts (eds) *Standard English: The Widening Debate*. London & New York: Routledge.

Miyazaki, S. (2001) Theoretical framework for communicative adjustment in language acquisition. *Journal of Asian Pacific Communication* 11 (1), 39–60.

Nebeská, I. (2016a) Jazyková norma [Language norm]. In P. Karlík, M. Nekula & J. Pleskalová (eds) *CzechEncy – Nový encyklopedický slovník češtiny* [CzechEncy – New Encyclopaedia of Czech]. On WWW at https://www.czechency.org/slovnik/JAZYKOVÁNORMA. Accessed July 30, 2018.

Nebeská, I. (2016b) Jazyková správnost [Linguistic correctness]. In P. Karlík, M. Nekula & J. Pleskalová (eds) *CzechEncy – Nový encyklopedický slovník češtiny* [CzechEncy – New Encyclopaedia of Czech]. On WWW at https://www.czechency.org/slovnik/JAZYKOVÁSPRÁVNOST. Accessed July 30, 2018.

Nebeská, I. (2016c) Teorie spisovného jazyka [Theory of standard language]. In P. Karlík, M. Nekula & J. Pleskalová (eds) *CzechEncy – Nový encyklopedický slovník češtiny* [CzechEncy – New Encyclopaedia of Czech]. On WWW at https://www.czechency.org/slovnik/TEORIESPISOVNÉHO JAZYKA. Accessed July 30, 2018.

Nekvapil, J. (2008) Language cultivation in developed contexts. In B. Spolsky & F. M. Hult (eds) *The Handbook of Educational Linguistics*. Malden, Oxford & Carlton: Blackwell, 251–265.

Nekvapil, J. (2012) From language planning to language management: J. V. Neustupný's heritage. *Media Komyunikēshon kenkyū / Media and Communication Studies* 63. Sapporo: Hokkaido University, Research Faculty of Media and Communication, 5–21.

Nekvapil, J. (2016) Language Management Theory as one approach in Language Policy and Planning. *Current Issues in Language Planning* 17 (1), 11–22.

Nekvapil, J. & Sherman, T. (2013) Language ideologies and linguistic practices: The case of multinational companies in Central Europe. In E. Barát, P. Studer & J. Nekvapil (eds) *Ideological Conceptualizations of Language: Discourses of Linguistic Diversity*. Frankfurt on the Main: Peter Lang, 85–117.

Nekvapil, J. & Sherman, T. (2015) An introduction: Language Management Theory in Language Policy and Planning. *International Journal of the Sociology of Language* 232, 1–12.

Neustupný, J. V. (2002) Language and power into the 21st century: A paper for the *International Conference on Language and Empowerment*, Malaysian Association of Modern Languages, Kuala Lumpur, Malaysia, April 11–13, 2002. On WWW at http://languagemanagement.ff.cuni.cz/bibliography. Accessed June 23, 2019.

Neustupný, J. V. & Nekvapil, J. (2003) Language management in the Czech Republic. *Current Issues in Language Planning* 4 (3/4), 181–366.

Pomerantz, A. & Heritage, J. (2013) Preference. In J. Sidnell & T. Stivers (eds) *The Handbook of Conversation Analysis*. Chichester: Wiley-Blackwell, 210–228.

Pravdová, M. & Svobodová, I. (eds) (2019) *Akademická příručka českého jazyka* [Academic Vade Mecum of the Czech Language]. 2nd expanded edition. Praha: Academia.

Pravidla českého pravopisu [The Rules of Czech Orthography]. Praha: Academia, 2005.

Příruční slovník jazyka českého [Concise Dictionary of the Czech Language]. Vol. I. Praha: Státní nakladatelství, 1935–1937.

Prošek, M. (2020) Processes of language enquiries: The case of the Prague Language Consulting Service. In G. Ch. Kimura & L. Fairbrother (eds) *A Language Management Approach to Language Problems: Integrating Macro and Micro Dimensions*. Amsterdam: John Benjamins, 197–213.

Prošek, M. & Smejkalová, K. (2011) Kodifikace – právo, nebo pravomoc? [Codification – right or mandate?] *Naše řeč* 94 (5), 231–241.

Šichová, K. (2017) K fenoménu správnosti a standardu ve výuce češtiny pro cizince [On the phenomenon of correctness and Standard Czech in teaching Czech for foreigners]. In M. Nekula & K. Šichová (eds) *Variety češtiny a čeština jako cizí jazyk* [Varieties of Czech and Czech as a Foreign Language]. Praha: Akropolis, 207–246.

Sidnell, J. & Stivers, T. (eds) (2013) *The Handbook of Conversation Analysis*. Chichester: Wiley-Blackwell.

Silverstein, M. (1979) Language structure and linguistic ideology. In P. Clyne, W. Hanks & C. Hofbauer (eds) *The Elements*. Chicago: Chicago Linguistic Society, 193–248.

Uhlířová, L. (2002) Jazyková poradna v měnící se komunikační situaci u nás [Language consulting service in the light of recent communication changes in the Czech Republic]. *Sociologický časopis / Czech Sociological Review* 38 (4), 443–455.

Uličný, O. (2013) K teorii českého pravopisu [The theory of Czech orthography]. In O. Uličný & M. Prošek (eds) *Studie k moderní mluvnici češtiny 5: K české fonetice a pravopisu* [Studies in Modern Czech Grammar 5: On Czech Phonetics and Orthography]. Olomouc: Univerzita Palackého, 119–121.

Weber, M. (1978) *Economy and Society: An Outline of Interpretive Sociology*. Berkeley, Los Angeles & London: University of California Press.

Woolard, K. A. (1998) Language ideology as a field of inquiry. In B. Schieffelin, K. Woolard & P. V. Kroskrity (eds) *Language Ideologies: Practice and Theory*. Oxford: Oxford University Press, 3–47.

Stephanie Rudwick

Language politics at Stellenbosch University, South Africa

Abstract This chapter examines language management processes in the higher education sector in South Africa as a deeply politicized domain which exhibits complex dynamics of interests and power. It primarily discusses how a student movement at Stellenbosch University (SU) embraced a discourse that has accentuated the power of English as the primary academic lingua franca of the country. This pro-English interest and discourse is juxtaposed with one that portrays the Afrikaans language (the previously main language of learning and teaching at SU) as a "tool of exclusion" and in holding on problematic power constellations which are a legacy of apartheid. The chapter is based on an analysis of the language politics unfolding at SU in the years between 2014 and 2016 and it argues that this context provides fruitful data for research into the socio-cultural politics of English as an academic lingua franca. Employing Language Management Theory (LMT) as analytical lens (Jernudd & Neustupný 1987; Nekvapil 2006; Nekvapil & Sherman 2015), I examine why and how macro and micro language management processes have triggered divisive and conflict-riddled language politics at SU. While there is continued polarization of interests among students, alumni and language policy makers about the role of English vis-à-vis Afrikaans, I would like to demonstrate that according to the LMT model of the micro-(meso)-macro-(meso)-micro cycle, the institutional language management exhibits, unlike some other South African universities, a certain success. There appears to be approximation, albeit restricted, to a complete language management cycle in a sense that demands of changes in the institutional language practices and metalanguage discourses at the micro level of SU have significantly informed the decisions and power dynamics at the macro level of the institution. This ultimately resulted in language policy changes on the macro level and specific implementations at the micro level.

Keywords Language politics, South Africa, Stellenbosch University, English, Afrikaans, language management cycle

1 Introduction

On March 3rd in 2016, a meeting organized by the South African Student Council Organization took place at Stellenbosch University (SU). About four hundred students and other university stakeholders came together to critically discuss the role of Afrikaans at the institution. Initiating the meeting, one of the 'black'[1] South African student council leaders, opened up by saying:

---

1 The four apartheid-based race categories (African [Black], Colored, Indian and European [White]) continue to serve bureaucratic purposes and are part of everyday

> Black children are brought here [to *Stellenbosch University*] to be educated, coming with the dreams of their families, so that they can have a good education, but when they get here, there are *obstacles in their way*. This obstacle, first and foremost, is being *taught in a language that they do not understand*. Let's get this clear, we never said we hate or dislike Afrikaans, it is one of the languages of this country, but *never must a language be enforced onto people*, never in this country. (my emphasis in italics)

The student's emphatic speech resonated with the crowd and there was much cheering in response. The broader South African language and identity politics it addresses are intriguing from a range of sociolinguistic and socio-political perspectives. The speech essentially contained a dual message: Firstly, Afrikaans, unlike English which is the language in which the student leader holds his speech, is not widely understood by African students and secondly, it is seen as politically illegitimate to enforce students to learn (in) Afrikaans or any other language for that matter. Implicit also is that Afrikaans is perceived as a tool of 'exclusion' and English is the accepted academic lingua franca for students (although English is not even mentioned). By emphasizing "this country," the student allures to the tragedy of the Soweto uprising in 1976 that will be explained in further detail below. Suffice it to state at this point: language management discourse in South African education has always been a much-politicized domain (Alexander 2004; Mwaniki 2011; Rudwick 2016), and language politics, in particular at South African universities, also have a history of being caught in static and technocratic views of language (Hill 2010).

In this chapter, I aim to address how English as a widely desired academic lingua franca at Stellenbosch (as asserted by the student movement *Open Stellenbosch* in 2015/16) is not without socio-political ambiguities. The assertion is not particularly surprising given that English has been the preferred ex-colonial language for the overwhelming majority of African people. This is the case not least because it has been the primary language of the country's liberation party (the African National Congress, ANC) that continues to be in power but also because of its complex international and academic value and its role as the most common lingua franca among educated Africans. Even speakers of isiZulu and isiXhosa whose languages are mutually intelligible (both are part of the Nguni language cluster) are often heard speaking to each other in English.

Although the language is indisputably linked to British interests and colonialism, as well as educational and economic privilege in South Africa, it is widely perceived as a relatively 'neutral' medium especially if contrasted to Afrikaans. However, even in relation to the official African languages which are often

---

discourse of most South Africans. Although reluctantly and uncomfortably, I maintain these racial classifications here in order to demonstrate how race matters to South Africans. I employ the categories in inverted commas to capture their ambiguity.

associated with ethnicity English fares quite well. English has been claimed to be a naturalized African language (Kamwangamalu 2007), but this does not necessarily include a language shift from African languages to English but rather increased bilingualism in which English might be taking a more dominant and leading role. I aim to demonstrate how the naturalized status of English has been playing out in the language politics at SU in recent years. As Kamwangamalu (2019: 11) recently argued that there is a need to "explore ways in which English, now irrevocably a naturalized African language rather [...], can co-exist with its sister languages, the indigenous African languages, in higher domains of language use, including the educational system."

African urban spaces provide rich data on the multiple entanglements of English and various African languages and the boundaries between so-called different ways of speaking have often become blurry. Post-colonial linguistics has shown the fallacies of Eurocentric scholarship on language as a bounded system and Herderian ideologies of 'pure' languages linked to 'pure' nations (Errington 2007; Bauman & Briggs 2003; Beck 2018). Nonetheless, current South African language politics have re-asserted the link between language and ethnicity (Makoni 2003; Rudwick 2018). While the complex and ambiguous role of English is far from benign and uncontested in the South African context (Rudwick 2021), this chapter aims to show how the perceived and managed role of English as a relatively neutral academic lingua franca has been asserted in power dynamics at SU. Of course, the academic power of English is also due to its economic power and the simple fact that good job opportunities are inextricably linked to proficiency in the language (Turner 2015; Posel & Zeller 2015).

In the next section, I provide a brief sociolinguistic background to relevant language issues in South Africa and the student protests that took place during 2015/16. Then, I examine the research paradigm of English as a lingua franca (ELF) for its relevance in the South African context. The section that follows shifts to Language Management Theory (LMT) (Jernudd & Neustupný 1987; Nekvapil 2006; Nekvapil & Sherman 2015) and the focus on interest and power which provides the analytical lens for examining the case study at hand. The chapter ultimately shows why and how macro-, meso- and micro-level processes triggered conflict-riddled language politics at SU from 2014 until 2016 when the language policy was officially changed. This text is informed by two ethnographic fieldwork periods in Stellenbosch during January–February 2015 and March 2016. For the purpose of this chapter, I also make use of the analysis of Facebook and Twitter postings during this period. Reflective practices on my position as a 'white' European female researcher also constituted an essential part of the research.

2 Brief socio-political background

In recent years, the reconciliatory ('rainbow') politics of the iconic Nelson Mandela have become increasingly criticized among 'black' students who argue that 'freedom' was only provided on a political level for African people, but not on an economic one (Horáková 2019). The majority of 'black' South Africans continue to live in poverty while the reality of 'white privilege' permeates facets of the society. Many among the 'black' youths feel that Mandela's reconciliation 'sold-out' Africans to the economic power of the 'whites.'

The year 2015 marked a watershed in South African higher education. Initiated at the University of Cape Town (UCT), the '#Rhodes must fall' (RMF) student campaign sparked off a complex process of countrywide student movements (most notable, #FeesMustFall) which had the broader aim to "decolonize education." The #RMF campaign succeeded in having the statue of imperialist Cecil Rhodes removed from UCT premises and the countrywide #FeesMustFall even achieved an unprecedented government commitment to a zero percent fee increment at all universities in 2016.

At SU, a predominately African student group founded *#Open Stellenbosch,* a movement that was primarily concerned with a language issue: the dominance of Afrikaans and Afrikaner ('white' Afrikaans speakers) indisputable dominance at the institution and in the town.[2] This cause, capturing a sociolinguistic injustice, was phrased as the complaint that Afrikaans was employed as a "tool of exclusion" at the institution. It quickly became clear: Afrikaans had not shed its stigma as the 'language of the oppressor' that it acquired during apartheid. Afrikaans was the mother tongue of apartheid architects and most commonly spoken by national security police of the apartheid state (Giliomee 2003: 14). Most South African school children were more or less forced to learn Afrikaans and in 1970 the Department of Education even enforced a strict 50:50 percent rule for Afrikaans and English as languages of instruction in 'black' schools (Hartshorne 1992). In response to this decree, African learners and teachers took to the street in 1976 in order to demonstrate against Afrikaans as a language of tuition. During these events, documented as the *Soweto uprising* many African children tragically lost their lives due to ruthless police intervention. A photograph featuring a small 'black' boy, named Hector Pieterson dying in the arms of his older brother shocked the entire world at the time, triggered further sanctions on South Africa at the time and continues to symbolize until today the atrocities of apartheid.

Today, mother-tongue Afrikaans speakers make up about 13.5% of the South African population and the majority of Afrikaans speakers are so-called 'colored' ('mixed-race') people, not 'white' Afrikaners. However, the variety spoken by the vast majority of 'colored' people is called Kaaps and it is quite different from the Afrikaner standard that guides the orthography. Despite the fact that many

2 Against the background that the RhodesMustFall protest initiated the call for decolonization, Dube (2017: 19) aptly remarks that the demand of replacing Afrikaans with English is quite ironic "in the sense that Rhodes, who is a symbol of everything colonial in South Africa, and whom the students would like to obliterate from history, is an iconic figure of the English culture in the whole of Southern Africa – a culture whose language is English."

'colored' people speak a variety of Afrikaans, the language remains stigmatized among many 'black' South African people who associate it with oppression and institutionalized racism. Several studies discussed the strong link between Afrikaans and Afrikaner ethnicity (Blaser 2007; Bosch 2000; Engel 1997; Kriel 2003; Webb & Kriel 2000). The saliency of the stigma of Afrikaans as the 'language of the oppressor' among 'black' South Africans and awareness of the horrors of apartheid is necessary in order to adequately understand socio-political events that unfolded between 2015 and 2016 at SU. The primary concern of the *Open Stellenbosch* collective was that the university did not sufficiently transform since the end of apartheid. And indeed, it cannot be denied that SU continued to represent a primarily 'white' Afrikaans-speaking, Afrikaner cultural microcosm despite being officially a public university. Many of the undergraduate programs at Stellenbosch were taught exclusively in Afrikaans and many 'black' students have insufficient knowledge of the language because their schooling was largely in English. This background is important to understand why English hit such fruitful ground in Stellenbosch in 2015. Given this saliency of English as an (academic) lingua franca in South Africa I would like to argue that the research field of ELF has relevance in the South African context and I will briefly turn to this research field below.

3 English as a lingua franca[3]

The beginning of systematic research on the phenomenon of 'English as a lingua franca,' including the use of the acronym ELF, can be traced back to the early 2000s. The scholars at the forefront of the field (Jenkins 2018; Mauranen 2018; Seidlhofer 2011) insist that ELF does not exclude English first language speakers and that it describes a linguistic contact phenomenon between speakers when at least one of them uses English as a second language. In other words, ELF is not a variety of English that could be "formally defined" but rather "a variable way of using it" (Seidlhofer 2011: 77), a complex discourse phenomenon so to speak. The *Routledge Handbook of English as a Lingua Franca* is testimony to the fact that ELF has been a thriving research field for some years, despite much criticism in the early years of its conception. Its center of research gravity, surprisingly, continues to be Europe and, to some degree, developed countries in Asia. This seems puzzling given that there are many other places, in particular British ex-colonial countries where English lingua franca communication is pervasive. As a result of not engaging sufficiently with Englishes in ex-colonies and postcolonial debates, critical issues in the sociocultural politics of global English have been neglected (Pennycook 2017). It cannot be denied that the overwhelming bulk of ELF work

3 For reasons of scope the discussion here merely focuses on selected aspects of ELF and does not engage with other, similar approaches to English spoken in multilingual environments, such as English as an International language (EIL, Modiano 2004), translingualism (Canagarajah 2013), etc.

has drawn from empirical data collected in the global North and that as such the field could be termed geopolitically Eurocentric. Pennycook (2017: ix) puts it this way: "the ELF approach has been able to avoid some of the problems of the World English focus [...] and can open up more flexible and mobile versions of English," but, at the same time, "it has likewise never engaged adequately with questions of power." I would like to add that critical issues around gender, class, ethnicity and 'race' have also not received the attention they deserve. Few ELF studies (e.g., Baker 2015, 2018) have conceptualized 'culture' in ELF communication more critically and there has been much focus on what might constitute a shared culture and identity through ELF. Many studies (Jenks 2013 is a noteworthy exception) continue to highlight the benign status and positive effects of ELF communication for people. This is problematic in post-colonial contexts. Given the pervasive multilingualism and the complex power dynamics involving the access to English, it seems that perspectives from Africa could contribute to a more critical engagement with what I would consider 'romanticized' views about ELF in some scholarship.

This is not to say that previous theorizing around ELF might not also be useful in post-colonial settings. Some ELF work (Kecskes 2007; Fiedler 2011) framed ELF as a 'third space' invoking the work of Homi Bhabha (2004). The conceptualization of ELF discourse as a third space is instructive in terms of disrupting formal-informal dichotomies that exist in many educational spaces. These conceptualizations can foreground hybridity, fluidity and idiosyncrasies as the 'norm' that are in line with the idea of "multilingualism as the new linguistic dispensation" (Singleton, Fishman, Aronin & Ó Laoireal 2013). However, at the same time, too narrow a conceptualization based on the positive and communicative status of ELF discourse might also lead to misguided perceptions that actors in this third space are horizontally located with no hierarchies involved, which is not the case in most South African English lingua franca contexts.

Therefore, critical perspectives towards some ELF paradigms are important in a place such as Africa where World Englishes scholars have long stressed that non-native Englishes are best seen as divergent rather than deficient. And yet, public opinion often perpetuates ideas of Standard English as the ultimate ideal. 'Black South African English' (BSAE) has been extensively examined[4] but BSAE is only one of several English lingua franca varieties or *similects* (Mauranen 2012, 2018) playing different roles in the country. Many different English varieties constitute pieces in the complex puzzle of English lingua franca discourse in Africa and this high variability of Englishes in educational contexts poses a challenge to some conceptualizations of ELF. Certain studies (Hynninen 2016; Mauranen 2011, 2014, 2018a) from the ELF university context have already portrayed the complexity in English as an academic lingua franca but European languages influencing ELF

4 Black South African English is a broad research field, see for example De Klerk & Gough (2002), Mesthrie (2006), Makalela (2004), Smit (1996), Van Rooy (2004), Wade (1996), Mesthrie & Bhatt (2008).

discourse dominate much of the data (i.e., the ELFA corpus). Furthermore, there are few ethnographically and, to the best of my knowledge, not a single intersectional approach to sociolinguistic power dynamics in ELF discourse available yet. Given this volume's focus on interests and power, I would like to emphasize that the lingua franca status of English does not simply provide it with neutrality and allows speakers to be impartial.[5] Admittedly, the default function of a lingua franca is commonly assumed to be that of a tool to solve communication between speakers of different languages (Sherman 2018: 115) and hence, it often carries a relative neutrality. Indeed, speakers might opt for a lingua franca because "other candidate varieties are laden with historical and political connotations and may signal a power imbalance" (Sherman 2018: 116). While English might be perceived as more 'neutral' than other languages in some contexts, different Englishes spoken in ELF communication might still be endowed with varying power potentials.

In terms of interest, power and language management, English might well have a more communicative function for one speaker and more identity related aspects for another. Any event involving English as the world's primary lingua franca inherently has consequences for the interlocutors' ways of being, although this might not be overtly evident. The dated proposal that English can represent a communicative tool alone (Hüllen 1992) without powers to trigger identity dynamics and inequality can safely be discarded at this point. In other words, interests and identities are always there, we are simply not able not to construct identities when communicating, whether in English or in any other language. Even if English is chosen as a lingua franca because of its relative neutrality and communicative value rather than as an act of identity, interlocutors nonetheless construct implicit identities as, for instance, global, communicative, cosmopolitan, educated, British, American or international people.

The few articles where English is discussed explicitly as a lingua franca in South Africa either mark its status as "failed" (Balfour 2002) or engage insufficiently with its sociocultural politics (Khokhlova 2015). Recently, Van der Walt & Evans (2018) also question the status of ELF in the country and their article is a manifest of how ambivalent South African researchers continue to feel towards the alleged lingua franca status of the language. This ambiguity of ELF shall serve as a springboard towards the more general observations that 'there are always two sides to one coin.' There is no neutral language in the South African context where colonialism, nativism and many other -isms play out in complicated ways in the everyday lives of people. But before I turn to more specificities of the South African context, I will briefly provide the theoretical framework of LMT in relation to interest and power in English lingua franca discourse.

5 English has been portrayed as a "neutral" language before (House 2014); even in some South African contexts, but to suggest that ELF is "bereft of collective cultural capital" (House 2003: 560) is removed from the realities of the cultural politics surrounding English in South Africa.

4 The language management approach

Lingua franca English, as a paradigm, is arguably based on a certain ideology, one, for instance, that gives value to the English language as an "international," "neutral," and "communicative" medium for people all over the globe. Writing about ideologies in the framework of LMT, Nekvapil & Sherman (2013: 86) argue that:

> language ideologies are not an end in themselves, but rather, they are used as the means to extralinguistic ends; in other words, their use produces social reality—language ideologies, for example, help reproduce the divisions between groups, they aid in the exclusion of individuals from a specific social or cultural group or, conversely, in the inclusion of an individual in such a group.

The scholars' comment is illuminating for the South African context. Mechanisms of inclusion/exclusion operate in myriad and complicated ways in South Africa and language ideologies often overlap with socio-political convictions. At the same time, the sociolinguistic situation of the country is extremely diverse and the many hybrid and fluid linguistic practices prevalent raise questions as to what actually constitutes a language. In recent years, several leading socio- and applied linguists have added terminologies such as superdiversity (Blommaert & Rampton 2011), translanguaging (Garcia 2009), translingual practice (Canagarajah 2013) or turbulence (Stroud 2015) in order to provide conceptual tools for the analyses of increasing multilingualism in society. In a country with such extensive levels of multilingualism (such as South Africa) language management might be considerably more complicated than in linguistically more homogenous territories. Given that the country has eleven official languages the interests of different language lobbies, and language policy stakeholders are often quite at loggerheads with each other.

As for 'interest,' Jernudd and Neustupný (1987: 76) suggest in their seminal paper that 'interests' need to be linked to each component of the management process and they further raise a number of valuable questions, such as where the interests differ in simple and organized language management, in which stages of the process which interests emerge or how group interests might change through time and space. They also suggest that linguistic and non-linguistic interests shall be differentiated but in the case of South Africa this is extremely difficult. Language is deeply political in the country and linguistic interests almost always merge with socio-cultural or socio-political interests. Macro level "top-down" language management has historical apartheid "baggage"[6] and is therefore heavily politicized. Nekvapil and Sherman (2015) distinguish the metaphors "top-down"

6 During apartheid the top-down language policy was providing only official status for the two ex-colonial languages, Afrikaans and English. No indigenous language had official national status, despite the fact that the majority population spoke African languages. For more detail on South Africa's language politics, see Webb (2002).

and "bottom-up" in the context of language management and conclude: "The 'top-down' impact is more complex and there is often the work of institutions behind it, which is why it is labeled as 'macro'" (Nekvapil & Sherman 2015: 2). In contrast, "the 'bottom-up' impact may be simpler, often the work of individuals, which is why it is understood as 'micro'" (Nekvapil & Sherman 2015: 2). South Africa has a long history of 'top-down' rather than 'bottom-up' language management. As mentioned earlier, the educational system during apartheid taught Afrikaans and English per decree and African languages were given little space for development.

As for 'power,' the link between English and power can be felt everywhere in South Africa, and in fact in many other African countries. LMT is a useful tool for analyses in English lingua franca research on the African continent because the framework highlights how socio-economic power relations influence linguistic choices (Sherman 2018: 116). In South Africa, and in fact most of Anglophone Africa, colonialism (and apartheid) complicate simple assumptions about the value of ELF.[7] As a paradigm of LMT organized language management ideally influences simple language management, and at the same time organized language management results (or rather should result) from simple language management (Nekvapil & Nekula 2006: 324). Multiple processes on a micro level might help a formulation of a macro language policy that feeds back onto the micro level. Although LMT has been critiqued with the argument that the "micro-macro duality seems to imply a certain hierarchy in which macro-level phenomena somehow take place on a different plane of existence from micro-level phenomena" (Hult 2010: 18), in the context of language planning and policy the two levels seem relevant. I would argue that it is useful, as LMT does, to distinguish macro-level management as endowed with larger (political) interests, executive power and serious implementation agency from micro-level management processes that require organization and collectivity before they might influence policy implementations on a larger scale. However, too sharp a distinction between micro and macro might not be useful when power hierarchies among different language stakeholders are blurry and uncertain. These considerations of the LMT framework in the analysis of the official Language Policy change at SU as it took place in 2016. While differentiating simple (micro) from organized (macro) acts at SU the discussion will show that there are various spaces in between the two levels. There might be sociolinguistic situations where different micro-level management processes conflict and form meso-level management with multi-level hierarchies. My focus here is on the interests of students and the power of what could be described as a meso- or semi-organized language management emerging: First, individual students, second, a

7 For example, access to so-called 'Standard' English is strongly dependent on socio-economic standing of a family, which again is also related to ethnicity and race. Due to persistent 'white' privilege, the African population has had a restricted access to what is widely perceived to be 'good' English, which represents a variety closest to the 'Standard' British English.

student collective, and third, a shared discourse with actors from the macro level. *Open Stellenbosch* students fought for English as the primary Language of Learning and Teaching at SU and ultimately succeeded in their main demand. The next section describes how language (Afrikaans vis-à-vis English) became a terrain of struggle in Stellenbosch and turned into what has been termed a "war of language" (Giliomee 2009).

5 Stellenbosch University

Since early in the twentieth century, SU had promoted "a distinctly Afrikaans academic institution" associated with Afrikaner nationalism and 'white' racist-supremacist politics (van der Waal 2015: 1). From 1930, the institution was almost entirely Afrikaans speaking and it represented an academic engine behind much of apartheid ideology. Only in the early 1990s, the university opened (or rather was forced to open) its doors to all South African students.[8] But Afrikaans continued to be the default language in the university and its town where Afrikaners have put vast financial investments. In the early 2000s, however, and more markedly from 2002 when Chris Brink took over as vice-chancellor of SU (Brink 2006), the largely monolingual institution started to transform into one that also offered English tuition.[9] It was during those years when the first *taalstryd* [language battle] unfolded. A protest petition fighting to protect Afrikaans against English at the institution was signed by 3,500 SU staff and students, as well as a letter signed by 143 prominent Afrikaans authors, was presented to the SU Council in 2005 in an attempt to safeguard the language. Afrikaans became a symbol of Afrikaner identity politics in the new South Africa and Stellenbosch was arguably among the most contested battlegrounds. Afrikaans speaking people have, more than any other ethnolinguistic group in South Africa, complained about lack of support for their language in the press and various other platforms (Orman 2008). A renowned Afrikaner historian has employed dramatic metaphors such as the 'lamb' [Afrikaans] being eaten by the 'lion' [English] (Giliomee 2009). Indeed, for most 'white' Afrikaans speakers, language is the primary point of reference in the social construction of their identity and ethnicity. Put succinctly, Afrikaans "acts as a creator and definer" of Afrikaner ethnicity, Afrikanerdom (Bosch 2000: 52).

From 2007, the university inaugurated a new vice-chancellor. Russel Botman was the university's first 'colored' vice-chancellor, and he tried conciliating the polarized language lobbies within the institution. On the one hand, he showed

8 This involved a whole range of complicated socio-political dynamics that for reasons of scope cannot be elaborated here (for more detail, see Giliomee 2001, 2003).

9 All South African universities that were so-called "Afrikaans universities" converted, more or less, into bilingual models during the first decade or two after apartheid, implementing English as the second Language of Learning and Teaching (Du Plessis 2003, 2006; Webb 2010).

commitment to Afrikaans, but he also allowed English to increasingly enter the institution. The language policy (LP) revisions of 2007 put an emphasis on multilingualism and make specific reference to safeguarding Afrikaans. Nonetheless, conservative Afrikaners and so-called *taalstreyders* [language fighters] regarded the LP as impeding further on Afrikaans. Botman tragically died in 2014, and it has been alleged in the media that emotional and psychological pressure (not least due to polarized language politics at the university) might have contributed to his untimely sad death.[10] In the absence of hard evidence relating to Botman's passing, we can only make assumptions about how sensitive and potentially devastating for some individuals the *taalstreyd* unfolded at Stellenbosch. Language is a sensitive issue for many people in South Africa but it is exceptionally emotional for many Afrikaners who see a threat to their language as a threat to their very existence. There is an acute concern among Afrikaners that Afrikaans would lose its status as a language of the higher domains of life (in Fishman's terms). The ideology of Afrikaans as a carrier of Afrikaner high culture and as a valuable academic and intellectual tool is prevalent to a noteworthy extent.[11]

In the wake of the #RMF campaign and other 'Fallist' movements in South Africa, student protests started against Afrikaans at SU in early 2015. Initially a small group of predominately, but not only 'black' students founded *Open Stellenbosch* in order to "purge the oppressive remnants of apartheid" (Facebook page). In the South African *Daily Maverick* on 28 April 2015, the collective identified three primary demands:

1. No student should be forced to learn or communicate in Afrikaans and all classes must be available in English.
2. The institutional culture at Stellenbosch University needs to change radically and rapidly to reflect diverse cultures and not only White Afrikaans culture.
3. The University publicly needs to acknowledge and actively remember the central role that Stellenbosch and its faculty played in the conceptualization, implementation and maintenance of Apartheid.[12]

Emphasizing that SU is a *public* tertiary institution in South Africa and therefore supposed to provide equal access to *all* South Africans, members of *Open Stellenbosch* demanded that the university management reconsidered and revised the language policy (Stellenbosch University 2014), due to it favoring Afrikaans. Shortly after the founding of *Open Stellenbosch*, in August 2015, the university

10 https://www.dailymaverick.co.za/article/2014-07-02-revealed-professor-botmans-torrid-final-week/#.WvqtbS-B1Bw (accessed 3 April 2019).

11 But more generally, also outside the sphere of Afrikaans politics, language policies in the South African educational sphere have been shaped often by ideological concerns (Manyike & Lemmer 2014; Rudwick 2017).

12 See: https://www.dailymaverick.co.za/article/2015-04-28-op-ed-open-stellenbosch-tackling-language-and-exclusion-at-stellenbosch-university/

management came further under pressure after a very negative portrayal of the institution featured in a documentary entitled *Luister* [Listen]. The film went viral on social media and outraged not only South Africans but also international viewers. *Luister*[13] is based on personal interviews that deliver a shocking account of discriminatory, oppressive practices that 'black' students endure in Stellenbosch. While much of the narrative is not about language but violent racism of diverse nature, some students also describe how Afrikaans is "killing" African students at SU because their proficiency in the language is inadequate. One student, in particular, describes how the language remains the "language of the oppressor" to him. Many sentiments brought forward in the film echo what Mabokela (2001: 72) argued, that is, that "for African students, using Afrikaans as a medium of instruction is like pouring salt into an open wound."

As a result of *Open Stellenbosch* and *Luister*, the macro 'structure' of SU language management started shaking and the institution's 'managers,' executives and VC became painfully aware that they needed to become proactive in order to counteract a devastating publicity of SU. Between mid-2015 and mid-2016, *Open Stellenbosch* organized countless demonstrations and demanded a clear change in the language policy. The Language Coalition of the *Open Stellenbosch* movement met repeatedly with the acting vice-chancellor, various university administrators, and 'managers' from the institution. It became clear that the university would have to make some major concessions in order to pacify the toxic climate that had emerged through students' dissatisfaction and the international negative media coverage. In mid-2016, the executive management agreed that a new language policy would be drafted, one in which English (and not Afrikaans) would become the primary language of learning and teaching. Given the stigma of Afrikaans as a 'language of the oppressor' on the one hand, and the strong international value of English on the other hand, it is not surprising that events in Stellenbosch unfolded in this way. While it seems that the lingua franca status of English asserted itself at the University, it is apt to caution that English (es) and English lingua franca academic discourse are far from 'neutral' communication and learning modes in South Africa. I will attempt to illustrate this further below.

6 English at Stellenbosch in LMT analysis

Throughout the twentieth century and also in the post-apartheid years, several authors have promoted the important role of ELF for the country. But the economic and socio-political hegemony of English in South Africa also resulted in a small 'black' elite who employs English as a first language and whose members are no longer proficient in an African language. The overwhelming majority of

13 The documentary is a compelling and quite personal account of thirty-two students and one lecturer at SU, available online: https://www.youtube.com/watch?v=sF3rTBQTQk4.

all 'black' South Africans, however, continue to speak an indigenous African language as so-called 'mother-tongue' (Census 2011). English serves, in many contexts and situations as an exclusionary device. The late Neville Alexander, who was one of the most ardent promoters of multilingualism in South Africa, also emphasized the value of English as a linking language in the country. However, he cautioned: "the use of English as a language of tuition at tertiary level because of its lingua franca function [...] is no guarantee of educational equity" (Alexander 2013: 84). While his warning continues to have currency, the majority of students in Stellenbosch are either Afrikaans or isiXhosa speaking and from this perspective, English arguably constitutes a kind of compromise, as it is a shared second language for most.

Some sociolinguists, for instance, have criticized the *Open Stellenbosch* collective for apparent univocal focus on and preference for English. On an Email based list-server engaging with sociolinguistic issues in 2016, one contributor described the demands of *Open Stellenbosch* as "short-sighted" for demanding English tuition (rather than a multilingual framework) at the institution. However, members of *Open Stellenbosch* repeatedly explained on public and social media platforms that they felt SU had primarily focused on Afrikaans development while hiding under the blanket of multilingualism. Also, support for African languages (in this case isiXhosa) is arguably also not uncontroversial (at least for 'white' people) as it draws rejection from at least two lobbies: First, those who regard English as the 'only' future and see vernacular promotion counter-productive to national progress and second, those who object to the involvement of non-'black' people in African language and cultural matters (Makoni & Makoni 2009: 116).

Furthermore, it appears that some positions of *Open Stellenbosch* have been (mis-) portrayed as perhaps presented too radical by some commentators in the media and press and on social networks. While certain extremist members of the movement might have wanted to see Afrikaans disused at SU in the future, the *Open Stellenbosch* collective as present on social media never called for the abolishment of Afrikaans. After all, it needs to be acknowledged that this student collective has been very diverse and its members also polarized as regards certain issues, such as gender, race and class. Be that as it may, the interests of the *Open Stellenbosch* group were made explicit. The *Memorandum of Demands*[14] published on 13 May 2015 read the following:

1. All classes must be available in English.
2. The use of translators and translation-devices must be discontinued, as they are ineffective, inaudible and highlight the place of non-Afrikaans speaking students at Stellenbosch as those who do not belong.

14 To view the entire document, see: http://www.sun.ac.za/english/management/wim-de-villiers/Documents/Open%20Stellenbosch%20Memo%2020150513.pdf.

3. All official and unofficial communication from management, faculty and university departments must be available in English. This includes communication between faculty and staff, and not simply the communique from management.
4. All residence, faculty, departmental and administrative meetings and correspondence must be conducted in English.
5. Afrikaans must not be a requirement for employment or appointment to leadership positions.
6. The University must stop using isiXhosa as a front for multilingualism when it has clearly invested minimal resources in its development on campus. Alternatively, significant investment must be directed at developing isiXhosa on campus.
7. All signage on campus must be available in English.

The above demands capture that "access" to all classes in English represents the main prerogative of the collective. Language ideologies manifest themselves in multiple ways in meta-linguistic discourse and while two individuals might have similar attitudes towards one and the same language, the motives behind those might be driven by different ideologies. At SU, certain 'black' African students might have rejected Afrikaans simply because they are not proficient in the language, others might reject it on political grounds. Importantly, there are multiple forms of interests and power at play in this setting. As for LMT in reference to Stellenbosch, the usefulness of a rigid distinction between macro- and micro-level management activities must indeed be questioned. In initial analysis, individual student activities on the ground, students' behavior towards language, and individual students' language political demands were seen as the micro-level management within an institution. In contrast, activities of the university management, i.e., the vice-chancellor's office and language policy makers were regarded as agents of the macro level. It became quickly clear, however, that some of the activities at the so-called (initial) micro level became rather "organized" through *Open Stellenbosch* and were in fact moving into a kind of meso- and semi-macro-level sphere which then was also endowed with collective interests and sufficient power to enact a change.

Between the years of 2015 and 2016, one could observe, at least to a certain extent, approximation to a complete LMT cycle in a sense that meta-linguistic discourses at the micro level of SU, i.e., *Open Stellenbosch* language demands sufficiently informed the meta-discourse and language planning activities on the macro level in order to trigger a language policy change. For this to happen, however, the language management as enacted by *Open Stellenbosch* individual members needed to become organized and move into a type of semi-macro sphere where language management was no longer the work of only individual actors but that of the collective. Once the Language Coalition of *Open Stellenbosch* was formed and once the collective met persistently during 2015–16 with the university executive in order to have their demands met, they also were able to negotiate change in the official language policy document. This resulted in the change of status of Afrikaans vis-à-vis English at the institution. The group continuously reported on these meetings via their Facebook and twitter accounts. As a result of these negotiations, the SU council approved, on 22 June 2016, a new language policy reflecting a change in the role of Afrikaans and English at the institution.

7 Language policy change at Stellenbosch University

In comparing the actual SU language policy documents from 2014 and 2016 (see Stellenbosch University 2014, 2016, available online), a superficial glance already reveals a fundamental difference between the two texts: their lengths. While the 2014 document comprises six pages, the 2016 version is twice as long. Each document has an initial heading termed "The essence of the Policy" which marks the first significant change between the two versions. The second sentence in the 2014 text states: "The University is committed to the use and sustained development of Afrikaans as an academic language in a multilingual context [...]" and this is omitted in the revised version. Instead, the current document reads in the last sentence of this section as "[...] we commit ourselves to multilingualism by using the province's three official languages, namely Afrikaans, English and isiXhosa." Under the heading "The multilingual context," the first sentence is scrapped from the 2014 version that initially stated: "the University contributes to multilingualism in such a way that Afrikaans can be used and advanced, while utilizing the value of English [...]." Furthermore, a sentence of the section "Policy principles" appearing in the 2014 version reading as "The University acknowledges the particular status of Afrikaans as an academic language and accepts the responsibility to advance Afrikaans as an academic language" is entirely omitted in the 2016 version. Suffice it to say, virtually all references specifically to Afrikaans and to its special role in the institution, which still appeared in the 2014 document, are removed in the 2016 revision.

The scope of this chapter does not allow for providing much more detail of the current Language Policy document; suffice it to quote one of the most significant passages representing the real policy change from the 2014 version. It reads:

> During each lecture, *all information is conveyed at least in English* and summaries or emphasis of content are also repeated in Afrikaans. Questions in Afrikaans and English are, at the least, answered in the language of the question [my emphasis in italics].

The above makes it clear that SU has committed itself to a Language Policy that has English as the primary Language of Learning and Teaching but also makes provisions for Afrikaans. To recapture the stages in which language management takes place: It was *noted*, initially by individual students and later by *Open Stellenbosch* as a collective, that privileged Afrikaans usage at the institution was perpetuating social injustices and disadvantaged 'black' African students. An interest group of students, forming into the collective *Open Stellenbosch evaluated* this as negative and inadequate for a post-apartheid public university. Students organized themselves more systematically as a collective endowed with interests and powers and worked on *planning an adjustment*. With an actual language policy change in mind, *Open Stellenbosch* as an initially "bottom-up" collective formulated a document demanding the university management to respond to their interests. After initial resistance in the executive of the institution, the negative publicity Stellenbosch received combined with public pressure led to the students' demands being met and *implemented* through a new official language policy. The above summary is only one of many interpretations in line with LMT that could be offered in relation to language issues at SU. Language matters and Afrikaans politics continue to be contested in many contexts and spaces at Stellenbosch and they will offer further data for sociolinguistic research.

8 Conclusion

This chapter discussed interests and power dynamics in language policy changes at a South African university by employing LMT as an analytical tool. There are essentially two arguments that have been brought forward, one imperial, and the other theoretical. Firstly, English as an academic lingua franca has a strong momentum at SU due to its dual functions as, first, a 'communicative tool,' and second, as a relatively 'neutral' lingua franca. I argued that the official language policy change occurring at SU in 2016 represents an unprecedented case of successful 'bottom-up' language planning at a South African university. It is suggested, that the interest and power dynamics at Stellenbosch triggered language management processes which entailed initial micro level language management (individual students' dissatisfaction with the status quo involving Afrikaans at the institution) to transform into a semi-organized, 'meso'-level language management (the *Open Stellenbosch* collective) in order to inform language management processes at the macro level (i.e., the university executive) and this is where the second argument is formulated: LMT can usefully be applied to language planning dynamics at SU but a more nuanced cycle of micro → meso → macro → micro might well be useful. As previously argued, the "'macro' and 'micro' represent extreme limits of social space ('continuum'), which could be further subdivided into 'macros' or 'micros' of various complexities" (Nekvapil 2006: 100). This study concurs with Nekvapil's assertion and argues that simple language management processes have to develop a socio-politically viable momentum and collective support at a meso level in order to ultimately influence macro-level organization and actual policy change.

Although the value of English as an academic lingua franca has been asserted in Stellenbosch during the years 2015–16, ELF discourse, whether in academia or at grassroots levels, has not a 'benign' status in South Africa and further studies are needed in order to closely examine diverse power hierarchies. There is no doubt that many Afrikaans speakers feel strongly disillusioned about the events in Stellenbosch and the decreasing status of their language in the higher domains. English, so much is evident, certainly does not represent a "neutral" medium to them. More scholarship is required which examines the multiple power dynamics that exist among the speakers of different Englishes in the institution.

Acknowledgments

This chapter emerged as part of a project funded by the German Research Foundation (DFG) and my sincere thanks go to this institution. I am also grateful to the Masters students Lorryn Williams and Reinette Meiring for research assistance. Last, I also owe thanks to the members of the Sociolinguistic Seminar at Charles University who commented on a presentation of this topic and, in particular, Tamah Sherman for many stimulating and critical discussions about ELF.

References

Alexander, N. (2004) The politics of language planning in post-apartheid in South Africa. *Language Problems and Language Planning* 28 (2), 113–130.

Alexander, N. (2013) *Thoughts on the New South Africa.* Auckland Park: Jacana.

Baker, W. (2015) *Culture and Identity through English as a Lingua Franca: Rethinking Concepts and Goals in Intercultural Communication.* Berlin: De Gruyter Mouton.

Baker, W. (2018) English as a lingua franca and intercultural communication. In J. Jenkins, W. Baker & M. Dewey (eds) *The Routledge Handbook of English as a Lingua Franca.* London & New York: Routledge, 25–36.

Balfour, R. (2002) Post-colonial twilight: English as a failed lingua franca. *The English Academy Review* 30 (1), 20–32.

Bauman, R. & Briggs, C. L. (2003) *Voices of Modernity: Language Ideologies and the Politics of Inequality.* Cambridge: Cambridge University Press.

Beck, R. M. (2018) Language as apparatus: Entanglements of language, culture and territory and the invention of nation and ethnicity. *Postcolonial Studies* 21 (2), 1–24.

Bhabha, H. K. (2004) *The Location of Culture.* Abingdon: Routledge.

Blaser, T. (2007) *Afrikaner Identity after Nationalism: Young Afrikaners and the "new" South Africa.* Unpublished Doctoral thesis. Submitted at University of the Witwatersrand, Johannesburg.

Blommaert, J. & Rampton, B. (2011) Language and superdiversity. *Diversities* 13 (2), 1–21.

Bosch, B. (2000) Ethnicity markers in Afrikaans. *International Journal of the Sociology of Language* 144, 51–68.

Brink, C. (2006) *No Lesser Place: The Taaldebat at Stellenbosch.* Cape Town: African Sun Press.

Canagarajah, S. (2013) *Translingual Practice: Global Englishes and Cosmopolitan Relations.* Abingdon: Routledge.

Census (2011) Statistics South Africa. Available online: http://www.statssa.gov.za.

De Klerk, V. & Gough, D. (2002) Black South African English. In R. Mesthrie (ed) *Language in South Africa.* Cambridge: Cambridge University Press, 356–380.

Du Plessis, T. (2003) Taalbeleid aan Universiteite in Suid-Afrika [Language policy at university website in South Africa]. *Acta Academics Supplementum* 2, 58–82.

Du Plessis, T. (2006) From monolingual to bilingual higher education: The repositioning of historically Afrikaans-medium universities in South Africa. *Language Policy* 5 (1), 87–113.

Dube, B. (2017) Afrikaans must fall and English must rise: Ironies and contradictions in protests by South African university students. *Africa Insight* 42 (2), 13–27.

Engel, U. (1997) Ethnische Konflikte und politischer Neubeginn in Südafrika [Ethnic conflicts and political new beginnings in South Africa]. *Afrika Spectrum* 32 (1), 25–47.

Errington, J. (2007) *Linguistics in a Colonial World: A Story of Language, Meaning, and Power.* Malden & Cambridge: Blackwell.

Fiedler, S. (2011) English as a lingua franca — a native-culture-free code? Language of communication vs. language of identification. *Apples – Journal of Applied Language Studies* 5 (3), 79–97.

García, O. (2009) *Bilingual Education in the 21st Century: A Global Perspective.* Malden & Oxford, UK: Wiley-Blackwell.

Giliomee, H. (2001) Die Taal- an Kulturele Uitdagigs van die Historiese Afrikaanse Universiteite in Suid-Afrika [The language and cultural challenges of the historical Afrikaans universities in South Africa]. DF Malherbe – Gedenklesing 20. *Acta Varia* 1, 1–46.

Giliomee, H. (2003) *The Rise and Possible Demise of Afrikaans as a Public Language.* Cape Town: PRAESA.

Giliomee, H. (2009) The deadly war of languages. *Mail & Guardian.* Online October 5. On WWW at https://mg.co.za/article/2009-10-05-a-deadly-war-of-languages. Accessed August 2, 2018.

Hartshorne, K. B. (1992) *Crisis and Challenge: Black Education 1910–1990.* Cape Town: Oxford University Press.

Hill, L. (2010) Language and status: On the limits of language planning. *Stellenbosch Papers in Linguistics* 39, 41–58.

Horáková, H. (2019) Challenges to political cosmopolitanism: The impact of racialised discourses in post-apartheid South Africa. *Modern African, Politics, History and Society* 6 (2), 95–118.

Hult, F. M. (2010) Analysis of language policy discourses across the scales of space and time. *International Journal of the Sociology of Language* 202, 7–24.

House, J. (2003) English as a lingua franca: A threat to multilingualism? *Journal of Sociolinguistics* 7 (4), 556–578.

House, J. (2014) English as a global lingua franca: A threat to multilingual communication and translation? *Language Teaching* 47 (3), 363–376.

Hüllen, W. (1992) Identifikationssprache und Kommunikationssprache: Über Probleme der Mehrsprachlichkeit [Language of identification and communication of language: About problems of multilingualism]. *Zeitschrift für germanistische Linguistik* 20 (3), 298–317.

Hynninen N. (2016) *Language Regulation in English as a Lingua Franca.* Berlin: Mouton de Gruyter.

Jenkins, J. (2018) Not English but English-within-multilingualism. In S. Coffee & U. Wingate (eds) *New Directions for Research in Foreign Language Education.* London & New York: Routledge.

Jenks, C. (2013) Are you an ELF? The relevance of ELF as an equitable social category in online intercultural communication. *Language and Intercultural Communication* 13 (1), 95–108.

Jernudd, B. & Neustupný, J. V. (1987) Language planning: For whom? In L. Laforge (ed) *Actes du Colloque international sur l'aménagement linguistique / Proceedings of the International Colloquium on Language Planning.* Québec: Les Presses de l'Universite Laval, 69–84.

Kamwangamalu, N. M. (2007) One language, multilayered identities: English in a society in transition, South Africa. *World Englishes* 26 (3), 263–275.

Kamwangamalu, N. M. (2019) English as a naturalized language. *World Englishes.* doi: 10.1111/weng.12395.

Kecskes, I. (2007) Formulaic language in English lingua franca. In I. Kecskes & L. Horn (eds) *Explorations in Pragmatics: Linguistic, Cognitive and Intercultural Aspects.* Berlin & New York: De Gruyter, 191–218.

Khokhlova, I. (2015) Lingua franca English of South Africa. *Procedia: Social and Behaviourial Sciences* 214, 983–991.

Kriel, M. (2003) Approaches to multilingualism in language planning and identity politics. A critique. *Society in Transition* 34 (1), 159–177.

Mabokela, R. O. (2001) Selective inclusion: Transformation and language policy at the University of Stellenbosch. In R. O. Mabokela & K. L. King (eds) *Apartheid No More: Case Studies of Southern African Universities in the Process of Transformation.* Westport: Bergin & Garvey, 59–72.

Makalela, L. (2004) Making sense of BSAE for linguistic democracy in South Africa. *World Englishes* 23 (3), 355–366.

Makoni, S. (2003) From misinvention to disinvention of language: Multilingualism and the South African constitution. In A. Ball, S. Makoni, G. Smitherman, A. K. Spears (eds) *Black Linguistics: Language, Society and Politics in Africa and the Americas.* London & New York: Routledge, 132–151.

Makoni, S. & Makoni, B. (2009) English and education in Anglophone Africa: Historical and current realities. In M. S. Wong & S. Canagarajah (eds) *Christian and Critical English Language Educators in Dialogue: Pedagogical and Ethical Dilemmas.* New York & London: Routledge, 106–119.

Manyike, T. V. & Lemmer, E. M. (2014) Research in language education in South Africa: Problems & prospects. *Mediterranean Journal of Social Science* 5 (8), 251.

Mauranen, A. (2011) *Exploring ELF in Academia.* Cambridge: Cambridge University Press.

Mauranen, A. (2012) *Exploring ELF.* Cambridge: Cambridge University Press.

Mauranen, A. (2014) Lingua franca discourse in academic contexts: Shaped by complexity. In J. Flowerdew (ed) *Discourse in Context.* London: Bloomsbury Academic, 225–246.

Mauranen, A. (2017) Conceptualising ELF. In J. Jenkins, W. Baker & M. Dewey (eds) *The Routledge Handbook of English as a Lingua Franca.* London & New York: Routledge, 7–24.

Mesthrie, R. (2006) Anti-deletions in an L2 grammar: A study of Black South African English mesolect. *English World Wide* 27 (2), 111–145.

Mesthrie, R. & Bhatt, R. M. (2008) *World Englishes. The Study of New Linguistic Varieties.* Cambridge: Cambridge University Press.

Modiano, M. (2004) Monoculturalization and language dissemination. *Journal of Language, Identity, and Education* 3 (3), 215–227.

Mwaniki, M. (2011) Language management in Africa: The dialectics of theory and practice. *Southern African Linguistics and Applied Language Studies* 29 (3), 243–257.

Nekvapil, J. (2006) From language planning to language management. *Sociolinguistica: International Yearbook of European Sociolinguistics* 20, 92–104.

Nekvapil, J. & Nekula, M. (2006) On language management in multinational companies in the Czech Republic. *Current Issues in Language Planning* 7, 307–327.

Nekvapil, J. & Sherman, T. (2013) Language ideologies and linguistic practices: The case of multinational companies in Central Europe. In J. Nekvapil, T. Sherman & P. Kaderka (eds) *Ideological Conceptualizations of Language: Discourses of Linguistic Diversity.* Frankfurt on the Main: Peter Lang, 85–118.

Nekvapil, J. & Sherman, T. (2015) An introduction: Language Management Theory in Language Policy and Planning. *International Journal of the Sociology of Language* 232, 1–12.

Orman, J. (2008) *Language Policy and Nation-building in Post-Apartheid South Africa.* Dordrecht: Springer.

Pennycook, A. (2017) *The Cultural Politics of English as an International Language.* London & New York: Routledge.

Posel, D. & Zeller, J. (2015) Language shift or increased bilingualism in South Africa? Evidence from census data. *Journal of Multilingual and Multicultural Development.* doi: http://dx.doi.org/10.1080/01434632.2015.1072206.

Rudwick, S. (2016) Afrikaans and institutional identity: A South African university in the crossfire. In H. Horáková & K. Werkman (eds) *Knowledge Production in and on Africa.* Berlin: LIT Verlag, 127–150.

Rudwick, S. (2017) Compulsory African language learning at a South African tertiary institution. *Language Problems and Language Planning* 41 (2), 116–137.

Rudwick, S. (2018) Language, Africanisation and identity politics in South African tertiary education. *Language, Identity and Education* 17 (4), 255–269. doi: https://doi.org/10.1080/15348458.2018.1460207.

Rudwick, S. (2021) *The Ambiguity of English as a Lingua Franca: Politics of Language and Race in South Africa.* London & New York: Routledge.

Seidlhofer, B. (2011) *Understanding English as a Lingua Franca.* Oxford: Oxford University Press.

Sherman, T. (2018) ELF and the EU / wider Europe. In J. Jenkins, W. Baker & M. Dewey (eds) *The Routledge Handbook of English as a Lingua Franca.* London & New York: Routledge, 115–125.

Singleton, D., Fishman, J. A., Aronin, L. & Ó Laoireal, M. (eds) (2013) *Current Multilingualism: The New Linguistic Dispensation.* Berlin & Boston: De Gruyter Mouton.

Smit, U. (1996) *A New English for a New South Africa? Language Attitudes, Language Planning and Education.* Vienna: Braumüller.

Stellenbosch University (2014) Language Policy of the University of Stellenbosch, LP – SU. On WWW at https://www.sun.ac.za/english/Documents/Language/Language%20Policy%202014%20Final%2012%20Dec%202014.pdf. Accessed July 20, 2018.

Stellenbosch University (2016) Language Policy of the University of Stellenbosch, LP – SU. On WWW at http://www.sun.ac.za/english/Documents/Language/Final%20Language%20Policy%20June%202016.pdf. Accessed July 20, 2018.

Stroud, C. (2015) Afterword: Turbulent deflections. In C. Stroud & M. Prinsloo (eds) *Language, Literacy and Diversity: Moving Words.* New York: Routledge, 303–316.

Turner, I. (2015) A matter of choice? The role of English and isiXhosa for university graduates in their early careers. *Modern Africa, Politics, History and Society* 3 (2), 43–74.

Van der Waal, C. S. (2015) Languages of identification and languages of teaching at Stellenbosch University. Paper written for the panel discussion on *Language and Transformation at Stellenbosch University,* June 4, 2015, University Museum.

Van der Walt, C. & Evans, R. (2018) Is English the lingua franca of South Africa? In J. Jenkins, W. Baker & M. Dewey (eds) *The Routledge Handbook of English as a Lingua Franca*. London & New York: Routledge, 186–198.

Van Rooy, B. (2004) Black South African English: Phonology. In B. Kortmann & E. W. Schneider (eds) *A Handbook of Varieties of English 1: Phonology*. Berlin: Mouton de Gruyter, 943–952.

Wade, R. (1996) *An Investigation of the Putative Restandardisation of South African English in the Direction of a 'New' English, Black South African English*. Unpublished MA thesis submitted at the University of Natal, Durban.

Webb, V. (2002) *Language in South Africa: The Role of Language in National Transformation, Reconstruction and Development*. Amsterdam: John Benjamins.

Webb, V. (2010) Afrikaans in higher education in S.A. *Alternation* 17 (1), 355–381.

Webb, V. & Kriel, M. (2000) Afrikaans and Afrikaner nationalism. *International Journal of the Sociology of Language* 144, 19–50.

Part II
Minority languages and minoritized languages

Roland Marti

Language management from above (and from below), from outside (and from inside): The case of Lower Sorbian

Abstract Lower Sorbian (LS) is a severely endangered minority language dominated by German, but in the past also by the neighboring minority language Upper Sorbian (US). This complicates language management (LM), especially organized LM. Speakers of LS (or of other minority languages) may choose a radical individual LM solution: the switch to the majority language, particularly in cases when measures of organized LM are not acceptable to them. Thus, in the post-war period organized LM, imposed by representatives of US, led to a large-scale language shift from LS to German. In recent years, organized LM has tried to correct ill-conceived measures of the past through a different kind of LM that respects the language use of native speakers, rejecting the US influence. It remains to be seen whether this new kind of organized LM, together with attempts at language revitalization through immersion programs, will be able to stop and reverse the language shift.

Keywords Lower Sorbian, minority languages, endangered languages, purism

1 Introduction

As far as I know, concepts of Language Management Theory (LMT) have not yet been applied to Lower Sorbian (LS), the only partial exception being some remarks by Nekvapil (2007) on the relationship between LS and US.[1] The main problem of using LMT is the importance that it puts on deviations from the (or a) norm, given the fact that the norms of LS are rather volatile, disputed in many respects and hardly ever applied correctly by anyone, as will be shown. On the other hand, LMT may be very helpful in understanding the development of LS, if the establishing of norms and not deviations from them are at the center of attention. At the same time it is also the macro-level and organized language management (LM) that are, albeit in a way that is quite different from other languages, important in the analysis of the behavior of speakers of LS. The weakness of norms due to the insecurity of most speakers of LS (who are today, as a rule, non-native speakers) makes the micro-level noting of deviations, their evaluation and the implementation of

1 There are two articles by Goro Kimura that deal with LMT as applied to Sorbian (Kimura 2014, 2015), but his object is US as it is used in the Catholic region, and that is sociolinguistically rather different from LS.

adjustments, as described in standard LMT (cf., e.g., Neustupný 2002; Nekvapil 2012) rather exceptional. Organized LM in the case of LS, on the other hand, is quite often the result of the activity of individuals and small groups rather than official bodies invested with power to impose norms. In the following, I will attempt to describe how LM worked and works in the case of LS in an historical perspective with special emphasis on the recent past and the present.[2]

2 Prehistory of Sorbian in a Slavic-German context

In the Central and Eastern part of Europe, two branches of Indo-European were rivals ever since the earliest written testimonies comment on the language of the people living in these areas: Germanic and Slavic.[3] The advancement of Slavic towards the West is essentially a consequence of the westward movement of Germanic speaking tribes on the continent during the Great Migration of Peoples: Slavic speaking tribes followed them a few centuries later and occupied the largely vacant regions. By the 9th century the maximum westward extension of Slavic was reached: Slavic speaking tribes settled as far west as the Elbe and even beyond (the Polabians)[4] and as far south as Franconia. From then on, the linguistic border was slowly pushed back towards the east to the detriment of Slavic until the early 20th century when the expansion was halted and eventually reversed as a result of World War I and II (in the latter case by a policy that is best described as 'linguistic cleansing') so that today the linguistic border between West Slavic and Germanic coincides with the political borders of Germany and Austria with their Slavic neighbors Poland, the Czech Republic, and Slovakia. The eastward movement of the linguistic frontier in the High and Late Middle Ages

2 For the present article, Nekvapil (2009) was most useful, since it deals particularly with contact situations and the interplay of micro- and macro-level as well as of simple and organized LM.

3 In the earlier period of their contacts, the Germans did not differentiate between the speakers of Slavic: they were generally referred to as *Wenden* [Wends] and their language as *Wendisch* [Wendish]. Later on, this general term would be specified and used for Sorbs and Sorbian. A variant, viz. *Windisch*, was used to designate Slovenian in Austria. In both cases, the use of these terms is resented by a part of the Sorbian- and Slovenian-speaking population today since they are considered pejorative (for Sorbian cf. Section 6 below).

4 In the region to the south of Hannover that is called *Wendland* to this day, Polabian was spoken as late as the 18th century. Cf. on Polabian Olesch (1983–87) and (1989). It is perhaps worth mentioning that Polabian is, to my knowledge, the only extinct Slavic language that has been revived, first in a keynote lecture at the VIIth International Congress of Slavists in Warsaw 1973 delivered entirely in Polabian (Olesch 1998), and recently for touristic purposes. It is doubtful, however, that a full revival with "secondary native speakers" (as, e.g., in the case of Cornish) will be attempted.

was largely the result of colonization and assimilation and was not often reflected upon in written sources,[5] exceptions being legal provisions regarding the use of Slavic in court and restrictions on membership in the regulations of guilds (the so-called *Wendenparagraphen* [Wendish paragraphs]).[6] This negligence of linguistic matters is not surprising since the language of the people did not really matter: the administration used Latin or (increasingly) German, the church exclusively Latin in writing: when addressing Slavic speaking subjects the representatives of state and church were expected to know and to be able to use Slavic or else they had recourse to interpreters. As far as the Slavic speaking population was concerned, they were "speechless" in a most literal sense since there are no sources expressing their point of view regarding the process of linguistic assimilation.

This situation changed profoundly with the Reformation. The Lutheran Reformation and the Reformed churches in general stressed the use of the language of the people, and this not only in speaking, but also and above all in writing. The basic texts, i.e., the Bible (at least a lectionary, if possible the New Testament with psalms, ideally the complete Bible), the liturgy, the catechism(s) and hymns had to be translated and the translations were, as a rule, eventually published.[7] Because of this, many 'smaller' languages developed a written tradition for the first time.[8] In linguistically mixed regions, it had to be decided whether all the languages should be considered or whether one should be given preference to the detriment of the other(s).

In the area east of the Elbe that was in a state of transition from Slavic to German, one group of Slavs was particularly affected by this change: the Sorbs living in Lusatia. Moreover, it is here that the history of LM can be studied from the time of the Reformation. The case of Sorbian is particularly illuminating because the area where Sorbian was spoken would soon become a linguistic island (and later an archipelago) in German-speaking surroundings, because German was the language of power, because Lusatia was politically very heterogeneous, lacking centralized power, and because a part of the Sorbian-speaking area remained Catholic. As a result, there were many different factors and many different actors interested in and influencing LM.

---

5 The best recent description of this process of linguistic assimilation is given by Stone (2016); cf. also Herrmann (1985) for the earlier period.

6 It should be borne in mind, however, that the *Wendenparagraphen* were based on ethnicity, not on language: those interested in becoming members of a guild of necessity had to master German since Slavic would not have been used in guild meetings.

7 Incidentally this also affected areas that did not accept the new faith (or reverted to Catholicism again) since the Counter-Reformation stressed the use of vernacular languages in writing, too, but mainly for proselytizing and not in the liturgy.

8 This did not necessarily save them from extinction, a case in point being the Baltic language (Old) Prussian with a short written tradition and its final extinction at the beginning of the 18th century (cf. Rinkevičius 2017).

The Sorbian case is particularly interesting, because it is not only the relationship between German and Sorbian that influences LM, but also an internal dualism, viz. that between US and LS. In addition, in this latter dualism there is a change of roles, since LS was originally the leader, but it was soon outperformed by US.

3 History of language management for Lower Sorbian from the reformation to World War II

The Reformation reached Lusatia rather early since its first stronghold, Wittenberg, was actually on the western fringe of the Sorbian language area.[9] As usual, the urban population was affected first, but they were mainly German speaking and the Sorbs living there were mostly bilingual. In the rural areas, where a monolingual Sorbian population has to be assumed, the Reformation spread somewhat later.[10]

It is impossible to reconstruct the spoken Sorbian of those days since we only have written sources and most of them are translations from German (or, to a lesser degree, Latin). Native speakers of German translated many of the texts and in any case, they betray a strong German influence. Therefore, it is safe to assume a certain, maybe even a considerable distance between the language of those texts and the real spoken Sorbian of the villagers.

The earliest longer Sorbian text conserved in written form is the translation of the New Testament by Mikławš Jakubica († ca. 1563) of 1548. In the colophon, Jakubica refers to the language simply as *Serpfky* [Sorbian].[11] The translator's linguistic basis was a now extinct dialect from the Eastern periphery usually described as being transitional from LS to Polish (cf. Schuster-Šewc 1967: XXXIII–XLIII). The choice was obviously dictated by the necessity to be understood by the parishioners. Since the translation remained in manuscript form and seems to have been forgotten until its rediscovery in the 19th century, it did not influence the further development of written Sorbian. It was different in the case of printed books, however, and this is already evident from the first two books printed in Sorbian, viz. Albin Moller's (1541–1618) calendar *cum* hymnal and catechism of 1574 and Wenceslaus Warichius's (1564–1618) catechism of 1595. They actually laid the basis for the division of Sorbian into LS and US as two distinct Sorbian written languages that all later translators, authors and printers adhered to and that would

---

9 Luther, it must be said, was not particularly inclined towards the Sorbs (or the Wends, as he called them), and his remarks referring to them in his *table talks* were neither flattering nor politically correct. Cf. on this Malink (1983), a slightly apologetic Malink (2017b), Stone (2016: 90–91).

10 Cf. for the beginnings Stone (2016: 70–93), Malink (2017b) and especially Buliš (2017), for later periods the respective articles in the collection published on the quincentenary of the Reformation (Malink 2017a).

11 Schuster-Šewc (1967: 415). All translations, unless noted otherwise, are mine.

eventually lead to the codification of two separate standard languages.[12] This division, dictated by practical considerations (viz. to use the variety of Sorbian best understood by the parishioners), was tacitly accepted and not called into question until the 19th century.[13]

The LS written language, then, reflected in some ways the spoken language, but in order to be used in a religious context and later on in literature this spoken language had to be adapted. The main source for this adaptation was, of course, German. Since, however, we only have the written texts it is difficult to determine the exact extent of German interference. As the population in the villages was largely monolingual, it may be assumed that the authors or translators introduced those linguistic aspects of Sorbian that have no parallel in other Slavic languages (or only in those that were under equally strong German influence, such as Slovene). The first translators, being faced with the enormous task of rendering highly complex texts in a heretofore unwritten language, probably did not worry too much about linguistic 'purity,' so there probably was not much conscious LM regarding the purity of the language they used, or stayed on the level of noticing. 'Purity' became an issue for later generations, and they tried to meet the theological demands regarding the correctness of their translations and the linguistic demands for correct and adequate LS.

The best example for these problems in the case of LS is the translation of the New Testament by Gottlieb Fabricius (1681–1741), first published in 1709. In the unpaginated German foreword *Dem Chriſtlichen Leſer* [To the Christian reader], he reflects on the problems of translation but also on linguistic matters:

> In der Sprache ſelbſt, die wegen Mangel der Schrifften ziemlich armſcheinet [sic!] an Wörter, hat man dahin geſehen, wie die Reinigkeit derſelben möge wieder hergeſtellet werden, und die eingeſchlichenen deutſchen Wörter, ſo viel, als ſich hat wollen thun laſſen, vermieden, und bißweilen andere, die eben noch nicht allenthalben ſehr bekant, aber doch [...] ihre Richtigkeit in dem Grunde haben, und leicht zu verſtehen seyn, eingeführet [...]. (Fabricius 1759)
>
> [As for the language itself that seems to be rather poor in its vocabulary due to the lack of written texts, we tried to re-establish its purity and to avoid as much as possible the

12 Moller, being the first to publish in Sorbian, referred to the language only as *Wendiſch*: *ein Wendiſches Gesangbuch* [...] *in Lateiniſcher und Wendiſcher Sprache* [...] *Auch der Kleine Catechiſmus* [...] *Wendiſch vertiret* [a Wendish hymnal [...] in the Latin and Wendish language [...] And also the Small Catechism [...] translated into Wendish] (Moller 1959: 3). In the introduction to his catechism Warichius refers to Moller's publication as *ein geſangbuch ſo Magiſter Albinus Mollerus in Niderlauſitzer ſprache Vertiret vnd in druck vorfertiget* [a hymnal that Master Albinus Mollerus translated into the Lower Lusatian language and published in print] (Schuster-Šewc 2001: 29). Warichius's own language is called *die Oberlauſentſche wendische Sprache* [the Upper Lusatian Wendish language] (Schuster-Šewc 2001: 31).

13 On the non-linguistic background for this development cf. for US Fasske (1985) and for LS Stone (1985).

German words that had entered it and to introduce sometimes others that, although not very well known yet [...], are basically correct and easy to understand [...].]

This is, as far as I know, the first expression of linguistic purism in LS, and Fabricius obviously tried to achieve his goal of 'pure' LS largely unaffected by German by presenting a model in the form of the New Testament.[14] In spite of this purism, German still heavily influenced the language of the New Testament, as a short random excerpt will show:

WOno pak ße ſtanu wó tich ßamich dńach,
ES begab sich aber in jenen Tagen,
až pſchikaſn wot togo Keyžora Auguſtußa wón hujžo,
daß ein Geboth vom Kayser Augusto ausgieng,
abü ſchyken ßwět ſapißani hordowal.
daß alle Welt geschätzet würde. (Lk 2, 1; Fabricius 1759: 221)[15]

[And it came to pass in those days, that there went out a decree from Cæsar Augustus, that all the world should be taxed.][16]

German influence is most noticeable in the choice of script (both the German and the LS texts were printed in black letter/Gothic script) and orthography (<*ß*> for [s], <*ſ*> for [z], <*ſch*> for [ʃ] etc.), but also in the use of the (definite) article (*wot togo* = vom [von dem]), of the detachable verbal prefix (*wón hujžo* = ausgieng), in the passive voice formed with the auxiliary *hordowaś* (morphologically adapted from *werden*, the auxiliary used for passive voice in German), a German loanword (*ſapißani hordowal* = geschätzet würde), and in word order (final position of the finite verb in subordinate clauses).[17]

14 In the text Fabricius refers to a previous (hand)written translation that, however, was apparently faulty in many (unspecified) ways. Therefore, the language of his translation was obviously the result of a full LM cycle of noting deviations and implementing adjustments, even inviting the evaluation and a new LM cycle by future editors.

15 The New Testament of Fabricius was a bilingual (German and LS) publication so that superiors could easily compare original and translation as to the orthodoxy of the translation. This also facilitated the task of the pastor since he often had to preach twice on Sunday, once in German and once in LS. It could also be interpreted as a sign of gratitude towards German-speaking authorities or nobility sponsoring the publication, and it might finally be seen as an attempt to familiarize the Sorbs with the German language (which would be a matter of interest for LM).

16 The English translation is that of the King James Bible.

17 It is interesting to compare the text to Jakubica's translation of 1548: *Stalo ſe pak ie w tich dnåch, aſch wyſſchla ie yedna prczykaſn wot tego Keyſchora Auguſta, aby / zaly Swett byl wopiſſany.* Jakubica's orthography is clearly inferior since it uses *ſ* for both the voiced and the voiceless consonant (the same is true for *ſch*), but it is more Slavonic in using *y* instead of Fabricius's *ü* or *i*. Jakubica also uses the indefinite article *yedna* under German influence. On the other hand, Jakubica does not use a

However, he 'managed' the language in other aspects as well since he also reflects on the dialectal basis of his language:

> Sonſt hat man ſich bey denen in der Wendiſchen Sprache ſehr häufigen und unterſchiedlichen Dialectis nach demjenigen gerichtet, der um Cotbus herum gebräuchlich iſt, und vor den zierlichſten und accurateſten gehalten wird [...].
>
> [Otherwise and in view of the very numerous and diverse dialects of the Wendish language we adhered to the one that is in use around Chóśebuz/Cottbus and that is considered the most delicate and accurate one [...].]

It is, of course, not surprising that the dialect chosen was that of the political and economic center of the region and that it is considered the most beautiful and the best. This is typical of many other languages (French with Paris, English with London, and Russian with St. Petersburg/Moscow etc.).[18] Although this was an individual choice, the passage quoted above indicates that Fabricius reached his decision based on the general opinion in the speech community. The fact that almost all of his successors in printing LS texts followed his example corroborates this assumption.

However, it is remarkable that for Fabricius this applies only to the written language. He states specifically that the pronunciation is not predetermined by his codification of the written language:

> Doch [...] kan ſchon ein jeder [...] es alſo leſen, wie es ſeines Ortes Gelegenheit mit ſich bringet [...].
>
> [However [...] everyone may [...] read it as it is customary in his village [...].]

Therefore, Fabricius only proposed a written norm. The spoken realization could be adjusted to the regional pronunciation. The spoken norm, then, was a matter of individual or even simple LM, as it were. This 'liberalism' as far as spoken LS is concerned comes as a surprise and it was not followed by his successors. Thus, the Chóśebuz/Cottbus pronunciation was later considered standard, at least for the use in church, even though it might be noted as a deviation (from the dialect norm) outside of the Chóśebuz/Cottbus dialect region.

Around this time, the first proposal to introduce one single written language for all the Sorbs was made. It emanated from the US area and, not surprisingly, advocated the exclusive use of written US to serve all the Sorbs:

---

detachable verbal prefix (*wyſſchla*) and has the Slavonic construction *to be + past passive participle* (*byl wopiſſany*) instead of the *hordowaś* construction to form the passive voice, typically Slavic features. In both cases, then, Fabricius's LS is more German.

18 Cf. on this Stone (1985: 100–101) who considers the choice of the Chóśebuz/Cottbus dialect to have been a deliberate choice by Fabricius to make the language as different from US as possible.

> Derowegen stünde wohl zu hoffen, wenn in der Niederlausiz sich die Herren Pastores des Oberlausizschen reinen Haupt=dialecti auf der Cantzel nur bedienen wollten, daß leichtlich dahin gebracht werden könnte, daß der gemeine Mann die hier oben ausgegangenen Kirchenbücher verstehen und zugleich nutzen würden [...]. (Muka 1881: 74)[19]
>
> [Thus, one might hope that if the ministers in Lower Lusatia were to use the Upper Lusatian pure main dialect from the pulpit, then this could easily result in the simple man understanding and at the same time using the church books published here [i.e., in Upper Lusatia, RWM].]

This proposal was a clear attempt to influence the LM of LS from the outside in order to establish one norm for the Sorbian language used in church. This idea, however, did not gain ground in Lower Lusatia. LS slowly developed further along the lines established by Fabricius, the German influence becoming stronger, especially in the 19th and 20th centuries, due to the increase of bilingualism among the Sorbs and because of economic and political development of the region (industrialization, increased mobility, centralization, and a more systematic policy of Germanization). It must be said, though, that there could have been much more borrowing than actually occurred. However, much of it was not needed because LS was essentially restricted to a few domains and for them the indigenous vocabulary sufficed.[20]

In the first half of the 19th century, the Slavic renascence movement reached the Sorbs from Bohemia. Its representatives elaborated the theory of Slavic reciprocity (cf. Kollár 1929), which led to important linguistic changes in Slavic standard languages. In the case of Czech, it resulted in a switch from black letter/Gothic script (considered German) to Roman, changes in the orthography ('German' *w* and *au* being replaced by more 'Slavic' *v* and *ou*) and a strong 'xenophobic' purism.[21]

The ideas of the movement were taken up in Lusatia and led to the Sorbian renascence, advanced mainly by representatives of US cultural life. As a result several far-reaching changes in the codification were proposed: the introduction of Roman script and a diacritic and slightly historical orthography (known as *analogiski prawopis* [analogous orthography]), puristic changes in the vocabulary (replacement of German loanwords by older native words, Czech loans or calques) and in grammar (ostracizing the use of the article(s) and of the passive forms modeled

19 The Lutheran minister and polymath Abraham Frencel (1656–1740) made the proposal, but it was not published in his lifetime and thus did not exert any influence on the further development of the written tradition.

20 Of the possible domains listed in Spolsky (2009) LS was essentially restricted to family, religion, the workplace of preindustrial times (agriculture and the crafts linked to life in rural areas), and local government. All other areas already required knowledge or even the exclusive use of German.

21 On the various forms of purism, cf. Thomas (1991), on purism as a form of LM cf. Neustupný (1989).

on the German *werden* passive etc.). At the same time, the movement advocated the unification of the Protestant and Catholic US written languages. In terms of LMT, it was not a deviation from the actual norm that was noted, evaluated and corrected, but with respect to an ideal norm, the actual norm itself was considered deviant, and important parts of it had to be replaced in favor of the ideal norm.[22] The proposals were successfully implemented only partially, because those advocating the changes did not have the power or authority necessary to impose the new norm. As a result, US was written in three different variants until World War II (Protestant, Catholic, analogous). Thus, the idea to strengthen the position of US through unification as proposed by the intellectual elite resulted in the opposite, viz. a further split within US between adherents of the traditional written languages and the Slavicizing unificators.

The Sorbian renascence movement also addressed the problem of the division between US and LS. In this case, however, it was not unification any more that was advocated,[23] but rather convergence.[24] Again, the main propagators were Upper Sorbs and essentially their efforts failed again. Still a LS variant of the analogous orthography was elaborated and finally codified in 1903, but it was used even less than the corresponding US codification. So until 1936, when the last LS publication appeared before the war, the written (and thus standard) language was split, too: there was a traditional variant using black letter/Gothic script and German orthography with strong German influence in vocabulary and grammar, and a

---

22 Adherents of the new norm practiced quite a rigid form of LM. Their publications were most carefully checked for deviations, and rumor has it that in their meetings people accidentally violating the new norm in conversation, e.g., by using an article, had to pay a fine.

23 In a footnote to the quote from Abraham Frencel above (cf. n. 19) the editor of the journal, Michał Hórnik (1833–1894), an important figure in Sorbian cultural life and an advocate of Sorbian renascence, explained why this was not possible any more: "To budźeše móžne było, hdy by so před 300 lětami tak zawjedło, hdy budźechu duchowni narodnje zmysleni byli a hdy budźechu šule w Hornjej a Delnjej Łužicy derje serbske bywałe. Ale Serbja su sebi wot Němcow powjedać dali a skónčnje sami wěrili, zo horni Serb delnjemu njerozymi a tak staj so wobě podrěči bóle dźěliłoj dyžli zjednoćałej." [This might have been possible if it had been introduced 300 years ago, if the ministers had had a [Sorbian, RWM] ethnic conscience and if the schools in Upper and Lower Lusatia had been thoroughly Sorbian. However, the Sorbs let the Germans tell them that an Upper Sorb does not understand a Lower Sorb and they finally believed it themselves. Thus, it came about that the two dialects diverged rather than converged.] (Muka 1881: 74) This is contradicted by the fact that the Sorbs themselves differentiated US and LS as early as the 16th century (cf. n. 12 above).

24 Nevertheless, even this convergence was lopsided since it usually meant bringing LS closer to US. Thus Hórnik (1880), even though claiming a mutual convergence in theory, actually proposed more changes reflecting an US bias than vice versa.

puristic variant written in Roman script and analogous orthography and only marginal German influence.[25]

Looking back at the period from the perspective of LM, one may say that the emergence and the development of written and later standard LS were largely the result of individual efforts of actors with interest and partially also with expertise, but with limited power.[26] The majority of speakers of LS did not hold the language in high esteem, an attitude that was strengthened by the Germanizing activities of the state (LS was officially not to be used in school except for the purpose of teaching the children German) and partly the church, and thus did not develop a particular interest in questions regarding standard LS. If the 'ordinary' speakers of LS practiced LM at all, then it occurred on the level of language choice, i.e., it was the decision to use either German or LS, and in most official contexts (with the partial exception of the church), it was to the detriment of LS. In the other sense, the few people that really practiced LM within LS, mostly preachers or teachers, therefore had a considerable influence on LS, and their individual decisions could actually alter the norm. According to their power given by authority based on expertise, their LM, although it was individual LM, could have the same influence as organized LM in other languages. Nevertheless, as in US, the lack of state or institutional power to impose norms seriously hampered these attempts of LM in LS.

25 In both cases (US and LS) the idea that Slavic languages should also have a 'Slavic' script and orthography misfired, whereas in the Czech lands it was successful, cf. Galmiche (2001). Obviously, it was unwise to replace a script and an orthography that was familiar to the Sorbs from German (the language used and taught in school and partly in church) by an innovation, whose only asset was the easier accessibility of other Slavonic languages. The closeness to their 'Slavic brethren,' however, was apparently something that most Sorbs, and Lower Sorbs in particular, were not very interested in.

26 A good example of this is the (only) LS weekly newspaper. A quantitative analysis of the language in the first fifty years of its existence shows that the frequency of passive constructions with the auxiliary *hordowaś* (from German *werden*), one of the primary targets of Sorbian purism (cf. above), increased with each change of the editor to drop slowly but continuously during the term of editorship. Obviously, each new editor started out with the intention to use a more popular and less puristic language and developed into a moderate purist as time wore on. It is interesting to note that in spite of these temporary upsurges of *hordowaś* constructions the overall development reduced the use of the construction drastically (cf. Bartels 2006). A similar analysis targeting US loanwords shows that the influence of the editor(s) was very strong in this area, too. Thus, the number of US loanwords increased significantly during the editorship of Bogumił Šwjela (1873–1948, editor 1916–1922) and Mina Witkojc (1893–1975, editor 1923–1931), both trying to reduce the high number of Germanisms (cf. Pohontsch 2002: 317–321, 339). To typology of actors, cf. Fenton-Smith & Gurney (2016).

In the first half of the 20th century, LM was less of an intra-Sorbian issue. It centered on the use of Sorbian (both US and LS) in the face of increasing Germanization. LM was essentially reduced to using Sorbian *tout court*, and encouraging others to do so, too. In the Third Reich, after an initial period of tolerance, Sorbian was practically ousted from public life, and Sorbian publishing activities were forbidden. Under these conditions, the organized LM within the Sorbian community with respect to standardization or convergence simply ceased to exist.

4 Sorbian revival after 1945

After having been virtually non-existent in the public sphere for about ten years, the re-establishment of Sorbian started almost immediately after the unconditional surrender of the Third Reich.[27] The Domowina, the national organization of the Sorbs, resumed its activities on May 10, 1945 in Upper Lusatia (i.e., in the Free State of Saxony), but only in 1949 in Lower Lusatia (Brandenburg), where LS was spoken. At first, there were plans by some representatives of the Sorbs to secede from Germany or to obtain some kind of political autonomy, but this was given up in favor of a promise of state support for Sorbian culture and a certain degree of cultural autonomy. This led to the promulgation of the Sorbian law in the Free State of Saxony (i.e., for Upper Lusatia) in 1948 and an Ordinance extending the provisions of this law to the State of Brandenburg in 1950. In exchange for the support of the politics of the Socialist party, the Domowina was given a quasi-official status as a so-called mass organization and had access to considerable financial means. In 1955 a member of the Politburo officially proclaimed the slogan *Łužica budźe dwurěčna* [US] – *Łužyca buźo dwojorěcna* [LS] – *Die Lausitz wird zweisprachig* [Lusatia will become bilingual].[28] At the end of the decade, however, the slogan was changed to *Łužica budźe socialistiska* – *Łužyca buźo socialistiska* – *Die Lausitz wird sozialistisch* [Lusatia will become socialist] (Elle 1995: 148).

Some of the earliest decisions taken by the Sorbian representatives that were now in a position of power concerned linguistic matters. Most urgent were decisions regarding script and orthography since Sorbian printing should be resumed as soon as possible. It was clear from the offset that only Roman script and analogous orthography would be permitted since those now in a position of power were adherents of those changes. The changes in orthography were minor for US.[29] LS, however, was an altogether different matter.

27 On the linguistic side of this revival, see Faska (1998).

28 Elle (1995: 43). Actually, this was not quite correct: the slogan should have been "Lusatia will become trilingual" since US and LS are considered two distinct languages.

29 The orthography was essentially changed in one respect: initial *kh-* was replaced by *ch-*, but it was still to be pronounced as [k^h].

The situation for LS was particularly difficult. There were few linguistically informed and active representatives of the language, there was even less "language pride" than in US, and thus the danger of a language shift to German was quite real. Furthermore, the Sorbs and thus also LS were given official protection later in Brandenburg, if compared to US in Saxony (see above), and the Domowina was essentially an US organization with headquarters in Budyšin/Bautzen, i.e., in US territory. Moreover, US printers often printed LS publications in Upper Lusatia.

The first LS publications, especially the revived weekly newspaper, used Roman script and a slightly modified analogous orthography based on US. The changes pointed towards US and this was openly admitted:

> Teke smy dolnoserbski pšawopis tšochu pśeměnili, aby jen zblížyli pšawopisoju gornoserbskeje rěcy, ale ńejo to wělike pśeměneńe. (*Nowy Casnik* 1949 no. 1, quoted in Pohončowa 2000: 9)
>
> [We also changed the LS orthography a little bit in order to bring it closer to the orthography of US, but this is not a great change.][30]

These were *ad hoc* LM measures to get LS publishing started. Then a linguistic tug of war started regarding LS orthography. Several commissions discussed the issue in 1951 and 1952.[31] In the first commission there were originally only US members, so two Lower Sorbs had to be invited later to have at least a minimal representation of those directly concerned. There seems to have been quite a lot of wrangling and political pressure exerted upon the LS members.[32] The main goal was always to bring US and LS closer together. The discussions also spilled over into the newspapers. It was even questioned whether LS should be considered as a separate language at all. Consequently, there were outside proposals to abandon LS altogether in favor of US. In the end LS was recognized as a language in its own right, but the following changes were introduced in its orthography:

1. *i* → *ě* in a few words (*nimski* [German], *źiśi* [children] → *němski*, *źěśi*, US *němski*, *dźěći*)
2. *h-* → *w-* before *o* and *u* (*hokno* [window], *humožnik* [savior] → *wokno*, *wumožnik*, US *wokno*, *wumóžnik*)
3. *ó* → *o* (*pód* [under], *Chóśebuz* [Cottbus] → *pod*, *Chośebuz*)
4. *ĆV/CjV* → *CjV* (*smužkowańe/jotowanje* → *jotowanje*, US *jotowanje*)[33]

30 The "we" in this case refers to the US editor-in-chief so it was clearly a decision from the outside and from above, since the LS speech community had not been consulted beforehand.

31 The history of this process is described in detail in Pohončowa (2000), essentially based on the minutes of the commissions and of articles published in this context.

32 The minutes of one meeting were signed and thus approved by a LS participant *aus taktischen Gründen* [for tactical reasons], and in another case the signatures of the LS participants are illegible, probably on purpose.

33 This refers to the rendering of palatalized consonants in writing when a vowel follows. LS in both traditional and analogous orthography had a mixed system of

Of these changes 1, 2, and 4 actually brought LS closer to US whereas 3 was neutral in this respect.[34] The discussions and the subsequent changes in orthography did not really concern the average speaker of LS at first since most of them had little contact with written LS, and the older generation that had learnt to read LS in religious instruction had difficulties with the new script and the new orthography. Moreover, the texts they used, i.e., mainly the Bible and the hymnal, were still accessible in the traditional script and orthography.

However, the whole discussion is instructive from the point of view of LM, at least as far as LS was concerned. First, there was a considerable amount of outside (mainly US) influence and even pressure. Secondly, the original changes were proposed not by representatives of LS, but by speakers of US; only at a later stage were the former invited but, as it seems, more for cosmetic reasons. Finally, the main changes (introduction of Roman script and analogous orthography) had been decided upon before and could not be discussed, even though they were symbolically very important, especially for the average speaker of LS.[35] Therefore, briefly, one may say that these decisions are examples of organized LM and of LM that did not come from the LS speech community itself, but from above and from the outside. It is also obvious that those changes could only be imposed because their advocates were now in a position of power.

5 Lower Sorbian after the reforms

In view of the late official support for LS (see above), one may say that the language did not really rebound until the early 1950s. This relaunch was heavily supported from the US side. Thus, the only LS newspaper first re-appeared as a supplement to the US *Nowa doba* [New Era], after a few irregular publications on a monthly basis, as of 1950 as *Nowy Casnik* [New Journal]. It was edited and published in Budyšin/Bautzen, i.e., in US territory. Only in 1955 did it become independent of *Nowa doba*, when finally the editorial office, publisher and printing were moved to Chóśebuz/Cottbus and it became a weekly paper. LS as a subject (not as the language of instruction) was officially introduced in the schools as of 1952 (at the same time the first LS high school was established in Chóśebuz/Cottbus). Later on, regular broadcasts in LS were introduced. In all these instances, the 'new' LS was used.

---

using the acute, i.e., *smužkowańe* (thus *ńasł* [carried]) or *j*, i.e., *jotowanje* (thus *wjas* [village]) that reflected the actual pronunciation quite closely. There had also been proposals advocating *smužkowańe* throughout.

34 US had *ó* as well but it was pronounced differently and the positions in which it appeared were different.

35 This aspect applies to US as well. It seems, however, that there the changes introduced (especially the change of script and orthography) were not felt to be too aggravating, since there was practically no public discussion.

These changes in favor of LS faced many problems. First, there was a lack of qualified LS personnel. In order to overcome this, speakers of US were recruited, but it seems that they were not always properly prepared, so in many cases their US linguistic background influenced their performance in LS. This was, of course, particularly problematic in the case of the teaching profession, and it led to the widespread impression that the language of the LS high school was US (see the quote below).

Another problem was the official language policy that was highly puristic for both US and LS. The elite had always been puristic, but in the past, they had to restrict purism to their own linguistic activity, so it was more or less simple LM. Now, however, they were in a position of power and could impose purism on others (organized LM). Furthermore speakers of US (whether on purpose or inadvertently is not relevant in this context) introduced numerous US loans in the lexicon, partly to fill lexical gaps but sometimes also to replace widely accepted German loanwords or even LS words.[36] The fact that in the German Democratic Republic (GDR) all publications had to undergo preliminary censure made it even easier to enforce linguistic uniformity.[37] Unfortunately, this attitude was coupled with a systematic denigration of dialectal varieties of Sorbian, so that the native speakers were made to feel ashamed for their language. In addition to this, school and mass media promoted a kind of spelling pronunciation so that the orthographic reform also had orthoepic consequences. This alienated even those speakers of LS that did not read their language but only spoke it. Finally, yet importantly, there was a problem of content: the official media and the school propagated socialism and atheism and this in a region that was (and still is) rather conservative and very religious. In sum, organized LM, coming (at least partially) from the outside and from above, artificially separated standard LS from its dialect basis.

Overtly there was little if any reaction to this type of LM. The 'new' LS reigned in the mass media, in school and on formal public occasions. Unofficially, the speech community reacted to this new situation in different ways. Most of the native speakers continued using their local dialect among themselves, but limited

36 An analysis of the lexicon of the LS weekly shows a peak in the use of US loans to be in the middle of the 1950s (i.e., at about the time the newspaper moved to Chóśebuz/Cottbus) and then a slow drop to a very low number in the mid-1970s (Pohontsch 2002: 298). It has to be borne in mind, however, that this records only the first use of the respective words: once introduced, the loans were likely to stay. Therefore, the drop in the mid-1970s perhaps indicates not so much a conscious decision not to introduce any more US loanwords but rather a saturation point.

37 In addition to the normal censor, whose task it was to ensure political and ideological correctness, the Sorbian publishing house that was state-owned (officially *volkseigen* [owned by the people]) also had a special proofreader to ensure linguistic correctness. His main task was to enforce purism. To my knowledge, this post still exists in the case of the US daily newspaper *Nowa doba* (after reunification reverting to its old name *Serbske nowiny*).

their participation in official contexts where LS was used since the 'new' LS was expected. More serious, however, was the decision of many speakers of LS not to transmit their language to their children.[38] This interrupted the intergenerational transmission of LS almost completely so that by the end of the 1980s there were practically no LS native speakers of childbearing age any more. This, of course, is an extreme consequence of organized LM from above on the level of family LM that might be dubbed *linguosuicide*.

The institutions that decided on organized LM never recognized this fact and so the policy was not changed to accommodate the native speakers who had the impression that the 'new' LS language was not their language any more:[39]

> Nejmarkantnjej jawi se to [mócny wliw górnoserbšćiny, RWM] we wucbnicach a wuwucowańskej rěcy na dolnoserbskem gymnaziumje w 50tych a 60tych lětach. Rěc w dolnoserbskich wusćełanjach a w Nowem Casniku njejo se w tej rigoroznej reformowanosći pokazała. Weto jo se wot cytarjow a słucharjow cesto posuźowała ako "njenaša rěc", a rěc na gymnaziumje ako gornoserbska. (Jenč & Starosta 1998: 249)

> [Most noticeable is this [the strong influence of US, RWM] in the textbooks and in the language of instruction used in the LS high school in the 1950s and 1960s. The language of the LS broadcasts and of the *Nowy casnik* [the LS weekly, RWM] was not so rigorously reformed. Still readers and listeners often considered it as "not our language," and the language of the high school as US.]

The partisans of the official position (officials, journalists, broadcasters, teachers, representatives of Sorbian cultural organizations), on the other hand, who were

---

38 This is a particular form of family LM typical for minority languages: if speakers disagree with changes introduced (often it is purism) they can always decide to switch to the majority language. Another example of this kind of reaction (albeit on quite a different scale) among the Slavonic languages is Belarusian in relation to Russian, cf. Zaprudski (2007) and Sloboda (2009), the main difference being that in this case there is a middle way, i.e., a mixed language generally referred to as *trasjanka* (on the latter and its Russian Ukrainian counterpart, *suržyk*, cf. Hentschel, Taranenko & Zaprudski 2014).

39 It was not true that the official representatives (especially those of the cultural organization, the *Domowina*) did not know about this. However, it was official policy that there were 100,000 speakers of Sorbian (both US and LS), and this number was propagated until the end of the GDR. Thus, Nowusch (1988: 13) writes: "In der politisch-staatlichen Tätigkeit wird die sorbische Bevölkerung mit annähernd 100 000 Menschen beziffert. Der Gesamtzahl liegen demographische Untersuchungen zugrunde [...]." [For the purposes of political and state activity the Sorbian population numbers almost 100,000 persons. This overall number is based on demographic research [...].] (The strangely obfuscated wording is probably an indication of the author's disbelief.) Actually, field research carried out in the 1950s had already revealed the number to be not more than 80,000 but these results could not be published in the GDR (see Elle 1995: 241–265).

often non-native or US native speakers, used standard language (i.e., the 'new' LS) in most, if not all contexts, supported puristic tendencies and adhered to spelling pronunciation. Few were those that tried to find a middle road. Therefore, LM policies that were intended to strengthen LS but were ill-conceived were countered by the reaction of many, if not most native speakers that decided not to transmit the language to the next generation. The result was a dramatic drop in the number of speakers of LS during the years of the GDR in spite of all the efforts to support LS, albeit only in its 'new' form.[40] It has to be admitted, though, that other factors, not related to LM, were important, too (industrialization, collectivization in farming, 'devastation' of Sorbian villages due to strip mining etc.). The fact that the drop in the number of speakers was much more pronounced in the case of LS, however, allows for the conclusion that in the case of LS the ill-conceived organized LM was an important factor.

6 Development after reunification

The reunification of Germany in 1990 brought with it changes for the citizens of the former GDR in almost all areas of life, and the Sorbs were no exception. In these times of change, it was important for the Sorbs that they were guaranteed continued protection and support in the treaty of reunification. In the future, however, it was not the republic that would be responsible for them: In the context of Sorbian, and in particular LS, the most important change was the substitution of centralism by federalism. Cultural matters (and minority questions were considered to belong to the domain of culture, at least according to the official view of the Federal Republic of Germany) were the responsibility of the individual states, not of the republic as a whole.[41] Both states where Sorbs lived, i.e., the Free State of Saxony and the State of Brandenburg, in due time enacted each a Sorbian law (to replace the old Sorbian law of 1948 and the Ordinance of 1950, respectively) and passed regulations regarding teaching, bilingual inscriptions, the use of the language in official contexts etc.

This originally merely administrative reordering gave a real boost to a widespread wish among speakers of LS to shake off the shackles of 'Budyšin/Bautzen centralism.' This took on many different forms. One of them was the fact that some Lower Sorbs did not want to be referred to as *Sorben* [Sorbs] and their language as

---

40 Fieldwork in selected communities carried out in the 1990s and an extrapolation based on it arrived at a maximum of 7,000 speakers mastering LS more or less fluently (Jodlbauer, Spiess & Steenwijk 2001: 39). For a detailed description of the intergenerational language change from LS to German in one village, see the case study by Norberg (1996).

41 The republic acted only as a subsidiary in financial matters, taking over half of the budget of the *Założba za serbski lud* [Foundation for the Sorbian People], the rest being financed by Saxony (two thirds) and Brandenburg (one third).

sorbisch [Sorbian] in German official texts, claiming that *Sorben* referred to Upper Sorbs only and *sorbisch* either to US or the 'new' LS language. The discussions on this topic were very heated and have not yet abated completely. This forced the State of Brandenburg to choose the politically correct formulations *Sorben/Wenden* and *sorbisch/wendisch* in official publications. The reaction of the state shows that it took into consideration the different opinions of the Lower Sorbs when making a decision.

More interesting from the point of view of LM, however, are the changes that took place in the language itself. The first sign of change was a different attitude towards the LS dialects that were now treated as a source of enrichment for standard LS rather than a depraved form of it. So elderly native speakers (often grand- or even great-grandparents) were invited to day nurseries and kindergartens to introduce the young generation to dialectal LS,[42] and interview partners in the media could use their language (including the Germanisms it was peppered with) without running the risk of being corrected. As a further result of this opening-up towards LS as spoken by native speakers the spelling pronunciation that had been enforced before was abandoned in the media and later on in teaching as well.[43] This, however, required changes in the orthography, viz. a reform of the reform, since practically all young speakers of LS have learned the language at school and rely on the written form for the pronunciation.

Thus, the *Dolnoserbska rěcna komisija* [LS language commission][44] started work on correcting the reforms introduced after 1945. Their first decision, taken in 1995, rescinded change 1 (*i* => *ě*), most likely because it was the least conspicuous, affecting only a few words. Still the uproar was considerable, so the commission was even more careful when advocating further steps. Change 3 (*ó* => *o*) was corrected only half-heartedly at first, reintroducing *ó* (or rather the acute) as an orthographic *Hilfszeichen* [auxiliary mark], then introducing it in the standard dictionary (Starosta 1999: 19), officially still as an auxiliary mark, and fully

42 Ironically, some of them might have been among those parents that in the past had decided not to pass on the language to their own children, thus effectively interrupting the intergenerational transmission chain.

43 I remember my surprise when, sometimes in the early 1990s, in the monthly TV program in LS (*Łužyca*) announcers that a month before had used spelling pronunciation all of a sudden switched to a pronunciation that was closer to the dialects, an example of simple LM that, however, soon became organized and is now considered to be standard.

44 Originally, there had been only one language commission for both US and LS. It was then split into two sub-commissions for US and LS, respectively. After the reunification of Germany, the LS commission declared full independence, changing its name from *Dolnoserbska podkomisija serbskeje rěcneje komisije* [Lower Sorbian sub-commission of the Sorbian language commission] to *Dolnoserbskaja rěcnaja komisija* [Lower Sorbian language commission].

sanctioning its introduction in 2006.[45] Change 2 (*h-* => *w-*) remained in writing but it was suggested that pronunciation should not follow spelling but rather dialectal usage, i.e., revert to [h] or a glottal stop. This half-hearted decision caused considerable protest again, and in church circles, the spelling with *h-* was (partially) reintroduced.[46] These changes or partial restorations show that the previous reforms had truly been LM decisions from above and from the outside and had never really been accepted. Thus, as soon as the possibility arose they were revoked, the commission more or less followed the majority opinion of the Lower Sorbs. Interestingly enough change 4 (*ĆV/CjV* => *CjV*, i.e., the introduction of general *jotowanje*) did not seem to bother anyone, so the commission did not see any reason to rescind it. To my knowledge, there are no individual attempts (simple LM) to revert to the old practice.

The symbolically most important change in the orthography reform after 1945, however, seems to have escaped the attention of the language commission, viz. the introduction of Roman script and analogous orthography. However, the faithful took an interest in it, since in church there were still some Lower Sorbs who had been introduced to the church language in black letter/Gothic script and traditional orthography and did not want to read church texts in the new script and orthography. So in 1991 the liturgy was published in a bi-scriptural edition (*Dolnoserbska liturgija* 1991), albeit with general *jotowanje*, and in 2007 the hymnal appeared in a fully bi-scriptural edition (*Duchowne kjarliže* 2007).[47] It is clear that within a few years no one will be left that is still used to black letter/Gothic script and traditional orthography, but it is noteworthy that the needs and the wishes of a small group were taken into consideration in a rather large publishing endeavor (the hymnal is a book of over 900 pages).[48]

45 In fact, it was not a full return to the *status quo ante* because the rules were different now and considerably less logical than the previous ones. They seem to reflect the predilections of the author of the standard dictionary, but they were upheld in spite of serious criticism. This would then be an example of individual LM that was forced upon the complete linguistic community.

46 This even spilled over into the LS newspaper: in the main body, it uses *w-* but on the church page, the authors are free to use *h-* or *w-*. It is said that the main reason for the insistence on the reintroduction of *h-* by religious Lower Sorbs is symbolic: a central word for them is *humóžnik* [Savior], and writing it with *w-* is felt to be a desecration. This is a clear case of an orthographic shibboleth.

47 Cf. Meschkank, Frahnow & Pernack (2007). For some time, there was also a bi-scriptural column in a regional newspaper but this attempt was soon given up.

48 The most recent case of reviving traditional script and orthography is digital: The complete LS Bible (Biblia 1868) is now accessible online in three versions: Black letter/Gothic script and traditional orthography, Roman script and traditional orthography, Roman script and analogous orthography (http://www.dolnoserbski.de/biblija/info).

Almost of equal importance is a principal change in the attitude towards non-puristic language that was formerly considered non-standard. The LS media (newspaper and broadcasting) are now highly tolerant towards it, and this regarding all levels of language. If formerly a word like *burstak* (from German *Geburtstag* [birthday]), quite normal in spoken LS, was replaced by *narodny źeń* or had to be put into quotation marks, it may now be used more or less freely, and so it is with many other German loan words. Interestingly enough there seems to be a new form of lexical purism at work, and its primary target are US loan words. Thus, the word *zajmny* [interesting], taken over from US in the 1920s (Pohontsch 2002: 268), has recently fallen into disfavor in the *Nowy Casnik* and is now more and more ousted by *interesantny*. Even more remarkable: some grammatical constructions, formerly banned completely from official LS, have been reinstated. Thus, the definite and indefinite articles reappeared, albeit inconsistently, and so did the *wordowaś/hordowaś* passive, both of them formerly primary targets of purism. The reasons for these changes are manifold: bringing standard LS closer to the spoken varieties and here especially the dialects, marking the independence of LS (especially with regard to US) after a long period that was perceived by many as one of US dominance, perhaps also the wish to make LS more easily accessible to the new speakers with German as a native language. This last aspect is particularly important since the almost complete absence of young native speakers of LS made it imperative to install a revitalization program (under the name *Witaj* [welcome]) since 1998 and to take into consideration the particular needs of this new group of speakers of LS.

The changes in the organized LM are very noticeable. The top-down, rigid, and institution-based tradition of the GDR has been replaced by a more tolerant and individualized approach that is essentially more bottom-up. The US influence that was so pervasive previously and resented by many has all but disappeared. Perhaps even more important is the fact that this new kind of LM is closely monitored by the speech community as a whole and flexible if problems arise. A case in point is the compromise found regarding *h-* and *w-*, allowing for a deviation from the norm in church publications.

7 Conclusion or: What can be learnt from the case of Lower Sorbian?

Looking back on the linguistic history of Sorbian and later LS it can be stated that it shared the fate of many, if not most, minority languages: the area where it was spoken diminished in favor of the majority language, German, because speakers did not transmit the language to the next generation for a variety of reasons. This process of assimilation intensified in the 19th and 20th centuries due to the process of modernization and official measures. Up to the 20th century, the language was mainly supported by the church through its publications but it was only marginally subjected to major changes since there were no institutions that could have enforced them. LM was thus a largely individual process, most visible in the elaboration of a written, later standard language by a few individual actors with authority based on expertise, and in the decisions of Sorbian-speaking parents either to conserve the minority language and pass it on to the next generation or to switch to German. It also was an internal LS affair.

This changed completely in the GDR. The new actors, claiming to come to the rescue of LS,[49] who had the power to introduce fundamental changes in LM, were perceived as representatives of institutions (the state and the party) responsible for the destruction of the two main pillars of traditional LS life: the church, the traditional mainstay of LS[50] that was completely ousted from public life, and the traditional rural community of small farms that was broken up by collectivization. On the level of the language itself, they proclaimed revolution instead of continuity. This kind of aggressive LM from the outside and from above led to reactions from the speech community that resulted in the exact opposite of what was intended: a dissociation from 'official' LS and, worse still, a refusal to pass on the language to the next generation. Since in the context of a totalitarian state the effects of official measures could not be evaluated (or if they were, negative results could not be published), it was not possible to remedy the situation. This could only be done after the reunification of Germany, and many of the measures proposed and introduced since then point to a direction in the development of LM that is more adequate for the particular situation of an endangered minority language. The only problem is that they are too late as far as the traditional speech community is concerned (the dialects are doomed). Moreover, the community of 'new' speakers is still far from being stable.

The example of LS shows that LM in the case of minority languages is more complicated and requires more dexterity than in the case of 'normal' languages. Above all, it calls for permanent evaluation and readjustment of measures in order to avoid negative consequences.

References

Bartels, H. (2006) Wordowaś: Wó ranych wopytach wutłocowanja póžyconki [Wordowaś: On Early Attempts to Eliminate a Loanword]. *Lětopis* 53 (2), 90–103.

Biblia (1868) *Biblia abo to zełe Sswěte Pißmo Starego a Nowego Teſtamenta, do ßerſkeje rėcy pſcheſtawjone, wot nowotki pilńe pſeglėdane a pſcheporėžane* [The

49 There is no doubt that they were convinced to fight for the right cause. They invested a lot of enthusiasm and were often unable to understand the unfriendly reactions of those they had come to support.

50 Little did it matter that there were only a few churches left where church service was held in LS: still it was traditional to sing hymns in LS, and religious traditions such as Easter singing kept the language alive.

Bible or the Complete Holy Scriptures of the Old and the New Testament Translated into the Sorbian Language, Diligently Reviewed and Corrected once more]. Halle: Canstein. On WWW at http://www.dolnoserbski.de/biblija/info. Accessed July 22, 2019.

Buliš, J. (2017) The introduction of the Reformation: An example of the "Lusatian uncertainty principle". In J. Malink (ed) *Five Centuries: The Wends and the Reformation.* Austin: Concordia University Press; Serbin: The Wendish Press, 6–11.

Dolnoserbska liturgija (1991) Bautzen: Domowina-Verlag.

Elle, L. (1995) *Sprachenpolitik in der Lausitz. Eine Dokumentation 1949 bis 1989* [Language Policy in Lusatia. A Documentation 1949–1989]. Bautzen: Domowina-Verlag.

Faska, H. (ed) (1998) *Serbšćina* [Sorbian]. Opole: Uniwersytet Opolski – Instytut Filologii Polskiej.

Fasske, H. (1985) The historical, economic and political bases of the formation and development of the Sorbian literary languages. In G. Stone & D. S. Worth (eds) *The Formation of the Slavonic Literary Languages. Proceedings of a Conference Held in Memory of Robert Auty and Anne Pennington at Oxford 6–11 July 1981.* Columbus: Slavica Publishers, 61–69.

Galmiche, X. (2001) *Romaine* contre *gothique*: aspects culturels des options alphabétiques et typographiques dans les Pays tchèques au XIXe siècle [*Roman* against *Gothic*: Cultural aspects of alphabetic and typographic alternatives in Bohemia in the 19th century]. *Slavica occitania* 12, 191–216.

Hentschel, G., Taranenko, O. & Zaprudski, S. (eds) (2014) *Trasjanka und Suržyk – gemischte weißrussisch-russische und ukrainisch-russische Rede. Sprachlicher Inzest in Weißrussland und der Ukraine?* [Trasjanka and Suržyk: Mixed Belarusian-Russian and Ukrainian-Russian Speech. Linguistic Incest in Belarus and the Ukraine?]. Frankfurt on the Main: Peter Lang.

Herrmann, J. (1985) *Die Slawen in Deutschland. Geschichte und Kultur der slawischen Stämme westlich von Oder und Neiße vom 6. bis 12. Jahrhundert; ein Handbuch* [The Slavs in Germany. History and Culture of the Slavic Tribes to the West of Oder and Neisse from the 6th to the 12th Century]. Berlin: Akademie-Verlag.

Hórnik, M. (1880) Wutworjenje našeje spisowneje rěče a jeje zbliženje z delnjoserbskej [The elaboration of our standard language and its convergence with Lower Sorbian]. *Časopis Maćicy Serbskeje* 33, 155–164.

Jenč, H. & Starosta, M. (1998) Leksika [Vocabulary]. In Faska, H. (ed) *Serbšćina* [Sorbian]. Opole: Uniwersytet Opolski – Instytut Filologii Polskiej, 238–255.

Jodlbauer, R., Spiess, G. & Steenwijk, H. (2001) *Die aktuelle Situation der niedersorbischen Sprache: Ergebnisse einer soziolinguistischen Untersuchung der Jahre 1993–1995* [The Present Situation of Lower Sorbian: Results of a Sociolinguistic Inquiry, Conducted in the Years 1993 to 1995]. Bautzen: Domowina-Verlag.

Kimura, G. C. (2014) Language management as a cyclical process: A case study of prohibiting Sorbian in the workplace. *Slovo a slovesnost* 75 (4), 255–270.

Kimura, G. C. (2015) Spracherhalt als Prozess: Elemente des kirchlichen Sprachmanagements bei den katholischen Sorben [Language maintenance as a process: Elements of ecclesiastical language management among the Catholic Sorbs]. *International Journal of the Sociology of Language* 232, 13–32.

Kollár, J. (1929) *Rozpravy o slovanské vzájemnosti* [Articles on Slavic Mutuality]. Prague: Slovanský ústav.

Malink, J. (1983) Die Beziehungen Martin Luthers zu den Sorben [The relationship between Martin Luther and the Sorbs]. *Lětopis* B 30 (1), 54–70.

Malink, J. (ed) (2017a) *Five Centuries: The Wends and the Reformation.* Austin: Concordia University Press; Serbin: The Wendish Press.

Malink, J. (2017b) Luther, Melanchthon and the Wends. In J. Malink (ed) *Five Centuries: The Wends and the Reformation.* Austin: Concordia University Press; Serbin: The Wendish Press, 1–5.

Meschkank, W., Frahnow G. & M. Pernack (2007) *Duchowne kjarliže.* Bautzen: Domowina-Verlag.

Moller, A. (1959) *Niedersorbisches Gesangbuch und Katechismus* [Lower Sorbian Hymnal and Catechism]. Berlin: Akademie-Verlag [Budissin 1574].

Muka, E. (1881) Frenceliana II: Abraham Frencel jako serbski rěčnicaŕ [Frenceliana II: Abraham Frencel as a Sorbian linguist]. *Časopis Maćicy Serbskeje* 34, 69–78.

Nekvapil, J. (2007) On the relationship between small and large Slavic languages. *International Journal of the Sociology of Language* 183, 141–160.

Nekvapil, J. (2009) The integrative potential of Language Management Theory. In J. Nekvapil & T. Sherman (eds) *Language Management in Contact Situations: Perspectives from Three Continents.* Frankfurt on the Main: Peter Lang, 1–11.

Nekvapil, J. (2012) From Language Planning to Language Management: J. V. Neustupný's Heritage. *Media and Communication Studies* 63, 5–21.

Neustupný, J. V. (1989) Language purism as a type of language correction. In B. H. Jernudd & M. Shapiro (eds) *The Politics of Language Purism.* Berlin: De Gruyter, 211–224.

Neustupný, J. V. (2002) Sociolingvistika a jazykový management [Sociolinguistics and language management]. *Sociologický časopis/Czech Sociological Review* 38 (4), 429–442.

Norberg, M. (1996) *Sprachwechselprozeß in der Niederlausitz: Soziolinguistische Fallstudie der deutsch-sorbischen Gemeinde Drachhausen/Hochoza* [The Process of Language Change in Lower Lusatia: A Sociolinguistic Case Study of the German-Sorbian Village of Drachhausen/Hochoza]. Uppsala: Uppsala University.

Nowusch, H. (1988) *Die Gleichberechtigung der Bürger sorbischer Nationalität in der DDR – verwirklichtes Menschenrecht* [Equality of the Citizens of Sorbian Nationality in the GDR: A Realized Human Right]. Bautzen: Domowina-Verlag.

Olesch, R. (1983–87) *Thesaurus Linguae Dravaenopolabicae* I–IV [Thesaurus of the Polabian Language]. Cologne & Vienna: Böhlau.

Olesch, R. (1989) *Gesammelte Aufsätze* I. *Dravaenopolabicae* [Collected Essays I. Polabian]. Cologne & Vienna: Böhlau.

Olesch, R. (1998) *Okcent venst'ă recĕ – Der dravänopolabische Wortakzent – Akcent wyrazowy w języku drzewiańsko-połabskim* [The Word Accent in Polabian]. Ed. by H. Rothe & A. Lauhus. Cologne, Weimar & Vienna: Böhlau.

Pohončowa, A. (2000) Procowanje wo pśibliženje gorno- a dolnoserbskego pšawopisa po lěśe 1945 [Attempts to bring Upper and Lower Sorbian orthography closer together after 1945]. *Lětopis* 9/47 (1), 3–21.

Pohontsch, A. (2002) *Der Einfluss obersorbischer Lexik auf die niedersorbische Schriftsprache. Ein Beitrag zur Entwicklungsgeschichte der niedersorbischen Schriftsprache* [The Influence of Upper Sorbian Vocabulary on the Lower Sorbian Standard Language: A Contribution to the History of the Development of the Lower Sorbian Standard Language]. Bautzen: Domowina-Verlag.

Rinkevičius, V. (2017) *Altpreußisch. Geschichte. Dialekte. Grammatik* [Old Prussian. History. Dialects. Grammar]. Hamburg: Baar.

Schuster-Šewc, H. (1967) *Das niedersorbische Testament des Miklawuš Jakubica 1548* [The Lower Sorbian New Testament of Miklawuš Jakubica from 1548]. Berlin: Akademie-Verlag.

Schuster-Šewc, H. (2001) *Die ältesten Drucke des Obersorbischen. Wenceslaus Warichius und Gregorius Martini: Eine sprachwissenschaftliche Analyse. Mit Faksimiledruck, Transliteration und Transkription* [The Oldest Printed Books in Upper Sorbian. Wenceslaus Warichius and Gregorius Martini: Linguistic Analysis with Facsimile, Transliteration and Transcription]. Bautzen: Domowina.

Sloboda, M. (2009) A language management approach to language maintenance and shift: A study from post-Soviet Belarus. In J. Nekvapil & T. Sherman (eds) *Language Management in Contact Situations: Perspectives from Three Continents.* Frankfurt on the Main: Peter Lang, 15–47.

Spolsky, B. (2009) *Language Management.* Cambridge: Cambridge University Press.

Starosta, M. (1999) *Dolnoserbsko-nimski słownik/Niedersorbisch-deutsches Wörterbuch* [Lower Sorbian-German dictionary]. Budyšyn/Bautzen: Domowina.

Stone, G. (1985) Language planning and the Lower Sorbian literary language. In G. Stone & D. S. Worth (eds) *The Formation of the Slavonic Literary Languages. Proceedings of a Conference Held in Memory of Robert Auty and Anne Pennington at Oxford 6–11 July 1981.* Columbus: Slavica Publishers, 99–103.

Stone, G. (2016) *Slav Outposts in Central European History. The Wends, Sorbs and Kashubs.* London & New York: Bloomsbury.

Thomas, G. (1991) *Linguistic Purism.* London & New York: Longman.

Zaprudski, S. (2007) In the grip of replacive bilingualism: The Belarusian language in contact with Russian. *International Journal of the Sociology of Language* 183, 97–118.

Ben Ó Ceallaigh

Interests, power, and austerity in Irish-language policy 2008–2018

Abstract In order to examine how macro-level economic developments can contribute to the decline of a minoritized language, this chapter examines the case of the Irish language in the wake of the 2008 economic crash and subsequent "Great Recession." The disproportionately severe effects of neoliberal austerity measures on the Irish-language community are detailed, with particular emphasis being placed on the consequences of such policies for the language's heartland areas (collectively known as the "*Gaeltacht*"). The chapter initially discusses the nature of neoliberalism and its crash in 2008, before examining how this affected both overt and covert Irish-language policy. The findings of ethnographic research conducted in some of the strongest remaining Gaeltacht communities between 2014 and 2016 are then discussed to add empirical weight to the policy analysis presented in the first half of the chapter. The effects of large-scale unemployment, intensive out-migration, the intersection of economic disruption and gendered aspects of language maintenance, as well as the increased use of English-language technologies as "surrogate child minders" by Irish-speaking parents are all detailed. Language revitalization policies, it will be argued, are fundamentally contraindicated to neoliberal policy prescriptions, and as such the Irish language received proportionally much greater cutbacks than other sectors in the post-2008 period, which was used as an opportunity to implement a large scale "roll-back" of state support for this sector.

Keywords Irish, Gaeltacht, minority languages, language policy, neoliberalism, austerity, language shift

1 Introduction

In attempting to explain the process through which languages cease to be spoken, literature on language loss and extinction frequently cites "economic forces" as being key to driving this process. Grenoble and Whaley, for instance, have claimed that economics "may be the single strongest force influencing the fate of endangered languages" (1998: 52), and similar statements by other scholars are commonplace.[1]

1 See, for instance, Baker 2011: 62; Crystal 2014: 175–176; Edwards 1984: 304; Herbert 2011: 403–422; Kamwangamalu 2003: 227; Kaplan & Balduf 1997: 280; Leonard 2015; McColl Millar 2005: 26; Nelde, Strubell & Williams 1996: 7–11; Nettle & Romaine 2000: 126–147; Ó Ciosáin 2013: 362; Ó Huallacháin 1991: 123; Ó Riagáin 1996: 36, 2001: 206; O'Rourke & Pujolar 2013: 54; Phillipson 2008; Romaine 2006: 456;

Despite the frequency of such declarations, as Grin (1999: 169) and Austin and Sallabank (2011: 21) have observed, there are very few studies which have offered a detailed explanation of how precisely macro-level socioeconomic changes contribute to the endangerment of languages, with most references to the topic being more rhetorical than analytical in their nature.

Using the example of Irish as a case study, this chapter will take some tentative steps to rectify this deficit in our knowledge. In order to demonstrate the power economic forces have over language vitality, it will examine the Irish-language management regime and sociological change in Irish-speaking communities in Galway and Donegal in the mid- and North-west of Ireland during the ten-year period which followed the international economic crash of 2008. Ethnographic data from Irish-speaking areas (known collectively as the "*Gaeltacht*") are used to illustrate some of the social mechanisms through which this macro-level economic disruption accelerated an ongoing process of language shift.

After the foundation of the Irish Free State in 1922 (known as the Republic of Ireland post-1937), Irish enjoyed a much greater level of institutional protection than most minoritized languages, with use of the language being supported in the public service, the education system and in the Gaeltacht. This support was particularly important for Gaeltacht communities, which are overwhelmingly located in poorer, peripheral areas in the west of the country. Although it is commonly accepted that state commitment to the language revitalization project began to wane in the 1970s, by which time the failure of fifty years of attempts to re-Gaelicize the country was apparent (Ó Giollagáin 2014; Ó Riagáin 1997: 23–24), what followed was a relatively incremental withdrawal of state support for the language. Nevertheless, when compared to other languages with a similarly sized population of speakers, Irish was still well served with institutional supports even after this reduction in state commitment. This was especially true in light of some important developments made in response to bottom-up resistance to the withdrawal of state provision, such as the founding of *Údarás na Gaeltachta* ("The Gaeltacht Authority," discussed below) in 1979.

Despite this legacy of support and its status as the first official language of the Republic of Ireland Irish is categorized as "definitely endangered" by UNESCO (2018). In 2016, out of a total population of 4,757,956 in the Republic, just 73,803 spoke Irish daily outside of the education system, some 20,586 of these being concentrated in the Gaeltacht (CSO 2017a: 8, 66). Furthermore, as will be demonstrated, the 2008–2018 period has seen a significant weakening of provision for the language, especially in the Gaeltacht. This has been the case despite a large-scale sociolinguistic report published in 2007 finding that in even the strongest of these distinct linguistic communities, Irish was under severe pressure and in need of significantly strengthened policy interventions to ensure its continued

Skutnabb-Kangas 2000: 436–476; Tabouret-Keller 1968: 113; UNESCO et al. 2003: 5; Williams 1991: 4.

intergenerational transmission (Ó Giollagáin, Mac Donnacha, Ní Chualáin, Ní Shéaghdha & O'Brien 2007). While the census and other official data on which this report was largely based has been critiqued by some commentators as unreliable (Ó Broithe 2012; Ó Riagáin 2018), it nonetheless broadly reiterated conclusions that had been previously reached in other research (e.g., Hindley 1990; Ó Cinnéide, Mac Donncha & Ní Chonghaile 2001).

With the "Great Recession" which began in 2008 ultimately being a crisis of the neoliberal model of capitalism, the first section of this chapter offers a brief overview of what precisely is meant by neoliberalism. Ireland's enthusiastic adoption of neoliberal policies over recent years will be described, as will the severity of the crash's effects—direct results of the neoliberalization of the Irish economy. These background sections serve to set the stage for subsequent discussions of the reforms to Irish-language management and to contextualize the extent of the withdrawal of state support for the language post-2008. Following Harvey (2005: 19), neoliberalism is understood as an expression of the interests and power of the international capitalist class. As such, this chapter offers a discussion of how precisely "language management" (Spolsky 2009) efforts are restricted by the power of greater structural forces.

Section three will examine the consequences of austerity measures introduced after the 2008 crash on both the content and implementation of official language promotion policies. Those areas which illustrate "covert" language policy (Shohamy 2006)—such as the vastly disproportionate level of cuts received by Irish-language promotion bodies—will be discussed in section four. The radical reforms implemented in the Irish-language management regime after the 2008 economic crash will be used to demonstrate how the interests of international finance took precedence over language revitalization measures, despite the pressing need for such supports being well documented. Language revitalization policies, it will be argued, are fundamentally contraindicated to neoliberal policy prescriptions, and as such received proportionally much greater cutbacks than other areas in post-2008 Ireland.

Section five will draw on ethnographic data collected between 2014 and 2016 in some of the strongest remaining Gaeltacht areas in Galway and Donegal, including extracts from fifty-two ethnographic interviews conducted with a wide range of community members throughout this time. These data will be used to demonstrate some of the key ways in which the disruptions caused by the 2008 crash led to a variety of deleterious social consequences for the Gaeltacht, including increased unemployment, widespread out-migration, etc.

To conclude, the substantial 11.2% decrease in the number of daily speakers of Irish in the Gaeltacht between 2011 and 2016 will be discussed, this decline being understood as largely a product of the dramatic decrease in state support for language revitalization efforts and the social dislocation caused in Gaeltacht communities by the economic crash.

2 Neoliberalism and economic crisis

Originally theorized between the 1940s and 1960s by economists such as Friedrich Hayek and Milton Friedman (Hayek [1944] 2001; Friedman [1966] 2002), neoliberalism, unlike more traditional neoclassical economic models, argues in favor of substantial state intervention in the market. Such intervention, however, should only take place in favor of capital, with the goal of aiding profit maximization (Mirowski 2013). By facilitating the generation of profit via pro-business intercessions, it is argued that wealth will "trickle down" and provide the greatest benefit possible to the greatest number of people, without any need for states to implement redistributive welfare policies, which were famously described by Hayek as "the road to serfdom," inevitably paving the way for totalitarianism ([1944] 2001).

Having developed into a relatively coherent theoretical position over the past several decades, neoliberalism has come to be associated with trade liberalization, privatization, and, more recently, bank bailouts designed to defend the interests of international investors. As Harvey explains:

> Neoliberalism is in the first instance a theory of political economic practices that proposes that human well-being can best be advanced by liberating individual entrepreneurial freedoms and skills within an institutional framework characterized by strong private property rights, free markets, and free trade. The role of the state is to create and preserve an institutional framework appropriate to such practices [...]. It must also set up those military, defence, police, and legal structures and functions required to secure private property rights and to guarantee, by force if need be, the proper functioning of markets [...]. But beyond these tasks the state should not venture (Harvey 2005: 2).

Although originally a fringe position, neoliberalism eventually began to emerge as a hegemonic political project in the early 1970s. This saw the beginning of the end for the Keynesian welfare state, with Keynesian macro-economic policy being held responsible for the rate of profit declining globally, a period known as the "stagflation" crisis, which was the most severe economic disruption since the Great Depression of the 1930s (Gamble 2009: 6).

In the context of this volume, it is significant that Harvey has argued that rather than simply aiming to continue the economic boom of the post-war era via the adoption of a more efficient set of macro-economic policies, this period of reform specifically aimed to exercise power with the goal of promoting one set of class interests at the expense of others. Neoliberalism, he contends, was adopted in order to restore class dominance "to sectors that saw their fortunes threatened by the ascent of social democratic endeavors in the aftermath of the Second World War" (2007: 22). This class bias continues to this day, with a wide range of literature demonstrating that austerity measures implemented to maintain the neoliberal system post-2008 affected the poorer sections of society most severely (Bisset 2015: 175–177; Varoufakis 2016). This fact has important implications for both language management regimes and the type of underdeveloped peripheral areas in which minoritized language communities are most often found (Nelde, Strubell & Williams 1996: 8), including, as will be seen, Ireland's Gaeltacht areas.

2.1 Neoliberalism and the Irish economy

Since originally being adopted by governments in the UK and US in the 1970s, neoliberalism has become the dominant economic ideology of not only transnational economic institutions such as the International Monetary Fund (henceforth "IMF") and the European Central Bank, but also the vast majority of the world's nation states (Harvey 2005; Allen & O'Boyle 2013: 13–20). It was during the "Celtic Tiger" period which began in the early 1990s that Ireland began to follow this trend, enthusiastically implementing neoliberal reforms. Having earned a reputation as the "sick man of Europe" during the early and mid-20th century due to its chronic underdevelopment, this time of high growth saw the country finally catch up with the rest of Western Europe in terms of economic progress (Kirby 2010). The Celtic Tiger economy was initially based on a heavy reliance on Foreign Direct Investment attracted via low tax rates, which led the country to become a tax haven for transnational corporations (McCabe 2011: 41–43, 164–170; Garcia-Bernardo, Fichtner, Takes & Heemskerk 2017). By 2007, a massive property bubble had emerged, with the construction sector comprising an enormous 25% of the Gross National Product (Glynn, Kelly & MacÉinrí 2013: 38) and property in Dublin selling for prices that surpassed London, New York or Hong Kong (O'Toole 2010: 3).

As with most of Western Europe, the international financial crash of 2008 had severe repercussions for the then-booming Irish economy. In response to what was reported to be its impending collapse, the Irish government opted to "bail out" the country's banking sector, which had been heavily invested in the international credit default swap market that imploded so dramatically at this time. As Blyth comments when describing the extent of the crash's impact on Ireland:

> The combined result of the property-bubble collapse and the banking system implosion was "the largest compound decline in GNP of any industrialized country over the 2007–2010 period." Government debt increased by 320 percent to over 110 percent of GDP as the government spent some 70 billion euros to shore up the banking system. Meanwhile, unemployment rose to 14 percent by mid-2011, a figure that would have been higher had it not been for emigration. (Blyth 2013: 66)

The costs of the bank bailout necessitated a severe program of austerity, the effects of which were still visible in state spending in 2018, which remained 10% below 2008 levels, despite strong growth having returned to the economy by this time (Taft 2018). As Mercille and Murphy (2015) have shown, the crisis was used to a large degree as an opportunity to accelerate the neoliberalization of a wide range of public policy in Ireland, a tendency also visible internationally during this time (Crouch 2011). Austerity, then, allowed for the intensification of neoliberalism's consolidation of certain class interests, serving to maintain "the power and privilege of some while extending and deepening the suffering of others" (Bisset 2015: 175).

While the issue has received only very limited attention in literature on either public policy or language revitalization, Irish-language policy also clearly exemplifies this trend of increased neoliberalization and the consolidation of certain class interests, as the following two sections will demonstrate.

3 Overt language management post-2008

As noted above, Irish is unusual in having a far greater range of institutional supports than other languages with similarly small speaker bases. These supports are a legacy of the important role the language revitalization movement played in politicizing the state's first generation of political leaders who took power in 1922, following the 1916 Rising and subsequent War of Independence (Garvin 1987: 80). While Irish continues to enjoy a higher level of protection than most threatened languages, the radical reform of public policy in Ireland since 2008 (Mercille & Murphy 2015) has seen the extent of this severely reduced.

Indeed, the two most significant changes regarding official Irish-language management introduced in the last several decades—the *20-year Strategy for the Irish Language 2010–2030* and the *Gaeltacht Act 2012* (Government of Ireland 2010, 2012) were both adopted while the Irish economy was under the supervision of the IMF, the European Central Bank and the European Commission, collectively known as the "Troika." These institutions, as Allen and O'Boyle note (2013: 13–20), are well-known for being central to the propagation of neoliberalism internationally. As Crenson explains in his influential work on agenda setting (1971: 125), the reputations of such powerful institutions often guarantee a favorable outcome without them having to actively exercise power. Significant investment in Irish-language management efforts would thus have been kept off the agenda purely by virtue of the reputations of these institutions, the exigencies of the crisis and the anxiousness of the Irish elite to end the recession as quickly as possible via budgetary contraction. The contributions of Bachrach and Baratz (1963) and Lukes (1974) to the community power debate—a seminal discussion in political science in the 1960s and 1970s about the nature of political power (Cairney 2012: 46–58)—are of great pertinence here. As these authors noted, the so-called "second face of power" is often exercised primarily to keep issues off the political agenda and away from public attention, as seems to have happened with the demands made for increased support for Irish just prior to the crash (Ó Giollagáin, Mac Donnacha, Ní Chualáin, Ní Shéaghdha & O'Brien 2007). Furthermore, as Hardiman and Regan (2012: 9) explained when writing at the time "[a]ll budget decisions must be cleared with the Troika, fiscal performance is subject to quarterly reviews and Troika personnel are embedded in the core government departments." Importantly for the present discussion, the conditions of the *Memorandum of Understanding* between Ireland and the Troika "required a continued liberalization of Ireland's political economy and increased marketization of previously protected public spheres" (Murphy 2014: 134).

It is therefore of little surprise that both the content and implementation of the *20-year Strategy* and the *Gaeltacht Act 2012* bear the mark of the trying economic circumstances which the country faced at the time of their introduction. Ó Giollagáin has described at length the numerous ways in which the policy provisions laid out in the *20-year Strategy* are inadequate to address the severity of the sociolinguistic crisis facing the Gaeltacht, amounting, in his terms, to a "fully-fledged policy of abandonment" of the language revitalization project (Ó Giollagáin 2014: 102). While introduced as an official policy response to the *Comprehensive Linguistic Survey on the Use of Irish in the Gaeltacht* (Ó Giollagáin, Mac Donnacha, Ní Chualáin, Ní Shéaghdha & O'Brien 2007), the *Strategy* paid little heed to the recommendations made in the 2007 study. Despite the weak nature of its proposals, the implementation of the *Strategy* has been extremely lackluster, with an implementation report issued by the Department of the Taoiseach (the Irish Prime Minister) at the quarter way point of *Strategy's* lifespan in December 2015 containing a mere 225 words. Research commissioned in 2018 by TG4, the Irish-language television station, showed that none of the structures proposed in the *Strategy* were functioning, and that the interdepartmental committee dedicated to its implementation had not met in over two years (Tuairisc.ie 2018a). As Ó Giollagáin has described, policies such as the *Strategy* and the institutions charged with their implementation "act as dismantlers at the behest of those in real positions of power whose primary concern at this stage is to effect budgetary contraction in the irksome domain [...] of minority language support mechanisms" (Ó Giollagáin 2014: 116–117).

The effects of neoliberal austerity measures are also very visible in relation to the *Gaeltacht Act 2012* which emerged from a proposal in the *Strategy*. As with the *Strategy*, the 2012 Act has been extensively criticized by both language promotion bodies and academic commentators (Conradh na Gaeilge 2012; Ó Giollagáin 2014: 106–112; Walsh 2014). Belying the fact that effective language revitalization was apparently not the sole (or even, perhaps, primary) goal of the act, in a statement of unusual candor the *Explanatory and Financial Memorandum* which accompanies the act claims that:

> It is estimated that Part 3 of the Bill [regarding the abolition of the election for the board of the Gaeltacht development authority, *Údarás na Gaeltachta*] will result in savings of approximately € 100,000 annually and up to € 500,000 every five years. It is not expected that the remaining Parts of the Bill will result in any additional costs to the Exchequer (Government of Ireland 2012: 44).

A key provision of the Act divides the official Gaeltacht into twenty-six "Language Planning Areas" and requires each of these to prepare a language revitalization plan in order to retain their Gaeltacht status. This work has been delegated by the department of state responsible for the Gaeltacht to *Údarás na Gaeltachta*. In light of the severe budget cuts the Údarás has received since 2008 (described in the following section), they have in turn delegated much of the preparation of these plans to voluntary community committees. Such committees are typically overseen by a community development group which receives funding from the Údarás. In many cases that I witnessed during my ethnographic fieldwork, even where an area has many thousands of residents, these committees consist of only a handful of individuals doing far more than their fair share of this important work. Although this work was delegated to volunteers, there was no coordinated Gaeltacht-wide publicity campaign aimed at getting people involved in the process, due, I was told, to the Údarás not having sufficient resources to fund such an effort. As such, many language planning committees consist in no small part of people who are employed by institutions which the Údarás funds, and who are fearful of being defunded should their area lose its Gaeltacht status due to not preparing a plan. As a member of one such committee told me:

> B: Go bunúsach tá Roinn na Gaeltachta ag rá [...] le Údarás na Gaeltachta "caithfidh sibh é a chur i gcrích nó bainfidh muid an t-airgead díbh" agus tá Údarás na Gaeltachta tar éis a rá leis an bpobal, "caithfidh sibhse é a chur i gcrích nó bainfidh muid an t-airgead díbh". Agus tá, tá mé lárnach sa gcóras sin mé féin, ar an receiving end mar a déarfá, agus sin atá ag tarlú.
>
> [B: Basically the department of the Gaeltacht is saying [...] to Údarás na Gaeltachta "you have to do this or we'll cut your funding" and Údarás na Gaeltachta has said to the community "you have to do this or we'll cut your funding." And I'm central in this process myself, on the receiving end as you might say, and that's what's happening.][2]

Further to such difficulties surrounding community ownership and participation in this process, the provision of funding for the implementation of those plans which have already been completed has been an enormously contentious issue. Indeed, the € 100,000 per plan per annum being offered amounts to less than 50% of that requested in one case, and at the time of writing the respective local committee was threatening to disband itself and boycott further engagement with state institutions as a result of their frustration with such inadequate support (Tuairisc.ie 2017).

While the state, then, claims that the language planning process under the *Gaeltacht Act 2012* promotes community ownership and participation in language revitalization, it in effect amounts to a classic example of the neoliberal "roll-back" of the state from an area which it had previously presided over, as famously described by Peck and Tickell (2002). Thus, under the guise of democratizing the Irish-language management regime, the state is in effect able to withdraw from its historic commitment to language revitalization. As Mercille and Murphy (2015) observe, such withdrawal of the state from the provision of services previously

2 Interviews were conducted in Irish. The translations given are the author's own.

seen as core duties is entirely in accordance with the neoliberal project of privatization and restructuring.

4 Covert language policies in an age of austerity

As the previous section detailed, official language management measures introduced in the wake of the 2008 crash clearly bear the mark of the austerity policies the Irish government adopted while attempting to navigate its way through the most severe economic crisis the state has ever faced. Further to the ignoring of the *20-year Strategy for Irish* and the problematic implementation of the *Gaeltacht Act 2012,* the full effects of this trend towards the neoliberalization of language policy can perhaps be seen even more clearly in the extent to which public funded provision for the language was cut in the post-2008 period.

While the decline in public spending in the wake of the recession had negative consequences for a great many sectors of Irish society (Nagle & Coulter 2015; O'Boyle & Allen 2013), provision for Irish language-focused institutions was hit particularly hard. An examination of the extent of these cuts allows for an interesting insight into "covert" language policy, understood as the "hidden agendas" which operate behind official policy, and which often have more significant consequences than the stated policies themselves. As Shohamy (2006: xvi) reminds us:

> [T]he real LP of a political and social entity should not be observed only through declared policy statements, but rather through a variety of devices that are used to perpetuate language practices, often in covert and implicit ways. Moreover, these devices, which on the surface may not be viewed as policy devices, are strongly affecting the actual policies, given their direct effects on language practice. Thus, it is only through the observations of the effects of these very devices that the real language policy of an entity can be understood and interpreted.

The reductions to the budget of Údarás na Gaeltachta offer one telling example of such "de-facto" language policy.

Initially established in 1979 to promote the economic development of Gaeltacht areas which had long since suffered from mass out-migration and unemployment, by 2008 Údarás na Gaeltachta had a budget of over € 25 million. By 2015, however, this had been cut by almost three-quarters, to € 6.7 million. The significance of this reduction becomes all the more apparent when compared to the budgets of the Industrial Development Agency and Enterprise Ireland, institutions which perform effectively the same duties as the Údarás, but in English-speaking communities outwith the Gaeltacht.

Table 1: Comparison of enterprise promotion agencies' budgets 2008–15

	Údarás na Gaeltachta	Enterprise Ireland	Industrial Development Agency
2008	€ 25.5 million	€ 56.4 million	€ 78.5 million
2015	€ 6.7 million	€ 52.7 million	€ 116 million
% change 2008–15	-73.7%	-6.6%	+47.8%

Sources: Údarás na Gaeltachta 2009a: 9, 2016: 11; Enterprise Ireland 2009: 48, 2016: 42; IDA 2010: 36, 2016: 33.

As Table 1 illustrates, concomitant to the Údarás losing over 73% of its budget, Enterprise Ireland lost just 6.6% of its funding and the Industrial Development Authority received an increase of over 47%. The budgetary adjustments of these latter two institutions would seem reasonable at a time when the creation of employment was a priority, with levels of un- and under-employment in Ireland having reached a "staggering" 23% by 2013 according to the IMF (2013: 26). As one of my interviewees commented when discussing the disproportionate cuts the Údarás received, "níl dabht ar bith ach go bhfuil teachtaireacht áirithe ansin" (there's no doubt but there's a certain message there).

As seen in the following section, these cuts had significant impacts for the agency's ability to attract businesses to locate in the Gaeltacht, with the Donegal Gaeltacht area in particular (which is in a very peripheral location) suffering greatly because of this (see Section 5.1).

In light of these cutbacks, Irish-language media reported in summer 2016 that staff morale in the Údarás was "at an all-time low" (Ó Gairbhí 2016). When interviewing an employee of the agency in the week after this story broke, I asked him how accurate such reports were, to which he responded as follows:

É: 100% cruinn. Tá rudaí níos measa ná sin fiú.
B: Dáiríre? Agus cén uair a thosaigh sé sin?
É: Trí nó ceithre bliain ó shin.
B: Mar gheall ar...?
É: Rationalization.
B: Na coinníollacha oibre agus é sin?
É: Yes. Tá an tríú cuid den fhoireann [imithe], nuair a imíonn daoine cuireann siad cosc duin' neacht eile a fháil. I bhfad níos mó oibre a dhéanamh le níos lú daoine [...] brú ón roinn [Gaeltachta] ag iarraidh an rud uilig a chúngú isteach, níl siad ag iarraidh seo agus siúd a chur i bhfeidhm [...]. Tá siad ar an chúigiú cuid den budget a bhí deich mbliana ó shin. Tá siad ar 30% níos lú foirne, tá an foireann atá fágtha aosta. Níl duine ar bith úr ag teacht isteach. Thit siad amach leis an cheardchumann. Tá siad seo ag iarraidh na rudaí seo a bhrú ar aghaidh gan pairtnéireacht ar bith, gan a ghoil i gcomhairle.

[É: 100% accurate. Things are worse than that, even.
B: Really? And when did this start?
É: Three or four years ago.
B: Because of…?
É: Rationalization.
B: Working conditions and things like that?
É: Yes. A third of the staff have been laid off, when people leave we're not allowed recruit someone to fill their place. [There's] much more work to do with less people […] pressure from the department [of state for the Gaeltacht] trying to narrow things down, they don't want to implement this and that […]. They're on a fifth of the budget they had ten years ago. They have 30% less staff, the staff they have are old. No one new is coming in. They fell out with the trade union. They're trying to push things through with no partnership at all, no consultation.]

Similar to the case of the Údarás, as the previous quote alludes to, the Department of Community, Regional and Gaeltacht Affairs (which is also responsible for language policy more generally) had 70% of its budget cut over the three-year period from 2008 to 2011 (O'Halloran 2016; Ó Murchú 2014: 210). Within this department the Gaeltacht subsector was targeted for the highest proposed cuts, some 58% (Guth na Gaeltachta 2010). This was the case despite the fact that this time also saw the introduction of the *20-year Strategy for Irish* and the *Gaeltacht Act 2012* which were described in the previous section, which the department is ultimately responsible for, although some aspects of their implementation have been delegated to the equally ill-funded Údarás. Like so many areas facing neoliberal restructuring, these institutions now have more work to do, but fewer resources to do it. As an interviewee from a major language promotion group told me:

M: [T]háinig an dá rud sin isteach ach níor cuireadh aon acmhainní breise ar fáil i ndáiríre […]. In aon polasaí rialtais eile thuigfeadh siad go mbeidh costas ag baint le polasaí chomh mór leis sin agus chomh fairsing leis sin a chur i bhfeidhm agus go mbeadh acmhainní breise curtha ar fáil. Y'know a mhalairt de sin—bhain siad airgead ón dá institiúid is mó a bhaineann leis ó thaobh cúrsaí maoinithe.

[M: Both of those came in but no extra resources were really made available […]. In any other government policy they would understand that there will be costs associated with implementing any policy that is as big and far-reaching as that, and extra resources would be made available […]. [I]t's the opposite of that—they took money from the two biggest institutions that are involved.]

While the full extent of the cuts to Irish language promotion initiatives is far too great to discuss in a chapter of this length, it is important to note that these cuts to the Údarás and the department of state responsible for Gaeltacht policy led to the discontinuation of a great many of those schemes previously used to incentivize the use of Irish and retain the population of the Gaeltacht. These included housing grants for Gaeltacht residents, university scholarships for people from the Gaeltacht and the support scheme for Gaeltacht parents raising their children with Irish.

Although, as noted in Section 2.1, state capital expenditure a decade after the recession began had reached 90% of its pre-crash level, capital expenditure on Irish in 2017 was just one seventh of what it had been in 2008, further illustrating the extent to which language management policies were transformed after the crash (Byrne 2018: 8). Although the government's National Development Plan 2018–2027, launched in February 2018, stated that annual funding for Údarás na Gaeltachta would increase to € 12 million over the duration of the plan, no time line was given for the provision of such funds, which, at any rate, would amount to less than 50% of the funding the organization had in 2008 (Government of Ireland 2018: 50; Tuairisc.ie 2018b). Furthermore, as research commissioned by campaign group *Teacht Aniar* subsequently demonstrated, the additional funding touted did not actually amount to an overall increase in spending on the Gaeltacht, which, based on the figures provided in the plan, will still be well below 2008 figures come 2028 (Byrne 2018: 11).

5 Micro-level sociolinguistic consequences of macro-level neoliberalism

5.1 Employment

As noted above, one of the ways in which the effects of the crash and ensuing recession were most clearly visible in Irish society was the rapid increase in unemployment. As the growth of the Celtic Tiger reached its zenith, the property bubble which was so central to its development swelled to an enormous degree, with more than one in five men employed in Ireland working in the construction sector in 2007 (O'Connell 2017: 240). When the banks withdrew credit from property developers in late-2008 as a way to ensure the banking sector's liquidity, however, the construction industry was plunged into crisis. By 2012 it had shrunk to make up less than 6% of GNP (Glynn, Kelly & MacÉinrí 2013: 38) and employment in the sector had declined enormously—"[falling] by 163,000 between 2007 and 2012, a contraction of over 60 per cent" (O'Connell 2017: 239).

Similar to the rest of rural Ireland, where, between 2008 and 2014, "[u]nemployment increased by double the rate of cities, at about 200%, largely as a result of the collapse of the construction sector" (O'Donoghue 2014: 19), the Gaeltacht was severely affected by this collapse. In accordance with other research on the matter (e.g., Glynn, Kelly & MacÉinrí 2013), this decline in employment opportunities in construction was often cited during interviews I conducted as a key reason for the recession having affected men more severely than women. A woman in her early 30s from the Galway Gaeltacht reflected on this trend as follows:

G: Tá chuile dhuine san Astráil, na fir óga. Abair an dream atá comhaois liomsa, a raibh mise ar an scoil leothab. Tá go leor acub imithe. Siod dream a bhí ag plé le siúinéireacht, ag obair ar shuíomhannaí tógála i nGaillimh agus rudaí den tsórt sin. Tá siad sin imithe. Tá leath de mo rang, déarfainn, san Astráil, nó i Meiriceá, nó i gCeanada nó áit eicínt. Agus tagann siad abhaile faoi Nollaig agus imíonn siad arís [...]. Ní dóigh liom go raibh éifeacht chomh mór sin ag cúrsaí ar na mrá.

[G: Everyone is in Australia, the young men. Say the people who are the same age as me, who I was at school with. Lots of them are gone. These are the people who were involved in carpentry, working on building sites in Galway city and the likes. They're gone. Half of my class, I'd say, is in Australia or America or Canada or somewhere. And they come home at Christmas and then leave again [...]. I don't think things affected the women so badly.]

Although, as Spillane (2015) describes, austerity measures often had severe consequences for women, labor market participation figures bear this informant's instincts out: on a national scale, the male unemployment rate rose from 5.2% in 2007 to 16.6% in 2012, falling to 10.4% in 2015. While female labor market participation remains lower in Ireland than that for males, it is notable that the rise in female unemployment, itself substantial, was less severe—increasing from 3.9% before the crash to 10.3% in 2013 and falling somewhat to 6.6% in 2015 (O'Connell 2017: 233).

The contraction of the industrial sector during this time also had a disproportionate effect on males, with females in Ireland more likely to work in the service or hospitality industries. Although not as extreme as that of the construction sector, the recession hit Irish manufacturing industry hard, with employment in this sector declining by 16.9% between 2007 and 2012, only recovering partially (by 4.7%) by 2015 (O'Connell 2017: 239).

The 73.7% cut to the budget of Údarás na Gaeltachta described in the previous section meant that the manufacturing sector's contraction affected the Gaeltacht particularly severely, as the agency was forced to greatly reduce grant aid to industry located therein. In 2008 the Údarás provided subsidies to 490 projects, but by 2015 this had fallen by almost three quarters, to 124. The Údarás' total expenditure on capital grants in 2008 was € 13,944,440 but fell to € 3,001,968 in 2015 (Údarás na Gaeltachta 2009b: 3, 2016: 3). As a result of this reduced aid, combined with challenging market conditions, many companies left the Gaeltacht to relocate overseas, particularly, as one Údarás employee told me, "comhlachtaí déantúsaíochta, traidisiúnta [...] comhlachtaí teicstíle, comhlachtaí leictreonacha" (traditional manufacturing companies [...] textile companies, electronics companies). Indeed, this same interviewee told me in 2016 that there were just 430 people employed on an Údarás-managed industrial estate which had provided employment for 1,300 before the crash. By November 2017 it was reported that of the 516 commercial units in the Údarás' property portfolio, 106 were empty, with 81 of these having been vacated during the previous decade (Ó Coimín 2017). Forty-five of these buildings were in Donegal, providing a further striking visible illustration of the effects of the recession on this county's Gaeltacht community.

As the following section will describe, the widespread unemployment caused by the economic crisis led to a steep increase in out-migration from rural areas such as the Gaeltacht, with notable consequences for linguistic and community vitality therein.

5.2 Emigration

With underdevelopment and poverty being a fundamental part of life in rural Ireland for the majority of the 20th century, emigration became firmly entrenched in the social consciousness of many Gaeltacht residents. Such was the extent of impoverishment in the Gaeltacht in the 1950s (when the economy of most of the developed western world was booming), that Ó hÉallaithe (2004: 174) has estimated that "two out of every three native Irish speakers" emigrated during this decade alone, typically heading to America or England. Although the Celtic Tiger period had seen such a transformation of the Gaeltacht's economic fortunes that many former emigrants were able to return (often, however, bringing monoglot English-speaking spouses or children with them), old patterns of out-migration were quickly re-established after 2008. As migration scholars have noted, previous emigration is typically a key factor driving current emigration (Brody 1974: 7). With patterns of "chain migration" so well established in Gaeltacht life, the return of this practice post-2008 was all but inevitable.

As described in the previous section, those made redundant by the collapse of key economic sectors such as construction were amongst the most likely to emigrate. While female emigration has historically been very common in Ireland, by 2009 the male rate of emigration was double that of females, reflecting the higher male unemployment rates resulting from the contraction of the construction and industrial sectors. Although the gender discrepancy amongst emigrants evened out on a national scale over the coming years, in areas with much higher than average numbers employed in agriculture (such as the Gaeltacht), a 2013 study found that the ratio of males to females was still very high, at 64:36 (Glynn, Kelly & MacÉinrí 2013: 32–33).

Although language shift can undoubtedly be driven by men in situations where the nature of the job market makes their integration into networks outside the local community more likely (Spolsky 2009: 6, 23; Holmes 2013: 61), in the Gaeltacht males are more often employed in domains which preserve Irish. This, combined with the linguistic conservatism males often display (Gal 1979: 167; Labov 2001: 292), and which can make them more likely to maintain minoritized languages, means that the higher rate of male emigration had obvious implications for the vitality of Irish in Gaeltacht communities. Indeed, several of my informants who were apparently unaware of sociolinguistic principles commented on the greater propensity of males to speak Irish. "'Siad na leaids sin is mó a labhródh Gaeilge" (It's those lads who'd speak Irish the most) as one young man, then a student in university, told me in reference to those from his home village in Galway who had not pursued education beyond secondary level (see, however, Eckert & McConnell-Ginet 2003: 283–288 for discussion of gendered aspects of language maintenance in various other contexts).

Interviewees frequently told me that they had close friends or family members who had emigrated after the crash, and often commented on the void in their communities that this population loss created. As one informant in Donegal stated:

> L: [N]uair a imíonn daoine tá tú ag sú nó ag tarraingt anam amach as pobal [...] pobal a raibh creidim láidir [...] nuair a bhí obair agus fostaíocht agus achan rud ag dul ar aghaidh [...]. Achan duine a imíonn bheireann siad píosa den phobal leotha [...]. Achan duine a fhágann is buille marfach don phobal atá ann, sílim. Agus an rud atá ann, tá tú ag cur le bánú na tuaithe [...]. An méid tithe [atá folamh], chan amháin tithe ach áiteacha a raibh fostaíocht iontu san am a chuaigh thart. Má tá tú ag tomaint thart agus má fheiceann tú na háiteacha atá fágtha fuar, fann, folamh a raibh beocht agus solas [...] ann am amháin, déarfá leat féin nach mór an trua [...] ach mór an náire é fosta
>
> [L: [W]hen people leave you're sucking the soul out of the community, a community that was I believe strong [...] when employment and things were going well [...]. Everyone who leaves takes a bit of the community with them [...]. Every person who leaves is a fatal blow to the community, I think. And it's all adding to the depopulating of the countryside [...]. The amount of houses [empty], not just houses, but places that employed people. If you drive around and if you see the amount of places left forlorn and empty where there had been life and light [...] you say to yourself isn't it an awful pity [...] but also an awful disgrace.]

In Galway I heard similar narratives, with the more remote parts of that county's Gaeltacht having been hit particularly hard by emigration:

> A: Tá ráta an-ard imirce agus 'sé is faide a théann tú siar 'sé is airde atá an ráta imirce [...]. Tá an áit bánaithe ar fad. Is beag duine óg atá fágtha [...]. Aon duine singil, óg tá siad bailithe as an áit.
>
> [A: There's a very high rate of emigration, and the further west you go the higher it gets [...]. The place is totally abandoned. There are very few young people left there [...]. Anyone single, young, they've left.]

As Ó Giollagáin, Mac Donnacha, Ní Chualáin, Ní Shéaghdha & O'Brien (2007) have shown, those areas furthest west mentioned in this quote are also those that are most strongly Irish speaking.

While the recession was obviously an intensifying factor, it is not the case that all of those who emigrated were doing so purely due to financial necessity. As one of my informants noted, "[s]in sórt 50% economic. Tá daoine ag iarraidh bogadh thart anyway" ([i]t's probably 50% economic. People want to move around anyway.) Although population movement from rural to urban areas is not a new phenomenon, and indeed is a key feature of our globalized world, emigration rates did notably increase as a consequence of the recession. All of the fifty-two key informants I interviewed confirmed findings of other research (e.g., Glynn, Kelly & MacÉinrí 2013: 38) that the search for employment was a key factor in prompting people to leave their communities.

While the overall population of the Gaeltacht between the 2011 and 2016 censuses declined only slightly, from 96,628 to 96,090 (CSO 2017a: 69), this small 0.6% reduction conceals considerable regional variation. Peri-urban Gaeltacht areas on the outskirts of Galway city saw their populations increase somewhat during this time, while more peripheral parts of the Gaeltacht experienced significant population loss (Pobal.ie 2017). Toraigh and Árainn Mhór, Gaeltacht islands in Donegal, for instance, lost 17.4% and 8.8% of their population respectively during this time, while Leitir Mealláin and Inis Mór in Galway also saw significant reductions, 15.4% and 9.8% respectively (CSO 2017b).

Further to the differential rates of male and female emigration, those who moved abroad were heavily clustered in the 20–34 age bracket. On a national scale, Glynn, Kelly & MacÉinrí (2013: 34) have shown that over 70% of emigrants were in their twenties. This pattern would seem to also pertain to the Gaeltacht, with this cohort being very noticeably absent at community events I attended during my fieldwork. A diachronic view of census data would appear to corroborate this observation: in the Galway Gaeltacht there were 10,972 in the 20–34 age group in 2006, which had fallen to 10,724 in 2011 and 9,339 in 2016 (-15% in the span of a decade) (CSO 2012a, 2017c). In Donegal this same cohort decreased in number from 3,805 in 2006 to 3,672 in 2011 and then further to 2,833 in 2016 (-25.5% in total) (CSO 2012b, 2017d). With the 20–34 age group being that most likely to form families and bear children, this decline is of obvious concern for intergenerational transmission of Irish in Gaeltacht communities. As one interviewee bluntly observed: "[m]airfidh sé sin an teanga, muna bhfuil daoine óga, cainteoirí dúchais, ag fanacht sa bhaile, sin deireadh" (that'll kill the language, if young people, native speakers aren't staying at home, that's the end).

5.3 Further implications of the Great Recession for the vitality of the Irish language

As stated in section one, even before the economic turmoil that began in 2008, the Irish language was under immense pressure in even the strongest Gaeltacht communities. The *Comprehensive Linguistic Survey of the Use of Irish in the Gaeltacht*, published the year before the crash, predicted that Irish was unlikely to remain the dominant community language anywhere for more than another 15–20 years (Ó Giollagáin, Mac Donnacha, Ní Chualáin, Ní Shéaghdha & O'Brien 2007: 431). Significantly, however, an update to this report published in 2015 observed that language shift was occurring at a faster rate than predicted, stating that "based on the findings presented here, [the 2007 survey] presented an overly optimistic conclusion regarding the sustainability of Irish as a community and family language" (Ó Giollagáin & Charlton 2015: 2, my translation), although this bleak picture was challenged by some non-academic commentators at the time (e.g., Mac an Iomaire 2015).

The results of the 2016 census confirmed the findings of these reports, however, illustrating the extent to which language shift had taken place since the previous census in 2011. In 2011, the total population of the Gaeltacht was 96,238, although only 66,238 of these claimed the ability to speak Irish, with the number of those speaking Irish daily outside the education system (the study of Irish at school is compulsory throughout the Republic) being lower again, at 23,175 (CSO 2012c: CD964, CD965). By 2016 the number of daily speakers outside of the education system in the Gaeltacht had fallen by 2,589 to 20,586, an alarmingly sharp drop of 11.2% since 2011 (CSO 2017e: EA055). Although the previous census in 2011 was conducted at the height of the country's economic difficulties, the lagged effect of macro-level events such as the Great Recession meant that the full scale of the recession's demographic and linguistic impacts were not fully visible in the 2011 figures, which included in-migration and growth patterns more correctly associated with the tail-end of the Celtic Tiger. Furthermore, many of the severest cuts to Irish-language funding occurred after 2011. The effects of this turmoil can be inferred by contrasting the 11.2% reduction during the intercensal period of 2011–16 with the 1.4% *increase* in the same category between the 2006 and 2011 censuses.

In light of the various sociological consequences of the economic crisis described above (as well as many others which are beyond the scope of a chapter of this length), such a higher than predicted rate of language shift would seem inevitable. While the deaths of older people known to be more likely to speak Irish was set to see numbers fall regardless of the economic crash (as noted in the reports cited above—i.e., Ó Giollagáin, Mac Donnacha, Ní Chualáin, Ní Shéaghdha & O'Brien 2007; Ó Giollagáin & Charlton 2015), the steep decline seen in the 2016 census was greater than could be accounted for by this factor alone. As Spolsky (2009: 3) reminds us, "language management in the family is partly under the control of family members, but its goals are regularly influenced by the outside community," and this was clearly the case for Gaeltacht families as a result of the recession. Further to emigration seeing the loss of a huge number of prospective parents in the 20–34 age category, many of those parents already raising children in the Gaeltacht were forced to work increased hours or take up work which involved long commutes or periods staying outside the Gaeltacht. Such changes in family life amounted to a further disruption of a domain key to Irish-language transmission, reducing the amount of parent-child interaction which is so fundamental for the reproduction of a minoritized language, with children and teenagers thus being all the more likely to shift to English.

The increased use of technology in recent years was also something that a great many of my informants mentioned in terms of explaining ongoing language shift in their communities. While this increase was sure to have occurred regardless of the economic crash, it is of note that, as many other studies have shown (e.g., Warren 2005; Rideout & Hamel 2006; Piotrowski, Jordan, Bleakley & Hennessy 2015: 169; Domoff, Miller, Khalatbari, Pesch, Harrison, Rosenblum & Lumeng

2017: 279), overworked parents and those in lower income households are much more likely to use television and computers as "surrogate child minders." As a great many of my interviewees told me, such technologies are a significant driver of children's shift towards English. One 18-year old who I interviewed explained this to me as follows:

> G: [T]á teilifís i mBéarla, tá idirlíon i mBéarla, má tá tú ag iarraidh goil ar Facebook, tá na posts ar fad i mBéarla. [...] Bhí mé ar an X-bosca agus ag labhairt i mBéarla le chuile dhuine air sin. So bhí, chaill mise an Ghaeilge níos luaithe ná [a dheirfiúracha atá níos sine]. Chaill mise é nuair a bhí mé timpeall 13—stop mise á labhairt den chuid is mó. Tháinig an teicneolaíocht isteach i mo shaol...
>
> [G: Television is in English, the internet is in English, if you want to go on Facebook the posts are all in English. [...] I was on the X-box talking in English with everyone on that. So I lost Irish earlier [than his older sisters]. I lost it when I was about 13, I stopped speaking it mostly. Technology came into my life...]

Another parent recounted hearing his five-year old daughter speak English for the first time during a holiday abroad:

> P: "Cá háit a d'fhoghlaim tú do chuid Béarla? Ní raibh 's agamsa go bhfuil Béarla mar sin agat!" "Á a dheaide, tá scoil bheag Béarla agamsa mé féin thíos i mo sheomra leapan ag coimhead Netflix".
>
> [P: "Where did you learn your English? I didn't know you could speak English like that!" "Ah daddy, I have a little English language school myself down in my bedroom watching Netflix."]

Furthermore, even when personally committed to the maintenance of Irish, parents faced with the "cognitive load" of struggling to pay bills, mortgages and so on (as a huge number of the Irish population were during the crash) have more pressing concerns than ensuring their children are getting sufficient Irish-language input. Addressing this point, one interviewee quipped that "[r]oimh an bpleanáil teanga caithfidh díon a bheith os do chionn agus caithfidh jab a bheith agat!" ([b]efore language planning you have to have a job and a roof over your head!) (see also Spolsky 2009: 21). Inglehart's conceptions of "materialist" and "post-materialist" values are brought to mind—as is the widespread move away from supporting post-materialist causes that has occurred due to the decline of welfare state provisions under neoliberalism (Inglehart 2018). As the majority of Irish speakers in the Gaeltacht are not employed in the language sector, Irish thus likely falls into the category of "post-materialist" issue for such individuals, as the previous quote suggests.

With small and medium enterprises in rural areas being severely affected by the crisis (CEDRA 2014: 45), informants often lamented the closure of such (typically locally owned) businesses in their communities. The loss of these, I was told, saw the contraction of another important domain in which Irish had previously been maintained:

B: [N]uair a dúnadh na hóstáin agus an t-infreastruchtúr sin uilig, ar chuir sé sin isteach ar an...
É: Teanga?
B: Sea.
É: Chuir. Because sin na daoine uilig ag obair san áit, cuid iníonacha s'acu, cuid mac s'acu, bhí siad ag fáil jabannaí samhraidh ann. D'obair mé féin cúig bliana i gceann de [na hóstáin a dúnadh le gairid], ní raibh an nduine le Béarla. Sin go háirithe infreastruchtúr a bhí millteanach dúchasach ó thaobh teanga dó agus tábhachtach.

[B: When the hotels and all that infrastructure closed, did it affect the...
D: Language?
B: Yeah.
D: It did. Because the people working in those places, their daughters, their sons, they were getting summer jobs there. I worked for five years in [one of these recently closed local establishments], there was no English there. That in particular was infrastructure that was extremely traditional and important in terms of language.]

The loss of such "safe harbor" domains where the use of Irish was strong, in addition to the decline of the construction and industrial sectors and the emigration this prompted, thus contributed to the weakening of the all-important "home-family-neighborhood-community" nexus (Fishman 1991: 95) in which Irish survives. When added to the flawed or non-implementation of official language policies and the severe cuts language management institutions and schemes received, it is of little surprise that the vitality of the language declined so significantly in the wake of the 2008 crash.

6 Conclusion

The Irish state's response to the 2008 financial crash and the "Great Recession" which followed it, as has been argued by many commentators (e.g., Mercille & Murphy 2015; Allen & O'Boyle 2013; Coulter & Nagle 2015), ultimately aimed to defend the interests of international investors and the financial sector. It involved the intensification of neoliberal policies of rationalization, privatization and a drastic reduction in state expenditure on social policy. This macro-level policy trajectory had significant consequences for much of Irish society, including, as has been shown, those areas where Irish remains a vernacular.

With the state's response to the crisis being driven by a neoliberal paradigm which sees no place for significant state intervention in spheres such as language revitalization, a wide range of language management measures were severely weakened post-2008, thus placing the vitality of Irish in an even more precarious position than it had been before the crash. Although the *Comprehensive Linguistic Survey of the Use of Irish in the Gaeltacht* (Ó Giollagáin, Mac Donnacha, Ní Chualáin, Ní Shéaghdha & O'Brien 2007) demonstrated in 2007 the need for significant additional interventions for Irish-speaking communities, the Great Recession which began the following year saw the discontinuation of many of those schemes which had supported the Gaeltacht before the crash. Compounding this difficulty, the unemployment crisis in the post-2008 period and resultant widespread out-migration of young adults aged 20–34, the cohort who are most likely to have families and thus raise a new generation of Irish speakers, provided a significant blow to the future intergenerational transmission of Irish in its heartlands. Despite the Irish economy having returned to rapid growth by 2016, reinvestment in the Gaeltacht is not taking place in a way anywhere near commensurate with the cutbacks recently implemented, highlighting the way in which the economic crisis was used as an opportunity to fundamentally reform state language policy through neoliberalization (cf. Klein 2007; Mirowski 2013; Krugman 2015).

Eminent Irish sociolinguist Pádraig Ó Riagáin has observed that large-scale language revitalization efforts for endangered languages like Irish will cost more than liberal democratic states have thus far been willing to commit (Ó Riagáin 1997: 283), a point with profound resonance in an era when so many of the world's languages are faced with near-term extinction. The intensification of neoliberal policies since 2008 and the reduction in state support that accompanies this therefore has significant implications for those involved in minority language planning and policy. The structural power and embedded nature of capitalist class interests in a globalized neoliberal economy provide a major challenge for revitalization-focused language management regimes, as efforts to counteract language shift are ultimately destined to collide with the power of these interests in the way that Irish-language revitalization attempts have done since 2008.

As has been demonstrated, the power of elites to defend their interests means that culturalist endeavors such as the revitalization of languages seen to lack significant market value in the neoliberal economy are left in a deeply precarious position. In light of this tendency, practical examples of which have been given in this chapter, it is unsurprising that the vitality of the Irish language in its core communities went from bad in 2008, to much worse a decade later.

References

Allen, K. & O'Boyle, B. (2013) *Austerity Ireland: The Failure of Irish Capitalism.* London: Pluto Press.

Austin, P. K. & Sallabank, J. (2011) Introduction. In P. K. Austin & J. Sallabank (eds) *The Cambridge Handbook of Endangered Languages.* Cambridge: Cambridge University Press, 1–24.

Bachrach, P. & Baratz, M. (1963) Decisions and nondecisions: An analytical framework. *The American Political Science Review* 57 (3), 632–642.

Baker, C. (2011) *Foundations of Bilingual Education and Bilingualism.* 5th edition. Clevedon: Multilingual Matters.

Bisset, J. (2015) Defiance and hope: Austerity and the community sector in the Republic of Ireland. In C. Coulter & A. Nagle (eds) *Ireland Under*

Austerity: Neoliberal Crisis, Neoliberal Solutions. Manchester: Manchester University Press, 171–191.

Blyth, M. (2013) *Austerity: The History of a Dangerous Idea.* Oxford: Oxford University Press.

Brody, H. (1974) *Inishkillane: Change and Decline in the West of Ireland.* Harmondsworth: Penguin.

Byrne, S. (2018) *An Plean Forbartha Náisiúnta agus an Ghaeltacht 2018–2027* [The National Development Plan and the Gaeltacht]. On WWW at https://teachtaniar.eu/proxy/pdf/anaili-s-ar-chaiteachas-an-rialtais-ar-an-ngaeltacht-agus-an-ghaeilge-leagan-deif-22052018-g/. Accessed June 23, 2018.

Cairney, P. (2012) *Understanding Public Policy.* Basingstoke: Palgrave Macmillan.

CEDRA (2014) *Energising Ireland's Rural Economy: Report of the Commission for the Economic Development of Rural Areas.* On WWW at https://www.teagasc.ie/media/website/rural-economy/CEDRA_Report.pdf. Accessed June 23, 2018.

Conradh na Gaeilge (2012) *Full Support for Opposition Dáil Walkout Over Gaeltacht Bill.* On WWW at https://cnag.ie/en/news/138-full-support-for-opposition-d%C3%A1il-walkout-over-gaeltacht-bill.html. Accessed June 19, 2018.

Coulter, C. & Nagle, A. (eds) (2015) *Ireland Under Austerity: Neoliberal Crisis, Neoliberal Solutions.* Manchester: Manchester University Press.

Crenson, M. (1971) *The Un-Politics of Air Pollution: A Study of Non-decision Making in the Cities.* London: Johns Hopkins Press.

Crouch, C. (2011) *The Strange Non-death of Neoliberalism.* Cambridge: Polity Press.

Crystal, D. (2014) *Language Death.* Cambridge: Cambridge University Press.

CSO (2012a) *Gaeltacht Area Galway.* On WWW at http://census.cso.ie/sapmap2011/Results.aspx?Geog_Type=GA&Geog_Code=03. Accessed February 19, 2019.

CSO (2012b) *Gaeltacht Area Donegal.* On WWW at http://census.cso.ie/sapmap2011/Results.aspx?Geog_Type=GA&Geog_Code=02. Accessed February 19, 2019.

CSO (2012c) *Statistical Product – Profile – What We Know – A Study of Education and Skill in Ireland: Tables CD964, CD965, CD959 & CD960.* On WWW at http://www.cso.ie/px/pxeirestat/Database/eirestat/Profile%209%20What%20we%20Know%20-%20A%20study%20of%20Education%20and%20Skills%20in%20Ireland/Profile%209%20What%20we%20Know%20-%20A%20study%20of%20Education%20and%20Skills%20in%20Ireland_statbank.asp?SP=Profile%209%20What%20we%20Know%20-%20A%20study%20of%20Education%20and%20Skills%20in%20Ireland&Planguage=0. Accessed February 19, 2019.

CSO (2017a) *Census 2016 Summary Results – Part 1.* On WWW at http://www.cso.ie/en/media/csoie/newsevents/documents/census2016summaryresultspart1/Census2016SummaryPart1.pdf. Accessed February 19, 2019.

CSO (2017b) Census of Population 2016, E2021 Population of Islands off the Coast 2011 to 2016 by Islands, Census Year and Sex. On WWW at http://www.cso.ie/px/pxeirestat/Statire/SelectVarVal/Define.asp?maintable=E2021&PLanguage=0. Accessed February 19, 2019.

CSO (2017c) Census 2016 Sapmap Area: Gaeltacht Ghaeltacht Na Gaillimhe [sic]. On WWW at http://census.cso.ie/sapmap2016/Results.aspx?Geog_Type=GAEL&Geog_Code=372FEC7C-DB30-4853-B7D4-BA6C2DCAF0F2. Accessed February 19, 2019.

CSO (2017d) Census 2016 Sapmap Area: Gaeltacht Ghaeltacht Dhún Na Ngall [sic]. On WWW at http://census.cso.ie/sapmap2016/Results.aspx?Geog_Type=GAEL&Geog_Code=865CD4F3-B2D8-4405-841E-0AB4CEA25B7B. Accessed February 19, 2019.

CSO (2017e) Statistical Product – Profile 10 – Education and Skills and the Irish Language: Table EA055. On WWW at http://www.cso.ie/px/pxeirestat/Database/eirestat/Profile%2010%20-%20Education%20and%20Skills%20and%20the%20Irish%20Language/Profile%2010%20-%20Education%20and%20Skills%20and%20the%20Irish%20Language_statbank.asp?SP=Profile%2010%20-%20Education%20and%20Skills%20and%20the%20Irish%20Language&Planguage=0. Accessed February 19, 2019.

Domoff, S. E., Miller, A. L., Khalatbari, N., Pesch, M. H., Harrison, K., Rosenblum, K. & Lumeng, J. C. (2017) Maternal beliefs about television and parental mediation in a low-income United States sample. *Journal of Children and Media* 11 (3), 278–294. doi: 10.1080/17482798.2017.1339102.

Eckert, P. & McConnell-Ginet, S. (2003) *Language and Gender.* Cambridge: Cambridge University Press.

Edwards, J. (1984) Language diversity and identity. In J. Edwards (ed) *Linguistic Minorities, Policies, and Pluralism.* London: Academic Press, 277–310.

Enterprise Ireland (2009) Annual Report & Accounts 2008. On WWW at https://www.enterprise-ireland.com/en/Publications/Reports-Published-Strategies/Annual-Reports/2008-Annual-report-eng.pdf. Accessed September 20, 2018.

Enterprise Ireland (2016) Annual Report & Accounts 2015. On WWW at https://www.enterprise-ireland.com/en/Publications/Reports-Published-Strategies/Annual-Reports/2015-Annual-Report-and-Accounts-English.pdf. Accessed September 20, 2018.

Fishman, J. (1991) *Reversing Language Shift.* Clevedon: Multilingual Matters.

Friedman, M. [1962] (2002) *Capitalism and Freedom.* Chicago: Chicago University Press.

Gal, S. (1979) *Language Shift: Social Determinants of Linguistic Change in Bilingual Austria.* New York: Academic Press.

Gamble, A. (2009) *The Spectre at the Feast.* Basingstoke: Palgrave Macmillan.

Garcia-Bernardo, J., Fichtner, J., Takes, F. W. & Heemskerk, E. M. (2017) Uncovering offshore financial centers: Conduits and sinks in the Global Corporate Ownership Network. *Scientific Reports* 7 (1) 6246, 1–10. doi: 10.1038/s41598-017-06322-9.

Garvin, T. (1987) *Nationalist Revolutionaries of Ireland 1858–1928*. Oxford: Oxford University Press.

Glynn, I., Kelly, T. & MacÉinrí, P. (2013) *Irish Emigration in an Age of Austerity*. On WWW at https://www.ucc.ie/en/media/research/emigre/Emigration_in_an_Age_of_Austerity_Final.pdf. Accessed May 1, 2018.

Government of Ireland (2010) *20-Year Strategy for the Irish Language 2010–2030*. Dublin: Stationery Office.

Government of Ireland (2012) Gaeltacht Act 2012 and Explanatory and Financial Memorandum. On WWW at https://data.oireachtas.ie/ie/oireachtas/bill/2012/53/eng/initiated/b5312s.pdf. Accessed May 11, 2018.

Government of Ireland (2018) Project Ireland 2040: National Development Plan 2018–2027. On WWW at http://www.per.gov.ie/wp-content/uploads/NDP-strategy-2018-2027_WEB.pdf. Accessed May 24, 2018.

Grenoble, L. & Whaley, L. (1998) Toward a typology of language endangerment. In L. Grenoble & L. Whaley (eds) *Endangered Languages: Language Loss and Community Response*. Cambridge: Cambridge University Press, 22–54.

Grin, F. (1999) Market forces, language spread and linguistic diversity. In M. Kontra, R. Phillipson, T. Skutnabb-Kangas & T. Varády (eds) *Language: A Right and a Resource*. Budapest: Central European University Press, 169–186.

Guth na Gaeltachta (2010) Open letter to An Taoiseach and An Tánaiste about the future of the Gaeltacht. On WWW at http://guthnag.com/summary.html. Accessed August 12, 2017.

Hardiman, N. & Regan, A. (2012) The politics of austerity in Ireland. *Intereconomics* 48 (1), 9–13.

Harvey, D. (2005) *A Brief History of Neoliberalism*. Oxford: Oxford University Press.

Harvey, D. (2007) Neoliberalism as creative destruction. *Annals of the American Academy of Political and Social Science* 610, 22–44. doi: 10.1177/0002716206296780.

Hayek, F. [1944] (2001) *The Road to Serfdom*. London: Routledge.

Herbert, W. (2011) Endangered languages and economic development. In P. K. Austin & J. Sallabank (eds) *The Cambridge Handbook of Endangered Languages*. Cambridge: Cambridge University Press, 403–422.

Hindley, R. (1990) *The Death of the Irish Language: A Qualified Obituary*. New York: Routledge.

Holmes, J. (2013) *An Introduction to Sociolinguistics*. New York: Routledge.

IDA (2010) Annual Report & Accounts 2009. On WWW at https://www.idaireland.com/IDAIreland/media/docs/About-IDA/IDA-AR09-24-June(lr).pdf. Accessed September 20, 2018.

IDA (2016) Annual Report & Accounts 2015. On WWW at https://www.idaireland.com/IDAIreland/media/docs/About-IDA/annual_report_2015.pdf. Accessed September 20, 2018.

IMF (2013) Ireland: Ninth Review under the Extended Arrangement, IMF Country Report No. 13/93. On WWW at https://www.imf.org/external/pubs/ft/scr/2013/cr1393.pdf. Accessed June 6, 2018.

Inglehart, R. (2018) The silent revolution in reverse: The rise of Trump and the authoritarian populist parties. In R. Inglehart (ed) *Cultural Evolution: People's Motivations are Changing, and Reshaping the World.* Cambridge: Cambridge University Press, 73–199.

Kamwangamalu, N. M. (2003) Social change and language shift: South Africa. *Annual Review of Applied Linguistics* 23, 225–242. doi: https://doi.org/10.1017/S0267190503000291.

Kaplan, R. B. & Baldauf, R. B. (1997) *Language Planning: From Practice to Theory.* Clevedon: Multilingual Matters.

Kirby, P. (2010) *Celtic Tiger in Collapse: Explaining the Weaknesses of the Irish Model.* 2nd edition. Basingstoke: Palgrave Macmillan.

Klein, N. (2007) *The Shock Doctrine: The Rise of Disaster Capitalism.* London: Allen Lane.

Krugman, P. (2015) *The Austerity Delusion.* On WWW at http://www.theguardian.com/business/ng-interactive/2015/apr/29/the-austerity-delusion. Accessed July 4, 2018.

Labov, W. (2001) *Principles of Linguistic Change: Social Factors.* Vol. 2. Oxford: Blackwell.

Leonard, J. L. (2015) *Revitalisation et documentation des langues en danger* [Revitalization and Documentation of Languages in Danger]. Paris: Michel Houdiard.

Lukes, S. (1974) *Power: A Radical View.* London: Macmillan.

Mac an Iomaire, R. (2015) *Irish and the Gaeltacht – They Haven't Gone away, you know.* On WWW at https://www.independent.ie/opinion/comment/irish-and-the-gaeltacht-they-havent-gone-away-you-know-31572643.html. Accessed August 19, 2018.

McCabe, C. (2011) *Sins of the Father: The Decisions That Shaped the Irish Economy.* 2nd edition. Dublin: The History Press Ireland.

McColl Millar, R. (2005) *Language, Nation and Power: An Introduction.* Basingstoke: Palgrave Macmillan.

Mercille, J. & Murphy, E. (2015) *Deepening Neoliberalism, Austerity and Crisis: Europe's Treasure Ireland.* Basingstoke: Palgrave Macmillan.

Mirowski, P. (2013) *Never Let a Serious Crisis Go to Waste: How Neoliberalism Survived the Financial Meltdown.* London: Verso.

Murphy, M. (2014) Ireland: Celtic tiger in austerity – Explaining Irish path dependency. *Journal of Contemporary European Studies* 22 (2), 132–142. doi: 10.1080/14782804.2014.902367.

Nelde, P., Strubell, M. & Williams, G. (1996) *The Production and Reproduction of the Minority Language Groups in the European Union.* Luxembourg: Euromosaic Office for Official Publications of the European Communities.

Nettle, D. & Romaine, S. (2000) *Vanishing Voices: The Extinction of the Worlds Languages.* Oxford: Oxford University Press.

Ó Broithe, É. (2012) Scéim Labhairt na Gaeilge: Feidhm agus Mífheidhm [The Irish speaking scheme: Use and misuse]. In C. Lenoach, C. Ó Giollagáin; B. Ó Curnáin (eds) *An Chonair Chaoch: An Mionteangachas sa Dátheangachas* [The Blind Alley: The Minority Language Condition in Bilingualism]. Indreabhán: Leabhar Breac, 237–268.

Ó Cinnéide, M., Mac Donncha, S. & Ní Chonghaile, S. (2001) *Polasaithe agus Cleachtais Eagraíochtaí Éagsúla le Feidhm sa Ghaeltacht: Tuarascáil Chríochnaitheach* [Policies and Practices of Various Organizations Operating in the Gaeltacht: Final Report]. Galway: An tIonad Taighde sna hEolaíochtaí Sóisialta, Ollscoil na hÉireann, Gaillimh.

Ó Ciosáin, N. (2013) The print cultures of the Celtic languages, 1700–1900. *Cultural and Social History* 3 (10), 347–367. doi: 10.2752/147800413X13661166397184.

Ó Coimín, M. (2017) *Cé mhéad foirgneamh folamh atá ag Údarás na Gaeltachta, cá bhfuil siad agus cén fhad atá siad le ligean?* [How Many Empty Buildings does Údarás na Gaeltachta Have, where are they and how Long Have they been Available to Let?]. On WWW at https://tuairisc.ie/ce-mhead-foirgneamh-folamh-ata-ag-udaras-na-gaeltachta-ca-bhfuil-siad-agus-cen-fhad-ata-siad-le-ligean/. Accessed April 4, 2018.

Ó Gairbhí, S. T. (2016) *An caidreamh idir foireann agus bainistíocht an Údaráis 'at an all-time low'* [Relationship between Staff and Management of the Údarás 'at all-time low']. On WWW at http://tuairisc.ie/an-caidreamh-idir-foireann-agus-bainistiocht-an-udarais-at-an-all-time-low/. Accessed July 14, 2018.

Ó Giollagáin, C. (2014) From revivalist to undertaker: New developments in official policies and attitudes to Ireland's 'first language.' *Language Problems & Language Planning* 38 (2), 101–127. doi: 10.1075/lplp.38.2.01gio.

Ó Giollagáin, C. & Charlton, M. (2015) *Nuashonrú ar an Staidéar Cuimsitheach Teangeolaíoch ar Úsáid na Gaeilge sa Ghaeltacht* [Update on the Comprehensive Linguistic Study of the Use of Irish in the Gaeltacht]. On WWW at http://www.udaras.ie/media/pdf/002910_Udaras_Nuashonr%C3%BA_FULL_report_A4_FA.pdf. Accessed September 21, 2018.

Ó Giollagáin, C., Mac Donnacha, S., Ní Chualáin, F., Ní Shéaghdha, A. & O'Brien, M. (2007) *Staidéar Cuimsitheach Teangeolaíoch ar Úsáid na Gaeilge sa Ghaeltacht* [Comprehensive Linguistic Study of the Use of Irish in the Gaeltacht]. Dublin: Stationery Office.

Ó hÉallaithe, D. (2004) From language revival to language survival. In C. Mac Murchaidh (ed) *Who Needs Irish?* Dublin: Veritas, 159–192.

Ó Huallacháin, C. (1991) *The Irish Language in Society.* Coleraine: University of Ulster.

Ó Murchú, H. (2014) *More Facts About Irish.* Vol. 2. On WWW at http://www.gaelport.com/uploads/documents/More%20Facts%20About%20Irish%20(2014)%20-%20Helen%20%C3%93%20Murch%C3%BA.pdf. Accessed March 3, 2018.

Ó Riagáin, P. (1996) Reviving the Irish language: 1893–1993: The first one hundred years. In M. Nic Craith (ed) *Watching One's Tongue: Issues in Language Planning.* Liverpool: Liverpool University Press, 33–55.

Ó Riagáin, P. (1997) *Language Policy and Social Reproduction: Ireland 1893–1993.* Oxford: Clarendon Press.

Ó Riagáin, P. (2001) Irish language production and reproduction 1981–1996. In J. Fishman (ed) *Can Threatened Languages Be Saved?* Clevedon: Multilingual Matters, 195–214.

Ó Riagáin, P. (2018) *Measures of Language Proficiency in Censuses and Surveys: A Comparative Analysis and Assessment.* Basingstoke: Palgrave Macmillan.

O'Connell, P. (2017) Unemployment and labour market policy. In W. K. Roche, P. J. O'Connell & A. Prothero (eds) *Austerity and Recovery in Ireland: Europe's Poster Child and the Great Recession.* Oxford: Oxford University Press, 232–251.

O'Donoghue, C. (2014) Introduction. In C. Ó Donoghue, R. Conneely, D. Frost, K. Heanue, B. Leonard & D. Meredith (eds) *Rural Economic Development in Ireland.* Carlow: Teagasc, 18–33.

O'Halloran, M. (2016) *State to buy almost 2,000 hectares in Dublin Mountains.* On WWW at https://www.irishtimes.com/news/environment/state-to-buy-almost-2-000-hectares-in-dublin-mountains-1.2743804. Accessed July 10, 2018.

O'Rourke, B. & Pujolar, J. (2013) From native speakers to "new speakers" – problematizing nativeness in language revitalization contexts. *Histoire Épistémologie Langage* 35 (2), 47–67.

O'Toole, F. (2010) *Ship of Fools: How Stupidity and Corruption Sank the Celtic Tiger.* London: Faber.

Peck, J. & Tickell, A. (2002) Neoliberalizing space. *Antipode* 34, 380–404.

Phillipson, R. (2008) The linguistic imperialism of neoliberal empire. *Critical Inquiry in Language Studies* 5 (1), 1–43. doi: 10.1080/15427580701696886.

Piotrowski, J. T., Jordan, A. B., Bleakley, A., & Hennessy, M. (2015) Identifying family television practices to reduce children's television time. *Journal of Family Communication* 15 (2), 159–174. doi: 10.1080/15267431.2015.1013107.

Pobal.ie (2017) *Deprivation Indices.* On WWW at https://maps.pobal.ie/WebApps/DeprivationIndices/index.html. Accessed May 10, 2018.

Rideout, V. & Hamel, E. (2006) *The Media Family: Electronic Media in the Lives of Infants, Toddlers, Preschoolers and their Parents.* Menlo Park: The Henry J. Kaiser Family Foundation.

Romaine, S. (2006) Planning for the survival of linguistic diversity. *Language Policy* 5 (4), 443–475. doi: 10.1007/s10993-006-9034-3.

Shohamy, E. (2006) *Language Policy: Hidden Agendas and New Approaches.* New York: Routledge.

Skutnabb-Kangas, T. (2000) *Linguistic Genocide in Education — or Worldwide Diversity in Human Rights?* New York: Routledge.

Spillane, A. (2015) The impact of the crisis on Irish women. In C. Coulter & A. Nagle (eds) *Ireland Under Austerity: Neoliberal Crisis, Neoliberal Solutions.* Manchester: Manchester University Press.

Spolsky, B. (2009) *Language Management.* Cambridge: Cambridge University Press.

Tabouret-Keller, A. (1968) Sociological factors of language maintenance and language shift: A methodological approach based on European and African examples. In J. Fishman, C. Ferguson & J. Das Gupta (eds) *Language Problems of Developing Nations.* New York: John Wiley & Sons, 107–127.

Taft, M. (2018) *Austerity's Hangover.* On WWW at http://notesonthefront.typepad.com/politicaleconomy/2018/01/austeritys-hangover.html. Accessed March 5, 2018.

Tuairisc.ie (2017) *Iarracht Roinn na Gaeltachta géarchéim na pleanála teanga a réiteach á meas ag Fóram Chois Fharraige* [The Department of the Gaeltacht's Attempt to Resolve the Language Planning Crisis Being Considered by Fóram Chois Fharraige]. On WWW at https://tuairisc.ie/iarracht-roinn-na-gaeltachta-gearcheim-na-pleanala-teanga-a-reiteach-a-meas-ag-foram-chois-fharraige/. Accessed June 24, 2018.

Tuairisc.ie (2018a) *Níl feidhm ar bith le haon chuid den struchtúr a bhí in ainm is an Straitéis 20 Bliain don Ghaeilge a chur i gcrích – taighde nua* [No Part of the Structure that was Designed to Implement the 20-Year Strategy for the Irish Language is Functioning – New Research]. On WWW at https://tuairisc.ie/nil-feidhm-ar-bith-le-haon-chuid-den-struchtur-a-bhi-in-ainm-is-an-straiteis-20-bliain-don-ghaeilge-a-chur-i-gcrich-taighde-nua/. Accessed June 23, 2018.

Tuairisc.ie (2018b) *Gan aon chinneadh fós faoi cathain a thabharfar maoiniú breise d'Údarás na Gaeltachta* [No Decision yet as to when Additional Funding will be Given to Údarás na Gaeltachta]. On WWW at https://tuairisc.ie/gan-aon-chinneadh-fos-faoi-cathain-a-thabharfar-maoiniu-breise-project-ireland-2040-dudaras-na-gaeltachta/. Accessed June 23, 2018.

Údarás na Gaeltachta (2009a) *Tuarascáil Bhliantúil agus Cuntais 2008/Annual Report and Accounts 2008.* On WWW at http://www.udaras.ie/wp-content/uploads/2012/06/2009-Annual-Report-and-Accounts.pdf. Accessed March 4, 2018.

Údarás na Gaeltachta (2009b) *TÁBLAÍ 2008 Aguisín don Tuarascáil Bhliantúil/TABLES 2008 Appendix to the Annual Report.* On WWW at http://www.udaras.ie/wp-content/uploads/2012/06/2008-Annual-Report-Tables.pdf. Accessed March 4, 2018.

Údarás na Gaeltachta (2016) *Táblaí 2015 Aguisín don Tuarascáil Bhliantúil/Tables 2015 Appendix to the Annual Report.* On WWW at http://www.udaras.ie/wp-content/uploads/2016/12/Tuarascail-Bhliantuil-Tablai-2015-D.pdf. Accessed March 5, 2018.

UNESCO et al. (2003) *Sharing a World of Difference.* On WWW at http://unesdoc.unesco.org/images/0013/001323/132384e.pdf. Accessed June 2, 2018.

UNESCO (2018) *UNESCO Interactive Atlas of the World's Languages in Danger: Irish.* On WWW at http://www.unesco.org/languages-atlas/index.php. Accessed September 17, 2021.

Varoufakis, Y. (2016) *And the Weak Suffer What They Must? Europe, Austerity and the Threat to Global Stability.* London: Bodley Head.

Walsh, J. (2014) An ceart ag an gCoimisinéir [The commissioner is correct]. *Comhar* 74 (1), 10–11.

Warren, R. (2005) Parental mediation of children's television viewing in low-income families. *Journal of Communication* 55 (4), 847–863. doi: https://doi.org/10.1111/j.1460-2466.2005.tb03026.x.

Williams, C. (1991) *Linguistic Minorities, Society and Territory.* Clevedon: Multilingual Matters.

Nadiya Kiss

Key actors in the organized language management of Ukraine: On the materials of language legislation development and adoption[1]

Abstract The chapter highlights language management in contemporary Ukraine from the Euromaidan period (2013–2014), during Petro Poroshenko's presidency (2014–2019) up to recent developments under the president elected in 2019, Volodymyr Zelenskyi. Based on an actor-centered approach, this study provides a detailed analysis of language legislation developments and adoption processes in different phases. The chapter examines the interests of different social groups and the power relations between various social and political actors. Through the content of law texts, media discussions, political rhetoric and expert interviews, the research gives an overview of language policy changes and competing interpretations of the language situation by various social actors. The study also pays attention to describing conflicts that occur between the actors in the process of decision-making.

Keywords language management in Ukraine, actor-centered approach, language laws, language policies

1 Introduction

In contemporary Ukraine, language management is in the process of a vivid development. Since Ukrainian independence in 1991, language policy strategies have changed many times according to the general policies of Ukrainian presidents and leading political parties. The history of language policy dynamics is described in detail in Besters-Dilger et al. (2009), Moser (2014), Bilaniuk (2017) and in Azhniuk (2017). Moreover, Ukrainian language policy has been considered from different perspectives in numerous studies—from the historical and sociocultural (Masenko 2008), to ideology battles (Kulyk 2010), language and speaker rights (Pavlenko 2011), as well as multilingualism (Pavlenko 2013).

1 This chapter is a part of a larger post-doc project "Language Policies in Contemporary Ukraine, Georgia and Moldova" which I am currently advancing in the frame of the LOEWE research group "Conflicts in the Eastern Europe" at the Justus Liebig Giessen University, Germany. Therefore, in this chapter I will try to develop a research model of actors in language management that I could further apply in a comparative analysis of contemporary Georgian and Moldovan language policies.

On the other hand, the very term "language management" is seldom mentioned in Ukrainian sociolinguistics (language policy and language planning are still the most frequently used terms), which creates a research gap for the presented subject. The exception is Spolsky's work where he described early Soviet language policy strategies (Spolsky 2011: 184) and highlighted the preservation of the Ukrainian language in Ukrainian diaspora communities in the USA (Spolsky 2011: 197). Hence, in a detailed overview of language management in post-Soviet countries, Hogan-Brun & Melnyk (2012) analyze the Ukrainian situation in different contexts, including the underlying process of Russification during the Soviet era and explain the main features of language management following Ukrainian independence, especially in the sphere of education and minority languages protection. More recently, Csernicskó & Ferenc (2016) provided a chronological classification of Ukrainian language policies from 1989 until the Russian-Ukrainian military conflict began in 2014.

However, the Euromaidan revolution (2013–2014), the Russian annexation of Crimea in February-March 2014 and its military aggression in Donbas (started in 2014 and still ongoing) have stimulated grassroots movements in different spheres of public life, including cultural and language policies. Nowadays, the actors in language management decisions are not only political parties and government bodies, but also language activist groups and organizations. The goal of this project is to call attention to the chief decision-makers in the process of language management in contemporary Ukraine and to describe the strategies they use to achieve their goals.

2 Methodology

Using the theory of language management by Jernudd and Neustupný (1987), I would like to shed light on the changes in Ukraine's *organized language management* after Euromaidan. Nekvapil gives a clear definition of the latter: "Organized management or also institutional management, [...] is management performed by institutions" (Nekvapil 2016: 15). In addition, he defines the main goals for the organized management research: "It is certainly of particular importance for organized language management to identify language problems, i.e. such deviations from the norm which are not only noted by individual speakers in particular interactions but also receive negative evaluation" Nekvapil (2006: 97).

Therefore, I will analyze (1) which actors note the deviation from language use (in the Ukrainian context it is mainly about the use of the Ukrainian vs Russian languages in such public domains as mass-media, education, government, and parliament); (2) how they evaluate this deviation (especially in mass-media discourses, featured in articles, blogs, interviews etc.); and (3) what measures they propose to adjust to this deviation. As Kimura (2014) points out, language management theory considers language policies to be a cyclical process. Therefore, it is important for this research to look not only at the results of language policy, but maybe more so at its formation and negotiation. Nekvapil and Sherman (2015: 1) themselves emphasized the importance of actors in language management: "Change can be initiated by various actors, such as politicians, government officials or experts appointed to solve language problems." Furthermore, they emphasize an analysis of the "interplay of bottom-up and top-down" (Nekvapil & Sherman 2015: 2). The actor-centric approach is crucial for this study, since the depiction of the involved actors assists in highlighting power and interest relations.

In this research, I also use a triangulation method, the main principle of which is an analysis of different sources and various discourses. Therefore, the material for this research is composed of laws and draft laws on language issues, and related mass-media discussions, political rhetoric texts, as well as ten expert interviews conducted in 2018 in Kyiv, Ukraine. The experts were selected via a "snowball technique," starting firstly with members of the working group on the language law and then asking for further contacts. As an interviewer, I tried to ask in detail about organized language management process, the role of different actors and their influence on the decision-making process. It is important to underline that it was partially a "participant observation," since I am Ukrainian with Ukrainian as my mother tongue, was born and educated in Ukraine, previously worked at a Ukrainian university for a number of years and am myself a member of the language policy expert community. I am aware of the fact that my personal language ideologies could partly affect my research, which is why the critical discourse approach was chosen as part of my methodology as well.

Therefore, in this chapter I will present the information about the actors who try to influence language policies in Ukraine (e.g., deputies, journalists, linguists, language activists etc.), the direction of change they choose, the political interests they represent, the coalitions they form, as well as the specific measures proposed in the laws and the ensuing reactions.

3 "Actor-centered approach" in language policies analysis

Language policy and planning (LPP) theory represents a wide spectrum of different approaches and methodological tools. In this research, I use an actor-centered analysis, since it allows us to highlight the main discursive events in contemporary Ukrainian language policies of, including such factors as power and interests. Therefore, this research seeks to understand which actors form, develop and (re) negotiate the present language policies in Ukraine.

Even in traditional LPP theory, which is often portrayed as idealistic and oriented towards a top-down present perspective, the role of actors is understood and underlined. For instance, Cooper proposed an accounting scheme for the research on language planning in which he defined several types of actors, namely—formal elites, influential, counter-elites, and non-elite policy implementers (Cooper 1989: 98). Grounding his scheme in behavioristic theory, Cooper counted other factors that were later summarized briefly by Hornberger (2005: 24): "Cooper's accounting framework, organized around the question 'What actors attempt to influence what behaviors of which people for what ends under what conditions by what means through what decision-making process with what effect?'." Hornberger, in turn, builds up her integrative model of LPP analysis, taking inspiration from the observations of the classical approach. Hence, the notion of actors has disappeared from this model, which concentrated more on the goals of language policies and the different processes within it than on issues of power, interest and agency. In addition, Dorner uses Cooper's question scheme to build-up her research tools investigating language policies concerning minority groups. As she assumed, "language policy and planning processes as an example of social human action are highly dynamic and therefore characterized by and dependent on the involvement of all social actors at all social levels" (Dorner 2012: 157).

The classical work by Jernudd and Neustupný (1987) describes the notions of linguistic (communicative) and non-linguistic (symbolic) interests. These two varieties of the interests involve different social groups. Further, the position of actors can change at various stages of language management process: "the interest of a social group may be limited to one or several stages of the management process only. Politicians may raise certain language problems in the discussion of evaluation of language during the process of organized management. It is in the interest of such politicians to assert their participation in order to attract the attention of the voting public. However, the same politicians may be completely indifferent in regard to selecting proper adjustment or implementation procedures [...]" (Jernudd & Neustupný 1987: 78).

Zhao and Baldauf also applied the classical LPP approach and proposed a systematic classification of actors, dividing them into four main categories—(1) *people with power*—national leaders, officials; (2) *people with expertise*—linguists, applied linguists, scientists from other fields, involved in LPP, for instance, in terminological committees; (3) *people with influence* (writers, celebrities, scholars (non-linguists), priests, civil rights lawyers, artists, ad hoc group lobbyists); (4) *people with interest*—ordinary citizens at grass-root levels (see for details Zhao 2011: 910). The authors also state that actors can play productive or receptive roles in language planning. This classification should be critically reconsidered, since people with power often have influence on and interest in the process of language development etc.; therefore, what the authors present as discrete categories largely overlap. Moreover, the same person can belong to multiple groups; for instance, a scientist can also be a public figure, or an applied linguist can be a writer at the same time; they even form coalitions or networks of actors. Nevertheless, this classification is helpful in putting accent on and prioritizing certain groups of actors.

Zhao and Baldauf also established the "I-5" model of the process of realizing language planning goals which includes initiation, involvement, influence, intervention and implementation (see for details: Zhao 2011: 911–912; Zhao & Baldauf 2012: 7–9). Different actors play key roles in different stages of this process. Continuing the development of this theory, Zhao and Baldauf describe actors' roles in diverse spheres of language planning, namely—status and corpus, language-in-education and prestige planning. The actor-centered approach is broadly applied in the domain of language-in-education scholarship. For instance, Brown (2010) defines schoolteachers as language policy actors while Johnson and Johnson introduce the notion of "language policy arbiters" defined as "individuals who have a disproportionate amount of impact on language policies" (in their case study, school administrators play this role) (Johnson & Johnson 2014: 222). Finally, Zhao and Baldauf propose an actor-stage model, in which the classification of actors and implementation stages are combined (Zhao & Baldauf 2012: 10). This model is based on an empiric study of the Chinese script reform and has since been used by McEntee-Atalianis (2016) in a study of language policies within the depiction of the United Nations. In another publication, Zhao describes the conflicts between groups of actors, analyzing the complex nature of relations within language management agencies. As he concludes, conflicts occur more often within the same language management institutions than between representatives of different groups (Zhao 2011: 917). Moreover, he considers power relations and interests to be the root cause for the appearance of such internal conflicts: "One major reason is that LPP is an interest-bonding enterprise and the members or representatives involved with the decision-making are invariably vested with various forms of regional and economic interest. In addition, there are also individual reasons, influenced by personal inclination or linguistic ideology" (ibid).

Taking into account the connection between sociolinguistics and political science, Schmidt underlines the key role of actors in language policy formation and transformation. He states that language policies become significant at the political stage, when "political actors believe that something important is at stake regarding the status and/or use of languages in their society, and that these stakes call for intervention by the state" (Schmidt 2009: 97). As he claims, without actors' intentions and activities, language policies would not draw public attention. Moreover, Peled (2015: 18) underlines that "national governments, community NGOs, global corporations and other political actors are all agents that are capable of realizing political and linguistic transformations." As he concludes, "human agency certainly plays a crucial part in the shaping of that interface, even if it is incapable of achieving complete control" (ibid).

In contemporary political theory, language policies are viewed as a part of public policy and are often undermined in the frame of comparative politics (see Lamoreux 2011; Lo Bianco 2000). For this research, Foucault's notion of governmentality is also essential, as Pennycook asserts, it drives language policy research from its classical normative top-down perspective into an analysis of discourses and macro-levels (Pennycook 2005: 65). This notion allows transferring from a single actor's perspective to an analysis of a variety of actors: "In so doing, it moves us away from a focus on the state as an intentional actor that seeks to impose its will on the people, and instead draws our attention to much more localized and often contradictory operations of power" (ibid).

In addition, McEntee-Atalianis (2016: 213) points out those actors should be as assigned to dynamic categories. She underlines that it is especially applicable in the domain of language policies and planning: "Moreover, LPP itself is acknowledged as dynamic and negotiable in time and space; its meaning is not seated 'in' one text or 'in' the reader of the policy document or language user but emerges via the actions and discourses of multiple agents, often in transaction with one another" (Ibid). Furthermore, Spolsky's theory of language management shifts the focus from a top-down perspective by emphasizing the grass-root initiatives that also could stimulate changes in state management. In his work *Language Management* (2011), Spolsky dedicated a whole chapter to analyzing language activist movements and their influence on language policies. Therefore, in present LPP theory, both top-down decision makers and bottom-up activists, are recognized as significant participants, responsible for language policies' formation and the depiction of the language situation. On the other hand, the actor-centric approach towards analyzing language policies has its pros and cons, especially in describing the comparative perspectives of different countries. For instance, advocates of the historical institutionalism approach criticize sociolinguists for proceeding "without analyzing specific political actors such as the state and its institutions or, for example, political parties as institutional intermediaries between the state and society" (Sonntag & Cardinal 2015: 12). Therefore, it is crucial for researchers to take into account all possible actors, which influence language policy decisions, their interactions, possible cooperation or confrontation, networks, and coalitions.

Moormann-Kimáková (2016) herself underlines the simplification of actor-focused analysis in many publications, describing language-related conflicts in terms "group vocabularies" of majorities and minorities. Moormann-Kimáková explains the complex nature of institutions including government, media, minority organizations and international NGOs, which may affect language policies. Finally, Moormann-Kimáková introduces her own typology of language-related conflict participants, providing criteria such as territorial concentration, group age, mutual intelligibility, status and origin. Based upon the last criteria, she differentiates between minorities created by marginalization, border-minorities, minorities caused by immigration, and minorities caused by the change of identification border (for details see Moormann-Kimáková 2016: 72–77). In my research, I take into account these critical considerations, as they are crucial for the Ukrainian case.

In the frame of critical discourse studies that are regarded as one of the foremost methodological trends for investigating language policies, the role of an actor-centric analysis is also emphasized. For instance, Wodak and Meyer (2016: 11) draw attention to the behavior of actors who mostly obey their societies' discursive rules. As other researchers point out, however, "there exist certain degrees of freedom for such actors, allowing them to act strategically and to also change power relations." In this research, I will also explicate the models of lobbying actors' interests as represented in the media. I will try to find answers to questions such as: how the media highlighted the role of actors in the field of language policies and how their interests are interpreted via medial means. Savski (2016: 51) argues further that the portrayal of present-day language policy practices is a challenging task for scholars because they should consider the variety of "actors involved in language policy, the different spaces policies are created and interpreted in, and the potential for actors in such spaces to gain agency or to establish hegemony."

From a comparative perspective, my research interest is grounded in finding links between actors' models of language policy in different post-Soviet countries, their similarities as well as their peculiarities.

4 Language management in contemporary Ukraine

As a post-Soviet country, Ukraine is marked by widespread Ukrainian-Russian bilingualism. As the most recent sociological data collected in the Razumkov Center survey in March 2017 shows, 68% of Ukrainians consider Ukrainian as their mother tongue and 14% of respondents consider Russian as their native language, while 17% responded that they speak both Ukrainian and Russian equally with 0.7% reporting another language (*Razumkov Center* 2017: 6). At the same time, 92% of the respondents identify as Ukrainians, 6% as Russians and 1.5% as other nationalities (ibid). In 2013–2019, many discursive events occurred which impacted Ukrainian language policies. First of all, in the wake of the Euromaidan protests (2013–2014), researchers, as evidenced by the results of sociological surveys, perceived the unilateral annexation of Crimea by the Russian Federation (2014) and the ongoing Russian-Ukrainian war in Donbas an identity shift in Ukrainian society. As Volodymyr Kulyk points out:

> One of the most noteworthy consequences of the recent events in Ukraine is a dramatic change in Ukrainian national identity. In various media one can regularly encounter assertions of individuals' increased self-identification as Ukrainian, greater pride in being a citizen of the Ukrainian state, stronger attachment to symbols of nationhood, enhanced solidarity with compatriots, increased readiness to defend Ukraine or work for Ukraine, and increased confidence in the people's power to change the country for the better. (Kulyk 2016: 588)

This shift is also reflected in language use, language attitudes and, consequently, in the language policies enacted by state authorities.

Researchers explicate the essence of bilingualism in Ukraine, as well as the risks of language bipolarity:

> While bilingualism is not a negative phenomenon in stable societies, the situation is quite different in Ukraine. On the one hand, after gaining independence in 1991, patriotic forces considered the revival and spread of the Ukrainian language to be an uncompromising task. On the other hand, the political forces in the regions where the Russian language prevails incite the population to resist the assimilation of languages under the slogan of the Russian language protection. (Matviyishyn & Michalski 2017: 189)

Kulyk explains the asymmetrical nature of the contemporary language situation in Ukraine, grounded on the consideration that many ethnic Ukrainians speak Russian, but simultaneously "fully support Ukraine's independence from Russia" (Kulyk 2017: 310). Therefore, language attitudes in contemporary Ukraine are more influenced by ideologies than by a sense of ethnic belonging. This factor also had a significant impact on the behavior of political elites in the sphere of language management.

4.1 Cancelation of the previous language law: Key actors

In his blog on the *Radio Liberty* website, Marusyk (2017) defines the key players in the language management process, namely: the Constitutional Court, the President, the Cabinet of Ministers, the Ministry of Culture, local councils, and civil-military administrations. Criticizing most of the actors for their ignorance or slow development of mechanisms and decision-making processes, Marusyk concludes that Ukrainian language policies are progressing thanks to bottom-up, not top-down initiatives. In this period, we can see that new actors appear on the language policies' stage during the military conflict. For instance, Marusyk alludes to civil-military administrations in Donbas (local government units, assigned by central authorities in Kyiv) as examples of different behavior aimed at influencing the language attitudes of the population in these regions. While the head of the Donetsk Regional Civil-Military Administration in territories controlled by the Ukrainian government communicates in Ukrainian, the head of the Luhansk unit uses Russian in communications with public servants (ibid).

In this chapter, I analyze the activities of these actors to estimate what interests are expressed in their undertakings. In February 2014, the Supreme Council of Ukraine canceled the previous language law *On the principles of the state language policy* that was adopted during Yanukovych's regime in 2012. The document, frequently called the "Kivalov-Kolesnichenko law" in reference to its authors, promoted the usage of Russian in all spheres of public life and proclaimed Russian as the regional language in many parts of Ukraine. The law's adoption in Parliament was heavily contested by Ukrainian-speakers supporters as well as due to numerous procedure violations (for details, see Moser 2014). Hence, Oleksandr Turchynov, interim-President after Yanukovych fled the country, refused to authorize canceling of the language law, explaining that at first a new law should be developed. Azhniuk (2017: 372) found that the "Temporary Special Commission for drafting a new language act was set up by the Parliament on 1 March 2014 to draft a new law instead." Petro Poroshenko similarly postponed language issues after a majority of votes in the first round of voting elected him as President in May 2014. Representatives of the East-South regions of Ukraine, where Russian is widely spoken, expressed the idea of the All-Ukrainian referendum concerning the status of Russian. They suggested the idea could be put into action, "in view of the escalation of the military conflict in the Donetsk and Luhansk regions, however, the idea found no response on either central or local levels" (Azhniuk 2017: 371). Therefore, state authorities were interested in putting the language issues aside and thus distracting the public from questions that could further polarize society in light of the ongoing military conflict.

However, certain politico-social groups were dissatisfied with these language policy developments. In July 2014, a group of national deputies applied to the

Constitutional Court to review the constitutionality of the above-mentioned law. In February 2018, after numerous postponements, protests by the right-wing party *Svoboda* and language activists, and three and a half years of deliberation, the Constitutional Court found the law to be "unconstitutional due to the violation of the personal voting procedure and a long consideration of the law in the Parliament" (Portal movnoji polityky 2018). The Court's final decision was made not just because of public pressure, but also due to the human factor, namely a personnel change. Two members of the Court retired, and before new judges assumed their offices, the majority voted to cancel the law. Besides, one of the judges actively cooperated with civil society from the very beginning to promote the annulment of the law.[2]

The Constitutional Court, however, is not a singular body and is composed of three authorities—the President, the Parliament, and the Congress of Judges (ibid 2018). These three actors delegate an equal number of representatives to the Constitutional Court. Therefore, despite the purported separation of powers between the legislative, executive and judicial branches in the Ukrainian Constitution, we can see groups of interests within the Court. In this regard, should the Court be considered an independent actor in language policies or as a representative of different groups of interests?

Thus, the previous language law was declared as unconstitutional; however, a new law had still not been adopted due to several factors, such as "the absence of a political will,"[3] and the proximity of parliament elections—politicians do not want to lose the electorate who do not support the law. Ihor Slidenko, a member of the Constitutional Court commented on these circumstances in an interview. In his opinion, the situation should encourage politicians to make a decision:

> Зараз ми маємо справу з правовою лакуною (прогалиною), коли суспільні відносини на законодавчому рівні не регулюються нічим, а лише нормами Конституції [...]. Ця ситуація повинна змусити народних депутатів пришвидшити свою роботу в плані підготовки нового закону, який би відповідав Конституції – і з точки зору його ухвалення, тобто без порушення процедури, і з точки зору змісту. (Portal movnoji polityky 2018)

> [Now we are dealing with a legal gap, when social relations at the legislative level are not regulated by anything, but only by the norms of the Constitution [...]. This situation should force the deputies to speed up their work in terms of preparing a new law that would conform to the Constitution—in terms of its adoption (without any procedural irregularities), and in terms of its content.] (Translation from the original Ukrainian texts here and below are mine.)

---

2 Interview with Taras Marusyk, ex-Deputy Chairman of the Coordination Council on the Application of the Ukrainian Language in All Spheres of Public Life under the Ministry of Culture of Ukraine, Kyiv, Ukraine, June 2018.

3 Interview with Zakhar Fedorak.

4.2 Development of the new language law: Key actors

Meanwhile, agents of diverse political parties and language activists have drafted new potential language laws. One of the working groups responsible for its development, led by renowned lawyer and diplomat Volodymyr Vasylenko, had been assembled under the Ministry of Culture between September and December 2016. In January 2017, three draft laws were put on the Parliamentary agenda, which elicited a considerable discussion in the media. The development of the three draft laws was connected to the competitiveness between opposing political parties. For instance, one of the members of the party *Blok Petra Poroshenka* visited the working group meetings under the Ministry of Culture, "behaving provocatively" and later presented its own draft law to the Parliament.[4] The hotly debated draft law No. 5670, dubbed so by the media as a *civic draft law* due to the veracity of its proponents and its support from different political parties, was taken as a foundational text for a new language law. The draft law titled *On ensuring the functioning of the Ukrainian language as a state language* was eventually accepted for the Parliamentary agenda with minor amendments. To block the Parliamentary adoption of the law, national deputies proposed around 2,000 amendments, which experts noted as an indication of dissention and absence of consensus concerning language issues in the Parliament. Nevertheless, after two years of consideration and particular amendments (for instance, the institution of Language Inspectorate was canceled), the law was adopted on 25 April 2019.

This occurred in a moment of transition in Ukraine, since Volodymyr Zelenskyi had been elected the next President of Ukraine on 21 April, gaining his official duties a month later on 20 May. In Zelenskyi's presidential campaign, language issues were seldom mentioned in his political rhetoric. For instance, in his pre-election program, Zelenskyi only once referred to language issues without defining his position and using generic human rights rhetoric

> Треба міняти країну і змінюватися самим. Треба брати відповідальність на себе й показувати приклад майбутнім поколінням. Треба єднатися усім, хто незалежно від статі, мови, віри, національності просто ЛЮБИТЬ УКРАЇНУ! (ZeKomanda 2019)
>
> [We must change the country and change ourselves. We must take responsibility and show the example for future generations. It is necessary to unite all those who, regardless of gender, language, religion, nationality simply LOVE UKRAINE!]

In addition, his campaign made strategic general statements concerning different fields of social life, in such a way as to embrace a larger audience.

4 Interview with Oksana Zabolotna, head of Parliament Secretariat, former coordinator of Working group for development of language draft law under the Ministry of Culture, Kyiv, Ukraine, January 2018.

Zelenskyi's main opponent, former President Petro Poroshenko appealed to support the state status of Ukrainian and its further support and promotion in his pre-election campaign. For instance, in a September 2018 speech addressed to Parliament, Poroshenko pointed out that,

> Утверджуємо українську мову – складову сили та успіху нашого народу. І надалі будемо вживати дієвих заходів для зміцнення державного статусу української мови, посилення і поширення її в усіх сферах публічного життя. (*Ukrajinska Pravda* 2018)
>
> [We support the Ukrainian language—a component of the strength and success of our people. We will continue to take effective measures to strengthen the official status of the Ukrainian language, empower and spread it in all spheres of public life.]

Similar messages were repeated in his political program:

> Ми захищаємо свою мову, вкладаємо кошти у підтримку української культури. [...] Продовжимо політику підтримки української мови як єдиної державної. [...] Розширимо підтримку культурних проектів – кіно, музики, книги та інших напрямів. (*Livyj bereh* 2019)
>
> [We are protecting our language; we are investing in support of the Ukrainian culture. [...] We will continue the policy of support for Ukrainian as the only state language. [...] We will widen support for cultural projects—films, music, books and other directions.]

Crucially, during Poroshenko's presidency, cultural management institutions such as the Ukrainian Cultural Foundation and the Ukrainian Book Institute were established and developed. One of the notable functions of these institutions is their financial support of Ukrainian cultural productions and, consequently, Ukrainian language promotion. Moreover, one of Poroshenko's election slogans was "Army, Language, Faith," while in his final campaign phase, this slogan was more subdued and general, stating merely "Think!" The parliamentary adoption of the law was accompanied by a mass gathering of language activists and the law's supporters, near the Parliament building (see Picture 1). The slogans on the placards reflect the link between language issues and the current military conflict: "Vote for language law! Protect language—vote for law! Language is our weapon! Language is our safety!" After the adoption in Parliament by 278 votes out of 348, Petro Poroshenko signed the law in one of the last decisions of his presidency. There were attempts by national deputies and representatives of *Oppositional Block* to prevent the Parliamentary speaker from signing the document, but they were rejected by Parliament.

Picture 1: Supporters of Ukrainization close to Parliament building, April 2019.
Source: https://www.radiosvoboda.org/a/istorychne-rishennya-zakon-pro-movu/29902793.html

The main idea of the law is the promotion of the state language in different spheres of public life by creating language management institutions like the State Language Department, providing free state courses of Ukrainian and introducing a language requirement for citizenship or government employment (public servants, national deputies, judges etc.). Newly-elected President Volodymyr Zelenskyi, who in his public speeches switched between Ukrainian and Russian (during the election campaign and after taking the office), criticized the new language law, stating "the state should assist in the development of the Ukrainian language by creating stimuli and positive examples, not by prohibitions and punishments, by complicating of bureaucratic procedures, by increasing the number of officials instead of shortening them" (official Facebook page of Volodymyr Zelenskyi, post from April 25, 2019). He also emphasized that the law was passed in a transitional period and that he will analyze it in detail during his presidency.

International actors were also involved in discussing the new Ukrainian language law. On May 17, 2019, the Russian Federation delegation asked the United Nations Security Council to convene a separate meeting to discuss the new language legislation, but the UN refused, as the request was rejected by the USA and certain EU member states (*UNIAN* 2019). Nevertheless, the Russian delegation made a second request, after which the UN scheduled a meeting concerning the law on July 16, 2019 (*Ukrinform* 2019); ironically, on the same day the language law was to enter into a force. Meanwhile, a group of fifty-one national deputies, led again by an *Oppositional Block* representative, applied to the Constitutional Court with a request to recognize the language law as unconstitutional. In this application, they stated that the law creates "an atmosphere of intolerance towards the historic linguistic diversity that is characteristic of the united and multinational people of Ukraine," and that "the procedure for the use of languages of national minorities in Ukraine is not regulated" (*Radio Svoboda* 2019). Therefore, we could see how opposing interest group use the identical strategies, namely in their applications to the Constitutional Court and protests of the language legislation. In her description of the current Ukrainian situation, Bilaniuk, concludes that two contrary competitive language ideologies dominate the country: "Language matters" and "Language does not matter" (see for details: Bilaniuk 2016). However, as she points out, discursive practices show that eventually language always matter (for some societal groups Ukrainian, for some Russian). As for the future, we can expect another shift in language policies towards regionalization with the Zelenskyi presidency giving more rights to Russian-speakers and national minorities, while shortening state programs for the support and development of the Ukrainian language. Another reason to expect such an outcome is that in his human resource policies, Zelenskyi has shown tight connections with ex-members *Party of Regions*—a political organization that, among other activities, promoted a widening of Russian language usage during the Yanukovych regime.

Yet it is important to underline that a broad coalition of actors formed in favor of the new language law. As Zakhar Fedorak of the Directorate of the State Language Policy under the Ministry of Culture comments: "Authors of the draft law on the state language created a strong background for its implementation thanks to a consolidation of efforts; many deputies supported this draft law as well."[5] Table 1 illustrates the different groups of actors at diverse steps of language policy development.

Table 1: Groups of actors at different stages of the development of the new draft law on language.

Stage	Period	Actors
Initiation	March 2014	National deputies, politicians
Involvement	September – December 2016	Language activists, lawyers, linguists, the Ministry of Culture
Influence	January 2017 – ongoing	Bloggers, journalists, writers, linguists, the Constitutional Court, language activists
Intervention	January 2017 – ongoing	Politicians, right-wing language activists
Implementation	Since July 16, 2019	Ministries, public servants, teachers, language management institutions

5 Interview with Zakhar Fedorak, expert of Directorate of State Language Policy under Ministry of Culture Kyiv, Ukraine, June 2018.

4.3 Conflicts between the actors during the new language law development

At the same time, several conflicts appeared between actors at different stages of language policy development. First of all, at the initiation stage, a dispute erupted between politicians concerning the general conception of a new language law in an argument about the structure of the law. Finally, national deputy Oksana Syrojid, a representative of the *Samopomich* party, put forward the winning idea to create two separate draft laws—one on the state language, and another concerning the languages of national minorities.[6] The draft law on minorities no. 6348 was also registered in the Parliament under the title *On amendments to some laws of Ukraine on provision of development and use of languages of national minorities in Ukraine*, but was not discussed in the media.

In addition, a conflict within a group of language activists appeared during the influence and intervention stages. As Zhao and Baldauf point out: "Intervention is the traditional term for the mediation of LPP problems, though intervention also may occur during implementation—with strongly negative results, since such involvement may lead to delay or discontinuation of the implementation. Intervention in this latter sense can occur at any stage in the continuum" (Zhao & Baldauf 2012: 8). The draft law on the state language had been promoted in the media as early as January 2017 by its developers and intelligentsia with a shared linguistic ideology of widening the sphere of state language usage. Representatives of the right-wing political party *Svoboda*, for instance, the national deputy and noted linguist, Iryna Farion, criticized the law for being too weak and liberal in its promotion of the state language, calling it a half-law (Farion 2018). In addition, Larysa Nitsoj, a child writer, also famous for her provocative behavior and blogs concerning language issues, criticized the draft law since "the status of the Ukrainian language, as a state language, cannot narrow the linguistic rights and needs of minorities" (Nitsoi 2017). These views were supported by right-wing activists, which provoked a split within the language activist community. As a result, experts have since accentuated the "radicalization of language issues."[7] As Zhao underlines, a conflict between actors can have positive consequences when compromises are found; at the same time, "it obviously creates a negative image of the actors and causes confusion among the public, which increases the difficulty of implementing LPP in practice" (Zhao 2011: 918).

In contemporary Ukraine, these conflicts draw the public's attention to language issues, but simultaneously stir up negative connotations of language policies in society and postpone decision-making procedures. As Oksana Zabolotna sums up: "Civil society does much more than authorities. [...] Civil society supports the

6 Interview with Oksana Zabolotna.

7 Interview with Anastasiia Rozlutska, head of NGO Free Courses of Ukrainian, Kyiv, Ukraine, June 2018.

language draft on the state language. A part of civil society criticizes this draft law [and their] actions are provocative."[8] Another expert, Jaryna Chornohuz, explains the reasons for such behavior: "For radical right-wing political parties it is profitable to keep language issues unsolved because in that case they can promise their electorate to solve them, for this reason they are blocking the adoption of the new language law."[9] At the same time, pro-Russian and Russian interest groups do not want an adoption of the new law on the state language,[10] since it will endorse the usage of Ukrainian.

4.4 Implementation stage in language management of contemporary Ukraine

According to Zhao and Baldauf's classification, language policy development in contemporary Ukraine mostly fail to reach the implementation stage. Moreover, Kimura proposes to add another phase to the cyclical model of language management—namely the post-implementation stage (Kimura 2014: 255). On the one hand, discourses concerning language in Ukraine are constructed and permanently supported by a vivid presence of the topic in the media. On the other hand, not many systemic changes are made in the process of language policy transformation.

Nevertheless, to fill the legal vacuum in the language sphere, ex-president Petro Poroshenko signed Decree No. 155/2018 in May 2018 *On urgent measures to strengthen the state status of the Ukrainian language and promote the creation of a united cultural space of Ukraine*. The decree foresees the development of a target state program for supporting the Ukrainian language. In this document, Poroshenko mentioned measures that echo the draft language law, for instance, a "certificate exam on the state language" (*Prezydent Ukrajiny* 2018). However, language policies experts regarded the decree as merely declarative and disappointing (Marusyk 2018).

One more document that appeared to fill a legal vacuum in the language domain is the *Strategy of popularization of the state language till 2030 "Strong language – strong state"* published by the Directorate of the State Language Policy under the Ministry of Culture. Kateryna Prytula, an expert at the Directorate explains this concept: "The Ukrainian language is the language of the future, it is a successful language, it is a marker of a valuable job, and it is not only the reason for healthy patriotism and identity-formation (our own, not remained from the former Soviet Union), but also a language for communication."[11] From a legal point of view,

8 Interview with Oksana Zabolotna.
9 Interview with Jaryna Chornohuz, the head of *Switch to Ukrainian* social movement.
10 Interview with Oksana Zabolotna.
11 Interview with Kateryna Prytula, expert of Directorate of State Language Policy under the Ministry of Culture of Ukraine, Kyiv, Ukraine, June 2018.

neither the decree nor the national strategy function as binding documents and therefore cannot introduce systemic transformations into language policies.

The prognoses of language policy researchers are connected to the development of the political situation in the country. As Azhniuk (2017: 382) underscores:

> The future of the language legislation greatly depends on the development of the military conflict in Eastern Ukraine. If the territories occupied by pro-Russian separatists remain under Kyiv's control, the regional status of the Russian language in Ukrainian legislation will most likely be preserved. If these territories are liberated from the separatists, the only language with a legal status in the country will be Ukrainian.

At the same time, despite the negative expectations of the experts, the implementation of the law *On ensuring the functioning of the Ukrainian language as a state language* has started during Zelenskyi's presidency. For instance, newly established language management institutions, such as the National commission on standards of the state language and Ombudsman on the protection of the state language begin to function. However, the implementation of the law, the conflicts between actors that appeared during this stage of language management, needs further exploration and is beyond the research scope of this chapter.

4.5 Adoption of the language legislation in the sphere of media and education: Key actors

On the other hand, the legislative initiatives in the sphere of mass-media Ukrainization were successful both in their adoption and in implementation. For instance, Ukrainian law *On amendments to the Law of Ukraine 'On television and radio broadcasting' (regarding the proportion of songs in the state language in musical radio programs)* was adopted in November 2016. According to the document, the broadcast of Ukrainian songs should be no less than 25% (with further growing) of the overall number of songs played on the radio, concerning the total time of transmission. The Ukrainian law *On amendments to laws of Ukraine regarding the language of audio-visual (electronic) mass media* was adopted in May 2017 and supported by President Petro Poroshenko. It demands that the national TV channels use the state language in 75% of broadcasted programs (60% in local TV channels). Both documents were broadly discussed in the media (with unofficial titles—laws on radio- and TV-quotas) concerning the details of their implementation and their influence on the Ukrainian media market.

Changes in language regulations within education also provoked a media outcry with the involvement of not only internal, but also external actors as well. In particular, language article no. 7 in the new law *On education* adopted in September 2017 requires an increased use of the state language in education at different levels—from primary schools to universities. The mechanisms of this law have started to be implemented in 2020, so the time has been allotted to prepare the reforms accordingly. The proposal is closely tied to the situation in the Zakarpattia region, which is densely populated by Romanian and Hungarian minorities. As the results of the External Independent Evaluation on university admission exams in 2016 showed, more than ¼ of pupils in the Zakarpattia region failed the Ukrainian language test (*Osvitnij portal Zakarpattia* 2016). Therefore, from the point of view of the Ministry of Education, new regulations should promote social integration and enable access to higher education in Ukraine for national minorities. However, external observers perceived it as a threat to the linguistic rights of national minorities. On the *Radio Liberty* website, numerous articles described this discursive event as Hungarian, Romanian, Polish, Bulgarian, Greek, Moldovan and Russian Federation officials actively participated in the discussion at the diplomatic level, and criticized the law for restricting the rights of minorities (*Radio Svoboda* 2017b). Official Hungarian representatives sent complaints to the Organisation for Security and Cooperation in Europe, European Union and United Nations, transferring the discussion of domestic policies to the international level (*Radio Svoboda* 2017a).

In turn, in October 2017, the Parliamentary Assembly of the Council of Europe passed a resolution, in which, on the one hand, criticized Ukrainian authorities for adopting the education law without previously consulting with the representatives of national minorities, and on the other hand, reiterated Ukraine's right to support and develop its own state language, taking into account the linguistic rights of minorities. Minister of Education Lilia Hrynevych went on to promise to clarify the phrasing in the language article (*Radio Svoboda* 2017b). Furthermore, in December 2017, the Venice Commission published an advisory opinion, in which the Commission members pointed out that the education law should be flexible enough to combine the promotion of the state language while preserving the languages of national minorities. The final recommendations include, in particular, "ensuring a sufficient proportion of education in minority languages at the primary and secondary levels, in addition to the teaching of the state language; to improve the quality of teaching of the state language; to amend the relevant transitional provisions of the Education Law to provide more time for a gradual reform, [...]; to ensure that the implementation of the Law does not endanger the preservation of the minorities' cultural heritage and the continuity of minority language education in traditional schools."[12]

Table 2 illustrates which actors were involved in the development of the language article at different stages. In this case, it is interesting to note that the intervention stage transpired on two occasions—first in June 2017 when language activists initiated a meeting with the Minister of Education to discuss the language article. After this meeting, eight of ten proposals submitted by the language activists were accepted by the Ministry of Education and introduced into the law. These amendments were mostly dedicated to strengthening the position of the state language in the education system. Later on, in September 2017, when the law was passed by Parliament, which provoked a discussion in media, the

12 Available at: http://www.venice.coe.int/webforms/documents/default.aspx?pdffile=CDL-AD(2017)030-e.

next phase of intervention began, led by diplomats and international organizations concerned about the suppression of the linguistic rights of minorities. These interventions had a positive effect, since they gave rise to a broader dialogue that involved the representatives of national minorities. At the same time, they revealed tensions between different social groups—those who encourage the promotion of the state language and those who are occupied with the preservation of minorities' rights. In case of the second group, the role of international actors was crucial. The discussion revolving around the possible discrimination on linguistic grounds was also fueled heated by external agents, not just by the internal minorities themselves. As Taras Marusyk suggests, those representatives of Ukrainian political parties who stoked the debate have tight cultural and financial relations with external actors, especially in Hungary.[13]

Table 2: Groups of actors at different stages of language article development in the new educational law.

Stage	Period	Actors
Initiation	April 2015	National deputies, politicians
Involvement	April 2015 – September 2017	The Ministry of Education
Influence	September 2017 – ongoing	Representatives of national minorities, journalists
Intervention	June 2017 September 2017 – ongoing	Language activists Diplomats, international organizations
Implementation	Has started in 2020	The Ministry of Education, school administrators, local authorities, teachers, language activists

Recent developments show that a compromise between representatives of national minorities and the Ministry of Education and Science has been struck. In 2019, the Ministry decided to differentiate between schoolchildren who came from national minorities' families and native speakers in their Ukrainian language assessments. However, this differentiation will only be in effect during the next two years (*The Babel* 2019). After-school Ukrainian language tests are extremely important for admission to universities, and the Ministry needs to minimize particular social barriers for representatives of national minorities.

Based on an analysis of Russian-speaking blogs in Ukraine, Maksimovtsova (2017: 10) defines two main rhetorical strategies—a rhetoric of loss and rhetoric of entitlement. The rhetoric of loss is often used by opposing camps:

13 Interview with Taras Marusyk.

> The frequent use of this argumentation pattern indicates that many Ukrainians feel that the position of the state language is 'threatened' and that the state needs to focus on preserving the unique cultural identity and territorial integrity of Ukraine. Like those social actors who argue that Ukrainian-speakers' rights are infringed in Ukraine, the second group of claim-makers admits exactly the opposite—total Ukrainization of the public space is the violation of the rights of Russian speakers. (Maksimovtsova 2017: 17)

This statement seems to be relevant for debates on the language article in a new education law as well, since both sides of the conflict use rhetorical strategies of loss and threat.

4.6 Language management in contemporary Ukraine: Key actors

The discursive events in Ukraine's organized language management have revealed that actors form coalitions to represent their interests and that conflicts appear between different actors or even within groups, which seem homogenous at first glance. Returning to Cooper's scheme of language planning analysis, we can see the combination of top-down and bottom-up initiatives in Ukraine's contemporary language policies. There is a continuous dialogue between the state and civil society concerning language policies. Different state institutions, such as the Constitutional Court, the Ministry of Culture, the Ministry of Education, the Parliament, and the President influence the transformation of different language policies. At the same time, language activists, represented by a number of organizations and movements, also actively participate in the decision-making processes. The media continuously highlight language policies, therefore journalists, writers, and bloggers should also be considered as actors in language policy development. All of these interrelations can be seen in Table 3.

Table 3: Language management in Ukraine (2013–2020) according to Cooper's scheme.

What actors	Representatives of the state institutions International organizations Media organizations Representatives of national minorities Cultural leaders Research institutions Language activists Teachers
To influence what behaviors	To encourage the learning of the Ukrainian language as the state language and to facilitate its use in different domains of public life (e.g., education, mass-media); to preserve the linguistic rights of national minorities
Of which people	Average citizens, journalists, pupils, students, minority representatives
For what ends	Social integration of minorities, access to higher education in Ukraine, Ukrainization, decrease of Russian influence in information space
Under what conditions	Russian-Ukrainian military conflict, economic crisis, migration
By what means	Legislative initiatives, draft laws, language article in law on education, new laws on language quotas in radio and television, new law on the state language, language activist movements
Through what policy decision-making process	Combination of the top-down and bottom-up models
With what effects	Public debates on language policies, Ukrainization of the media and education, shift in identities, creation pf language management institutions

Language management is always tightly linked to the socio-political situation of a given country. In present-day Ukraine, the context of reorientations of language policies is the ongoing Russian-Ukrainian military conflict, its ensuing economic crisis, and migration patterns. The general trend in language policies is a Ukrainization of different spheres of public life, in such a way that diminishes Russian's influence, especially in the information space. At the same time, the issues of preserving the rights of linguistic minorities are also on the agenda. Not all initiatives have been implemented, nevertheless, the draft laws also shape public discourses on language issues in the media.

5 Conclusions

In this chapter, I have analyzed language policies in contemporary Ukraine, applying Cooper's (1989) scheme for language planning research, as well the actors-stage model developed by Zhao and Baldauf (2012). As the results of the analysis have shown, these methodological tools reveal the main participants in the language policy process and shed light on the power relations and interests expressed or hidden in these circumstances. Different actors cooperate in language policy formation presenting strategies that are connected with their group belonging, linguistic ideologies, socio-political status, economic interests and values. These characteristics could also provoke conflicts between participants. Looking to the future, I plan to advance the typology of actors to analyze the complex nature of language policy development.

As the analysis of media and expert interviews revealed, different actors are involved at the different stages of language policy development in Ukraine. Some stages, for instance intervention, could have positive (amendment of current policies) or negative (blocking the decision-making process) effects on language policy development. Contemporary Ukraine is an informative case for the study of different, often contradicting interests of language policy participants. Consequently, these findings could be applied to an extent to other post-Soviet contexts. However, the behavior of actors is mostly a compilation of various sociocultural discursive practices, so the socio-political context should always be considered.

References

Azhniuk, B. (2017) Ukrainian language legislation and the national crisis. In M. Flier & A. Graziosi (eds) *The Battle for Ukrainian: A Comparative Perspective.* Cambridge: Ukrainian Research Institute, Harvard University, 365–387.

Besters-Dilger, J. (ed) (2009) *Language Policy and Language Situation in Ukraine. Analysis and Recommendations.* Frankfurt on the Main: Peter Lang.

Bilaniuk, L. (2016) Ideologies of language in wartime. In O. Bertelsen (ed) *Revolution and War in Contemporary Ukraine. The Challenge of Change.* Stuttgart: Ibidem-Verlag, 139–160.

Bilaniuk, L. (2017) Purism and pluralism: Language use trends in popular culture in Ukraine since independence. In M. Flier & A. Graziosi (eds) *The Battle for Ukrainian: A Comparative Perspective.* Cambridge: Ukrainian Research Institute, Harvard University, 343–363.

Brown, K. (2010) Teachers as language-policy actors: Contending with the erasure of lesser-used languages in schools. *Anthropology & Education Quarterly* 41 (3), 298–314.

Cooper, R. (1989) *Language Planning and Social Change.* Cambridge: Cambridge University Press.

Csernicskó, I. & Ferenc, V. (2016) Transitions in the language policy of Ukraine (1989–2014). In M. Sloboda, P. Laihonen & A. Zabrodsskaja (eds) *Sociolinguistic Transition in Former Eastern Bloc Countries. Two Decades after the Regime Change.* Berlin: Peter Lang, 349–377.

Dorner, D. (2012) Social actors and the language policy and planning process: A case study from German-speaking Lorraine (France). In P. Studer & I. Werlen (eds) *Linguistic Diversity in Europe: Current Trends and Discourses.* Berlin & Boston: De Gruyter, 157–175.

Farion I. (2018) Pro movu dlia hibrydiv: "na vymohu" chy "pryjniatnu dlia storin" [About language for hybrids: "on demand" or "acceptable for both sides"]. On WWW at https://blogs.pravda.com.ua/authors/farion/5a8ba660df572/. Accessed February 20, 2018.

Hogan-Brun, G. & Melnyk, S. (2012) Language policy management in the former Soviet sphere. In B. Spolsky (ed) *The Cambridge Handbook of Language Policy.* Cambridge: Cambridge University Press, 592–616.

Hornberger, N. H. (2005) Frameworks and models in Language Policy and Planning. In T. Ricento (ed) *An Introduction to Language Policy: Theory and Method.* Oxford: Blackwell, 24–41.

Jernudd, B. & Neustupný, J. (1987) Language planning: For whom? In L. Laforge (ed) *Actes du Colloque international sur l'aménagement linguistique / Proceedings of the International Colloquium on Language Planning.* Québec: Les Presses de l'Université Laval, 69–84. On WWW at http://languagemanagement.ff.cuni.cz/en/system/files/documents/jernudd_neustupny_1987.pdf. Accessed July 23, 2018.

Johnson, D. C. & Johnson, E. J. (2014) Power and agency in language policy appropriation. *Language Policy* 3, 221–243.

Kimura, G. C. (2014) Language management as a cyclical process: A case study on prohibiting Sorbian in the workplace. *Slovo a slovesnost* 75 (4), 255–270.

Kulyk, V. (2010) Ideologies of language use in post-Soviet Ukrainian media. *International Journal of Sociology of Language* 201, 79–104.

Kulyk, V. (2016) National identity in Ukraine: Impact of Euromaidan and the war. *Europe–Asia Studies* 68 (4), 588–608.

Kulyk, V. (2017) Language attitudes in independent Ukraine: Differentiation and evolution. In M. Flier & A. Graziosi (eds) *The Battle for Ukrainian: A Comparative Perspective.* Cambridge: Ukrainian Research Institute, Harvard University, 309–341.

Lamoureux S. A. (2011) Public policy, language practice and language policy beyond compulsory education. *Cahiers de l'ILOB* 3, 123–140.

Livyj bereh (2019) Peredvyborna programa Petra Porošenka [Pre-election program of Petro Poroshenko]. On WWW at https://ukr.lb.ua/news/2019/02/11/419445_peredviborna_programa_petra.html. Accessed July 4, 2019.

Lo Bianco, J. (2000) Making languages an object of public policy. *Agenda* 7 (1), 47–61.

Maksimovtsova, K. (2017) Language policy in education in contemporary Ukraine: A continuous discussion of contested national identity. *Journal of Ethnopolitics and Minority Issues in Europe* 16 (3), 1–25.

Marusyk, T. (2017) 2017 rik u movnij sferi: pidstavy dlia pozytyvu zbil'šujut'sja [2017 year in language sphere: bases for positive are increasing]. On WWW at https://www.radiosvoboda.org/a/28947735.html. Accessed July 24, 2018.

Marusyk, T. (2018) Novyj movnyj ukaz: rozčaruvannja i deklaracija [New language decree: disappointment and declaration]. On WWW at https://www.radiosvoboda.org/a/29268590.html. Accessed July 26, 2018.

Masenko, L. (2008) *Umovna Ukrajina* [Conditional Ukraine]. Kyiv: Tempora.

Matviyishyn, Y. & Michalski, T. (2017) Language differentiation of Ukraine's population. *Journal of Nationalism, Memory & Language Politics* 11 (2), 181–197.

McEntee-Atalianis, L. J. (2016) A network model of language policy and planning: The United Nations as a case study. *Language Problems & Language Planning* 40 (2), 187–217.

Moormann-Kimáková, B. (2016) *Language-Related Conflicts in Multinational and Multiethnic Settings: Success and Failure of Language Regimes.* Wiesbaden: Springer.

Moser, M. (2014) *Language Policy and the Discourse on Languages in Ukraine under President Viktor Yanukovych (25 February 2010 – 28 October 2012).* Stuttgart: Ibidem-Verlag.

Nekvapil, J. (2006) From language planning to language management. *Sociolinguistica* 20, 92–104.

Nekvapil, J. (2016) Language management theory as one approach in language policy and planning. *Current Issues in Language Planning* 17 (1), 11–22.

Nekvapil, J. & Sherman, T. (2015) An introduction: Language management theory in language policy and planning. *International Journal of Sociology of Language* 232, 1–12.

Nitsoj, L. (2017) Ukrajincjam haplyk, jakščo Rada uchvalyt' zarejestrovani zakony pro osvitu, movu j nacmenšyny [Ukrainians will not survive if parliament will adopt registered laws on education, language and national minorities]. On WWW at http://politicua.com/politika/8492-8492.html. Accessed July 26, 2018.

Osvitnij portal Zakarpattia (2016) Rezul'taty ZNO: Zakarpattja – sered najhiršych iz ukrajins'koji, istoriji, matematyky, heohrafiji ta biolohiji [Result of external independent tests: Zakarpattia region is among the worst concerning results on Ukrainian language, history, mathematics, geography and biology]. On WWW at http://osvita.uz.ua/rezultaty-zno-zakarpattya-sered-najgirshyh-iz-ukrayinskoyi-istoriyi-matematyky-geografiyi-ta-biologiyi/. Accessed July 24, 2018.

Pavlenko, A. (2011) Language rights versus speakers' rights: On the applicability of Western language rights approaches in Eastern European contexts. *Language Policy* 10, 37–58.

Pavlenko, A. (2013) Multilingualism in post-Soviet successor states. *Language and Linguistics Compass* 7 (4), 262–271.

Peled, Y. (2015) Normative language policy: Interface and interferences. In T. Ricento, Y. Peled & P. Ives (eds) *Language Policy and Political Theory: Building Bridges, Assessing Breaches.* Wiesbaden: Springer, 7–21.

Pennycook, A. (2005) Postmodernism in language policy. In T. Ricento (ed) *An Introduction to Language Policy: Theory and Method.* Oxford: Blackwell, 60–76.

Portal movnoji polityky (2018) Movnyj zakon mih buty skasovanyj sudom šče u 2014 roci – suddja KSU [Language law could have been cancelled already in 2014]. Interview with Ihor Slidenko. On WWW at http://language-policy.info/2018/03/movnyj-zakon-mih-buty-skasovanyj-sudom-sche-u-2014-rotsi-suddya-ksu/. Accessed July 24, 2018.

Prezydent Ukrajiny (2018) Ukaz Prezydenta Ukrajiny No. 156/2018 "Pro nevidkladni zahody ščodo zmicnennja deržavnoho statusu ukrajins'koji movy ta spryjannja stvorennju jedynoho kul'turnoho prostoru Ukrajiny" [Decree of the President of Ukraine No. 156/2018 "On urgent measures to strengthen state status of Ukrainian language and to assist creation of united cultural space of Ukraine"]. On WWW at http://www.president.gov.ua/documents/1562018-24258. Accessed July 25, 2018.

Radio Svoboda (2017a) Uhorščyna zvernulasja do OBSJE, OON i JES čerez movnu stattju ukrajins'koho zakonu pro osvitu [Hungary appealed to OBSCE, UN and EU concerning language article in Ukrainian law on education]. On WWW at https://www.radiosvoboda.org/a/news/28729757.html. Accessed July 25, 2018.

Radio Svoboda (2017b) U PARJE uchvalyly rezoljuciju ščodo zakonu pro osvitu v Ukrajini [The PACE adopted resolution regarding law on education in Ukraine]. On WWW at https://www.radiosvoboda.org/a/news/28789627.html. Accessed July 25, 2018.

Radio Svoboda (2019) 51 deputat zvernuvsja do KSU ščodo zakonu pro ukrajins'ku movu [51 national deputies applied to Constitutional Court regarding law on Ukrainian language]. On WWW at https://www.radiosvoboda.org/a/news-ksu-zakon-pro-movu-podannya/30012752.html. Accessed June 21, 2019.

Razumkov Center (2017) Osnovni zasady ta šljachy formuvannja spil'noji identyčnosti hromadjan Ukrajiny [The basic principles and ways of forming the common identity of Ukrainian citizens]. On WWW at http://razumkov.org.ua/images/Material_Conference/2017_04_12_ident/2017-Identi-3.pdf. Accessed July 24, 2018.

Savski, K. (2016) State language policy in time and space: Meaning, transformation, recontextualisation. In E. Barakos & J. W. Unger (eds) *Discursive Approaches to Language Policy.* London: Palgrave Macmillan, 51–70.

Schmidt, R. (2005) Political theory and language policy. In T. Ricento (ed) *An Introduction to Language Policy: Theory and Method.* Oxford: Blackwell, 95–110.

Sonntag, S. K. & Cardinal, L. (2015) State traditions and language regimes: A historical institutionalism approach to language policy. *Acta Univ. Sapientiae, European and Regional Studies* 8, 5–21.

Spolsky, B. (2011) *Language Management.* Cambridge: Cambridge University Press.

The Babel (2019) Vypusknykam škil z movamy nacmenšyn na dva roky sprostyly ZNO z ukrajins'koji movy (2019) [After-school test on Ukrainian language is simplified for graduates from schools with national minorities for the period of two years]. On WWW at https://thebabel.com.ua/news/29428-vipusknikam-shkil-z-movami-nacmenshin-na-dva-roki-sprostili-zno-z-ukrajinskoji-movi. Accessed April 26, 2019.

Ukrajinska Pravda (2018) Poslannia Prezydenta Ukrajiny Porošenka do Verkhovnoji Rady Ukrajiny [Message of the President of Ukraine Petro Poroshenko to the Supreme Council of Ukraine]. On WWW at https://www.pravda.com.ua/articles/2018/09/20/7192645/. Accessed September 20, 2018.

Ukrinfrom (2019) Rosija znovu sklykaje Radbez OON ščodo ukrajins'koho „movnoho“ zakonu [Russia again gathers United Nations Council of Safety meeting concerning Ukrainian language law]. On WWW at https://www.ukrinform.ua/rubric-polytics/2731600-rosia-znovu-sklikae-radbez-oon-sodo-ukrainskogo-movnogo-zakonu.html. Accessed July 1, 2019.

UNIAN (2019) Rada Bezpeky OON vidmovylasja obhovorjuvaty ukrajins'kyj zakon pro movu na vymohu Rosiji [United Nations Security Council refused to discuss Ukrainian law on language on Russia's demand]. On WWW at https://www.unian.ua/politics/10556508-rada-bezpeki-oon-vidmovilasya-obgovoryuvati-ukrajinskiy-zakon-pro-movu-na-vimogu-rosiji.html. Accessed July 1, 2019.

Wodak, R. & Meyer, M. (eds) (2016) *Methods of Critical Discourse Studies.* Los Angeles: Sage.

ZeKomanda (2019) Peredvyborča prohrama kandydata na post Presydenta Ukrajiny Volodymyra Zelens'koho [Pre-election program of Volodymyr Zelenskyi, candidate for post of President of Ukraine]. On WWW at https://program.ze2019.com/. Accessed July 4, 2019.

Zhao S. (2011) Actors in language planning. In E. Hinkel (ed) *Handbook of Research in Second Language Teaching and Learning.* Vol II. New York & London: Routledge, 905–923.

Zhao, S., & Baldauf, R. B. (2012) Individual agency in language planning: Chinese script reform as a case study. *Language Problems & Language Planning* 36 (1), 1–24.

Solvita Burr (née Pošeiko)

The interaction of nationalist language ideology and the interests of individual actors: An unresolved dispute over language use on Latvian house number signs

Abstract The chapter examines a trilingual house number sign which has repeatedly been defined by Latvia's public bodies as a language problem due to its use of foreign languages in addition to the state language. These metalinguistic actions have caused two-year-long discussions not only on language use on the sign, but also on normative documents which regulate language use in Latvian public signage. The actors who had the need/chance to express their views and attitudes towards the case under consideration can be placed into two interest groups: those with nationalist interests seeking to establish or maintain monopolistic use of the state language, and those who advocate for the right of minority groups to use their mother tongue in private (a house being a private environment). The theoretical framework of Language Management Theory is used to discuss multiple language management cycles at micro, meso and macro levels, to analyze motives, argumentation and strategies of both sides in the context of language policy, and in discussing the strengths and weaknesses of the actors in solving language problems. The main question is: What does the language management process tell us about the actors' capacity (power) to deal with a language problem in the linguistic landscape of Latvia?

Keywords trilingual street name, official signage, linguistic landscape, language problem, language management, language policy, power and weakness

I Introduction

Building number signs are plaques that show partial postal addresses, provide easier orientation, and facilitate the work of public services (e.g., emergency medical services, fire brigades, police). They are attached to residential, commercial and administrative buildings. Usually, the street name and a building number are included on them; additionally, text indicating ownership may be added. In Latvia, the production and placement of building number signs must comply with city or county standards that determine their visual design, location and linguistic content. However, building owners or managers are responsible for the cost of producing and placing these signs.

Due to the top-down management of signs and their strictly standardized form and content, building number signs—along with road signs, official announcements, and name signs of government institutions—are treated as signs of the official sphere of linguistic landscape (hereinafter the *LL*) (Gorter 2006; Gorter, Marten & Van Mensel 2012). LL studies show that official signs reflect a state's ideology or ideology of autonomous provinces and their language policy more accurately (e.g., Marten 2010; Puzey 2012; Pošeiko 2015b). A change in language use in official signs is often a result of a change in political power. For instance, at different times, streets in Latvia have been officially named in German, Russian and Latvian (for more on this, see Balode 2008; Pošeiko 2015b, 2018).

The chapter utilizes Language Management Theory to examine one of the most contentious "metalinguistic cases" surrounding a house number sign with a street name in three languages in Liepāja, one of Latvia's biggest cities, which, based on the sign owner's initiative, was ruled upon by the Constitutional Court of the Republic of Latvia—the highest authority at the national level. The process of this case is complicated due not only to the use of foreign languages (English and Russian)[1] on the official sign, but also because the right of the Russian minority to use their own language, and the compliance of some Articles of the Official Language Law (1999) with the Constitution of the Republic of Latvia (1922) and other legal national and international documents, are issues often subjected to discussion. Therefore, the resolution of the case involves both the single-language practice and the discourse on language use in the Latvian LL.

The aim of the chapter is to analyze the aggregate cycle of multi-level language management of the house number sign, focusing on actors' expressed beliefs, statements and metalinguistic activities. The chapter's underlying questions are thus:

1. Who has defined the house number sign with a street name in three languages as a language problem and what is the legal basis for this judgment? What other problems (language problems, language-related social problems) has it raised?
2. What are the actors' language-related interests and aims?
3. What arguments have been used to accept or deny the trilingual sign and what strategies have been used to influence the language management process?
4. What does the language management process tell us about actors' capacity (power) to deal with a language problem in the LL of Latvia?

In order to examine the language management of the trilingual house-number sign, a content analysis of the documents of Constitutional Court Case Nr. 2017-01-01 (Constitutional Court 2017a) that are available in the archives of the Constitutional Court; of online, publicly available information; of the case's final ruling

1 According to the Official Language Law (1999), "The official language in the Republic of Latvia is the Latvian language [...]. Any other language used in the Republic of Latvia, except the Liv language, shall be regarded, within the meaning of this Law, as a foreign language."

(Constitutional Court 2017b); and of the case's closure (Constitutional Court 2017c) has been carried out.

The chapter consists of seven sections. After the introduction, the second section discusses Language Management Theory in the LL in the context of language policy in Latvia. The third section briefly describes the ethnolinguistic situation in Liepāja. The most extensive is the fourth section. It includes first a brief overview of language use on street name signs at various times in Latvia's history; second, one example is given to demonstrate that foreign languages have been accepted on unofficial street name signs; third, a scrupulous characterization of the multi-level language management of the house number sign and involved actors' interests and applied strategies is provided. This section is followed by a discussion on language management stages and language problem management of the house number sign. The sixth section shares the houseowner's views on the trilingual sign. In the final section, theoretical and practical questions are summarized and the most significant conclusions are presented.

2 Theoretical framework

2.1 Language Management Theory and language management

First defined in the 1980s and later discussed by many scholars (e.g., Jernudd & Neustupný 1987; Nekvapil 2016; Fairbrother, Nekvapil & Sloboda 2018), Language Management Theory (LMT) is a theoretical framework that allows one to analyze and interpret various metalinguistic activities on a language and communication in different settings. According to theory, language management (LM) is a language-related behavior with respect to linguistic issues (mainly problems). The process of LM traditionally consists of five stages:

1. Deviations from norms (linguistic, communicative, or sociocultural) are intentionally introduced or accidentally occur.
2. Deviations from norms are noted.
3. The noted deviations are evaluated (or not evaluated).
4. (Correction) adjustment designs are selected to remove the deviations (or not selected).
5. The adjustment designs are implemented (or not implemented). (Jernudd & Neustupný 1987; Sloboda 2009: 17)

If the second and third stages are related to the recognition and formulation of a problem, then later stages refer to its management: planning, implementation, and possibly evaluation of a solution (for more on this, see Lanstyák 2018: 71). Depending on the involved actors and situation, a process can be simple management that occurs at the micro level or organized management that occurs trans-situationally. LM cycle(s) can incorporate both contexts combining and contrasting actions and responses of individual actor(s) and public authority (-ies). Thus, LMT is also a useful tool for investigating power relationships between actors and their language-related interests.

Some questions should be considered when thinking about LM of public signs in Latvia: What is meant by *norm* in the context of LL? What factors can affect the appearance of deviations? Who evaluates deviations? How does implementation of an adjustment design into practice look? The next section draws attention to these questions, theoretically defining types of language problems and their management in the context of LL and practically outlining the legal ways of managing them in Latvia.

2.2 Language problems in LL and their management in Latvia

In LMT, "language problems are the linguistic, communicative and associated socio-cultural phenomena that are not only noted but also evaluated negatively" (Nekvapil 2012: 160). In other words, there is only a problem if someone (e.g., author, recipient, inspector) sees it as such.

In Latvia, the State Language Center (SLC) is the public body which is responsible for the implementation of state language policy into practice, monitoring and controlling language use, and ensuring dominance of Latvian in the public domain. SLC has legal right to demand remedial action for an identified language problem. Its duty is also to understand the nature of the normative documents that regulate language use in Latvia and explain them to the public in a way that there would be no uncertainties regarding the use of language in sociolinguistic domains, including LL (SLC 2017). In this sense it functions as a mediator between prescriptive norm and practice.

However, it is useful to understand what constitutes a language problem in the LL. Firstly, public signs can be described with respect to linguistic norms in terms of problems if they are based on grammar or spelling mistakes (e.g., a lack or improper use of diacritics in Latvian text) and stylistic awkwardness. Such problems are first related to the concept of "correctness" with respect to a standard norm. In Latvia, language problems in the LL, especially in advertisements, are most often seen, analyzed and criticized from a prescriptive point of view, accompanied by suggestions of corrections which conform to prescriptive norms (e.g., Ragačevičs & Zilgalve 2015; Ločmele 2015). According to the SLC, such language problems can usually be resolved easily and quickly. Sign owners tend to become frustrated in instances of large-format ads or expensive signage, as the replacement entails significant financial expense (Interview in SLC, 20.02.2018). They do not oppose the language culture; dissatisfaction is due to economic reasons.

Secondly, a language problem may be described with respect to communicative norms in terms of sociolinguistic problems if the choice of linguistic code (dialect or language) or its visual layout for a public sign is not in accordance with the proposed language situation and its language regime, i.e., language choice in the official or commercial sphere of the Latvian LL.

The Official Language Law, issued and adopted by Parliament of Latvia in 1999, is the main normative document that must be considered for planning and evaluating language use in texts placed in the LL by private individuals, companies, municipal authorities and government. Several parts of Articles 18 and 21 of the State Language Law apply directly to public texts in Latvian LL. These regulate that public signage must be in Latvian only where state duties are concerned (including, most prominently, public bodies and road signs). On commercial signs, however, a Latvian-plus rule applies: other languages are explicitly allowed as long they are used in addition to Latvian and if they are not more dominant than Latvian. The law does not regulate unofficial communication, internal communication between national or ethnic groups, or religious activities. Thus symbolic signs with unofficial house or village names or historical city names, and notices of religious communities can be published in foreign languages.

The legal understanding of the term "foreign language" and the use of foreign languages in various sociolinguistic domains are the most controversial topics of discussion at present in relation to the Official Language Law (e.g., Burr 2021).

If a norm itself is questioned (e.g., a specific article of the Official Language Law or a provision by the Cabinet of Ministers), it can be seen as a discursively produced metalinguistic language problem or a metaproblem—a "generalized language problem" (Lanstyák 2018: 69)—within the organized LM. It is a macro-level problem which may lead to further language problems due to the potential scope of its interpretations.

The next paragraphs examine excerpts from the Official Language Law and subordinate regulations of the Cabinet of Ministers and municipal rules which directly regulate official signage, keeping in mind that "the language law represents one of rather strictly institutionalized discourses of metalinguistic character" (Dovalil 2015: 364). More specifically, attention is paid to the first part of two articles of the Official Language Law (see Table 1). On one hand, they have been used to support the rejection of the trilingual sign. On the other hand, they have also been contested as unconstitutional (incompatible with the Constitution of the Republic of Latvia), and have been mentioned and discussed as complex metalinguistic language problems. This will be discussed further in the chapter.

Article 18 of the Official Language Law is associated with Regulation No. 50 of the Cabinet of Ministers (see the middle column of Table 1). Both normative documents specify that place names are to be created and used in Latvian. According to Paragraph 45 of Regulation No. 50 of the Cabinet of Ministers, most names of Latvian places and geographic objects must be registered in the Place Name Database.[2] Street names are not included here; each municipality is responsible for street names' compilation and publication.

2 The Place Name Database is available in Latvian at https://vietvardi.lgia.gov.lv/vv/to_www.sakt. Accessed August 12, 2018.

Table 1: Excerpts from normative documents which regulate language use in the LL (the official English translation)

Article of Official Language Law (1999)	Relevant Regulations of the Cabinet of Ministers	Liepāja's Municipal Rule 2
Article 18. (1) Place names in the Republic of Latvia shall be created and use thereof shall be in the official language.	3. Geographical names in Latvia shall be created in Latvian according to the norms of Latvian. 45. Official geographical names and official parallel names shall be made public. Each geographical name authority has a duty to ensure the availability of official geographical names and official parallel names assigned thereby to users. (Regulations No. 50, 2012)	1.3. Number signs on buildings are to be deployed and maintained by the owners or managers of the building. 3.8. Text on number signs identifying buildings, street or squares must be in the official language. 3.9. Street names should be used in accordance with Annex 1 to this regulation. The enforcement of the binding rules is controlled by the local authority, Liepāja Municipal Police.
Article 21. (1) Information provided for public information purposes by State and local government institutions, courts and institutions constituting the judicial system, State and local government undertakings, and companies in which the greatest share of capital is owned by the State or a local government, shall be provided only in the official language, except in cases determined in Paragraph five of this section. This provision is also applicable to private institutions, organizations, companies, and self-employed persons, who perform, on the basis of laws or other regulatory enactments, specific public functions, if the provision of information is related to the performance of the relevant functions.	2. The institutions and persons referred to in Article 21 of the Official Language Law may provide information in a foreign language concurrently with the official language in information that is intended for public awareness in places accessible to the public if this information is related to: international tourism; international measures; safety reasons; free circulation of goods of the European Union; epidemics or dangerous infectious diseases; the rights and obligations of foreign citizens placed in places of imprisonment; emergency situations. (Regulations No. 130, 2005)	

Table 1: Continued

Article of Official Language Law (1999)	Relevant Regulations of the Cabinet of Ministers	Liepāja's Municipal Rule 2
(5) Observing the purpose of this Law, [...] the Cabinet of Ministers shall determine cases where a foreign language may be used concurrently with the state language in information that is intended for public awareness in places accessible to the public.		

In 2009, the municipal government of the city of Liepāja published Rule No. 2, "Directions for the Placement of Signs Indicating Building Number, Street or Square Names," which reiterates the necessity of using the state language on signs indicating the building number and street or square names (see the right-hand column of Table 1). A complete list of street names in Liepāja is provided in Annex 1, mentioned in Article 3.9 of the regulation. The list includes *Rucavas iela* ('Rucava Street'); the name's use on a Liepāja house number sign will be discussed in more detail below.

As the process of the case is complicated, it is therefore worth looking at Lanstyák's theory of language problem management (Lanstyák 2014, 2018). Lanstyák, focusing on the resolution process for language problems and discourse-related problem situations, has defined nine involvement strategies that actors use to deal with a language problem (see Table 2).

Table 2: Involvement strategies and their main aim (following Lanstyák 2018: 79–88)

Involvement strategy	Aim
Devolution	to transfer the burden of the problem onto somebody else (an individual or a group)
Alleviation	to reduce the problem without getting rid of it, to create a partial solution
Solution	to resolve the problem, to completely remove it
Ignoring	to act as if the problem did not exist
Denial	to disclaim the problem's existence
Belittlement	to create impression that the problem is less serious than it is in reality
Mitigation	to mentally lessen the problem without managing the outer circumstances of the problem situation
Elimination	to get rid of the problem by reinterpreting the problem situation
Acceptance	to mentally justify the need to live together with the problem as it is

However, in practice all actors (including both those who do or do not consider a sign to be a language problem) have limited ability to initiate and apply strategic actions, as each actor's practical scope is limited to his/her position's official duties and obligations (e.g., to challenge administrative protocol, examine the complaint, or evaluate the resolution process of the language problem), following a formal legal framework. Actors' strategies may be aimed at changing the discourse, the circumstances of language use or the ideas, thoughts, or opinions of other actors. Actors may be spurred by a desire to maintain or change language policy and thus public discourse on languages to be accepted in the Latvian LL. Actors may also hold the desire to replace one language practice with another (e.g., changing multilingual street sign to monolingual sign). But the reason for the application of a strategy may simply be an actor's desire to reasonably convince other actors of the inaccuracy of his/her view.

As the ethnolinguistic and sociolinguistic situations in a city can function as a useful example in the LM process, the next section gives an overview of the ethnic composition in Liepāja and language situation in the LL.

3 Ethnolinguistic situation in Liepāja

Liepāja is the third largest city in Latvia, located on the west coast of Latvia. Liepāja's population is 76,604, of which 56.08% are ethnic Latvians, 29.75% Russians, 4.75%

Ukrainians, 3.14% Belarusians, 2.98% Lithuanians and 1% Poles.[3] Public organizations for ethnic minorities in the city include a Russian society with more than 600 members,[4] two Ukrainian organizations, one Belarusian community, a Lithuanian society, a Polish society and a German association.

Research on the Liepāja LL was carried out in May 2018; it methodologically followed the traditional study of LL in the cityscape (e.g., Gorter 2006; Backhaus 2007; Gorter, Shohamy 2009), providing photographs, coding and analysis of all written texts visible along the streets. In total, 1,320 signs were photographed and analyzed according to criteria which can be divided into five groups: placement, type of sign, ownership, language use, and information in each language. Quantitative data analysis shows that Latvian was used on 1,159 signs (87.8%), English on 315 signs (23.9%), Russian on 39 signs (2.9%), and German on 7 (0.5%). Of the LL signs in Russian, 13 were official signs (e.g., multilingual city maps and reference information on historical heritage buildings).

4 Street names and street names signs under language ideology in Latvia

4.1 Unofficial street name signs as proof of multilingualism

Alongside official street name signs which comply with the relevant normative documents, there are still Soviet-era bilingual signs extant in some places—mostly villages and small parish centers—in the Latvian LL. In some instances, symbolic bilingual or multilingual signs placed next to official street name signs and house number signs refer to language practices, linguistic identity and the value of language over time. For example, Figure 1 shows three LL signs. The first from the top is the official street name sign in Latvian, below which is a symbolic trilingual sign in Russian, German and archaic Latvian, which had all at some point in history been used for street name signs at that location.

3 Information on population by ethnic group is published by the Office of Citizenship and Migration Affairs, on WWW at http://www.pmlp.gov.lv/lv/assets/documents/1aaaa/ISPN_Pasvaldibas_pec_TTB.pdf. Accessed July 4, 2018.

4 The Liepāja Russian Society is one of the most active Russian organizations in Latvia, whose members include not only Russians, but also Ukrainians, Belarusians and Latvians. Available:http://www.lro.lv/683.html. Accessed July 16, 2018.

Figure 1: From top: official street name sign, symbolic name sign and informative sign on languages used in the Soviet period (Pošeiko 2018)

The official sign differs from the symbolic sign in its color, size and boldface text. Below this sign is an additional sign which provides cultural-historical information in Latvian and English about language use on street name signs until the Soviet period; namely, that until 1877, street names were in German; until 1902 they were in two languages (German and Russian); and from 1902 to 1918, three languages (German, Russian and Latvian). In the Soviet period, street name signs were bilingual in Latvian and Russian.

The illustrated example shows the possibility of placing unofficial street name signs in other languages or scripts in the Latvian LL, as long as they differ visually from official signs (i.e., do not attempt to imitate official signs), and are placed below official street name signs (e.g., under or to the right).

However, in 2012, after the referendum on the elevation of Russian to the status of a second official language in Latvia,[5] a discussion was started by Yevgeniy Osipov, a representative of the "Native Language" organization, to allow street name signs in Latvian and Russian in cities where a majority of the local population voted for Russian as a second official language. Although only 20% of Liepāja's residents voted for the elevation of Russian to the status of a second

5 The results of the language referendum on the promotion of Russian to the status of a second official language were 24.9% (273,347) FOR and 74.8% (821,722) AGAINST.

official language (NeoGeo 2012), Osipov placed a house number sign with a street name in Latvian and Russian on his parents' house in Liepāja.

Bearing in mind the theoretical, legal and practical issues that have been discussed so far, and the language situation of Liepāja's LL, a number sign placed by Ljudmila Rjazanova on her Liepāja home in 2015 will be analyzed, describing its LM. The broader discussion will be on actors' role in the process, their motivations, power, interests and arguments, and on the language problem management involved in this case.

4.2 Exposition of the multi-level LM of the trilingual house number sign

This section consists of six subsections and provides a description of the language management cycles of a trilingual house number sign.

In May 2015, Ljudmila Rjazanova, a deputy of Liepāja's City Council who was elected from the Social Democratic party "Harmony Center,"[6] placed a house number sign with a street name in three languages: Latvian, English, and Russian (see Figure 2). On the other side, she left the old sign, on which the street name is only in Latvian. This sign lost its relevance in 2009, when Liepāja Municipality approved new rules for number signs' visual design (Liepāja's Rule 2, 2009).

Figure 2: From the left: trilingual house number sign and house number sign in Latvian (Pošeiko 2018)

---

6 The Social Democratic party "Harmony Center" is an ideologically left-wing party which actively advocates for favorable relations with Russia and is constantly critical of Latvia's participation in NATO. The party also pushes for minority rights and friendly interethnic relations. The party is currently in power in large Latvian cities, including Riga, Daugavpils and Rēzekne.

4.2.1. Development of the LM at local, regional and state levels

After about a month, a Liepāja police officer noticed the sign and filed an administrative protocol about a street name appearing also in foreign languages. The sign owner (hereinafter referred to as the *owner*) challenged the Liepāja Municipal Police (hereinafter the *Municipal Police*), which resulted in the Deputy Chief of the Municipal Police's terminating of the previous decision, because the sign complied with Liepāja's Rule No. 2. This LM cycle ended in an outcome favorable to the owner. The most powerful actor (the Deputy Chief of Police) reviewed the case, and in evaluating the language problem identified by his subordinate determined that there was no violation as the "text on the number sign *is* in the state language" (Liepāja's Rule 2, 2009; emphasis by author).

In the beginning, the SLC was only involved remotely, requesting that the owner correct the violation in two weeks. This was ignored. In October 2015, the SLC received a complaint from the Municipal Police about a possible violation of the Official Language Law. Reacting to this complaint, an SLC inspector went to the address listed, where she identified a language problem in terms of language regime and drafted an administrative protocol about the use of foreign languages. The owner was found to have violated Articles 18 and 21 of the Official Language Law (see Table 1). The owner challenged the ruling again, but on January 19, 2016, the SLC director approved the administrative issue and levied a 75 EUR fine. The owner fought the case in Liepāja Municipal Court in April of 2016. After losing this case, she appealed to the next higher authority, the Kurzeme Regional Court, which rejected the appeal. The final decision states that "street names are public information which concern legitimate public interests and are intended to provide public information. A number sign is placed by a private individual; however, it must follow the local government's procedures as to how it should be done and how the information provided to the public is presented" (Constitutional Court 2017a). The Regional Court agreed with the decision of the Liepāja Court and refused to change the ruling simply because the owner disagreed with it.

It appears that an employee of the Municipal Police[7] did not agree with the first result and reported the trilingual sign to the relevant public authority. As the SLC is obliged to respond to received submissions, the sign was re-evaluated, this time by a person who knew the legal rules on language use in LL and who had experience with resolving language problems.

At this stage the sociolinguistic language problem was likely viewed more broadly, in the context of a stronger legal document: holistically, all local government regulations on language use in the public space are subordinate to the Official Language Law. However, an agreement between the inspector and the owner

7 Constitutional Court Case No. 2017-01-01 does not indicate a specific plaintiff but rather, is submitted on behalf of the Municipality as a whole.

was not reached due to differing views. Therefore, litigation was initiated at a local and regional level. This LM cycle was not the last one.

4.2.2. The owner's complaint to Constitutional Court

On November 3, 2016, the Constitutional Court received the Constitutional Complaint (hereinafter the *Complaint*) from the owner. Lawyers of the Latvian Human Rights Committee[8] were involved in its preparation; one of them also represented the owner in the Constitutional Court.

The Complaint consisted of the list of disputed normative documents and a description of the circumstances of the case, which included the depiction of the then-current LM process, the judgment of the Kurzeme Regional Court and references to the historical and contemporary language situation in Latvia. In the beginning, the complainant mentioned several sections of national and international documents (articles and points), which were violated in applying the previously-mentioned norms, according to the owner and her lawyers. In other words, the owner requested that the Constitutional Court recognize that the first parts of Articles 18 and 21 of the Official Language Law (see Table 1) were incompatible with multiple regulatory documents:

- The Constitution of the Republic of Latvia (precisely Articles 91 and 96, the first sentence of Article 100, Article 114) (Constitution 1922)
- The Framework Convention for the Protection of National Minorities (precisely Section 1 of Article 1, Section 1 of Article 10, Parts 1 and 3 of Article 11) (Minority convention 2005)
- The Convention for the Protection of Human Rights and Fundamental Freedoms (precisely Articles 8 and 10) (Convention 1997)
- The international Covenant on Civil and Political Rights (precisely Section 1 of Article 17, Section 1 of Article 19, Article 27) (Preamble 1992)

These documents are related primarily to the idea of privacy, equality, the freedom of verbal expression, and the right of minorities to use and develop the spoken and written forms of their language, ethnic cultural preservations and privacy.

In the complaint, the owner stated that Article 4 on the "Framework Convention for the Protection of National Minorities" (Latvia declares Article 11, Part 3 as binding, insofar as it is not incompatible with the Constitution and other normative acts in force in Latvia regulating the state language use) is incompatible with Article 19, point C "Pretexts" (Vienna Convention 1969). The case also cited articles from other documents: "Law on Administrative Territories and Populated Areas"

8 The Latvian Human Rights Committee is a human rights non-governmental organization founded in 1992. Its primary concerns are tenant rights, minority rights and the legal status of individuals.

(Administrative Territories 2008), "Liepāja's Rule No. 2" (see Table 1) and "Latvian Administrative Violations Code" (Administrative Violations Code 1984).

In the complaint, the owner repeated that she added a sign at her own expense and that the street name was written in Latvian as well. She also pointed out that text in Latvian was first on the sign and highlighted with uppercase letters, and that the old house number sign was only in Latvian. She emphasized that "[she] belongs to the Russian minority and the community of Russian speakers in Latvia. [She] has a right to preserve and develop her native language, which includes communicating her place of living to members of her community in their language" (Constitutional Court 2017a). Repeatedly mentioned is Article 11 of the "Framework Convention for the Protection of National Minorities" regarding the right of minorities to place information in their own language in publicly-visible locations if that information is personally important. However, the owner had been asked to place the sign in Latvian only. The complaint disagreed with the Latvian reservation that Part 3 of Article 11 of the Convention is binding insofar as it does not contradict the Constitution and other normative documents regulating the use of the state language.

In addition, the complainant quoted the opinion of the EU Consultative Committee from 2013, which regrets that there has been no change in the recognition of the use of minority languages in Latvia, and she reiterated that "the open use of minority languages alongside the state language in place names, street names, and other topographical names has a significant symbolic value in terms of integration, as it confirms that the minority is valued in a given region and is a valuable segment of society. It increases the sense of trust in minority communities and contributes to social cohesion" (Constitutional Court 2017a). The complaint also pointed to the unequal treatment of linguistic communities: "She is a representative of the Russian minority," wrote the complainant, "which is in an unequal position with the representatives of a second minority (in number)–Latgalians. This is demonstrated by the SLC's acceptance of a road sign in Kārsava with text in the Latgalian written language in addition to Latvian"[9] (Constitutional Court 2017a).

The Complaint recalled that Latvian did not historically disappear in the context of social bilingualism during the Soviet era, and that the street name signs in Latvian and Russian have not been the reason for the decline of the role of Latvian. It argued that Latvian is no longer in need of additional protection, since all the inhabitants of Latvia have good knowledge of the state language. The share

9 Kārsava is a city in the Latgale region, which placed street name signs, road signs, business name signs exclusively or also in the Latgalian written language in addition to Latvian after a local municipal initiative. The SLC ruled against the municipality because the text in Latgalian written language was dominant on some signs. However, municipality successfully legally convinced the SLC, arguing that the Latgalian written language is a historical variety of the state language, which means that it is still Latvian, just with a different written tradition.

of Latvian as well as the number of speakers of Latvian among minorities has increased (Constitutional Court 2017a).

Some conclusions can be drawn about the Complaint. First, in the complaint the case of the house number sign is considered broadly, challenging the legitimate nature of articles of the State Language Law in the context of other national and international documents and thus defining these articles as metalinguistic language problems. This has led to a situation in which multilingual building number signs in Latvia are considered a sociolinguistic language problem.

Second, minorities' right to equality, non-discriminatory treatment and the free use of their language (including in LL), was highlighted. Therefore, the parallel with the Latgalians is drawn. One group is not allowed to publish official information in their own language while another is accepted, according to the arguments of the owner and her defenders. Here alleviation and mitigation are used as the strategies of language problem management (see Table 2).

Third, only one sentence indirectly justifies the use of another foreign language: English. Tourism is mentioned as the main criterion for choosing a language. This allows one to consider that the main "battle" (linguistic interest) is over the recognition of the use of Russian in a sign.

Fourth, the monolingual sign mentioned by the owner (see Figure 2) is inappropriate according to municipality's rules on the visual design of building number signs (Liepāja's Rule No. 2, 2009). This, similarly to the examples mentioned previously, can be described as a symbolic house number sign which no longer functions to provide official information.

4.2.3. Metalinguistic behavior of the Constitutional Court

The Constitutional Court evaluated this case as complicated, and therefore its evaluation period was extended. The decision to initiate proceedings was announced on January 4, 2017. It stated that "the Constitutional Court can assess the compliance of Latvian national law with international agreements entered into by Latvia which are not in conflict with the Constitution" (Constitutional Court 2017b). For further LM, it is important that the Constitutional Court:

- rejects the owner's claim of a restriction of rights as a minority representative because she is a citizen of Latvia and has not legally demonstrated in the Compliant that her case is related to any group's desire to preserve their intrinsic features over a long period of time. Such evidence would be consistent with the definition of *minority* in UN documents and the Minority Convention ratified by Latvia. (From the documents it is not immediately clear how the owner should express the will to preserve the uniqueness of the ethnic group, as it must be demonstrated in practice to be legally accepted.)
- emphasizes that Article 91 of the Constitution must be read in conjunction with Article 4, which details the constitutional status of Latvian in Latvia. There is no

legally grounded claim of a person to write a street name in foreign language that would follow from Article 91.
- points out that Latgalians have the *de facto* right to use their own language, and that there is no legal basis for comparison between the two groups.

In general, the Constitutional Court concluded that the Complaint lacks legal arguments for a claim of incompatibility with national and international documents or a violation of fundamental rights established in the Constitution.

The Constitutional Court decided to initiate a case "On the compliance of the first section of Article 18 and the first section of Article 21 of the Official Language Law with Article 96 of the Constitution," but refused to initiate proceedings regarding other claims specified in the application (see above). Article 96 of the Constitution reads as follows: "Everyone has the right to inviolability of his or her private life, home and correspondence" (Constitution 1922). The *Saeima* (Parliament of Latvia), as the institution that issued the challenged law, was obliged to submit a response to the Constitutional Court with a description of the factual circumstances of the case and the legal basis.

4.2.4. Response of the Saeima

In March 2017, the Constitutional Court received a response from the *Saeima,* in which it was stated that Article 18 of the Official Language Law is in compliance with Article 96 of the Constitution, whereas proceedings regarding the compliance of Article 21 with the Constitution should be terminated, as it is not binding to the applicant. The owner in this case was not among the actors to which this article of the law applies; she was not a self-employed person engaged in informing society and performing public functions (see Table 1). The application of this provision was a metalinguistic mistake committed by an SLC employee. The *Saeima* informed that

> the monopolistic use of the state language [was] justified not only socially and linguistically, but also psychologically: the need for a unified address system for successful postal work; maintaining Latvian as a national value in the context of increased language competition, and increasing its influence on the Latvian cultural environment; the right of Latvian citizens to receive public information in the state language; gaps between knowledge of the state language and use to achieve legitimate goals. (Constitutional Court 2017a)

In addition to mentioning the promotion of integration in Latvia, the promotion of positive linguistic attitudes towards the state language as an economically and symbolically valuable language was mentioned as an important reason why place names should be solely in Latvian. At the response's end, it was highlighted that the placement of the sign in Latvian was not related to the freedom of expression, nor did it prevent the owner from using their preferred language in private. Societal interests supersede individual interests in language choice for street names.

The *Saeima's* response ended with the conclusion (and implicit recommendation to the owner) that street names in several languages are publishable in private texts, including signs in the private sphere (see above for a symbolic number sign), but are not acceptable in the official sphere.

4.2.5. *Involving experts to obtain convincing arguments*

After about a month, the term of the responsible judge expired, and he was replaced. This meant that the case was taken over by another person who had to familiarize himself with the circumstances of the problem situation and the current process. Firstly, the new judge asked the *Saeima* to submit documents (minutes of *Saeima* meetings, decisions, opinions of external experts), illustrating the procedural progress of the adoption of the Official Language Law, in order to find out the essence of the challenged norms and their compliance with international standards. Secondly, he invited experts to reply in writing to specific questions within their area of competence and comment on the case filed. The invited actors were: (1) the Ministry of Justice, which organizes supervision of compliance with the Official Language Law; (2) the Ombudsman, which promotes the protection of the human rights of individuals; (3) Latvia's representative in international human rights institutions; (4) SLC; (5) Professor Ina Druviete of the University of Latvia, with scholarly expertise in language policy and sociolinguistics.

In general, the actors agreed with the arguments offered by the *Saeima* in its reply. The Ministry of Justice emphasized the national significance of Latvian: "The state, with all the means available to it, should maximally promote the use of Latvian in Latvia – the only place in the world where the Latvian nation is based" (Constitutional Court 2017c). The Ministry also rejected the owner's idea of the number sign's association with her privacy: "She knows her address, the informative sign on the outside of the home is in no way related to her private life or housing, but is focused on informing society" (Constitutional Court 2017c).

The Ombudsman joined the conclusion of the *Saeima* and the Constitutional Court that the first section of Article 21 did not apply to the owner in this case; therefore proceedings related to this article were terminated. The Ombudsman emphasized that

> for the use of Latvian in street name signs and other place name signs has a legitimate aim: to strengthen the use of the state language and to ensure the comprehensive use of Latvian in the public space as the basis of a consolidated society. The state may regulate the use of Latvian in compliance with fundamental human rights [...]. The restriction established in section 1 of Article 18 of the Official Language Law is necessary for the achievement of a legitimate aim in a democratic society. (Constitutional Court 2017c)

Latvia's representative in international human rights institutions raised an issue with the interpretation of the first section of Article 18 of the Official Language Law:

> It is necessary to find out whether the text of the first section of Article 18 of the Official Language Law gives an individual a clear idea of the legislature's desire to regulate what information may be included in the number sign – either the legislature wanted to define the minimum requirement, namely that information in Latvian is compulsory, but under certain conditions also allow for the parallel use of other languages, or it wished to establish the maximum regulation that the use of foreign languages in the number sign is not permissible. (Constitution 2017c)

The Constitutional Court, in reviewing the process of the adoption of the Official Language Law, concluded that the information in the first section of Article 18 is the maximum regulation. Only the state language is possible, without exception.

The SLC pointed out that there had been two similar cases in Liepāja over the past year, but that those were exceptions, because people mostly have a clear understanding of the regulatory framework. The institution as of yet has not received information that tourists have been unable to find an address due to the Latvian language. Here, the SLC also justified the mistake made by the employee in applying to the owner the first section of Article 21:

> Since violations have been detected since 2012, such as displaying a street name in a number sign in a foreign language, this article is also applicable in such cases. Section 1 of Article 21 of the Official Language Law is applicable only in Liepāja, because the binding regulations of the municipality do not provide for administrative liability for such an offence. (Constitutional Court 2017c)

According to the SLC, there are exceptions to the application of the specific provision. For example, if there is a lack of legal regulation at the local level, there is a metalinguistic problem. In its report the SLC appeared to interpret the Official Language Law as it stands. Thus, the first section of Article 21 in this case closed the loophole; Liepāja's Rule No. 2 is a requirement for Latvian on street name signs, but the Liepāja City Administrative Liability Regulations "do not specify punishment for the lack of Latvian or its use in conjunction with foreign languages" (Constitutional Court 2017c).

Druviete referred in her response to theoretical papers in language policy and the latest sociolinguistic studies in Latvia (including Pošeiko's dissertation on LL in the Baltic states, cf. Pošeiko 2015a). She stated that "the task of language policy is to protect the national language necessary for the existence of a state while also guaranteeing minority language rights [...]. The monopoly in certain areas of existence of Latvian, and hence the Latvian ethnic group, is a question of independence" (Constitutional Court 2017c). She also highlighted that "the exclusion of individuals from the scope of the first section of Article 21 of the Official Language Law is considered a weakness of this law and may have an adverse effect on the language use in Latvia" (Constitutional Court 2017c). Druviete emphasized the close connection between language and national identity as well as between language and the social cohesion of the inhabitants of Latvia. According to her, such a metalinguistic language problem can have a negative impact on language use at state level, which may indirectly contribute to the emergence of future sociolinguistic language problems in the Latvian LL.

The opinion on the preparation of the case for consideration was announced in May 2017. Three additional actors were invited to attend the following month: the Ministry of Foreign Affairs, University of Latvia lecturer Māris Lejnieks and Associate Professor at the University of London Mārtiņš Paparinskis, who provided opinions on the compliance of Article 4 of the Law "On the Convention on the Protection of National Minorities" with the objects and purposes of this Convention. All unanimously concluded that this article does not contradict the object and purpose of the Convention.

4.2.6. The final decision of the Constitutional Court

Following the session of the Constitutional Court, in which seven judges participated, everyone was given an opportunity to familiarize themselves with the case materials and express written opinions. By September 28, the only written opinion they had received came from the owner herself. She wrote: "The agreement on the EU Charter of Fundamental Rights, Article 22 confirms Latvia's commitment to linguistic diversity. The use of multiple languages in the public space had not threatened Latvian in the period from 1918 to 1934, when the knowledge of Latvian among minorities was less than it is now" (Constitutional Court 2017a). Here it was again emphasized that the owner is a Russian and that information in Russian and English is a matter of private rights. The owner did not agree that in this case the use of Latvian had been unacceptably restricted. In her opinion, everyone interested had been given the right to receive information in the state language. The text in Latvian was furthermore visually prominent. Moreover, she noted that Russian has been used in street names since the 1960s (Constitutional Court 2017a).

The final decision of the Constitutional Court was announced on November 17, 2017. First, general conclusions about the case were presented. The first conclusion already showed the court's ruling that the house number sign must be only in Latvian:

> In preparing signs, private persons have the responsibility to hold to official defined place and street names. The responsibility to use the state language in place names, as defined in section 1 of Article 18 of the Official Language Law, cannot be narrowed by applying it to government institutions, and applies to private persons. The prohibition to use a foreign language alongside Latvian on the building number sign follows from section 1 of Article 18 of the Official Language Law, which was applied according to the municipal code of Liepaja City Council, which reiterates this opinion. (Constitutional Court 2017a)

The ruling emphasized that

> Article 4 of the Constitution reflects the constitutional status of Latvian [...]. The state language is an integral part of the constitutional identity of Latvia. Latvian confers

> the state a certain – a specifically Latvian – national cultural identity [...]. The principle of a national state imposes not only a negative obligation on the state not to do anything that could weaken Latvia's Latvian identity, but also – and in particular – the positive obligations to strengthen it in various ways. The state has the responsibility to ensure with all available tools that Latvian fulfils its function as the state language – being the language of communication and society and the language of democratic participation. Ensuring the language's status in public visual information has a vital role in language acquisition and improving societal cohesion. Place names are part of the cultural heritage of Latvia, and the state has a responsibility to preserve and defend them. However, street name signs are public information which are necessary for public communication [...]. The reproduction of the content of the sign and its placement is not communication of the building owner with either society as a whole nor any member of it. (Constitution 2017c)

The final decision of the Constitutional Court was "the prohibition of the use of a foreign language parallel to Latvian on a building number sign does not violate the rights to the inviolability of private and domestic life defined in Article 96 of the Constitution" (Constitution 2017c).

The symbolic timing of the decision's announcement must be emphasized: the day before Latvia's Proclamation Day. At the state level, the owner and society certainly were reminded of Latvian constitutional values, including the state language. The language's role in the creation and feeling of a national cultural identity (the micro level) and constitutional identity of the Latvian state (the macro level) was highlighted in the response letter from the *Saeima*, the opinions of those invited by the Constitutional Court, and in the conclusions of the Constitutional Court. Thus, in the view of the public bodies, the result of LM in this case was a strengthening of the discourse about the state language as being an important element of national identity and common language in Latvia.

The uncovering of one case about a house number sign in this section demonstrates the consequential application of multiple LM models in two years, the complication of the LM process and consequential continuity, including many actors. The discussion of the metalinguistic actions of the actors will be continued in the next sections.

4.3 Interests and strategies of the actors

The actors in this case can be divided into two groups: those defending and those against the multilingual house number sign. Each actor assessed the legal justification (or lack thereof) of foreign language use, metalinguistically discussing and strategically using different normatives in national and international documents. Each side used excerpts of documents and expert opinions that they agreed with and which were situationally useful to the prosecution or defense.

To use Lanstýak's terms, the defense (the owner and her advocates) tried belittlement as its first strategy of language problem management (see Table 2), repeatedly mentioning that the state language was included in the house number sign. When this failed, they used the parts of national and international normative acts which were unclear, contradictory or misunderstood, which could have been interpreted as being in favor of the owner if they were not viewed in the context of other points within these or other documents (i.e., if they were decontextualized). After losing in the municipality court, it was clear that in the current circumstances, the owner could not legally keep the unaltered sign. Consequently, her strategy was to contest the articles of the Official Language Law at the state level in order to ensure that the sign was not legally a problem. Here they applied elimination as the strategy of language problem management (see Table 2); the main idea was that the problem was not the multilingual sign, but some parts in the Official Language Law.

Legal arguments (see the list of normative documents above), linguistic arguments (knowledge and use of the state language) and personal arguments (native language, private communication with family members) were all used. The situation was also compared to the use of Latgalian written language in official signs. The owner's initiative contributed to the legal process in which those responsible for the norm (*Saeima*, language policymakers and inspectors) had to re-evaluate parts of the State Language Law, justify their legitimacy and extend them to the owner's language practice (the trilingual number sign).

The purpose of the metalinguistic activities of the two groups was based on linguistic discourse and the attempt to change the opposite group's view. Advocates of the trilingual sign sought official recognition of the use of Russian in a public space, followed by changes of language practices in the LL. The owner initiated a change in discourse from the idea of the state language being threatened to the idea of its "sociolinguistic security." She sought to change public opinion about Latvian as a specially protected language because, according to her, use and knowledge of the state language was (is) high.

In turn, the aim of LM by those responsible for the normative language issues (the *Saeima*) and the additional actors invited by the Constitutional Court (including the SLC) was to prevent such a change in public discourse (in particular sections of society) by defending the national ideology, strengthening the idea of legitimacy of the Official Language Law and holding a monopoly for the state language in official LL signs. The most useful argument in the process was the obligation of the state to protect Latvian by avoiding of an alternative language hierarchy, preventing Latvian from being "squeezed" out of official public domains. The role of Latvian in the creation and preservation of national identity and communication between the Latvian citizens (i.e., the symbolic and integrative functions of the language) was emphasized in different contexts.

Actors can also be defined as those who, in addition to analyzing the language problem, also assessed the language problem management. The *Saeima* and the Constitutional Court evaluated not only the language problem, metalinguistic problem (the State Language law's compliance with the Constitution) and social problem (in this case, the concept of privacy), but also the whole resolution process of defined language problems. Consequently, they were responsible both for language practices and for assessing the metalinguistic activities of advocating and controlling institutions within the framework of normative acts. This LM process included two metalinguistic problems: the misinterpretation of language use in a number sign by a municipal policeman and the incorrect interpretation by a SLC inspector of the first section of Article 21 of the Official Language Law.

5 Discussion

5.1 Noting

The description of the proceedings shows that trilingual house number sign was spotted and identified at its location as a language problem by two public officials (a city policeman and an SLC inspector) over the course of few months. Previously defined and relatively clear metalinguistic activities began at this point. However, the language problem was re-identified with each subsequent actor involved; it was noticed again when looking at a photograph and getting to know the circumstances of the case. Thus, it can be argued that the language problem is detected as many times as actors are involved in LM issues.

5.2 Evaluation and selection of adjustment design

Many actors (state institutions, non-governmental organizations, experts) assessed the language problem in a narrow or broad context on many occasions. Each actor had the right, the need and/or the obligation to express his/her opinion, advocate individual and linguistic group interests, though each of them had their own tasks and motivations (e.g., to comment on the rights of ethnic minorities, to describe the use of Latvian, to defend nationalist interests). Thus, the language problem was associated with other socially significant problems: minority rights, divisions of the private and public spaces, language acquisition, language situation (in particular, the use of Latvian in different public domains).

Public bodies unanimously expressed that the proper solution of the language problem was a monolingual sign in Latvian. Although each used their own arguments, the general idea was related to the protection of a national state, including concerns for and responsibilities to constitutional values, i.e., Latvian as the state language in order to function as the basis for national identity and a common language in all sociolinguistic domains. There was no suggestion of the equivalent functioning of Russian in such signs, so that the idea of bilingualism did not develop more widely or become established as an acceptable language practice.

In turn, the owner and her lawyers did not perceive the number sign as a language problem or claimed an incompatibility between the two articles of the Official Language Law and other national and international documents related to the regulation of language use. Although they offered no direct amendments or additions to existing norms explicitly, their objective at the macro level was to attempt to change the Official Language Law providing for a wider use of minority languages in Latvia. At the micro and meso level, their goal was to justify the street name in three languages in the current legal context.

5.3 Implementation

A clear indication of the necessary changes (in this case, a new house number sign only in Latvian) was repeatedly expressed and communicated to the owner. However, she implemented none, even after receiving the decision of the Constitutional Court. The language practice remained unchanged; on August 28, 2018, the sign remained in its original place.

A resolution of the language problem has not followed the judicial result. Implementation has not occurred, and the owner has left the sign unchanged. None of the actors have the legal right to go and remove the sign themselves, replace it with an alternative that complies with language policy in Latvia, or enjoin the owner to do so herself. Though the owner lost the case, in practice, state institutions (and especially the SLC) have thus far shown themselves to be powerless in enforcing normative documents or compliance with court decisions at a state level. A situation has arisen in which it is impossible to achieve the desired result—an official sign only in the state language—in a lawful way if the owner does not make the change herself in good faith.

Thus, in this case, there is a partial solution of the language problem; the use of foreign language in building number signs is recognized as a deviation from the norm, but adjustment design has not been implemented in practice. In turn, the metalinguistic problem has been resolved; the powerful public body has ruled that section 1 of Article 18 of the State Language Law does not infringe the right to privacy, complies with other national and international normative documents and is binding on Latvian citizens. However, it has not helped to change the views of the owner and to influence the language practice at the micro level. A logical question arises: who is responsible for the final resolution of such a language problem?

The public affairs specialist for the Liepāja Municipal Police explained via email that

> Liepāja Police enforce the 2009 binding Rules No. 2 'Procedure for the placement of building number, street or square name signs in Liepāja'; however, the Constitutional Court's decision mentioned that it is the State Language Law which was violated, which the Municipal Police do not control. The execution of a court decision is controlled by a bailiff, not by the Municipal Police, and observance of the State Language Law in Latvia is supervised by the State Language Center. Ensuring the sign's change is not in the jurisdiction of the Municipal Police. (email, May 17, 2018)

The SLC, on the other hand, transferred liability to the Municipal Police, arguing that the SLC did not have the right to oblige an institution/person to change a sign (Interview in SLC, February 20, 2018.). Both actors used devolution as the strategy of language problem management (see Table 2) to shift responsibility for this phase of language problem resolution or its consequences. The Municipal Police also shifted responsibility to the Constitutional Court, demonstrating an inaccurate understanding of the Court's decision. This is not related to the language problem (i.e., does the number sign violate the State Language Law), but rather with the metalinguistic language problem (i.e., do the first section of Article 18 and the first section of Article 21 of the State Language Law infringe upon the right to privacy and home inviolability provided for in the Constitution). It is not legally defined in any normative document who is entitled or obliged to remove a sign and replace it with an official sign if the sign owner refuses to do so. A legally formulated action plan for such cases in an administrative procedural law, municipal regulation or the court decision would be necessary for LM to be effective not only legally, but also practically.

Considering the case discussed above, the overall LM process of the house number sign can be divided into the following cycles:

1. Management cycle without additional experts at the municipal level.
2. Management cycle at the regional level.
3. Management cycle under SLC supervision.
4. The defense's management cycle for the preparation of the complaint.
5. The Constitutional Court's management cycle for initiating the case.
6. The management cycle of experts invited by the Constitutional Court.
7. The Constitutional Court's management cycle for conclusion and decision making.
8. The management cycle for practical implementation of the result.

6 The owner's thoughts about language management and language use in Liepāja

As the owner's Constitutional Court complaint is not publicly available, her opinion is published on the website sputniknews.lv, which is subject to mixed public opinion and is known for its bias against the Latvia state. A journalist tells readers that the owner

> deemed it necessary that the street name on her home was written not only in the state language, but also in her mother tongue, as well as in the international language, English, so that guests from anywhere in the world could find the home and that her children could memorize their address in their native language. On one hand, this is due to personal reasons; on the other, there is no reason to believe that any rights were violated. On the contrary, the street name was written in larger letters in the state language than it was in English or Russian. (Dorofejevs 2017)

It should be noted that argument does not hold water when considered in context: the street name is not translated differently in either of the two languages, so its memorization could not possibly be a problem for children or tourists.

In order to get the owner's opinion, I asked several questions over email on April 22, 2018 about the house number sign, linguistic identity, her attitude towards language policy and the language situation in Liepāja and Latvia, and preferred languages in Liepāja's LL. A letter with her answers, dated May 3, after her request, is published in full:[10]

> I was born and raised in Liepāja. Latvia is my Motherland, and I do everything in my power so that our Latvia develops. I am Russian, my mother tongue is Russian. I speak Russian and Latvian fluently and can also understand and respond in Lithuanian. Maybe I make mistakes when writing in Latvian and I cannot be a writer, but my knowledge does not prevent me from working or communicating with people. And I believe that people are richer if they know several languages. Then there are no boundaries to communication... I am FOR Latvian as a state language... It is only necessary to find a way for citizens to learn the language. I learned the Latvian language from playing with children and attending meetings, at college, school, technical school and university.
>
> I learned the song "Who's in the Garden?" when we took part in Christmas activities at mom's workplace... I learned how to sing the song "Blow, Breezes" in the choir while studying at the Russian-Latvian high school and participating in the choir's performances... I know the poems of Rainis by heart... My colleague told me that she danced in a dance collective in the 1960s. They also danced Latvian folk dances... Therefore, when they write and tell us that speaking Latvian was forbidden or impossible, it's not true...
>
> When our grandchildren from Russia, England and Latvia meet and come together–they do not agree on which language they will communicate in: they just find common language, communicate and play... Our children and grandchildren speak several languages...
>
> I believe that pitting ethnic groups against one another benefits our political leadership, for as long as we quarrel over language issues, they do good and not-so-good things. They live by the "divide and conquer" principle... One example is OIK (*Obligātā iepirkuma komponentes* 'Compulsory Procurement Components')... A disproportionate burden affects our companies' ability to compete, citizens are forced to pay inappropriate payments for electricity. Therefore, several companies do not survive!
>
> We need to pay attention to the fact that for all of the talk about integration, what is going on in life? Why is it that when Russian-speaking children go to a Latvian kindergarten, only ONE of the six children remain in the group in a year's time, waiting to be given a place in the Russian kindergarten? Because the kindergarten teachers do not like the fact that children cannot speak Latvian and must be trained... it's easier

10 The letter is originally written in Latvian; though it contained some spelling mistakes, they do not hinder the reader's understanding of the sentences or the idea of the text. Translation in English is provided by the author. The text contains all original text's highlights and punctuation.

> to force children out of the kindergarten… none of the parents argue, because if you go to complain, what will the attitude be towards the children? And I have many such examples for other themes.
>
> Why do we live so poorly at this time? Because we are tackling issues that do not contribute to economic growth… Why are so many people leaving Latvia?… Why are taxes so high and incomes so low?… I am more in touch with such questions than who speaks what language. We have a very good relationship with our Latvian neighbors; we help each other… We have an advantage—our people are familiar with different languages, we could establish good economic relations with neighboring Russia—we've lost the latter, and the Latvian railway is an example of this…
>
> A sign with a street name in three languages is not a violation. The name of the street is indicated on the sign in Latvian, in accordance with Liepāja City Council binding regulations. The three languages used are our family's languages… Why doesn't anyone complain about people speaking English in companies, or an advertisement only in English?
>
> I hope I have answered your questions.

The letter expresses the owner's positive linguistic attitude towards Latvian. She believes that language knowledge and use is a prerequisite for successful communication between different ethnic groups. According to her, in Soviet times, it was possible to practice Latvian activities and to speak Latvian. This fact, in her opinion, is not considered in many cases.

Alongside language issues she actualizes some social problems too, including integration policy and its arguable practices in educational settings. Only the last paragraph directly justifies the number sign's presence in the LL of Liepāja. She states that the sign is not a legal violation, as it complies with city regulations. The language choice is based on the languages used in her family. According to her, the use of English in Latvian companies is insufficiently considered as a language problem. She also highlights the use of English in an advertising, which she says accepted by default. However, this ignores the fact that this type of language sign belongs to the commercial sphere, which is regulated by different articles of the Official Language Law and is not comparable to official signs.

The letter does not answer all the questions asked. It is implied that the sign will not be removed, as the owner does not see it as a violation of language policy. She does not comment on the use or necessity of other foreign languages (e.g., Lithuanian, Polish, Belarusian, Roma, Spanish, etc.) in Liepāja's LL. Thus, owner does not defend the rights of all minority or foreign language speakers, but rather advocates for the right to use her "mother language."

7 Conclusion

The language situation in LL, in particular in its official sphere, creates an understanding of which languages are necessary and can be used in public signs. To some extent, it provides an example of what to do in similar cases. Therefore, language policy advocates, and controllers are actively following, the use of the state language in LL, in particular on signs which contain information on national culture and history. An important and powerful "player" in language regulation and interpretation, as well as in the application of regulatory acts, is the SLC, but the example illustrated has shown that the SLC's capacity (power) is not endless.

A language problem which is based on language use which does not conform to legal norms points to the language practice of a subset of society in private and other domains, including some linguistic expectations; for example, that their language would be approved or accepted. Sociolinguistic language problems arise when personal and collective interests do not align with the interests of the state and when language users (micro level) and the state (macro level) have different opinions about language choice in the public sphere in general as well as specifically on one or another type of sign.

Standardization is a hallmark of official signs in the LL. Their visual appearance and content are largely fixed at local, regional and national levels, as presented in the case of Liepāja. State and municipal institutions, companies owned by these institutions, and self-employed persons performing public functions may officially only place texts in the state language, but in certain cases exceptions are allowed (e.g., language signs related to international tourism, public safety). House number signs with street names placed by private individuals, however, are no exception and must be only in the state language. Although street name signs have been in more than one language in the Latvian LL during certain historical periods, bilingual or multilingual street names currently are only legally accepted in the case of symbolic signs placed as a supplement to official signs.

The chapter has examined the repeatedly identified, analyzed and metalinguistically reviewed language problem: an official house number sign containing language use non-compliant with normative documents. Although multilingual signs of LL's official sphere are usually related to tourism indicated by topic and co-presence of English, this sign shows the multilingual language practice in a different domain.

This sociolinguistic language problem has been viewed holistically in the context of normative documents, as well as in the context of other sociolinguistic and metalinguistic language problems (the gap between language knowledge and use; language competition in the business environment; the incompatibility of the Official Language Law with the Constitution) using mainly political and sociolinguistic arguments. The metalinguistic language problem, i.e., the compatibility of two sections of the Official Language Law with the Constitution, has been resolved through standard LM processes. However, the sociolinguistic language problem remains unresolved. This means that the number sign with the street name in three languages has not been replaced with a version compliant with the normative documents, remaining unchanged in linguistic practice (i.e., there is no official number sign at the house on Rucava street with the street name in only Latvian).

In Latvia, the implementation of language adjustment is problematic; language problem management is not legally codified. Analysis of normative documents, studies of the functions, tasks and rights of responsible state institutions, as well as interviews with the advocates and controllers of the language policy showed that there is a lack of legal mechanism by which to achieve the desired sociolinguistic result, that is, the implementation of adjustment for a language problem, which in the context of LL would mean the placement of a new language sign. Consequently, it is possible that similar cases will occur if the practical outcome of the case is discussed more widely in the public space and people begin to understand the SLC's inability to remove and replace a language sign or to oblige another state institution to do so.

In our present case, the owner or better to say her layers, probably aware of the limited ability of state/municipal institutions to fully resolve the issue, has not used the opportunity to place a symbolic multilingual number sign. This would be a compromise between the two "players" in the case: the owner and the state (including SLC as a responsible authority). Therefore, it is now the case that the multilingual number sign is allowed by default. This situation (and possibly other later cases) arises due to the powerlessness of state institutions (SLC, municipal police) to ensure the implementation of prescriptive norms given by law if the owner either does not comply with or chooses to ignore legal decisions. It can be concluded that the sociolinguistic resolution in LL of a language problem does not necessarily follow from the legal resolution of a language problem (in this case, the legal decision that the number sign does not comply with normative documents and the finding that no human rights were violated).

Acknowledgments

This chapter has been produced within the framework of the ERAF postdoctoral research project "Linguistic Landscape of the City as a Multifaceted Resource in the Baltic States: Linguists,' Entrepreneurs' and Students' Perspectives" (No 1.1.1.2/VIAA/1/16/011).

References

Administrative Territories (2008) *Law on Administrative Territories and Populated Areas.* On WWW at https://likumi.lv/ta/en/en/id/315654-law-on-administrative-territories-and-populated-areas. Accessed December 20, 2021.

Administrative Violations Code (1984) *Latvian Administrative Violations Code.* On WWW at https://likumi.lv/ta/en/en/id/89648-latvian-administrative-violations-code. Accessed December 20, 2021.

Backhaus, P. (2007) *Linguistic Landscapes: A Comparative Study of Urban Multilingualism in Tokyo.* Clevedon: Multilingual Matters.

Balode, L. (2008) Varas atspulgs Latvijas vietvārdos [Reflection of power in Latvian place names]. *Latvijas Universitātes raksti. Valodniecība. Latvistika,* 7–16.

Burr, S. (2021) Chances for and restrictions against publishing texts in foreign language in the official sphere of the Latvian linguistic landscape. In A. Vershik (ed) *Acta Humaniora: Multilingual Practices in the Baltic States.* Tallinn: Tallinn University Press, 56–88.

Constitution (1922) The Constitution of the Republic of Latvia. On WWW at http://www.saeima.lv/en/legislation/constitution. Accessed July 21, 2018.

Constitutional Court (2017a) *Satversmes tiesas lieta Nr. 2017-01-01* [Constitutional Court Case No 2017-01-01]. Satversmes tiesas dokumenti Satversmes tiesas Kancelejā. On WWW at https://www.satv.tiesa.gov.lv/cases/?search[number]=2017-01-01. Accessed October 30, 2021.

Constitutional Court (2017b) *Satversmes tiesas lēmums par lietas izskatīšanu* [Decision of the Constitutional Court on the examination of the case]. On WWW at http://www.satv.tiesa.gov.lv/web/viewer.html?file=http://www.satv.tiesa.gov.lv/wp-content/uploads/2017/01/2017-01-01_Lemums_ierosinasana-1.pdf#search. Accessed May 16, 2018.

Constitutional Court (2017c) *Satversmes tiesas lēmums par tiesvedības izbeigšanu lietā Nr. 2017-01-01* [Decision of the Constitutional Court on termination of legal proceedings in Case No 2017-01-01]. On WWW at https://www.satv.tiesa.gov.lv/web/viewer.html?file=/wp-content/uploads/2017/01/2017-01_01_Lemums_izbeigsana.pdf#search=. Accessed October 18, 2021.

Convention (1997) *Convention for the protection of human rights and fundamental freedoms.* On WWW at https://likumi.lv/ta/en/starptautiskie-ligumi/id/649-convention-for-the-protection-of-human-rights-and-fundamental-freedoms. Accessed May 16, 2018.

Dorofejevs, V. (2017) *"Pretvalstiskās" plāksnītes lieta Liepājā* [The case of the "anti-state" plaque in Liepaja]. On WWW at https://sputniknewslv.com/20170118/Valsts-valodas-centrs-ielas-plaksnite-Liepaja-Rjazanova-3677850.html. Accessed December 20, 2021.

Dovalil, V. (2015) Language management theory as a basis for the dynamic concept of EU language law. *Current Issues in Language Planning* 16 (4), 360–377.

Fairbrother, L., Nekvapil, J. & Sloboda, M. (eds) (2018) *The Language Management Approach: A Focus on Research Methodology.* Berlin: Peter Lang.

Gorter, D. (ed) (2006) *Linguistic Landscape: A New Approach to Multilingualism.* Bristol: Multilingual Matters.

Gorter, D., Marten, H. F. & Van Mensel, L. (eds) (2012) *Minority Languages in the Linguistic Landscape.* London: Palgrave Macmillan.

Jernudd, B. H. & Neustupný, J. V. (1987) Language planning: For whom? *Proceedings of the International Colloquium on Language Planning.* Québec: Les Presses de L'Université Laval, 69–84.

Lanstýak, I. (2014) On the process of language problem management. *Slovo a slovesnost* 75 (4), 325–351.

Lanstýak, I. (2018) On the strategies of managing language problems. In L. Fairbrother, J. Nekvapil, M. Sloboda (eds) *The Language Management Approach: A Focus on Research Methodology.* Berlin: Peter Lang, 67–97.

Liepāja's Rule 2 (2009) Liepājas noteikumi 2. Ēku numurzīmju, ielu vai laukumu nosaukumu norāžu izvietošanas kārtība Liepājā [Liepaja's Rule 2: Procedure for the Placement of Building Number Plates, Street or Square Name Signs in Liepaja]. On WWW at https://likumi.lv/ta/id/188335-eku-numurzimju-ielu-vai-laukumu-nosaukumu-norazu-izvietosanas-kartiba-liepaja. Accessed May 16, 2018.

Ločmele, G. (2015) Latviešu valodas ilgtspēja, kvalitāte un konkurētspēja reklāmā [Sustainability, quality and competitiveness of the Latvian language in advertising]. *Scriptus Magnus* 2, 61–83.

Marten, H. F. (2010) Linguistic landscapeunder strict state language policy: Reversing the Soviet legacy in a regional centre in Latvia. In E. Shohamy, E. Ben-Rafael & M. Barni (eds) *Linguistic Landscape in the City.* Bristol: Multilingual Matters, 115–132.

Minority convention (2005) Framework convention for the protection of national minorities. On WWW at https://likumi.lv/doc.php?id=109252. Accessed May 16, 2018.

Nekvapil, J. (2012) Some thoughts on "noting" in Language Management Theory and beyond. *Journal of Asian Pacific Communication* 22 (2), 160–173.

Nekvapil, J. (2016) Language Management Theory as one approach in Language Policy and Planning. *Current Issues in Language Planning* 17 (1), 11–22.

NeoGeo (2012) Tautas nobalsošanas rezultātu karte [National referendum results map]. On WWW at http://neogeo.lv/?p=12864. Accessed June 14, 2018.

Official Language Law (1999) Official Language Law. On WWW at https://likumi.lv/ta/en/en/id/14740-official-language-law. Accessed June 12, 2018.

Pošeiko, S. (2015a) *Valodas un to funkcionalitāte pilsētu publiskajā telpā: Baltijas valstu lingvistiskā ainava* [Languages and their Functionality in Urban Public Space: The Linguistic Landscape of the Baltic States]. Doctoral thesis in Latvian. Rīga: LU.

Pošeiko, S. (2015b) The Latvian language in the linguistic landscape of Daugavpils (the middle of the 19th century – today). *The Journal of Education, Culture, and Society* 2, 320–336.

Pošeiko, S. (2018) Rīgas centra lingvistiskās ainavas izkārtnes 20. gs. pirmajā pusē [Linguistic landscape of the center of Riga in the first half of the 20th century]. In I. Vītola (ed) *Dzīves lingvistika: veltījumkrājums profesoram Jānim Valdmanim* [Linguistics of Life: A Festschrift in Honour of Jānis Valdmanis]. Rīga: LU Akadēmiskais apgāds, 145–171.

Preamble (1992) International Covenant on Civil and Political Rights. Preamble. https://likumi.lv/ta/en/starptautiskie-ligumi/id/705-international-covenant-on-civil-and-political-rights. Accessed May 16, 2018.

Puzey, G. (2012) Two-way traffic: How linguistic landscapes reflect and influence the politics of language. In D. Gorter, H. F. Marten & L. V. Mensel (eds) *Minority Languages in the Linguistic Landscape*. London: Palgrave Macmillan, 127–147.

Ragačevičs, V. & Zilgalve, E. (2015) Lekcija par valodu reklāmā „Pielāgo valodu!“ [Lecture about language in advertisements "Adapt the language!"]. On WWW at https://www.youtube.com/watch?v=4IwNL-0XILQ. Accessed July 12, 2018.

Regulations No. 50 (2012) *Regulations Regarding Geographical Names Information*. On WWW at https://likumi.lv/ta/en/en/id/243610-regulations-regarding-geographical-names-information. Accessed December 20, 2021.

Regulations No. 130 (2005) *Regulations regarding Use of Languages in Information*. On WWW at Cab._Reg._No._130_-_Use_of_Languages_in_Information.doc (live.com) Accessed December 20, 2021.

Shohamy, E. & Gorter, D. (eds) (2009) *Linguistic Landscape: Expanding the Scenery*. New York: Routledge.

SLC (2017) Valsts valodas centrs: Par mums [State Language Center: About us]. On WWW at http://vvc.gov.lv/index.php?route=product/category&path=65_169. Accessed July 20, 2018.

Sloboda, M. (2009) A language management approach to language maintenance and shift: A study from post-Soviet Belarus. In J. Nekvapil & T. Sherman (eds) *Language Management in Contact Situations: Perspectives from Three Continents*. Frankfurt on the Main: Peter Lang, 15–47.

Vienna Convention (1969) *Vienna Convention on the Law of Treaties*. On WWW at https://legal.un.org/ilc/texts/instruments/english/conventions/1_1_1969.pdf. Accessed December 20, 2021.

Part III
Foreign language policies, teaching and learning, and use

Lisa Fairbrother

Interests and power in English education policy in Japan: A focus on the high school 'Teaching/Learning English in English' policy

Abstract Focusing on the 'Teaching/Learning English in English' policy for high schools, this chapter examines how interests and power influence the language management of English language education policy in Japan. By investigating the language management processes occurring at the different stages of the formulation, evaluation, implementation, and post-implementation of the policy, it reveals the broad range of pedagogical, economic, and political interests involved and the power relations of agents and actors from the national level right down to the individual classroom. In practice, the policy's effectiveness is questioned by some, and it is argued that the government's failure to ensure the full implementation of the policy enables it to be avoided or resisted. Additionally, there are doubts whether the policy will be improved in the future, as it is unclear whether the government is paying attention to the concerns of teachers and students post-implementation.

Keywords Japanese English education policy, the policy-making process, pre- and post-implementation evaluations, power, interests, norms

1 Introduction

The state of English language education in Japan has been the focus of debate for a number of decades. Although English is taught as a compulsory subject during the six years of junior and senior high school, the English language teaching system in schools has been criticized for its emphasis on reading skills over speaking and listening skills (Koike 1978; Barker 2018), students' lack of conversation skills (Honna 1995; Fukunaga 2016), a lack of adequate teacher training and ineffective teaching materials (Browne & Wada 1998; Barker 2018), a lack of in-service training opportunities (Fukunaga 2016), a lack of reform in the university entrance exam system (LoCastro 1996; Barker 2018), and an emphasis on private-sector examinations, such as the Test of English for International Communication (TOEIC), which focus heavily on grammatical knowledge (Seargeant 2009).

The Japanese government has implemented a number of policy initiatives since the 1980s to try to improve the general state of English language education in schools. For example, the Japan Exchange and Teaching (JET) Programme was set up to hire English-speaking teaching assistants, English Oral Communication classes were introduced to the high school curriculum, and more money was provided for teacher training. However, despite these changes, it seems that no great progress has been made in the improvement of the communicative English language skills of the population as a whole (Keidanren 2000; Barker 2018). This suggests that there is a gap between language education policy and the subsequent learning outcomes from schools and individual classrooms. Aspinall (2013) even goes so far as to describe the Japanese government's recent English policies as mere "policy window-dressing."

This situation clearly raises a number of questions for those interested in both language education and language policy and planning (LPP). Despite the considerable number of policy initiatives, why are the English skills, particularly speaking skills, of the Japanese population still considered inadequate by both educators and policy influencers (Seargeant 2009; Barker 2018)? If school students' English proficiency is not improving, this suggests that there must be some issues relating to the government's policies. However, do the problems lie in the policy itself or are they more related to its implementation, or rather lack of implementation?

Although several researchers have focused on problems relating to English education policy in Japan and policies introduced to improve it (Honna 1995; Seargeant 2009), little research has focused on the processes underlying policy development and tried to trace it to its ultimate implementation (Bouchard 2017). One exception is Fukunaga's (2016) study of the Japanese *New Course of Study* (MEXT 2009a), which examined the development of the policy through to its implementation at both the institutional and individual teacher level. Fukunaga's research highlights the need to investigate more thoroughly the issues of who determines what the problems are, why and how they should be removed and how, or if, strategies designed to remove those problems are actually being implemented. In this sense, language management theory (LMT) (Jernudd & Neustupný 1987) is a useful framework for tracing the processes underlying language policy, from the noting and evaluation of deviations, to the design of adjustment plans and their implementation.

Of course, language policy is never created and implemented in a vacuum; it is always subject to the interests and power relations of the people involved. According to Neustupný's (2002: 4) definition, "Interests are aspirations for a certain state of affairs that is favorable to the subject. Power operates on interests. Power is the capacity to implement one's interests." Consequently, power can take many forms and rather than being seen as a monolithic entity, it "needs to be understood in relation to other elements in a complex web of force relations" (Kubota 2009: 244). Researchers working with LMT have shown how interests can affect the evaluation of deviations (Son 2017) and how power relations can affect who is able to implement adjustments to remove language problems (Fairbrother 2015a, 2015b, 2018). Therefore, in order to fully understand why problems occur in the formulation and implementation of language education policy, it is also important to examine how interests and power relations affect these processes.

This chapter will thus attempt to examine the interests and power underlying the language management of English language education policy in Japan, with a particular focus on the policy that Yamada (2010) has termed the 'Teaching/

Learning English in English' policy, introduced in Japanese high schools from 2013. This policy is of particular interest because although it advocates that high school English classes should be conducted through the medium of English, many high school graduates, including some of the current author's own students, claim that this was never actually implemented in their schools. This chapter, therefore, aims to investigate the language management processes occurring at the different stages of the formulation and implementation of the policy, and the interests and power dynamics reflected at each stage, in an attempt to understand why the policy is considered by some to be ineffective, or at least not fully implemented.

2 Problems associated with English language education and policy in Japan

The problems with Japanese English language education have been pointed out by numerous researchers and educators since the 1970s (Seargeant 2009). As Honna (1995: 57) explains:

> People have not developed proficiency in English as a language for international communication [...]. Many government, industrial and educational leaders expressed concern and proposed reforms. However, no significant change has been witnessed.

Research on English education policy in Japanese schools has shown that, in practice, there is still an emphasis placed on translation and sentence-level reading, which is commonly blamed on the importance given to passing Japanese university entrance examinations (LoCastro 1996; Barker 2018), which have traditionally placed a heavy focus on being able to answer tricky multiple-choice questions, without much attention given to the production of language. Traditionally, English classes were taught through the medium of Japanese, much like a classical language such as Latin might be taught in other parts of the world, and Aspinall (2013) argues that English is still taught like this in many schools. Subsequently, as the majority of teachers learned English in this way, their English communicative proficiency has often been regarded as low. This situation has resulted in little emphasis being placed on speaking or broader communication skills (Honna 1995). Additionally, the general tendency to focus on examinations has led to a very lucrative private preparatory school industry and an even more lucrative homegrown English language testing industry, including the TOEIC and the Test in Practical English Proficiency (EIKEN) examinations. English language education is clearly big business in Japan, but this then begs the question of why Japanese people in general are considered to have low English skills despite all this investment. Indeed, Fukunaga (2016: 21) points out the "mismatch between the abundant resources available for English education and the unsuccessful outcomes."

A number of scholars have claimed that part of the problem is ideologically and politically motivated, with some even arguing that the Japanese government does not actually want to improve the population's foreign language skills (Hayes 1979;

Befu 1983; Aspinall 2013). These arguments relate to the ideological position often referred to as *nihonjinron*, that is, the 'discourses of Japaneseness' (Ko 2010), which advocates the uniqueness and separateness of Japan and the Japanese people versus the Other. Indeed, as Hashimoto (2013: 30) argues, "English remains the Other in Japan." A number of scholars have further argued that ineptitude in English is actually an intentional decision. For example, Hayes (1979: 372) argues that:

> It may very well be that the Japanese do not want to learn English or, for that matter, any foreign language, as the bilingual and those having spent any time abroad are 'deviant' in the Japanese eye, not to be entirely trusted [...], [they] may be 'contaminated' and no longer 'pure' Japanese.

The anthropologist Harumi Befu (1983: 242) has also argued that "[i]t is as if ineptitude of foreign language instruction and learning is maintained (though needless to say, unconsciously) for the very purpose of convincing millions of Japanese of their separateness from foreigners." Over thirty years later Barker (2018: 145) argues that "there is still a strong prejudice against the idea of Japanese people using English with each other," stemming from what he sees as traditional views of English as "the language of the enemy."

Nihonjinron has also been seen to influence the goals of English language education in Japan. Liddicoat's (2013) analysis of Japanese policy documents demonstrates that the primary goal of teaching English is not to learn about other cultures and people but, rather, "to foster Japanese identity" (54) and to help Japan be correctly understood by people from other countries:

> Intercultural relationships therefore are ones in which the Japanese express their perspectives through the medium of English. Thus, foreign language learning is seen as a vehicle for the expression of Japaneseness through other languages rather than as a way of mediating between Japanese and other perspectives. (Liddicoat 2013: 57)

As Liddicoat's comparison of foreign language learning policies around the world demonstrates, this is one way in which the Japanese government's approach to foreign language education differs from that of other countries. On the other hand, Bouchard (2017: 175) warns us also not to overlook the emphasis on "international cooperation" and "international understanding" often mentioned in policy documents, and not to forget the "complex (if not contradictory) nature of policy discourse."

A number of policies and initiatives have been implemented over the years in an attempt to improve the general standards of English education in Japan. For example, the JET Programme was founded in 1987 "with the purpose of increasing mutual understanding between the people of Japan and the people of other nations" and promoting "internationalization in Japan's local communities by helping to improve foreign language education and developing international exchange at the community level" (CLAIR 2015). As part of this program, Assistant Language Teachers were recruited from overseas to teach at junior and senior high schools around Japan. Then, from 1989, English Oral Communication classes, focusing on communicative skills, became mandatory in high schools. *The Action Plan to Cultivate "Japanese with English Abilities"* (MEXT 2003) was announced in 2003. It outlined a series of goals to be achieved by 2008, including the establishment of sixteen (later increased to fifty) specialized 'Super English Language High Schools,'[1] targets for the number of high school students studying abroad, test score requirements for English teachers, an increase in the number of Assistant Language Teachers, the introduction of English conversation activities in elementary schools, and goals for the improvement of English classes in junior and senior high schools, including the specification that the "majority of an English class will be conducted in English and many activities where students can communicate in English will be introduced." Despite these reforms, it has been difficult to argue that these measures have actually brought about wide-reaching change. At least in terms of international English test scores, in 2010 Japan's Test of English as a Foreign Language (TOEFL) scores were still very low, ranking 135th out of 163 countries in total, and 27th within Asia (ETS 2011). Although Japan's TOEFL ranking within Asia had moved up from the second lowest place in 2003, it was still the 4th lowest ranked in 2010, surpassing only Cambodia, Laos, and Tajikistan. There appears to be a gap, therefore, between policy initiatives and the development of students' actual proficiency.

Indeed, despite the best intentions of governments and policy makers, research has shown that language education policy is often not implemented as intended. As Kaplan and Baldauf (1997: 150) argued, "implementation requires much more than a set of top-down decisions," including the proper allocation of adequate resources. Chua (2008: 195) has also pointed out the necessity of the inclusion of micro-level planning, arguing that "macro language planning needs micro language planning in individual schools if it is to be effectively implemented." Kaplan and Baldauf (1997) also pointed out the importance of the establishment of strong evaluation mechanisms to check the effectiveness of the policy and to drive future modifications. Therefore, to further understand this complex situation, it is vital to investigate the influence of different actors at each stage of the policy process and to see how different interests manifest themselves and the power dynamics that underlie each stage.

1 From 2002 until 2010 a number of high schools were designated by the Japanese Ministry of Education, Culture, Sports, Science and Technology as 'Super English Language High Schools' with the aim of enabling Japanese high school students to be able to communicate more effectively in English. The designated schools received special funding over a three-year period in order to research ways to provide more opportunities for students to communicate in English, including curriculum development, and increasing the number of foreign teachers and chances to study overseas.

3 Research on language management and language education policy

It is often challenging to trace the interplay of different agents on the government level of policy development with the institutional and discourse level of actual policy implementation. It is also sometimes difficult to understand why disparities occur between macro-level policy and its implementation on the micro level. LMT has proven to be a useful framework for investigating the relationship between these different levels (Nekvapil & Nekula 2006) and also to help reveal where certain conceptualizations of language problems come from. LMT is particularly suited to this type of research because the theory looks at all types of language problems as a circular process connecting different levels, referred to as the "language management cycle" (Nekvapil 2009) or the "micro-macro management cycle" (Kimura 2020). Indeed, one of the key tenets of the theory is that language problems should not be considered solved until all problems have been removed from discourse:

> Any act of language planning should start with the consideration of language problems as they appear in discourse, and the planning process should not be considered complete until the removal of the problems is implemented in discourse. (Neustupný 1994: 50)

Because of the theoretical strengths of the framework, a number of scholars have analyzed foreign and second language education policy through the lens of LMT. One area of focus has been the language education policies of universities, highlighting the deviations noted by different actors and the successes and limitations of different adjustments. For example, Marriott (2004, 2013a, 2013b) examined the institutional policies of an Australian university relating to the support provided for incoming international students. She found that although there were policies in place to support students' academic writing in English, little attention was paid to differences in academic practices and genres. Her research further revealed that there was resistance from the university administration to the introduction of a coherent independent language policy. Rudwick (2018) also applied the LMT framework to her investigation of the effects of a policy to make a university in South Africa bilingual in Zulu and English. Although many students were strongly in favor of the introduction of Zulu-medium education from an ideological position, in reality students opted for courses taught in English, due to their perceptions of the importance of this language for their future careers. Thus, there was a clear gap between the evaluation of the policy and the actual adjustments that individuals made to their choice of language.

Other studies have applied the LMT framework to the development of university language education programs. For example, Fan (2008, 2009) used the language management process as the basis for the development of a university Japanese language program for overseas students, highlighting the lack of national guidelines for the teaching of Japanese as a foreign/second language in Japan. Ali,

Baldauf, Shariff, and Manan (2018) also applied LMT to their development of an interview method to examine how students, lecturers, and administrators managed the implementation of a university English-medium-of-instruction engineering program in Malaysia.

However, to date very little research has been conducted on the language management processes involved in the development of national-level language education policy through to its implementation on the institutional and micro levels, including the development and implementation of language education policy in schools. One exception is Dovalil's (2018) study of foreign language education policy in the Czech Republic, where he investigated the factors that determine whether students will choose to learn English or German. He found that despite the economic opportunities for German speakers in the Czech Republic, there seems to be a stronger preference for English education rather than German, stemming from national-level policy, ideologies presented by certain sections of the media, institutional constraints, and parents' and students' beliefs.

As these past studies illustrate, because of its systematic focus on "behavior toward language" (Fishman 1972: 1), its processual model that looks at not only the products of management but the often-neglected processes leading up to it, and its emphasis on the connection between the macro and micro, LMT is clearly a useful framework for examining the complex processes underlying the development and implementation of language education policy. However, no studies so far have applied LMT to the analysis of English education policy in Japan, and in particular the recent high school policy of 'Teaching/Learning English in English.' Additionally, no previous studies have specifically addressed the influence of interests and power at each stage of policy development and implementation, from the perspective of different actors and agents at various levels of society. This chapter aims to fill that gap by focusing primarily on how interests and power are reflected through each stage of the development and implementation of the 'Teaching/Learning English in English' policy. In particular, it will examine why this policy was developed, what interests underlie the decision-making processes leading up to its formulation, and how interests and power relations ultimately influence the implementation, or lack of implementation, of the policy.

4 Method

The aim of this study is to examine the language management processes involved in the development of the 'Teaching/Learning English in English' policy, and to investigate how interests and power are reflected in these processes. Towards this aim, the study focuses on the following three research questions:

1. What deviations triggered the formation of this policy and, in particular, who noted and evaluated them?
2. How far is the policy implemented or not? And, what are the reasons for this?
3. How has the policy been evaluated?

In order to answer these questions a number of data sources were used. Firstly, publicly available documents produced in English and Japanese by English education policy-making/-influencing agencies in Japan were analyzed.[2] In particular, documents produced by the Japanese Ministry of Education, Culture, Sports, Science and Technology (MEXT), The Japan Business Federation (Keidanren), and the Prime Minister's Commission on Japan's Goals in the 21st Century were examined to pinpoint the agents involved in the policy-making process at different levels, the reasons given for education policy changes, and the official assessment of those policies after implementation. Secondly, academic studies published in relation to the implementation of the 'Teaching/Learning English in English' policy were reviewed to investigate how far independent researchers believe the policy has been implemented and to pinpoint any subsequent problems. Finally, a semi-structured interview was conducted with Professor X, one of the recent members of the Japanese government's English Education Expert Advisory Committee (英語教育の在り方に関する有識者会議 Eigokyōiku no arikata ni kansuru yūshikisha kaigi) that currently formulates English education policy, to find out how the committees function and how the decision-making process is actually carried out. Professor X is a university professor specializing in English language education and has been invited by MEXT to work on English education policy on a number of occasions.

The LMT framework was applied to each stage of the policy-making and implementation process, with particular attention paid to the noting and evaluation of deviations and their underlying norms and expectations, and the adjustments designed and implemented to remove those deviations. By looking at the language management processes undertaken on different levels of the policy formulation and implementation, the following sections will reveal how interests and power manifest themselves at each stage of the process.

5 Deviations noted by policy makers regarding English language education in Japan

Documents published by politicians and government agencies, which outline current problems and future goals often reveal the triggers or justifications for policy changes. The same is true for language education policy in Japan. There are two documents in particular that are frequently cited by researchers as the catalysts for the recent changes in education policy: The Prime Minister's Commission on Japan's Goals in the 21st Century report entitled *The Frontier within: Individual Empowerment and Better Governance in the New Millennium* (The Prime Minister's Commission 2000) and the Japan Business Federation's report entitled グローバル化時代の人材育成について (*Development of Human Resources in the Age*

2 In this chapter, I refer to the wording and content of the official English versions of the documents when available.

of Globalization, Keidanren 2000).[3] The report of the Prime Minister's Commission on Japan's Goals in the 21st Century, based on a 1999 meeting with Japanese business leaders, emphasizes the necessity of developing Japanese citizens' "global literacy," defined as "the ability to access and converse with the rest of the world, meaning that they can freely and immediately obtain information, understand it, and express their own ideas clearly" (The Prime Minister's Commission 2000: 4). The document goes on to explain the clear political motivations behind this policy, namely, that

> mastery of global literacy by the people of a country will determine whether that country's power in the international politics of the twenty-first century will wax or wane—and is also likely to determine whether the country rises or falls. Countries whose standard of global literacy is low will not attract superior human resources. (The Prime Minister's Commission 2000: 4)

Therefore, it is clear that, at least from the point of view of the Prime Minister's Commission, the concept of global literacy is closely related to Japan's future position in international politics. The document then goes on to outline how English is a central component of this global literacy:

> The basic components of this new literacy are the mastery of information-technology tools, such as computers and the Internet, and the mastery of English as the international lingua franca. In addition to these basics, communication skills [...] will also be important. (The Prime Minister's Commission 2000: 4)

The document further illustrates the deviations that politicians noted regarding English language ability in particular:

> Today's Japanese are lacking in these basic skills. Their English-language abilities as measured by their TOEFL scores in 1998 were the lowest in Asia. The Japanese themselves are painfully aware of the inadequacy of their communication skills. Though they would like to convey their country's good points and its real situation to the rest of the world, many of them feel unable to do so adequately. (The Prime Minister's Commission 2000: 4)

The noting and negative evaluation of a number of deviations is revealed in these brief excerpts. Firstly, the report claims that Japanese are deficient in these skills, using the term "lacking." Japan's low TOEFL scores, particularly in comparison with other Asian countries, are used to corroborate this claim. The report also evaluates average Japanese communication skills as "inadequate" and clearly posits the role of English as the means to convey Japan's "good points" to the outside world.

3 I quote the first document from the official English version, the second from the Japanese version.

The report published by the Japan Business Federation (Keidanren 2000) in the same year is based on a 1999 survey of Japanese companies, looking into their current needs. The Japan Business Federation is an independent body of business people which has considerable influence on Japanese government policy (Mouer & Kawanishi 2005). Although they do not take part in the final policy decisions, they do prepare extensive policy suggestions and these reports are usually taken very seriously by the government and taken up extensively by the media.

The Japan Business Federation report (Keidanren 2000) found that there was a general lack of English skills in the workforce necessary to participate in international meetings and business. They also noted that companies have to spend a lot of time and money on English education necessary for work because English education in schools and universities focuses primarily on reading and writing, while speaking and listening skills are not improving. Again, there is reportedly "a lack" of general English skills (英語力の不足 *eigoryoku no busoku*) in the workforce, which are needed to participate in international business. They also criticize the Japanese education system, which does not adequately develop students' speaking and listening skills and ends up costing companies dearly in time and resources because they are the ones who have to then pay for proper language training for their employees.

Both the Prime Minister's Commission and the Japan Business Federation suggested a number of adjustment plans in order to remove the deviations that they highlighted in their respective reports. First, the report of the Prime Minister's Commission (2000) sets out its overall goal as making sure that "all Japanese acquire a working knowledge of English—not simply as a foreign language but as the international lingua franca [...] by the time they take their place in society as adults." In order to do this within the context of education, it suggests organizing classes based on competency rather than age, providing more teacher training and increasing the number of foreign teachers, although no specifics are provided.

The recommended adjustments of the Japan Business Federation (2000) also emphasize the importance of more teacher training to improve teachers' English abilities (英語力 *eigoryoku*) and educational techniques (教育技術 *kyōiku gijutsu*), and the use of TOEFL and TOEIC standardized test scores to measure teachers' English proficiency. In addition, they suggested starting English language education from elementary school,[4] with a focus on listening, on teaching practical English (particularly speaking skills) at all levels of education, and hiring more English native-speaker teachers.

4 English activities were introduced in elementary schools from 2002 and English instruction became compulsory from the 5th grade in 2011.

6 Underlying norms and interests influencing the policy makers and influencers

A simple way to reveal the interests of policy makers and politicians is to examine their noted deviations and recommendations for adjustments in order to pinpoint the norms or expectations that are underlying them. Although Spolsky (2006: 97) warns us that the "stated" problem or motivation is sometimes different from the "most important" motivation behind a policy, it is at least possible to see the ideal situation that particular agents are publicly envisioning and the interests that those ideals represent. Additionally, sometimes one norm can be seen to reflect more than one single interest. In the examples presented here, the underlying norms or expectations are represented in italics.

First, when the Prime Minister's Commission's report (2000) claims that "[t]oday's Japanese are lacking in these basic [English] skills," the expectation is that *Japanese people should have basic English skills*, which can be seen as a pedagogical interest, regardless of how these skills are defined. Similarly, when the report mentions "the inadequacy of their communication skills," the underlying expectation is that *Japanese people should have adequate communication skills*, which can also be construed as a pedagogical interest. In addition, when the Japan Business Federation report (Keidanren 2000) points out that Japanese people's "English conversation skills are not improving" because of the education system's over-emphasis on reading and writing, the underlying expectation is that *the Japanese workforce should have practical English conversation skills and the education system should be responsible for developing this.*

Expectations regarding the proficiency of teachers could also be seen. For example, both the Prime Minister's Commission (2000) and the Japan Business Federation (Keidanren 2000) emphasize the necessity of providing more teacher training, including for in-service teachers. The expectation here appears to be that *if teachers are trained better in both their English and teaching skills, then students' proficiency levels will improve.* However, at the same time both bodies call for the hiring of non-Japanese teachers. The underlying expectation here seems to be that *having more foreign teachers* (Prime Minister's Commission) *or more native-speaker teachers* (Japan Business Federation) *will improve Japanese students' English proficiency.* Scholars researching native-speakerism, however, have argued that this favoring of native-speaker teachers actually covers up the assumption that *foreign/native-speaker teachers are better than local teachers* (Holliday 2006). This suggestion could, however, be seen as ironic because native-speaker teaching assistants, many with teaching credentials in their home countries, have been actively recruited as part of the JET Programme and its forebears since the 1980s without, according to these documents, any significant improvements in the ability of Japanese students to use English for communication purposes.

There are other pedagogical interests reflected in the recommendations that are still open to some debate in the Japanese academic community. For example, the Japan Business Federation's (Keidanren 2000) call for English education to commence from the elementary level reveals the assumption that *Japanese learners need to start learning English at elementary school in order to become proficient in the language.* Furthermore, their call for the teaching of more practical English reveals the assumption that *Japanese students need to learn practical English skills in order to become proficient in English.* On the other hand, the Prime Minister's Commission's (2000) recommendation to place students in classes with students of a similar ability, rather than students of the same age, points to another perceived deficiency in the current English language education system, namely that *Japanese students' English proficiency will not improve unless their classes are streamed according to ability.* However, it should be noted that no empirical research is cited in the reports to corroborate any of these pedagogical assumptions.

When the report of the Prime Minister's Commission (2000) mentions that Japanese "English-language abilities as measured by their TOEFL scores in 1998 were the lowest in Asia," the underlying expectation is that *Japanese people should have higher TOEFL scores, especially in comparison with other Asian countries.* While on the one hand, this can be seen as a pedagogical interest, the emphasis on Japan's relation to other Asian countries implies that this interest also contains political undertones. Similarly, when the report claims that "[t]hough they would like to convey their country's good points and its real situation to the rest of the world, many of them feel unable to do so adequately," the underlying expectation is that *Japanese people should have good enough English skills to be able to convey their country's good points and its real situation to the rest of the world.* Again, although this could be explained as a pedagogical interest, using English to convey only selective, positive attributes of one's country to the outside world could also be seen to reflect political interests.

Other excerpts from the public documents produced by policy makers reveal much clearer political and economic interests. For example, when the report of the Prime Minister's Commission (2000) claims that "mastery of global literacy by the people of a country will determine whether that country's power in the international politics of the twenty-first century will wax or wane—and is also likely to determine whether the country rises or falls," this reveals an explicit political interest. Namely, *global literacy, including English skills, is perceived as a factor that can determine a country's position within the international political hierarchy and its long-term success or failure in comparison with the international community.*

Other political interests seem to be intertwined with economic interests. For example, when the report of the Prime Minister's Commission (2000) claims that "[c]ountries whose standard of global literacy is low will not attract superior human resources," the underlying expectation here is that *a country needs a high level of global literacy (i.e., strong English and IT skills) to attract "superior human resources."* This reveals both political and economic interests: politicians want Japan to be a country with a high international reputation and one that can attract people with the best skills from overseas to work in Japan and contribute to the Japanese economy. Similarly, when the Japan Business Federation (Keidanren 2000) points out that there is a lack of workers with high enough English skills to be able to participate in international business and international meetings, the underlying expectation is that *Japanese workers should have good enough English skills to be able to participate in international business and meetings.* In this way, the ideal Japanese worker is one who can use their English for the economic and political interests of the country. Finally, when the Japan Business Federation blames the Japanese education system for the inadequate English skills of its workers, resulting in the financial burden of their language training being placed on individual companies, a clear economic interest can be seen. In other words, the Japan Business Federation's expectation is that *Japanese companies should not have to bear the financial burden of paying for employees' English education.*

These examples demonstrate the variety of interests that can be found in public discourse on English education policy in Japan. As well as a repetition of the pedagogical interests cited in the research literature, the documents produced by these political and economic agencies also reveal economic and financial interests as well as political and nationalistic aspirations underlying the conceptualization of the problems in English education. Clearly, not only educators and specialists in pedagogy, but also politicians and business people play a role in the conceptualization of language problems and the subsequent policies that derive from the noting and evaluation of these deviations. Considering the power differentials of these different agents in Japanese society, it is difficult to presume that all interests will be pursued equally.

7 Interests and power in the actual policy-making process

The first mention of the plan to have high school English classes conducted in English was in the *Action Plan to Cultivate "Japanese with English Abilities"* (MEXT 2003), which stated the goal that English should be used in the majority of class time. This then became an official requirement when the 'Teaching/Learning English in English' policy for high schools in Japan was announced in March 2009, as part of the *New Course of Study* (高等学校学習指導要領 *Kōtōgakkō Gakushū Shidō Yōryō*) (MEXT 2009a), which is the main education policy document produced by MEXT, revised every ten years in general. In this document, the implementation of the new policy was set to commence four years later, in April 2013. The document makes clear references to the promotion of communication skills in English, which was a key concern raised in both the report of the Prime Minister's Commission (2000) and the Japan Business Federation (Keidanren 2000) mentioned in the previous sections. The *New Course of Study* posits an overall goal "to develop students' communicative abilities" (MEXT 2009a: 87) and requires that:

> [...] 生徒が英語に触れる機会を充実するとともに、授業を実際のコミュニケーションの場面とするため、授業は英語で行うことを基本とする。その際、生徒の理解の程度に応じた英語を用いるよう十分は配慮するものとする。(MEXT 2009a: 92)

> [[...] classes, in principle, should be conducted in English in order to enhance the opportunities for students to be exposed to English, transforming classes into real communication scenes. Consideration should be given to use English in accordance with the students' level of comprehension.]

Thus, conducting classes through the medium of English is seen as a means to turn classrooms into "real communication scenes" in order to develop students' communicative skills in English.

However, a proviso regarding the use of Japanese was included in the *New Course of Study Guide* (高等学校学習指導要領解説 *Kōtōgakkō Gakushū Shidō Yōryō Kaisetsu*), published in December 2009:

> 「授業は英語で行うことを基本とする」こととは、教師が授業を英語で行うとともに、生徒も授業の中でできるだけ多く英語を使用することにより、英語による言語活動を行うことを授業の中心とすることである。[...] しかし、授業のすべてを必ず英語で行わなければならないということを意味するものではない。[...] 必要に応じて、日本語を交えて授業を行うことも考えられるものである。 (MEXT 2009b: 43–44)

> ["Classes, in principle, should be conducted in English" means that teachers will conduct their classes in English and students will use as much English as possible in class, so that language activities conducted in English will be the central focus of the class. [...] However, this does not mean that all the class will have to be conducted in English. [...] [W]hen necessary, it is possible to conduct classes including some Japanese.]

It is clear that some use of Japanese will be permitted in class but the documents published by MEXT do not go into detail concerning the extent or function of Japanese use that they regard to be permissible.

Yet, in order to fully understand the influence of interests and power in the formulation of language education policy, it is important not only to examine the policy document produced but to try to find out how language education policies are actually formulated and whose interests are most influential in the negotiations over the wording of the final policy. One way to do this is to look at who is involved in the actual policy-formulation process and how the process is usually carried out.

MEXT's policy revisions relating to English language education, published periodically in the *Course of Study* policy documents, are based on recommendations prepared by the English Education Expert Advisory Committee (henceforth the Advisory Committee). According to Professor X, the Advisory Committee is created by MEXT "to gain professional opinion concerning a policy they want to implement." Thus, MEXT decides the general overall policy but "they need professional input in order to come up with the details." The Advisory Committee, therefore, does not have the power to design the direction of new policy; however, in Professor X's experience, MEXT takes the results produced by the Advisory

Committee very seriously and generally the document they produce forms the basis of the future *Course of Study* policy document.

The Advisory Committee usually consists of around eleven members, chosen directly by MEXT or recommended by previous participants. According to the MEXT website, the members in 2014[5] were as follows:

Four university professors
Three school principals (elementary, junior high, and high school)
The head of a regional board of education
A director of a private English education company (whose services include university entrance exam preparation courses)
The president of Rakuten, an online shopping, travel, and banking company that uses English as its official corporate language
The president of a private business consulting research institute

As can be seen from this list, the Advisory Committee is not composed of merely education specialists but also representatives of a number of business interests. In addition, although the university entrance exam system is often criticized by scholars as one of the central problems of the current English education system, it is of particular interest that a director of an entrance exam preparatory school also has a place on the committee. Just from the make-up of the committee members, the potential for the presence of "competing managers [...] with divided and competing goals" (Spolsky 2006: 97) is clear.

Then, how is policy development actually managed within the Advisory Committee and whose interests come to be promoted? The interview with Professor X provided some useful information regarding how the decision-making process within the Advisory Committee functions and revealed the underlying power dynamics. Although Professor X was not a member of the committee that set up the recommendations for the 'Teaching/Learning English in English' policy, he provided some valuable insights into how decisions are ultimately made when education policy is being developed. Firstly, although the presence of business interests on the committee could be considered by many external observers as a conflict of interests in the formulation of education policy, Professor X strongly disagrees. He believes that having business people on the committees is a good thing because basically they want to improve the current education system and the government takes notice of them. As he succinctly explained, "[the government] won't listen to educators, so they're not listening to us; they're listening to the business community." In other words, rather than creating a conflict of interests between the business community and education specialists, the education specialists felt that

---

5 This committee was not the actual committee that compiled the recommendations that later formed the basis of the 2009 *New Course of Study*, but it is representative of the type of people that have participated in English education policy-making committees in the past according to Professor X.

the presence of business people actually gave them more leverage to further their own interests, that is, the improvement of Japanese English education policy.

According to Professor X, a much greater hurdle to the improvement of education policy regarding communication skills is the presence of other intellectuals on the committee who strongly oppose the introduction of communication skills into English education. In Professor X's words, "as far as [MEXT] was concerned, they wanted both sides." Within the context of Japanese consensus-building practices, this suggests that innovative ideas will always be watered down to some extent. Indeed, Professor X explained that the role of the head of the committee is "to summarize what everyone is trying to say and try to get them to move to the center" and this may involve a certain level of compromise, such as, for example, explicitly stipulating a requirement for the comparison of English with Japanese linguistic structure in the final policy. However, as MEXT deliberately includes people with strongly opposing views on the committees, it could be argued that this dilution of innovation may be a deliberate strategy.

Professor X, however, also revealed how the head of the Advisory Committee (who was a university professor in the 2014 committee) can manage the different interests in the committee. The head of the committee writes the final report and ultimately decides how the main recommendations will be formulated and which ideas will just get a minor mention. As he explained, "the final decision of what to include in the final report is up to [the head of the committee]. [...] [A]t times we have to put in some notes to say that although this is the way we want to go, there were other kinds of opinions as well." Therefore, even if there are stark differences of opinion, representing different interests, occurring within the committee negotiations, the head of the committee may be able to skillfully incorporate all the opinions raised in the committee, while highlighting certain interests over others in the final recommendations document. This suggests that the head of the committee is entrusted with a certain degree of power to ultimately shape the final recommendations, even though the ideas initially submitted to the committee may be watered down considerably.

Another strategy used by senior committee members to balance the different interests in the policy formulation process is to recommend members when new advisory committees are set up. Some committee members have been able to recommend people to MEXT to become members of subsequent advisory committees and often the people recommended are former students of those committee members now holding important positions in education and research. Because former students will generally be expected to conform to the Japanese system of hierarchical relationships, this usually means a number of allies with similar interests can be secured. Indeed, Professor X pointed out that certain senior committee members had been able to recommend a number of their former students to become members of subsequent advisory committees, implying the continuation of those senior members' power and influence on policy.

8 Evaluations of the adjustment plan

The 'Teaching/Learning English in English' was not to be implemented until 2013, but as soon as the *New Course of Study* was announced, the adjustment plan was critiqued from a number of perspectives, particularly from the academic community, teachers and students, who pointed out many of its potential weaknesses. In language management terms, they noted deviations regarding certain aspects of the 'Teaching/Learning English in English' policy and, in many cases, they evaluated them negatively. Yamada (2010) gives examples of a number of Japanese scholars who claimed that the 'Teaching/Learning English in English' policy would be ineffective from a pedagogical standpoint. For example, Erikawa (2009) argued that it is more appropriate to use the students' L1 in a foreign language-teaching environment and that there is no proof that 'Teaching/Learning English in English' is more effective than other methods. Indeed, this is a reasonable claim to make, considering that MEXT's policy does not show any empirical evidence in order to justify its policy change. Furthermore, Terashima (2009) argued that teaching the four skills of listening, speaking, reading, and writing will not automatically lead to improved communication skills, and teaching writing and speaking will not be possible under the current system with its large class sizes.

Negative responses were also recorded from in-service teachers. In their survey of teachers in Fukui prefecture, Yamada and Hristoskova (2011) discovered that although 52.7% of Japanese teachers totally or partially agreed with the introduction of the policy, almost 15% completely disagreed with it. In the same study, 34% of high school students in academic courses and 45% in vocational courses reported that they would be worried about the introduction of the 'Teaching/Learning English in English' policy. Some teachers also voiced their worries. For example, the two pre-service and two in-service Japanese teachers interviewed by Nagamine (2012) in his study on perceptions towards the new policy all felt various levels of pressure and anxiety. The two in-service teachers felt the threat of native-speakerism, fearing they would be disadvantaged compared to native-speaker English teachers, and one pre-service teacher voiced the opinion that MEXT's ultimate plan is to get rid of Japanese teachers with lower-level speaking skills. The two in-service teachers expressed their dislike of MEXT, with one teacher even reporting that he felt betrayed by the government and politicians. Other negative responses from teachers related to pedagogical and ideological concerns. One pre-service teacher felt that students would not be receptive to 'Teaching/Learning English in English' because the use of English in the classroom would make them feel uncomfortable. Moreover, none of the teachers in Nagamine's interviews had ever personally experienced being taught English through the medium of English at school so they questioned whether teachers would realistically be able to do it themselves. One in-service teacher even vowed that she would never use English to teach in her classroom. Additionally, a pre-service teacher expressed rather ethnocentric views, highlighting Japan's differences compared to other countries, and claiming that there is a Japanese way of teaching most suited to the local context (i.e., without using English as a medium of instruction).

Many of these pre-implementation evaluations of the adjustment plan can be interpreted as the manifestation of interests resistant to change. Pedagogy-based arguments from certain scholars could be seen to reflect their interests in maintaining the status quo, possibly because their status is somehow entwined with the maintenance of other educational methods. Similarly, general, non-specific expressions of concern over the new policy could be seen as reflecting a fear of change (Bouchard 2017).

It is therefore important to consider why there might be such resistance to change, particularly considering the situation of foreign language education overseas where the 'Teaching/Learning English in English' might not seem particularly radical at all. One possible explanation may stem from the ideological issues previously mentioned relating to the commonly perceived binary relationship between Japan and the Other. Hashimoto (2013) also points out that the 'Teaching/Learning English in English' policy is deliberately not referred to as 'English as a medium of instruction,' because bilingualism is not its aim. Rather, she sees it as a manifestation of the Othering of English in Japan. Although is it debatable as to how far these ideological positions are present in the conscious formulation and evaluation of the 'Teaching/Learning English in English' policy, as was shown in the previous description of the workings of the Advisory Committee, the fact that MEXT deliberately includes academics in the Advisory Committee who are resistant to the idea of communicative language teaching cannot be overlooked.

9 Implementation of the 'Teaching/Learning English in English' policy

The 'Teaching/Learning English in English' policy was officially implemented from the beginning of the school year in April 2013, four years after its initial announcement in the *New Course of Study*. Although there is some debate as to whether the *Course of Study* documents should be considered a policy (see Fukunaga 2016), Professor X's understanding is that "the *Course of Study* is law. It's a legal document, which means teachers should, or will have to follow what is in this document." The gravity of this statement suggests that the 'Teaching/Learning English in English' policy will be implemented quite thoroughly. However, many of the current author's undergraduate students claim that their high school English classes were not taught in English at all. Therefore, it is worth investigating how the policy is actually being implemented. One way of gauging the implementation of the policy is to look at the data that MEXT has published based on a nationwide survey of high schools (MEXT 2016a, 2016b, 2017). The results published in 2016 and 2017 show very similar tendencies. In high schools with special English courses,[6] over 80% of teachers and students were reported to be using English for over half their class time, which shows that while a clear majority of teachers are following the *New Course of Study* guidelines in these schools, 20% of teachers are not. Furthermore, in schools without special English courses, over 50% of both Japanese teachers and students reported using English for less than half of their time in class and 15% of students reported using English for less than 25% of their time in class. According to the data provided by MEXT, it can be concluded that the extent of the implementation of the policy is limited.

Even in schools where language education policy is reported as being fully implemented, it is important to examine exactly how the policy is being implemented to check for issues of consistency and quality. For example, Saito's (2017) interviews with three high school teachers and observations of their classes revealed that although all the teachers and students had very positive attitudes towards the 'Teaching/Learning English in English' policy, the amount of English used in the classroom varied significantly among individual teachers. Some teachers used English for 95% of class time, while others used it for only 35% of the time.

According to Takegami's (2016) questionnaire and interviews conducted with thirty Japanese teachers of English teaching at private secondary schools in Hokkaido, the majority of teachers responded that they *do* use English for more than 50% of their class time. However, observations of the actual classes revealed that the English being used in the classroom was mainly limited to classroom instructions and directions. Tsukamoto and Tsujioka (2013) made similar findings in their survey of teachers in western Japan. They also found that teachers interpreted the concept of communicative language teaching in very different ways, with the majority of teachers limiting their use of communicative English in the classroom to merely formulaic expressions, such as greetings and classroom instructions.

These results then beg the question of why the policy is not implemented consistently. One issue may be related to awareness, namely to what extent schools and teachers are actually aware of the content of the policy. In his interview, Professor X made a comment that "many teachers have actually read it," which implies that the policy makers themselves do not expect all classroom practitioners to be familiar with the actual policy. Indeed, he also added that "[a] lot of teachers don't know [what's in the guidelines]." Moreover, even if they do actually read the policy, it does not guarantee that teachers and schools will interpret it in the way it was intended. Indeed, the teachers in Fukunaga's (2016) study, who attended a mandatory in-service seminar on the *New Course of Study*, selectively listened to the information provided and they only focused on information that they believed might be useful when teaching their own individual classes. The teachers in her

6 In addition to the general course of high school studies, some schools offer specialized courses. According to the data provided by MEXT (2017), there were eighty-six high schools that offered courses with a special focus on English education, where more frequent and intensive English classes were provided.

study did not read the *New Course of Study Guide* thoroughly, nor did they try to learn its content. In their study of the implementation of the Common European Framework of Reference (CEFR) in the European Union, Byram and Parmenter (2012: 4) point out that "like any text, the intentions of its authors may not be read by its users." Clearly, this cannot be seen as a solely Japanese issue.

However, concerning the Japanese policy document specifically, the wording of the guidelines gives the impression that teaching and learning in English could be optional. For example, the *New Course of Study Guide* (MEXT 2009b) uses the term "in principle" when referring to the teaching of English classes in English. In Japanese, the term "in principle" (基本とする *kihon to suru*) gives a strong impression that something is optional and people will not be penalized for not following the guidelines. Thus, the use of this term in the *New Course of Study Guide* gives a clear message to readers of the document that the policy will not be enforced strictly.

In fact, MEXT's aim for implementation of the policy from the onset appears to be partial. According to Professor X, full implementation of the policy has never been the main goal:

> Ultimately, the government basically said when we're talking about teaching English in English, we're basically talking about teaching at least half of one class hour in English. [...] [W]hen a teacher is teaching this much in English then they're teaching English in English.

Therefore, MEXT's overall expectations for the implementation of the policy appear to have been relatively low and this seems to be corroborated by the previously mentioned findings from their nationwide surveys (MEXT 2016a, 2016b, 2017). Indeed, while the *New Course of Study Guide* explicitly states that it is possible to use the Japanese language in class, when necessary, because there is no clear explanation of when the use of Japanese might be deemed necessary, this wording leaves the door open for a wide range of interpretations.

It can be argued that these low expectations for policy implementation, originating from the policy makers themselves, are a reflection of the slow pace of social change in Japanese society as a whole. As can be seen in the time lag between the initial announcement of the 'Teaching/Learning English in English' policy and its actual implementation four years later, policy change in Japan takes considerable time. Some researchers have also pointed out that, whatever the English education policy, there is often a notable gap between policy and practice (Yoshida 2003; Aspinall 2013; Bouchard 2017).

Other issues that influence the implementation of the 'Teaching/Learning English in English' policy are institutional constraints and individual teachers' beliefs and abilities. For example, Fukunaga (2016) found that generally there was a lack of planning by regional authorities, districts, and individual schools. Some schools lack the internal organizational systems necessary to implement new policy changes. For example, there may be a lack of shared understanding amongst teachers concerning how to teach the new curriculum as a team, a lack of shared understanding of what pedagogical changes would be needed, and no clear leader of the implementation. Fukunaga (2016) found that teachers also felt individual pressures from their institutions. They were often forced to work excessively long hours but not given enough time to discuss and collaborate with other teachers. Additionally, policy implementation was left to individual teachers to fathom by themselves, rather than being planned as a strategy for the whole English teaching department in their schools. The teachers also felt pressured to give priority to university entrance exam preparation and complained that it was unrealistic to implement the new policy with large class sizes of forty students or more.

Some teachers' beliefs were also found to be an obstacle to the implementation of the new policy. Some teachers felt that their English skills were not good enough to teach communicative English, while others held the strong belief that grammar has to be taught via the L1, that is, Japanese (Takegami 2016). Other teachers expressed concern that they might confuse students if they used English above their current level (Tsukamoto & Tsujioka 2013; Takegami 2016). Therefore, it can be seen that a wide range of external and internal pressures on both the institutional and individual levels can affect policy implementation. On the one hand, competing interests appear to impede the full implementation of the policy, whereas on the other hand, participating agents do not appear to be able to exercise power effectively in order to ensure implementation. Subsequently the responsibility for implementation is left to individual teachers, who do not appear to suffer repercussions if they fail to implement the policy in their classrooms.

10 Post-implementation evaluations

Kimura (2014, 2020) has argued that in order to assess the effectiveness of adjustments and to position LMT research in the context of other language policy and planning (LPP) research, it is necessary to include a post-implementation/feedback stage. Indeed, a number of recent studies have examined responses to the 'Teaching/Learning English in English' policy after implementation, particularly the evaluation of the implemented adjustments. For example, the teachers in Takegami's (2016) and Fukunaga's (2016) studies positively evaluated the overall goals of the policy, and the high school students in Mori's (2013) study felt that their attitudes towards English were becoming more positive. On the other hand, a number of post-implementation issues have been raised. For example, Mori (2013) found that almost 75% of the students in his study felt dissatisfied when the class was completely taught in English, but their levels of satisfaction rose when the proportion of Japanese was increased. These levels of satisfaction are undoubtedly linked to students' proficiency levels. Indeed, some teachers negatively evaluated the policy for not taking into account students' low levels of English proficiency and the perceived need to teach grammar in Japanese (Takegami 2016). Fukunaga (2016) further questions how students can be expected to develop communicative competence in English when they are not even taught communicative skills in Japanese. She also highlights how the 'Teaching/Learning English in English' policy ignores teachers' other responsibilities, particularly the heavy emphasis that schools place on university entrance examination preparation and administrative work, which leaves them little time to focus on planning their lessons and developing new materials.

The post-implementation evaluations reported in recent research seem to reflect issues of powerlessness for both teachers and students. Both express concerns regarding the constraints of students' limited language and communicative proficiency and teachers further express their powerlessness in situations where they have conflicting responsibilities. In an ideal management cycle, this post-implementation feedback will be taken up by language education policy makers to improve future policy; however, in the Japanese context, there seems to be little evidence of this so far. This, presumably, is related to the structure of English education policy-making in Japan mentioned in Section 7, whereby the experts on the English Education Expert Advisory Committee are involved in preparing the details and wording of a policy previously decided by MEXT, but not its implementation. Thus, the agents involved at different stages of the policy process appear to lack sufficient power to guarantee implementation of the policy, particularly in light of the institutional and pedagogical constraints mentioned here.

11 Conclusions

This chapter has examined the development of the Japanese 'Teaching/Learning English in English' policy from its initial formulation to its implementation and examined the language management processes occurring at each of the stages, tracing the underlying norms and expectations triggering the conceptualization of the policy right down to its implementation and post-implementation evaluation. Based on this research, a number of observations can be made regarding the function of interests and power in the management of English language education policy in Japan.

Firstly, an examination of the norms and expectations underlying the noted deviations and adjustment plans recommended by policy makers and influencers reveal a wide variety of interests, including not only pedagogical interests but also clear economic and political interests. Some of these interests conflicted with others and also, as could be seen in the recommendation to hire more foreign teachers, seemed to favor a continuation of the past education policy of relying on native-speaker teachers to teach communicative skills rather than training Japanese teachers.

Regarding the negotiations over the wording of the actual policy, the power dynamics underlying the decision-making process were examined. It could be seen that the power of others can be utilized to further one's own interests. For example, rather than being considered a hindrance, the presence of business leaders on the English Education Expert Advisory Committee was seen by education specialists as a way to get English education policy moving forward, because of the government's tendency to take the views of business leaders more seriously than their own. Conversely, it could be argued that MEXT's inclusion of academics in the English Education Expert Advisory Committee, who actively oppose the introduction of communicative skills in English language education, could be seen as a means to fulfill their ideological interests to not drastically change school language education, resulting in a watering down of any innovative policies.

Secondly, an examination of the general language management processes occurring in the English Education Expert Advisory Committee negotiations revealed that the individual actor who controls the management of the language of the final recommendations report can ultimately determine which policy suggestions will be highlighted, and subsequently given more power, and which will not be included, or just given a minor mention in the footnotes. Furthermore, former members of the committee are granted the power to recommend members of new committees, predominantly allies, to make it potentially easier to further their own interests in the formulation of future policy. Thus, the decision-making process itself could also be seen as a process of power.

Concerning the actual implementation of the policy, however, neither education specialists, business leaders nor the government appear to have the power, or will, to fully implement the policy. In fact, MEXT's own low expectations for the amount of English use required in the classroom suggests that a great deal of leeway is being given regarding the interpretation of the policy. In practice, implementation can be easily avoided or resisted on the institutional and individual classroom level. It is MEXT's rescinding of power at the implementation stage, by means of not requiring full implementation of policy, that means that the multiple interests in local boards of education, schools and individual classrooms can allow non- or only partial implementation of a policy without much obstruction. Furthermore, it is unclear how far the post-implementation evaluations of teachers and students are being heard by policy makers. Although teachers' limited language proficiency and excessive workloads have been reported as serious concerns, it is doubtful that these micro-level deviations are being noted by agents who can influence future policy. As long as at least some teachers follow the policy, MEXT appears to be satisfied. In this way, the policy can be ignored or resisted, as long as overall change can be seen to be progressing slowly in the intended direction.

This study has also shown that an examination of the power relations and interests underlying the language management of agents involved in the development of the 'Teaching/Learning English in English' can help reveal the complexities of the development of language education policy and also highlight some of the reasons why policies may or may not be implemented. From an LMT perspective, it also clearly highlights the fact that there is not just one macro and one micro level, but many, often competing, interests operating at different levels and stages of the process, with different degrees of power (Neustupný 1997). This leads to a complex web of overlapping and intersecting management processes (Fairbrother 2020) at various stages of policy formulation and implementation, including the pre-implementation and post-implementation stages, which have so far received little attention in LMT-based research. I hope that this chapter has demonstrated the unique potential that LMT has for furthering our understanding of language issues and future avenues for the development of the theory itself, particularly regarding the pre- and post-implementation stages of language policy.

References

Ali, N. L., Baldauf, R. B., Shariff, N. M. M. & Manan, A. A. (2018) Utilisation of language management theory in framing interview pro formas. In L. Fairbrother, J. Nekvapil & M. Sloboda (eds) *The Language Management Approach: A Special Focus on Research Methodology*. Frankfurt on the Main: Peter Lang, 141–156.

Aspinall, R. W. (2013) Globalization and English language education policy in Japan: External risk and internal inertia. In D. B. Willis & J. Rappleye (eds) *Reimagining Japanese Education: Border, Transfers, Circulations, and the Comparative*. Oxford: Symposium Books, 127–146.

Barker, D. (2018) Fundamental problems with English education in Japan. *Annual Report of the Faculty of Education, Gifu University* 20, 139–148.

Befu, H. (1983) Internationalization of Japan and Nihon bunkaron. In H. Mannari & H. Befu (eds) *The Challenge of Japan's Internationalization: Organization and Culture*. New York: Kodansha International, 232–266.

Bouchard, J. (2017) *Ideology, Agency and Intercultural Communicative Competence: A Stratified Look into EFL Education in Japan*. Singapore: Springer.

Browne, C. & Wada, M. (1998) Current issues in high school English teaching in Japan: An exploratory survey. *Language, Culture and Curriculum* 11 (1), 96–111.

Byram, M. & Parmenter, L. (eds) (2012) *The Common European Framework of Reference: The Globalisation of Language Education Policy*. Bristol: Multilingual Matters.

Chua, C. S. K. (2008) Singaporean educational planning: Moving from the macro to the micro. In A. J. Liddicoat & R. B. Baldauf (eds) *Language Planning in Local Contexts*. Clevedon: Multilingual Matters.

CLAIR (The Council of Local Authorities for International Relations, Japan) (2015) Japan exchange and teaching (JET) programme: History. On WWW at http://jetprogramme.org/en/history/. Accessed March 11, 2020.

Dovalil, V. (2018) Qual der Wahl, or spoiled for choice? English and German as the subject of decision-making processes in the Czech Republic. In T. Sherman & J. Nekvapil (eds) *English in Business and Commerce: Interactions and Policies*. Berlin: De Gruyter Mouton, 276–309.

Erikawa, H. (2009) Eigokyōiku jihyōzaikaishukenshita no kōkō shidō yōryō [The high school course of study at the time when English education is under the sovereignty of the financial world]. *Eigokyōiku* [English Education] 57 (13), 41.

ETS (Educational Testing Service) (2011) Test and score data summary for TOEFL internet-based and paper-based tests. January 2010-December 2010 test data.

On WWW at https://www.ets.org/Media/Research/pdf/TOEFL-SUM-2010.pdf. Accessed December 17, 2021.

Fairbrother, L. (2015a) The management of language and power in intercultural contact situations in Japan. *International Journal of the Sociology of Language* 232, 59–78.

Fairbrother, L. (2015b) The 'multiform' linguistic, sociolinguistic and sociocultural practices of plurilingual employees in European multinationals. *The Japanese Journal of Language in Society* 18 (1), 162–175.

Fairbrother, L. (2018) The management of everyday interactions in the Japanese branches of European multinationals. In T. Sherman & J. Nekvapil (eds) *English in Business and Commerce: Interactions and Policies.* Berlin: De Gruyter Mouton, 149–171.

Fairbrother, L. (2020) Diverging and intersecting management: Cases of the simultaneous management of deviations by multiple parties in contact situations. In G. C. Kimura & L. Fairbrother (eds) *A Language Management Approach to Language Problems: Integrating Macro and Micro Dimensions.* Amsterdam: John Benjamins, 133–156.

Fan, S. K. (2008) Teaching Japanese interaction as a process of language management. In P. Heinrich & Y. Sugita (eds) *Japanese as Foreign Language in the Age of Globalization.* Munich: Iudicium, 139–163.

Fan, S. K. (2009) Language planning or language management: Treatment of problems for the development of 'Japanese in context.' *Ibunka Komyunikēshon* [Intercultural Communication] 21, 7–35.

Fishman, J. A. (1972) *The Sociology of Language: An Interdisciplinary Social Science Approach to Language in Society.* Rowley: Newbury House.

Fukunaga, S. (2016) *Implementing English Education Policy in Japan: Intersubjectivity at the Micro-, Meso-, and Macro Levels.* Unpublished PhD thesis, University of Washington.

Hashimoto, K. (2013) 'English-only', but not a medium-of-instruction policy: The Japanese way of internationalising education for both domestic and overseas students. *Current Issues in Language Planning* 14 (1), 16–33.

Hayes, C. (1979) Language contact in Japan. In W. Mackey & J. Ornstein (eds) *Sociolinguistic Studies in Language Contact: Methods and Cases.* Sydney: Language Australia, 363–376.

Holliday, A. (2006) Native-speakerism. *ELT Journal* 60 (4), 385–387.

Honna, N. (1995) English in Japanese society: Language within language. *Journal of Multilingual and Multicultural Development* 16 (1–2), 45–62.

Jernudd, B. H. & Neustupný, J. V. (1987) Language planning: For whom? In L. Laforge (ed) *Actes du Colloque international sur l'aménagement linguistique /*

Proceedings of the International Colloquium on Language Planning. Québec: Les Presses de L'Université Laval, 69–84.

Kaplan, R. B. & Baldauf, R. B. (1997) *Language Planning: From Practice to Theory*. Clevedon: Multilingual Matters.

Keidanren [The Japan Business Federation] (2000) Keidanren ikensho: Gurōbarukajidai no jinzai ikusei ni tsuite [Written opinion of the Japan Business Federation: The development of human resources in the age of globalization]. On WWW at http://www.keidanren.or.jp/japanese/policy/2000/013/. Accessed September 5, 2017.

Kimura, G. C. (2014) Language management as a cyclical process: A case study on prohibiting Sorbian in the workplace. *Slovo a slovesnost* 75 (4), 255–270.

Kimura, G. C. (2020) The bridging role of the researcher between different levels of language management: The case of a research project at the German-Polish border. In G. C. Kimura & L. Fairbrother (eds) *A Language Management Approach to Language Problems: Integrating Macro and Micro Dimensions*. Amsterdam: John Benjamins, 237–253.

Ko, M. (2010) *Japanese Cinema and Otherness: Nationalism, Multiculturalism and the Problem of Japaneseness*. London: Routledge.

Koike, I. (ed) (1978) *The Teaching of English in Japan*. Tokyo: Eichosa.

Kubota, R. (2009) Rethinking the superiority of the native speaker: Toward a relational understanding of power. In M. Neriko (ed) *"Native Speakers" Revisited: Multilingualism, Standardization, and Diversity in Language Education*. Berlin: Mouton de Gruyter, 233–247.

Liddicoat, A. J. (2013) *Language-in-Education Policies: The Discursive Construction of Intercultural Relations*. Clevedon: Multilingual Matters.

LoCastro, V. (1996) English language education in Japan. In H. Coleman (ed) *Society and the Language Classroom*. Cambridge: Cambridge University Press, 40–63.

Marriott, H. (2004) A programmatic exploration of issues in the academic interaction of Japanese students overseas. *Journal of Asian Pacific Communication* 14 (1), 33–54.

Marriott, H. (2013a) A programmatic exploration of issues in the academic interaction of Japanese students overseas. *Journal of Asian Pacific Communication* 14 (11), 33–54.

Marriott, H. (2013b) Multilingualism among university staff: A case study of language management at an Australian university. *International Journal of Multilingualism* 10 (4), 454–468. doi: 10.1080/14790718.2013.832126.

MEXT (Ministry of Education, Culture, Sports, Science and Technology) (2003) *Action plan to cultivate "Japanese with English abilities."* On WWW at https://www.gifu-net.ed.jp/kyoka/eigo/CommunicativeEnglish/Regarding%20the%20Establishment%20of%20an%20Action%20Plan%20to%20Cultivate%20%A1%C8Japanese%20with%20English%20Abilities%A1%C9.htm. Accessed March 11, 2020.

MEXT (Ministry of Education, Culture, Sports, Science and Technology) (2009a) Dai 8 setsu gaikokugo [The high school new course of study. Clause 8, foreign languages]. In *Kōtōgakkō gakushū shidō yōryō* [The New Course of Study], 87–92. On WWW at https://www.mext.go.jp/a_menu/shotou/new-cs/youryou/kou/kou.pdf. Accessed June 11, 2018.

MEXT (Ministry of Education, Culture, Sports, Science and Technology) (2009b) *Kōtōgakkō gakushū shidō yōryō kaisetsu. Gaikokugohen eigohen* [The high school new course of study guide: Foreign language section, English section]. On WWW at http://www.mext.go.jp/component/a_menu/education/micro_detail/__icsFiles/afieldfile/2010/01/29/1282000_9.pdf. Accessed September 9, 2019.

MEXT (Ministry of Education, Culture, Sports, Science and Technology) (2016a) *Heisei 28 nendo kōritsukōtōgakkō/chūtōkyōikugakkō (kōkikatei) ni okeru eigokyōiku jisshijōkyōchōsa: kōtōgakkō shūkeikeika* [The Heisei 28 survey on the implementation of public high school and secondary school (later course) English education: Tabulation results for high schools]. On WWW at http://www.mext.go.jp/component/a_menu/education/detail/__icsFiles/afieldfile/2017/04/07/1384236_06.pdf. Accessed September 5, 2017.

MEXT (Ministry of Education, Culture, Sports, Science and Technology) (2016b) *Heisei 28 nendo eigo kyōiku jisshijōkyōchōsa (kōtōgakkō) no kekka* [The results of the Heisei 28 survey on the implementation of English education (high schools)]. On WWW at http://www.mext.go.jp/component/a_menu/education/detail/_icsFiles/afieldfile/2007/04/07/1384236_02_1.pdf. Accessed September 5, 2017.

MEXT (Ministry of Education, Culture, Sports, Science and Technology) (2017) *Heisei 29 nendo eigo kyōiku jisshijōkyōchōsa (kōtōgakkō) no kekka* [The results of the Heisei 29 survey on the implementation of English education (high schools)]. On WWW at https://www.mext.go.jp/component/a_menu/education/detail/__icsFiles/afieldfile/2018/04/06/1403469_02.pdf. Accessed December 19, 2021.

Mori, K. (2013) "Jugyō wa eigo de" wa hontō ni kanō ka [Is the policy, "English classes should be conducted in English," really possible in Japanese high school classrooms?]. *Journal of the Chubu English Language Education Society* 42, 45–52.

Mouer, R. & Kawanishi, H. (2005) *A Sociology of Work in Japan*. Cambridge: Cambridge University Press.

Nagamine, T. (2012) Pre-service and in-service EFL teachers' perceptions of the new language education policy to "conduct classes in English" in Japanese senior high schools. *Japanese Senior High Schools Multiculturalism in Asia: Proceedings of the Second Afrasian International Symposium*, 123–139.

Nekvapil, J. (2009) The integrative potential of language management theory. In J. Nekvapil & T. Sherman (eds) *Language Management in Contact Situations: Perspectives from Three Continents*. Frankfurt on the Main: Peter Lang, 1–11.

Nekvapil, J. & Nekula, M. (2006) On language management in multinational companies in the Czech Republic. *Current Issues in Language Planning* 7 (2–3), 307–327.

Neustupný, J. V. (1994) Problems of English contact discourse and language planning. In T. Kandiah & J. Kwan-Terry (eds) *English and Language Planning: A Southeast Asian Contribution*. Singapore: Academic Press, 50–69.

Neustupný, J. V. (1997) Gengo kanri to komyuniti gengo no shomondai [Language management and issues of community languages]. In *Tagengo, tabunka komyuniti no tame no gengo kanri: sai o ikiru kojin to komyuniti* [Language management for multilingual and multicultural communities: Individuals and communities which live the difference]. Tokyo: National Language Research Institute, 21–37.

Neustupný, J. V. (2002) Language and power into the 21st century. A paper for the *International Conference on Language and Empowerment*, Malaysian Association of Modern Languages, Kuala Lumpur, Malaysia, April 11–13, 2002. Also available on WWW at http://languagemanagement.ff.cuni.cz/bibliography.

Rudwick, S. (2018) The struggle to promote an African language at a South African university: A language management perspective. In L. Fairbrother, J. Nekvapil & M. Sloboda (eds) *The Language Management Approach: A Special Focus on Research Methodology*. Frankfurt on the Main: Peter Lang, 157–183.

Saito, Y. (2017) High school teachers' cognition of the policy of "English classes in English", and their classroom practice. *The Language Teacher* 41 (1), 3–7.

Seargeant, P. (2009) *The Idea of English in Japan: Ideology and the Evolution of a Global Language*. Bristol: Multilingual Matters.

Son, M. (2017) International student participants' evaluations and interests in situations when receiving support in Japanese. In H. Muraoka (ed) *Ritual Interaction in Contact Situations: Language Management in Contact Situations*, Vol. 14. *Research Project Reports no. 309*. Chiba: Chiba University Graduate School of Humanities and Social Sciences, 41–61.

Spolsky, B. (2006) Language policy failures. In M. Pütz, J. Fishman & J. Neff-van Aertselaer (eds) *'Along the Routes to Power': Explorations of Empowerment through Language*. Berlin: Mouton de Gruyter, 87–106.

Takegami, F. (2016) An exploratory study on the impact of the new Teaching English Through English (TETE) curriculum policy in Japan: A case study of three teachers. *International Journal of Social and Cultural Studies* 9 (3), 15–45.

Terashima, T. (2009) *Eigokyōiku ga horobiru toki: "eigo de jugyō" no ideorogī* [The Moment when English Education will Die: The Ideology of "Classes in English"]. Tokyo: Akashi.

The Prime Minister's Commission on Japan's Goals in the 21st Century (2000) *The Frontier within: Individual Empowerment and Better Governance in the New Millennium.* On WWW at http://www.kantei.go.jp/jp/21century/report/pdfs/. Accessed September 7, 2017.

Tsukamoto, M. & Tsujioka, N. (2013) Teaching English through English to senior high school students in Japan: Towards the implementation of the new course of study. *Shitennoji University Bulletin* 55, 309–324.

Yamada, H. (2010) Teaching/learning English in English at Japanese senior high schools: The debate. *Jin-Ai University Research Bulletin* 9, 43–53.

Yamada, H. & Hristoskova, G. (2011) Teaching and learning English in English in Japanese senior high schools: Teachers' and students' perceptions. *Fukui eigokenkyūkai kaihō* [Bulletin of the Fukui Prefecture English Teachers' Association] 69, 3–33.

Yoshida, K. (2003) Language education policy in Japan: The problem of espoused objectives versus practice. *The Modern Language Journal* 87 (2), 290–292.

Hiroyuki Nemoto

The investment in managing interests and power through study abroad: Literacy and identities from a translingual perspective

Abstract With respect to language management, this chapter explores the ways Japanese university students invest in managing their interests and power relations with others in order to mediate literacy and identities, while socializing themselves into academic and social contexts during and after study abroad. Drawing upon the concept of investment (Norton 2010), the L2 motivational self system (Dörnyei 2009), and the concept of translingual practice (Canagarajah 2013a, 2013b, 2013c), an in-depth investigation is made about how their management of interests and power as well as (re-)negotiations of a sense of self affects their investments in literacy practices and enhances their translingual development of literacy and identities in the socialization processes. This study employed a mixed methods approach by collecting the qualitative data through a case study of sixteen Japanese university students as well as the quantitative data through a questionnaire survey of fifty-seven students in an intensive study abroad program. Further qualitative data were collected from three of the participants who undertook a one-academic-year-long study as exchange students in Australia after completing this intensive program. Their re-socialization processes into L1 literacy practices in Japan after a yearlong exchange were also analyzed. The findings suggest that a perspective of Language Management Theory (Jernudd & Neustupný 1987; Neustupný 1985, 1994, 2004) enables us to apply an analytical lens to the roles which negotiations of interests and power play in the processes of literacy socialization, and contributes to elucidating the intricate nature of identity negotiation and literacy development during and after study abroad.

Keywords language management, investment, translingual literacy, translingual identity, study abroad, community of practice, individual network of practice

1 Introduction

With the increasing recognition of study abroad (SA) contexts as one of the most fertile research fields for applied linguists, SA research has placed greater emphasis on epistemological and methodological diversity by following not only experimental and cognitive approaches to second language acquisition (SLA) but also sociocultural ones, including language socialization, Vygotskian sociocultural theory, and other poststructuralist approaches (cf. Kinginger 2013a). These sociocultural approaches to SLA have increasingly enabled researchers to analyze the positive impacts of L2 learners' overseas academic participation on their negotiation of identities and development of literacy instead of merely regarding them as linguistically deficient members in overseas host communities. Indicating that L2 users cannot always be construed as "newcomers" who stress the integrative and instrumental purposes of L2 learning, Higgins (2011: 12) claims that those users can re-fashion their identities in response to global forces by maximally utilizing the resources that additional language learning and use provide them with. Furthermore, given the growing sociolinguistic awareness about languages as mobile resources in a globalized world (Blommaert 2010), it is imperative to re-conceptualize students' socialization into SA contexts from a translingual perspective. Canagarajah (2013a: 1–2) has claimed that from the translingual perspective, communicative competence is considered as the ability to merge different language resources in situated interactions for new meaning construction. He also clearly distinguishes between two confusing concepts, "translingual" and "multilingual," by stating that whereas "multilingual" perceives the relationship between languages in an additive manner, "translingual" addresses the synergy that treats languages as constantly being in contact and mutually influencing each other (Canagarajah 2013b: 41). In order to analyze such synergy, in addition to SA contexts, it is crucial to investigate pre- and post-SA socialization into L2 and L1 literacies and to gain insight into how students socialize themselves into L2 literacy prior to departure, consolidate their acquired academic skills in L2 after returning home, and apply those skills in L1 literacy.

Based on the theory of language socialization (Duff 2010; Schieffelin & Ochs 1986), the present study examines the ways Japanese university students invest in managing interests and power relations with others, developing literacy, and transforming their identities, while socializing themselves into various academic and social contexts during and after SA. The focus of this study is placed on the three different stages: an intensive program involving the preparation for and initial orientation to SA organized by a public university in Japan, a yearlong exchange program in Australia, and the post-SA stage. Drawing upon the concept of investment (Norton 2010), the L2 motivational self system (Dörnyei 2009), and the concept of translingual practice (Canagarajah 2013a, 2013b, 2013c), an in-depth investigation is made about how their management of interests and power as well as (re-)negotiations of a sense of self helps them invest in literacy practices and develop literacy and identities translingually in the socialization processes. Language Management Theory (LMT) (Jernudd & Neustupný 1987; Neustupný 1985, 1994, 2004) is furthermore employed as an analytical tool for exploring the correlations among students' mediation of interests and power, negotiations of a sense of self, investments in literacy practices, and translingual development of literacy and identities.

2 Conceptual framework

Owing to the globalization of higher education, SA programs have been actively incorporated into university curricula in many countries to develop students' interactive competence and consolidate their academic literacy in English prior to sending them into the workforce. Considering this educational movement, more empirical studies of SA students' participation in overseas academic contexts need to be undertaken to provide universities with more comprehensive findings that are applicable to these programs. Given that academic discourse should not be regarded merely as an entity but considered in relation to a social, cognitive, and rhetorical process, positioning, representation, and stance-taking (Duff 2010: 170), it is crucial for research on SA to adopt sociocultural theories of SLA and take into consideration not only students' cognitive processes of L2 learning but their negotiations of interests and power with others when they engage in discursive academic and social practices in L2. Several studies have adopted the theory of language socialization in the sociocultural and sociolinguistic investigation of SA students, but a dearth of SA research has employed longitudinal data collection procedures particularly for dealing with such negotiations in the developmental processes of literacy and/or identities (cf. Kinginger 2013a).

The conceptual framework of the present study integrates some specific sociocultural perspectives into students' literacy socialization processes through which they manage interests and power, (re-)negotiate a sense of self, and develop translingual literacy and identities. Several different theories and concepts are employed in the framework, including language socialization (Duff 2007, 2010; Ochs 1986), poststructuralist and psychological approaches to L2 identity (Dörnyei 2005, 2009; Norton 2000, 2010; Norton & McKinney 2011), community of practice (CoP) (Lave & Wenger 1991), individual network of practice (INoP) (Zappa-Hollman 2007; Zappa-Hollman & Duff 2015), and the aforementioned concept of translingual practice (Canagarajah 2013a, 2013b, 2013c). Language socialization refers to language learning through interactions with others who are more proficient in the target language explicitly and/or implicitly providing novices with the knowledge of the relevant sociocultural practices and normative ways of using the target language (e.g., Duff 2007, 2010; Ochs 1986). As a broad framework, this theory thus enables us to investigate the impacts of interactions and power relations with others on the developmental processes of linguistic, cultural, and communicative competence (Duff & Talmy 2011). However, given such broadness, it needs to be reconsidered and expanded by incorporating more specific analytical perspectives into it to explore language behavior and behavior toward language more comprehensively.

In the present study, students' power negotiations in their socialization processes are analyzed in relation to their identity transformations using the two above-mentioned approaches to L2 identity. The poststructuralist approach emphasizes the relationship between identity and power in SLA and addresses the dynamic nature of identity and multiple identity positions, focusing on power relations with others, contexts, language users' understanding of their own relationship to the world, the processes of their constructing that relationship across time and space, and their understanding of the possibilities for the future (Norton 2000, 2010; Norton & McKinney 2011). From this perspective, Norton has stressed that an identity is thus regarded as a site of struggle and changing over time. The poststructuralist approach has been further elaborated by the concept of "investment" (Norton 2010). This concept helps us explore interests and power in relation to learners' ambivalent desire to learn the target language, sociocultural constraints on learning, their changing identities, language learning commitment, and intentional choice (Darvin & Norton 2015, 2016; Kramsch 2013; Norton 2010; Norton Peirce 1995). The psychological approach is represented by Dörnyei's (2005, 2009) L2 motivational self system, which involves ideal and ought-to L2 selves. An ideal L2 self is based on the desire to be an ideal L2 user and to reduce the discrepancy between our actual and ideal selves, whereas an ought-to L2 self refers to what learners think they should possess to meet expectations and to avoid possible negative outcomes (Dörnyei 2009).

The concept of a CoP furthermore contributes to specifying relations of power in students' literacy socialization processes by enabling us to examine the communities where novice members participate in a variety of social situations in multiple ways to be fuller participants (Lave & Wenger 1991). However, some researchers have problematized the tightly circumscribed sense of discourse socialization (Duff 2007; Duff & Talmy 2011; Haneda 2006; Zuengler & Miller 2006). Hence, the present study also considers the newly emerged concept of INoP that emphasizes opportunities for learning not only in a specific community but also through various others and enables us to analyze an individual's personal relationships within or beyond a social group, community, or institution (Zappa-Hollman 2007; Zappa-Hollman & Duff 2015). Among the theoretical concepts employed in the framework, the concept of translingual practice plays a central role in shaping the developmental trajectories of each participant's literacy socialization, allowing this longitudinal study to pay close attention to the ways L1 and L2 synergy affects the ongoing and dynamic processes of literacy development and identity transformations.

Figure 1 illustrates the conceptual model of this study that explores Japanese students' management of interests and power in their literacy socialization processes. The participants in this study were expected to increase their socialization through three different stages: intensive SA, yearlong SA on exchange, and the post-SA stage. The study hypothesized that they would manage interests and power relations with others in their INoPs and CoPs while (re-)negotiating a sense of self by forming ideal and/or ought-to L2 and L1 selves. From a sociocultural perspective of SLA, such negotiations through management of interests and power are deemed as a site of struggle which provides the participants with opportunities to adjust their own social positionings in INoPs and/or CoPs and promote agency, empowerment, and a sense of belonging. Therefore, the interests and power which are dealt with in this study do not only pertain to (non-)linguistic interests and power in language management but also involve those in "sociocultural management" and/or "communicative management," which focus on the sociocultural dimension of behavior toward language and the components of communicative acts (Nekvapil 2016: 16–17). Considering the dynamic nature of identity and students' multiple identity positions in literacy socialization processes, it is also presumed that their management of interests and power as well as (re-) negotiations of a sense of self can promote and be promoted by their investments in discursive literacy practices, development of translingual literacy, and co-construction of translingual identities with others. The present study explores the relational, temporal, and situational factors affecting these correlations in the processes of students' literacy socialization.

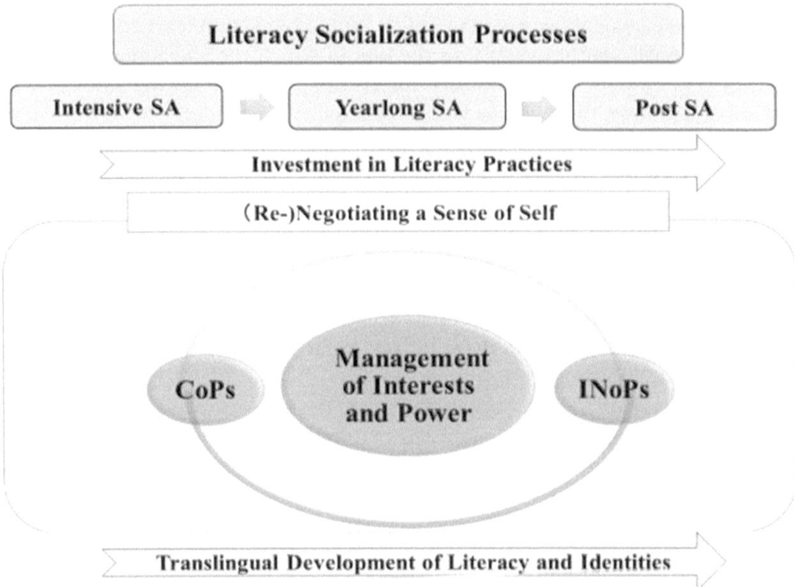

Figure 1: The conceptual model

3 Methodology

Employing a mixed methods approach, which integrated quantitative data with qualitative research, this longitudinal study began by collecting quantitative data from fifty-seven Japanese students who participated in the intensive SA program through a public university in Japan and by conducting a case study of sixteen students from this cohort. Further qualitative data were collected from three of the participants who undertook a SA program for one academic year as exchange students in Australia after completing the intensive program. Their re-socialization processes into L1 literacy practices in Japan after the yearlong exchange program were also analyzed.

3.1 The intensive program for the initial orientation to SA

The intensive program for the initial orientation to SA that involved two separate components—a three-month pre-departure course and a five-week English for Academic Purposes (EAP) program at an Australian university—was offered as one of the elective subjects at a public university in Japan, aiming to prepare students for yearlong SA. One of the main characteristics of the pre-departure course was the intercultural task-based computer-mediated communication (TB-CMC) project in which Japanese students engaged in online interactions with learners of Japanese at the same Australian university as the one in which the abovementioned EAP program was offered. While casually interacting and establishing rapport with learners of Japanese, the students were also required to conduct online interviews with them to complete a two-A4-page written assignment in English at the end of the pre-departure course. The students were provided with explicit written instructions for this assignment on how to analyze the elicited information and integrate the main findings into their texts to support their own arguments logically. If necessary, they were encouraged to use other relevant quotations, facts, and statistics to consolidate the findings in their written assignment. This project furthermore expected Japanese students to develop online L2 learning networks prior to departure and expand them to face-to-face networks while they were in Australia.

In the five-week EAP program in Australia, the students were offered various academic English classes and workshops that helped them improve their English literacy and prepare for the International English Language Testing System (IELTS). After finishing the fourth week, the students were required to actually take the IELTS and were provided with an opportunity to self-measure their own learning achievements.

3.2 Participants

From a cohort of fifty-seven informants in the intensive SA program, sixteen students participated in a case study, and then three of them were selected for the longitudinal case study. As presented in Table 1, this study explored the cases of one male and two female students—Keita, Masako, and Yurina—who majored in International Studies and Social Welfare. All the three participants are referred to using pseudonyms in this study. The data for their yearlong study at an Australian university were collected in two different academic years (2015 and 2016) based on the periods during which the three students were enrolled at the university. Keita and Masako studied at this Australian university as exchange students in 2015, and Yurina followed a year later.

Keita participated in the intensive SA program in 2012 and obtained an IELTS score of 6.0 when he was a first-year student. Masako also joined the program in her first year in 2013, and her IELTS score was 5.5, whereas Yurina gained an IELTS score of 6.0 during the intensive program when she was in her third year in 2014. Before applying for student exchanges, they needed to meet the minimum English language entry requirement of an IELTS score of 6.5. Although Keita and Masako successfully achieved the required score, Yurina had a score of 6.0 when applying for her enrollment in November 2015. She was thus given a conditional offer that allowed her to enroll in the undergraduate course at the university in the second semester in 2016 if she could obtain a score of 6.5 in the first semester. Yurina enrolled in the IELTS preparation course at the university-affiliated language center in February 2016, and after she achieved an IELTS score of 6.5 in April, she was accepted for the university course for the second semester.

Within a few months after returning to Japan, all of them took the Test of English for International Communication (TOEIC) and gained very high scores. Since the TOEIC score was considered as persuasive evidence of English competence in job applications in Japan, they considered that it would be advantageous for them to take the test, particularly at a time when they still had efficient listening skills. Keita and Masako obtained 930 and 935 out of 990 respectively, whereas Yurina's score of 890 was below 900 but still high enough to prove her achievement through SA.

Table 1: The profiles of the three exchange students

	Gender	*Major*	*IELTS during intensive SA/ Year level in Japan*	*IELTS before exchange/ Year level in Japan*	*TOEIC after exchange/ Year level in Japan*
Keita	Male	International Studies	6.0 (2012)/ 1st year	6.5 (2014)/ 3rd year	930 (2016)/ 5th year
Masako	Female	International Studies	5.5 (2013)/ 1st year	6.5 (2014)/ 3rd year	935 (2016)/ 5th year
Yurina	Female	Social Welfare	6.0 (2014)/ 3rd year	6.0 (2015)/ 4th year 6.5 (2016)/ 5th year	890 (2017)/ 6th year

3.3 Data collection and analysis

The quantitative data were collected through a questionnaire survey of fifty-seven Japanese students who participated in the intensive SA program from 2012 to 2016. The two questionnaire surveys with the same fourteen closed- and open-ended questions were conducted after the third week of the EAP course and after the students returned to Japan. The first survey results were subsequently compared with those of the second one. These questions predominantly aimed to discover how the students perceived their own improvements in reading, listening, speaking, and writing skills, how they socialized with peers who were studying English as a second language (ESL) in the program, how they interacted with teachers and their host family, and how the TB-CMC project impacted their development of L2 networks and task management in the EAP program. A four-point Likert scale, including "very," "somewhat," "not really," and "not at all" was used for responses to the closed-ended questions, while the open-ended questions were used to explore the specific reasons for each closed-ended answer.

The study also collected qualitative data through a case study of sixteen participants who were randomly selected out of fifty-seven Japanese students in the same program. Based on the weekly reflective journals, which these students were asked to compose during the five-week course, follow-up interviews were conducted with them to supplement the quantitative data and elicit detailed accounts of the students' engagement in the discursive activities in L2. Their IELTS results and course academic records were also collected in this study. Further qualitative data were collected from Keita, Masako, and Yurina during their participation in the exchange program and in the processes of their literacy socialization back in Japan. The interviews were conducted once per semester during their year-long SA and twice at the post-SA stage—a few weeks after returning to Japan and in their final semester of university study. This longitudinal approach provided "developmental evidence that can otherwise only be inferred" and enabled a thick and detailed description of the findings and triangulation of the data (Duff, 2008: 43). The integration of two different research methods also allowed the researcher to corroborate qualitative findings using quantitative data, to provide the richness and the details of the findings, and to offer new interpretations of them in this study (cf. Dörnyei 2007; Rossman & Wilson 1985).

In this study, micro-level sociocultural data analyses were undertaken based on LMT to explore the students' internal representations while undertaking situated interactions. Along with the traditional model in which norm deviations are followed by noting and evaluating the deviations, adjustment planning, and implementation of strategies to rectify the deviations, this study employed the positive flow of language management, which involves participants' encountering of intercultural phenomena and their positive evaluation of such phenomena in contact situations (cf. Nekvapil 2011; Nemoto 2004, 2011; Neustupný 2003). Adopting these two different perspectives in the data analysis, LMT played a role in discovering the intricate correlations between the theoretical concepts in the conceptual framework and in probing the factors that affected the students' negotiations of interests and power in the developmental processes of their literacy socialization.

4 Findings and discussion

Using micro-level sociocultural analyses, this study found that the students adopted discursive language management approaches to gain a critical awareness of how power operated in literacy practices and develop literacy and identities translingually in the processes of L2 socialization and L1 (re-)socialization during and after SA. After identifying the general characteristics and major factors of their socialization through quantitative analysis, the findings of the case study will delineate the ways in which the students managed interests and power by noting the complexity of L2 socialization, evaluating social positionings and situated identities, and investing in literacy practices in their INoPs and CoPs.

4.1 Overview of questionnaire survey results

Table 2 presents the results of the questionnaire surveys that this study administered after the students' third week of the EAP course and after SA. Each option was scored as one of four grades: "very = 4," "somewhat = 3," "not really = 2," and "not at all = 1." As indicated in the table, most of them clearly recognized their improvements in speaking, listening, and writing skills in English. In particular, the highest rate (M = 3.35 and SD = 0.64 after SA) was found in relation to listening skills. By contrast, they did not consider their learning in the EAP course as substantially affecting their development of L2 reading skills (M = 2.60 and SD = 0.82 after the third week and M = 2.88 and SD = 0.57 after SA). The open-ended findings about such skills revealed that the students evaluated their engagement in situated English discourse in the authentic L2 academic and social environments as productive L2 learning experiences. However, at the same time, they admitted that their own participation in such discourse practices was not always active on the grounds that they were occasionally overwhelmed by the power of norms in the host community and imbalanced power relations with other ESL students and local community members. Despite the problems with such power negotiations, the students sufficiently developed their INoPs with peers (M = 3.28 and SD = 0.65 after SA), teachers (M = 3.07 and SD = 0.65 after SA), and their host family (M = 3.14 and SD = 0.55 after SA) toward the end of the course.

Table 2: Survey results (N = 57)

	Mean (M)			*Standard Deviation (SD)*		
	Week 3	**Post SA**	**Difference**	**Week 3**	**Post SA**	**Difference**
Speaking skills	3.04	3.12	+0.08	0.65	0.54	−0.11
Listening skills	3.18	3.35	+0.17	0.50	0.64	+0.14
Writing skills	3.12	2.96	−0.16	0.60	0.60	±0
Reading skills	2.60	2.88	+0.28	0.82	0.57	−0.25
Peer networks in L2	3.21	3.28	+0.07	0.53	0.65	+0.12
Interactions with teachers	3.33	3.07	−0.26	0.55	0.65	+0.10
Interactions with host family	3.32	3.14	−0.18	0.47	0.55	+0.08
Impacts of the project on L2 networks	2.58	2.72	+0.14	1.07	0.96	−0.11
Impacts of the project on task management	2.67	2.65	−0.02	0.79	0.72	−0.07

Very = 4, Somewhat = 3, Not really = 2, Not at all = 1

On the other hand, the impacts of the pre-departure TB-CMC project on their development of L2 networks (M = 2.58 and SD = 1.07 after the third week as well as M = 2.72 and SD = 0.96 after SA) and task management (M = 2.67 and SD = 0.79 after the third week and M = 2.65 and SD = 0.72 after SA) were limited to the extent that they were not able to significantly recognize the positive relationships between online and actual face-to-face interactions as well as the commonality of task management processes between Japan and Australia. The analysis of open-ended findings helped elaborate on students' lower evaluations of these two categories. Some students struggled to receive online messages from their Australian partners in the project and such irregular responses prevented them from seeking their interests in experiencing successful online interactions and collecting interview data before departure. However, more importantly, judging from the positive comments made by several students on the impacts of the project, these evaluations depended on the ways they interpreted learning events and power relations in the host community and related previous learning experiences to their development of INoPs and task management processes in intensive SA (cf. Byram 1997, 2008).

On comparing Week 3 with post-SA surveys, Table 2 furthermore indicates that in general, the longer they socialized themselves into SA contexts, the better they became able to manage their L2 socialization. However, it was found that students had limited perceptions of their subsequent improvements in writing, interacting with their teachers and host family, and impacts of the project on task management. As a result of multiple analyses of open-ended findings, this study discovered that their higher awareness of the complexity of academic writing, intercultural interactions, and task management gradually made them more meticulous about their socialization into SA contexts. On the contrary, such awareness further encouraged them to proceed to the subsequent phases of language management where they evaluated their own struggles while considering the power of norms and other people in host communities, and then planned how to negotiate interests and power relations with others through their investments in literacy practices. These quantitative findings will be elaborated upon by the qualitative ones from a case study of Japanese students.

4.2 Noting the complexity of L2 socialization

The qualitative findings revealed that the students' management of interests and power resulted from their noting of the complexity of L2 socialization primarily by encountering the intercultural diversity of ESL speakers, identifying differences in academic genres between Japan and Australia, striving to organize their own speech acts, and experiencing difficulty with the logical structure of academic discourse. The students' struggles in dealing with the diversity of ESL speakers occurred particularly at the initial stage of the intensive EAP course. Regarding her difficulty in socializing with her ESL classmates in the course, Masako commented as follows:

> アジアとか中東からきているクラスメートが訛のある英語を早口で話すので聞き取れないことがしょっちゅうある。他の国から来た人たちは違う英語を話すことに気がついたし、私たちが日本で習った英語がすべてではないとわかった。 (Masako's journal entry, Week 2 of the intensive SA)
>
> [My classmates from other Asian and Middle Eastern countries speak accented English so fast, so I can't catch them often. I realized that people from different countries speak different types of English. Now I understand that the English we learned in Japan isn't the only one.]

There existed some different varieties of English which were affected by ESL students' native languages in this multicultural ESL CoP. In fact, several other students reported that discussions and conversations were dominated by classmates from Southeast Asia and the Middle East who had relatively higher interactive competence in L2. It thus seems that the Englishes used by those classmates constituted more powerful and dominant varieties of ESL in the community and created hierarchical relationships among ESL learners who tended to be viewed as a homogeneous group. Learning ESL may not be straightforward in this type of multicultural CoP on the grounds that students need to manage culturally different power and linguistic norms to establish a favorable position as ESL learners in the community. In this study, their awareness of this diversity led the participants to reconfirm that their L2 selves cannot be developed in a manner detached from the world they live in. The participants' encounter with otherness and interpretation of the other facilitated how they evaluated and determined who and what they were in the CoP (Burgat 2003; Prior 2011). This approach also encouraged them to consider how they can gain or lose power and negotiate their right to speak with peers and new power relationships in their INoPs and CoPs.

The participants also noted the complexity by confronting challenges to their "habitus" (Bourdieu 1991), which refers to "more or less permanent ways of being and behaving" (Kinginger 2013b: 340; Kramsch 2009: 112) and by recognizing the differences in academic genres between Japan and Australia, such as teacher- and student-centered or unidirectional and reciprocal teaching styles, students' roles as a passive recipient of knowledge and an active interlocutor, and so on. In particular, the participants in the intensive program struggled to accustom themselves to the highly interactive learning environments in Australian classes where reciprocal interactions between teachers and students were flexible and frequent. The three students who subsequently studied at an Australian university on exchange became more sensitive to their difficulty in adjusting themselves to this type of CoP at the initial stage of their one-academic-year SA. They realized that they were expected to voice their opinions as active participants, but their habitus consisted of a different type of agency, which was closely related to gaining a deeper understanding of a subject content through attentive listening rather than through interaction. Such noting of deviations from linguistic and communicative norms tentatively undermined their sense of membership in the classroom CoPs. However, recognizing their powerlessness gradually led them to reconsider their habitus as a more powerful approach to task management which allowed them to concentrate on collecting relevant information regarding their forthcoming assignments. In this way, they developed their own agentive selves who implemented a strategy of applying their habitus translingually and adhering to being attentive listeners in class intentionally rather than forcing themselves to be more than they could be.

The other factor that enhanced the participants' awareness of the complexity pertained to their experiences of difficulties in balancing power relations with others by organizing their own speech acts in authentic L2 interactions. At the interviews after the third week of the intensive course, most of them stressed that they experienced some problems with word combinations when they spoke English. Their insufficient organization of spoken texts resulted from their failure to put certain words together and to make complete sentences as well as the lack of ability to use a "because" clause to describe reasons after stating their own ideas. One of the participants mentioned in the interview, "I know it's not good at all, but I'm always using just a few words or short phrases and then trying to make myself understood." Admitting their own excessive reliance upon others to read between the lines and to even have a tacit understanding of their utterances, the participants, as powerless members in their CoPs and INoPs, noted the necessity of improving social positionings in intercultural contact situations and the importance of the speaker's agency and responsibility to specify their own intentions and realize and maintain their interests. Their limited L2 competence to express their own opinions and interests could be understood as a deviation from an ideal norm of communicative symmetry, and this norm contributed to enhancing the students' feelings of powerlessness and threatening their situated identities.

Toward the end of the EAP course and during their yearlong exchange, the participants' noting of the complex nature of L2 socialization was further triggered by their struggles with the logical structure of academic discourse in both spoken and written texts. In the interview conducted at the end of the first semester of his exchange, Keita emphasized that he felt satisfied with his achievement of interactive competence in English, but confessed that one of his weaknesses was his insufficient ability to logically organize his own text in written assignments. He also referred to the limitation of his speaking skills in the academic settings by mentioning, "Once I try to explain slightly complicated things regarding my study, my speech becomes ungrammatical." By noting the deviations from such linguistic norms, the students recognized that their insufficient academic competence could negatively affect their realization of academic interests and ongoing negotiations of a sense of belonging in the academic CoPs. Such recognition triggered their agency to enhance their literacy socialization.

As Zappa-Hollman and Duff (2015: 336) claim, the process of language socialization should not be merely considered as cultural transmission by those with institutional power and compliance by novices but understood as involving students' active negotiation and contestations of norms and practices in relation to their agency, goals, abilities, and preferences. Their noting and subsequent negative evaluation of new relations of power, challenges to their habitus, and their powerlessness and insufficient agency in SA contexts led them to develop attitudes toward tackling cultural contact, negotiating norms and practices, gaining knowledge of situated interactions, and improving L2 competence in informal and academic CoPs. This study indicates that noting the complexity of L2 socialization allowed the participants to reconsider the importance of securing their interests to increase cultural capital, which represents "knowledge, educational credentials and appreciation of specific cultural forms" (Bourdieu 1986; Darvin & Norton 2015: 44) in the processes of negotiating power relations with others. Such reconsideration contributed to their investment in managing interests and power to improve L2 academic literacy, construct L2 identity, and develop translingual practice at the subsequent stages.

4.3 Evaluating social positionings and situated identities

A language management perspective enabled this study to discover that the participants' struggles with L2 learning in contact situations, which were construed as a deviation from the communicative norm of symmetric communication, were conducive to their evaluation of their own social positionings in INoPs and CoPs and transformation of their situated identities. During their intensive SA, as they recognized their positionings in their INoPs and CoPs, the participants noted their own L2 selves that were based on their status as legitimate peripheral participants in the contexts and then negatively evaluated such existing L2 selves. Consequently, while planning to avoid negative outcomes that they might have encountered if they remained in peripheral positions in their CoPs, they gradually developed the fundamental component of their ought-to L2 selves in the SA contexts. Recognizing the situatedness of interactions with others, they implemented communicative and sociocultural management to become more communicative agents and more active negotiators of their interests to empower themselves and consolidate their English competence by using it rather than being passive learners.

Furthermore, at the stage of their yearlong exchange, the three exchange students more frequently evaluated power relations with others to secure their interests in their CoPs. In doing so, they became more highly motivated to be fuller participants in their host academic communities and L2 users as global citizens who were not concerned about whether their linguistic status was native or non-native. In this way, they evaluated deviations from the specific linguistic and communicative norms which were shown in the previous section on the background of negotiation of sociocultural norms. Such evaluation caused them to develop a more specific ought-to L2 self that necessitated them to be more proactive community members who deliberately negotiated power relations to position themselves in a favorable way in contact situations.

After completing student exchanges and returning to their home university in Japan, the three students had a strong awareness of their L1 selves when readjusting themselves to the host L1 communities and undertaking job-hunting activities. In particular, while they were frequently required to engage in formal L1 literacy practices in job-hunting contexts, this study found that they exerted agency with a partial L2 self whereby they strategically mixed their identity as native speakers of Japanese with their L2 selves in the processes of securing their interests to gain "economic capital" which would guarantee their future incomes (Bourdieu 1986). For example, when appealing their interculturality and problem-solving skills, which they had developed in contact situations, they maximized their own L2 originality in job interviews by exemplifying academic and sociocultural experiences during their intensive and long-term SA. Furthermore, their lenient attitudes toward diverse ways of thinking, which they had gained through intercultural interactions with others during SA, enabled them to respect individual differences in L1 opinions, and to be more open to suggestions and seek constructive criticisms in L1. Keita commented in one of the interviews:

> オーストラリア留学中は友達と意見が食い違うことも珍しくなかったので、日本でも他の人が僕と違う意見の時は、拒否しないでまず話をよく聞いて、どうやってうまく受け入れて折り合いをつけるか考えるようにしています。
> (Keita, second post-SA interview)

> [It wasn't unusual to have some disagreements with my friends when I studied in Australia. So, even in Japan, when other people have different opinions from me, I try

not to reject them but to listen and consider how to accept them and to work out a compromise carefully.]

As Keita's case reveals, the participants' investment in harmonizing differing interests with their interlocutors in SA contexts occasionally triggered such translingual application of L2 practices in L1.

The students' management of L2 (re-)positionings in overseas INoPs and CoPs furthermore generated their acceptance of marginal positions in L1. After overcoming various types of cultural contact during SA, all the three students emphasized that they did not get daunted easily even when they were treated unfairly. For example, Masako stated, "I often felt out of my comfort zone when I studied abroad, so I don't feel down easily even if I get the cold shoulder from company interviewers during job hunting." Through the multiple analyses based on LMT, this study found that the three students compared their L2 selves in Australia with their L1 selves in Japan and then noted that being a peripheral participant in L1 situations was less stressful to them compared to that in L2. Particularly, the last two cases indicate that the students employed cultural capital and norms of intercultural interactions that they had gained in SA contexts as the criteria for evaluating power negotiations in L1 situated interactions back in Japan. The findings demonstrated that the ways in which the students managed their own social positionings and situated identities in their INoPs and CoPs through SA were translingually applicable to their management of interests and power in L1 contexts and contributed to their exerting a hybrid type of agency which integrated L2 into L1 selves.

4.4 Investment in literacy practices in INoPs and CoPs

Based on their situated identities at each stage, the students enhanced their literacy socialization and managed interests and power by investing in literacy practices in their INoPs and CoPs in different ways. The students' investments predominantly emerged in the form of power negotiations during intensive SA. Such negotiations led the three exchange students to transform their cultural and social capital into valuable resources in new contexts during their yearlong exchange (Darvin & Norton 2015) and to construct other fundamental components of their ought-to selves and specify ideal selves in both L2 and L1 after SA.

4.4.1 Power negotiations during intensive SA

During intensive SA, this study identified that the participants' investment and language management actions in L2 literacy practices resulted in four types of power negotiations, including their establishment of an equitable relationship and rivalry with ESL peers, engagement in collaborative scaffolding of situated interactions in L2, expansion of online networks to face-to-face INoPs, and involvement of host family in academic INoPs. Their negotiating attempts to build equitability with their ESL classmates occurred particularly at the beginning stage when they felt that their classmates treated them like children due to their insufficient interactive competence in English. Reflecting upon the unfair treatment, some students stated, "I don't want to be in that kind of position anymore," and even fostered competitive rivalry with their classmates. One of the students commented, "I'm trying hard to be a better English user than my Asian classmates, because I can feel confident about myself when I think that my English skills are slightly higher than those of others." Such rivalry gradually expanded to occasional collaborative L2 interactions with their ESL classmates. The participants invested in co-constructing peer interactions in English as a lingua franca by providing ongoing collaborative scaffolding with each other to discover situationally appropriate expressions in English and compensate for their insufficient utterances in both academic and social contexts.

Furthermore, some of the students who undertook frequent online interactions with their Australian partners in the predeparture TB-CMC project effectively expanded such online INoPs into face-to-face ones by directly meeting their online partners and engaging in casual interactions, predominantly in English and sometimes in Japanese. Keita was the one who regularly met his Australian partner with an Asian ethnic background on the weekends. He emphasized the importance of this type of INoP in one of his weekly journals:

> オンラインパートナーと会って話すのはいつもとても楽しい。いつもJポップの話をして、パートナーは僕のたどたどしい英語をとても辛抱強く聞いてくれる。日本語も上手いので、英語で言葉が浮かばない時には、会話の流れを止めないように所々日本語を混ぜて話すこともある。 (Keita's journal entry, Week 4 of the intensive SA)
>
> [It's always great fun to meet and talk to my online partner. We usually talk about Japanese pop culture, and he listens to my clumsy English very patiently. He is also good at Japanese, so whenever I don't come up with proper English words, I use some Japanese words in English sentences to keep the flow going.]

His investment in peer interactions in this INoP allowed Keita and his partner to explore mutual interests and establish an equitable and productive relationship between them. His partner's curiosity about the authentic and latest information pertaining to pop culture in Japan resulted in Keita applying his individual L1 resources as cultural capital to the interactions, whereas this INoP constituted Bourdieu's (1986) social capital which refers to "connections to networks of power" (Darvin & Norton 2015: 44). It seems that he unwittingly empowered his investment in literacy practices by implementing adjustment strategies of drawing upon his cultural capital in peer interactions and consolidating his INoP as social capital.

Others built rapport with their host family and made efforts to form temporary academic INoPs and increase their social capital at home by involving host family members in academic discussions and relying on them as informal discussion partners. For example, when she had dinner with her host mother, Yurina was frequently requested to describe what she learned from the EAP course. Such an interactive atmosphere was conducive to her engaging in language management actions, including reviewing and evaluating what she had discussed in class on the day and preparing for the forthcoming in-class discussions by practicing stating her opinions about the assigned topics beforehand.

According to these findings, it is evident that language socialization research needs to pay attention to not only the learners' agentive, strategic, goal-directed efforts, and resourcefulness but also to the role played by peers and others as very powerful agents of (co-)socialization and identity work (Zappa-Hollman & Duff 2015: 358). In fact, by analyzing investment in power negotiations based on LMT, this study confirmed that "the conditions of power in different learning contexts can position the learners in multiple and often unequal ways, leading to varying learning outcomes" (Darvin & Norton 2015: 37). These students' cases nevertheless demonstrated that due to their efforts to negotiate the conditions of power and ongoing investments in L2 literacy practices, they noted and evaluated their L2 selves and also developed their skills of discovery and interaction whereby they acquired knowledge of the norms and practices that ESL students in SA contexts should follow and interacted based on the knowledge (Byram 1997, 2008). Furthermore, their investments in language management facilitated their re-evaluating their L2 selves, negotiating alternative and more powerful ought-to L2 selves to avoid remaining in peripheral positions, and becoming friendly rivals with peers, collaborative L2 users, providers of information about Japan in L2 interactions, and active recipients of L2 academic support. The findings suggest that SA students can manage interests and power and construct their situated identities depending on the contexts they are in by "resisting ascribed positionalities and developing subject positions based on their projected visions of who they are" (Higgins 2011: 10).

4.4.2 Transformation of cultural and social capital during yearlong SA

During their participation in discipline-specific courses at an Australian university for one academic year, the three exchange students in this study managed interests and power by more actively investing in new literacy practices in their out-of-classroom CoPs and INoPs. In particular, it is notable that the students used cultural capital that they already possessed as affordances and transformed such capital into valuable resources in new non-academic contexts (Darvin & Norton 2015: 45). Keita joined a local Kyudo (Japanese archery) community in the city where his host university was located and taught Kyudo to other local members. In addition to acting as captain of the Kyudo club at his home university in Japan prior to participating in the yearlong exchange, he won the high school Kyudo tournament in his prefecture and then played in the national competition in his third year of senior high school. Although he realized that the uniqueness of this traditional Japanese sport such as Judo and Kendo can attract Australian people through intensive SA, he was frustrated by his lack of linguistic ability to explain the characteristics of Kyudo properly. Thus, prior to his departure for the yearlong exchange, he allocated enormous efforts to prepare for explaining Kyudo. While he employed Kyudo expertise as his cultural capital in interacting with others at the beginning of his yearlong SA, he obtained information about the local Kyudo community from one of his friends who studied Japanese at the same university as him. Once he started to participate in it, the community constituted his CoP where he placed himself in a favorable position as a volunteer instructor but a legitimate member. This CoP also enabled Keita to transform his cultural capital, which involved his knowledge and skills of Kyudo, into resources for negotiating his interests and power relations with local Australian members.

Masako's case revealed that her transformation of cultural capital into L2 interactional resources led her to invest in managing interests and power in cooking INoPs in her dormitory. In the situated social interactions at the shared kitchen and dining space, while sharing how to cook culturally different meals with her friends, she employed her knowledge of traditional Japanese meals as a tool of interactions. Masako furthermore demonstrated her skills in eliciting cultural information from others that had been previously developed through the interviewing activities in the pre-departure TB-CMC project in the intensive SA program. As a result of her ongoing negotiations of interests and power, the INoPs that Masako formed through cooking gradually expanded to those where she shared various cultural topics with her friends. Such networks were even transferred to her social capital in the form of academic INoPs, which enabled her to gain academic support from them and secure her academic interests. In this way, as discussed by Zappa-Hollman and Duff (2015), informal interactions with members of her INoPs helped Masako to access and construct academic and disciplinary knowledge.

Yurina transformed her experiences in constructing social capital in Japan into affordances to develop her networks of power in yearlong SA. Yurina, who had played volleyball since she was 13 years old, participated in a volleyball club at the host university, the membership of which allowed her to negotiate interests and power with other members in team discussions about game plans. Although she was initially reluctant to voice her opinions in the discussions, her team members gradually expected her to provide suggestions or comments, because her strategic playing style, tactics, and dedicated contribution to the team, which she had gained through her social capital in Japan, led them to consider her as one of the leading players in the team. Her team members' respect enhanced Yurina's solidarity with them and empowered her to be a legitimate speaker in the team who felt more responsible for her own voice. She stated in the interview in her second semester:

> チームミーティングでチームメートが議論するのをよく観察してきましたが、説得しようとするときは本当に上手にこまかく理由を話すんです。私もチームメートを真似て話を組み立てようとずっと心がけていて、今ではどうやってチームメートを説得すればいいかなんとなくわかってきました。
> (Yurina, second interview in the yearlong SA)

> [At our team meetings, I have carefully watched the way my team members argue with each other, because whenever they try to convince other members, they state

detailed reasons very well. I've tried to structure my speech by mimicking what they do. Now I've somehow learned how to persuade my team members.]

In Yurina's case, her language management behavior including noting and evaluating her own position in this CoP allowed her to familiarize herself with local norms of interactions and to experiment with local discursive practices rather than rejecting new behaviors (cf. Jackson 2013: 182). Such an attitude contributed to the development of her argumentation skills by observing and emulating others as a model of situated interactions. These skills were also applied in her development of logical reasoning in academic contexts and helped her improve L2 academic literacy.

Through investment in L2 literacy practices in their own INoPs and/or CoPs, the exchange students secured their interests while harmonizing the differing interests of others and formed specific ought-to L2 selves. His response to members' expectations and avoidance to form a wrong impression about a traditional Japanese sport enabled Keita to manage power relations with members and realize that he needed to be one of the representative Kyudo players in Japan and to teach Japanese chivalry in L2. Similarly, Masako's social behavior to avoid adhering to her stereotypical view of other cultures and to discover authentic cultural information in intercultural interactions allowed her to negotiate mutual interests and deem herself an active listener and a provider of knowledge of traditional and contemporary Japan in L2. In Yurina's case, her growing awareness of her own position in the team contributed to her balancing power relations with team members and triggered her sense of self as a game planner who needed to explain the team tactics in L2 properly in order to win the inter-university competitions. From the perspective of language management, this study revealed that the students' investment in L2 interactions with their peers extended beyond building rapport with them and played a crucial role in noting and evaluating expected roles in their CoPs and INoPs. Such noting and evaluation empowered them to maximize cultural and social capital by implementing personal and cultural resources in communication, to establish favorable positions to increase social power in their CoPs and INoPs, and to improve L2 literacy to secure not only their memberships but also their academic interests in SA contexts. The students' strategic transformation of cultural and social capital into affordances constituted sociocultural management and also led to their implementation of communicative management in the situated interactions.

4.4.3 Re-negotiating L1 and L2 selves after SA

After returning to Japan, all the three students had limited INoPs and CoPs in L2. In Keita's case, his INoP with a Malaysian student in the Kyudo club at his home university provided him with some opportunities for L2 interactions. Masako's L2 INoPs in Japan consisted of her social capital gained through SA, which was transformed into her Skype networks with friends in Australia and involved her academic network with the American supervisor of her graduation research. Yurina's INoPs were limited to temporary ones where she took care of foreign customers as a part-time salesperson at a department store. In contrast to such limited investment in L2 INoPs, they actively invested in formal literacy practices in L1 in job-hunting activities through which they re-negotiated their L1 selves and increased their awareness of their ought-to L1 selves so as to manage their interests and power. It is common for Japanese university students to search for employment and make their career decisions in the final year of their four-year university study. By reviewing the strengths and weaknesses of their status as former exchange students, they realized that merely having SA experiences did not suffice in making themselves appealing in job interviews on the grounds that a large number of former short-term SA students and working holiday makers were in the same job-search competition. Such noting triggered their language management to develop their ought-to L1 selves and resulted in them placing a primary focus on their academic selves as well as cultural capital, both of which they had improved through SA. Such a focus caused the students to apply L2 academic norms and practices, which they had invested in but struggled to learn during SA, in the job-hunting discourse, particularly using the logical organization and rhetorical style in L2 written and spoken texts in L1. Yurina, for example, explained her strategy of being assertive in job applications and interviews.

> いつも意見のメインポイントをまず言うようにして、それから具体例を使って詳しく説明するようにしていました。これは留学して覚えたことで、このやり方で口頭での説明もエントリーシートの文章も上手くまとめることができたと思います。 (Yurina, second post-SA interview)
>
> [I always tried to introduce the main points of my opinions first and then explained details using examples. That is what I learned through SA. I think that this strategy helped me strengthen my speeches and application documents as well.]

The findings indicate that as a result of language management, the students "discovered their own rhetorical strengths and preferences as they adopted different strategies for voice" and integrated L2 rhetorical strengths into L1 to pursue their interests and transform their cultural capital into future economic capital (Canagarajah 2013b: 63).

Another major requirement for these three students to accomplish in their final year of university study was to complete their graduation theses. This study found that their academic selves in L2 and cultural capital, which had increased through L2 academic literacy practices, were also applied in their management of interests in the home academic contexts and contributed to them reframing their own academic power in the process of completing their graduation research. For example, since Keita and Masako were required to compose their graduation theses in English, they were empowered by maximizing the skills that they had developed during their yearlong exchange, particularly in relation to data collection and analysis, L2 text structure and organization, and logical development of ideas in written texts. Keita's case also revealed that reconstructing his ought-to L2 self in the home academic contexts led him to promote his transcultural self-management and apply metacognitive skills, which he had obtained through SA, in his graduation research. His sustained efforts to tackle many weekly readings and written assignments at his host university in Australia allowed him to review his performances, manage his time, make daily, weekly and monthly schedules, and set up several different short-term goals. His transcultural perspective of the task management based on his reconstructed ought-to L2 self facilitated applying such skills in the process of his research and thesis writing on returning to Japan. Keita and Masako furthermore re-negotiated their academic selves in L2 at their home university and activated the disciplinary knowledge as their cultural capital, which they had gained through SA, in their graduation theses in order to explore their academic interests. Keita expanded what he had learned in Pacific Studies and composed his thesis, which dealt with the dynamics of a Samoan family. Masako's thesis topic, "Filipina in Japan," derived from her interest in migrants and ethnic minorities that she had learned in the subject entitled "Crossing Borders: Diasporas and Transnationalism." She formed the theoretical framework of her research and composed the literature review of the thesis by referring to the articles that she had read on this subject.

From the perspective of language management, the findings imply that various types of investments in literacy practices, which resulted from the students' "ingenuity, resourcefulness, and agency," constituted adjustment strategies for mediating their interests and power in the processes of L2 socialization and (re-) socialization into L1 literacy practices (Duff & Anderson 2015: 338). Through investment, the students made some attempts to balance interests and power relations with others and then (re-)evaluated and (re-)negotiated their L1 and L2 selves by applying their cultural and social capital in various literacy practices during and after SA. Their investments further helped them consider how they should develop an ideal professional self during job hunting. Keita and Masako received official job offers from global logistics companies, whereas Yurina was accepted into a global telecommunication company. Those offers encouraged them to re-evaluate how to transform their cultural capital into future economic capital, imagine their ideal selves more clearly, and then establish a goal of becoming a translingual human resource who can leverage hybrid identities as well as both L1 and L2 literacies in global business settings. The findings demonstrated that the analysis of students' investments in managing interests and power based on LMT suitably equipped this study to explore "how learners are positioned, constrained or empowered as they navigate diverse spaces and perform a range of identities" (Darvin & Norton 2016: 34).

5 Conclusions and implications

The findings indicate that the LMT perspective enables us to apply an analytical lens to the roles that negotiations of interests and power relations with others play in students' investment in the processes of literacy socialization and contributes to elucidating the intricate nature of identity negotiation and literacy development during and after SA. In particular, this study highlighted that their language management behavior led the students to (re-)consider not only how to mediate linguistic and non-linguistic interests but also how to adjust social positionings in their INoPs and CoPs. Such behavior also resulted in their conducting translingual negotiations of norms, negotiating senses of selves across time and space, transforming cultural capital into valuable resources in new literacy contexts, and integrating L2 rhetorical strengths into L1 as an adjustment strategy for promoting literacy socialization.

As a result of exploring interests and power from the perspective of language management, this study reinforced the view of literacy socialization as "bidirectional, reciprocal, or multidirectional and always temporally, socially, and spatially situated and contingent" (Duff & Anderson 2015: 338). Importantly, in addition to the multiple relationships among experts, novices, and peers, there existed bidirectional effects between literacy practices in academic and social contexts in the processes of students' socializing themselves into the SA and post-SA contexts. The participants' language management actions from observing and engaging in discursive literacy practices in their local and/or out-of-classroom INoPs and CoPs were conducive to securing their subjective positions, developing networks of power as their social capital, and consolidating academic literacy during SA. They also employed their cultural capital as power and adopted academic language management approaches by applying L2 academic competence in job-hunting contexts and graduation research.

Furthermore, this study demonstrated that while negotiating norms in relation to translingual repertories and practices, the students enhanced their sensitivity to similarity-in-difference and difference-in-similarity which empowered them to perceive common practice in the process of yielding diverse textual products and identify the mediated and hybrid nature of standardized products (Canagarajah 2013c: 9). Such translingual competence allowed them to reframe power relations with others, evaluate situated interactions critically, assess cultural differences in a neutral manner, and discover intercultural commonalities. Their translingual practices also helped them demonstrate metacognitive skills in reviewing L2 literacy socialization and L1 literacy (re-)socialization and in re-positioning themselves in their INoPs and CoPs. After returning to Japan, the participants further developed hybrid, in-between, transcultural, and translingual identities and skills to find new ways of belonging and balance power relations with others (Higgins 2011: 2) and improved translingual literacy to secure economic and academic interests by using their cultural capital and norms of intercultural interactions in SA contexts as criteria for evaluating L1 situated interactions.

This study has contributed to expanding research on translingual competence and power dynamics using LMT in the aforementioned ways. However, future research needs to collect more comprehensive qualitative and quantitative data on the processes of students' language management in situated activities, investment in literacy practices, and negotiations of power, considering Canagarajah's (2013a: 2) claim that "translingual literacies are not about fashioning a new kind of literacy but about understanding the practices and processes that already characterize communicative activities in diverse communities." Particularly, given that written texts have been predominantly analyzed to explore translingual literacy, greater focus should also be placed on identity, agency, power, and capital through spoken interactions as in the case of this study.

From a pedagogical perspective, it is implied that home universities should preliminarily scaffold outgoing SA students' management of various linguistic and cultural contact phenomena by promoting students' development of interculturality and translingual practice, based on which they act upon critical awareness of their own and other academic cultures as well as integrate their L1 rhetorical strengths into L2. The findings of language management research should also be more thoroughly incorporated into a post-SA education system so that universities can help post-SA students apply cultural capital that they have increased in contact situations to their further study and career development.

References

Blommaert, J. (2010) *The Sociolinguistics of Globalization.* Cambridge: Cambridge University Press.

Bourdieu, P. (1986) The forms of capital. In J. F. Richardson (ed) *Handbook of Theory and Research for the Sociology of Education.* New York: Greenwood Press, 241–258.

Bourdieu, P. (1991) *Language and Symbolic Power.* Cambridge: Harvard University Press.

Burgat, F. (2003) Veils and obscuring lenses. In J. L. Esposito & F. Burgat (eds) *Modernizing Islam: Religion in the Public Sphere in the Middle East and Europe.* New Brunswick: Rutgers University Press, 17–41.

Byram, M. (1997) *Teaching and Assessing Intercultural Communicative Competence.* Clevedon: Multilingual Matters.

Byram, M. (2008) *From Foreign Language Education to Education for Intercultural Citizenship: Essays and Reflections.* Clevedon: Multilingual Matters.

Canagarajah, A. S. (ed) (2013a) *Literacy as Translingual Practice: Between Communities and Classrooms.* New York: Routledge.

Canagarajah, A. S. (2013b) Negotiating translingual literacy: An enactment. *Research in the Teaching of English* 48 (1), 40–67.

Canagarajah, A. S. (2013c) *Translingual Practice: Global Englishes and Cosmopolitan Relations.* New York: Routledge.

Darvin, R. & Norton, B. (2015) Identity and a model of investment in applied linguistics. *Annual Review of Applied Linguistics* 35, 36–56. doi: 10.1017/S0267190514000191.

Darvin, R. & Norton, B. (2016) Investment and language learning in the 21st century. *Langage et Société* 157, 19–38. doi: 10.3917/ls.157.0019.

Dörnyei, Z. (2005) *The Psychology of the Language Learner: Individual Differences in Second Language Acquisition.* Mahwah: Lawrence Erlbaum.

Dörnyei, Z. (2007) *Research Methods in Applied Linguistics.* Oxford: Oxford University Press.

Dörnyei, Z. (2009) The L2 motivational self system. In Z. Dörnyei & E. Ushioda (eds) *Motivation, Language Identity and the L2 Self.* Bristol: Multilingual Matters, 9–42.

Duff, P. A. (2007) Problematising academic discourse socialization. In H. Marriott, T. Moore & R. Spence-Brown (eds) *Learning Discourses and the Discourses of Learning.* Melbourne: Monash University Press, 1.1–1.18.

Duff, P. A. (2008) *Case Study Research in Applied Linguistics.* New York: Routledge.

Duff, P. A. (2010) Language socialization into academic discourse communities. *Annual Review of Applied Linguistics* 30, 169–192. doi: 10.1017/S0267190510000048.

Duff, P. A. & Anderson, T. (2015) Academic language and literacy socialization for second language students. In N. Markee (ed) *The Handbook of Classroom Discourse and Interaction.* Malden: Wiley-Blackwell, 337–352.

Duff, P. A. & Talmy, S. (2011) Language socialization approaches to second language acquisition: Social, cultural, and linguistic development in additional languages. In D. Atkinson (ed) *Alternative Approaches to Second Language Acquisition.* New York: Routledge, 95–116.

Haneda, M. (2006) Classroom as communities of practice: A reevaluation. *TESOL Quarterly* 40, 807–817. doi: 10.2307/40264309.

Higgins, C. (ed) (2011) *Identity Formation in Globalizing Contexts: Language Learning in the New Millennium.* Berlin: De Gruyter Mouton.

Jackson, J. (2013) The transformation of "a frog in the well": A path to more intercultural, global mindset. In C. Kinginger (ed) *Social and Cultural Aspects of Language Learning in Study Abroad.* Amsterdam: John Benjamins, 179–204.

Jernudd, H. B. & Neustupný, J. V. (1987) Language planning: For whom? In L. Laforge (ed) *Actes du Colloque international sur l'aménagement linguistique / Proceedings of the International Colloquium on Language Planning.* Québec: Les Presses de L'Université Laval, 69–84.

Kinginger, C. (ed) (2013a) *Social and Cultural Aspects of Language Learning in Study Abroad.* Amsterdam: John Benjamins.

Kinginger, C. (2013b) Identity and language learning in study abroad. *Foreign Language Annals* 46 (3), 339–358. doi: 10.1111/flan.12037.

Kramsch, C. J. (2009) *The Multilingual Subject.* Oxford: Oxford University Press.

Kramsch, C. J. (2013) Afterword. In B. Norton (ed) *Identity and Language Learning: Extending the Conversation.* 2nd edition. Bristol: Multilingual Matters, 192–201.

Lave, J. & Wenger, E. (1991) *Situated Learning: Legitimate Peripheral Participation.* Cambridge: Cambridge University Press.

Nekvapil, J. (2011) The history and theory of language planning. In E. Hinkel (ed) *Handbook of Research in Second Language Teaching and Learning.* New York: Routledge, 871–887.

Nekvapil, J. (2016) Language management theory as one approach in language policy and planning. *Current Issues in Language Planning* 17 (1), 11–22. doi: 10.1080/14664208.2016.1108481.

Nemoto, H. (2004) The cross-cultural academic communication and study management of Japanese exchange students. *Journal of Asian Pacific Communication* 14 (1), 113–136. doi: 10.1075/japc.14.1.08nem.

Nemoto, H. (2011) *The Management of Intercultural Academic Interaction: Student Exchanges Between Japanese and Australian Universities.* Newcastle upon Tyne: Cambridge Scholars Publishing.

Neustupný, J. V. (1985) Problems in Australian-Japanese contact situations. In J. B. Pride (ed) *Cross-Cultural Encounters: Communication and Mis-Communication.* Melbourne: River Seine, 44–63.

Neustupný, J. V. (1994) Problems of English contact discourse and language planning. In T. Kandiah & J. Kwan-Terry (ed) *English and Language Planning: A Southeast Asian Contribution.* Singapore: Times Academic Press, 50–69.

Neustupný, J. V. (2003) Japanese students in Prague. Problems of communication and interaction. *International Journal of the Sociology of Language* 162, 125–143. doi: 10.1515/ijsl.2003.033.

Neustupný, J. V. (2004) Theory and practice in language management. *Journal of Asian Pacific Communication* 14 (1), 3–31. doi: 10.1075/japc.22.2.09neu.

Norton, B. (2000) *Identity and Language Learning: Gender, Ethnicity, and Educational Change.* Harlow: Pearson Education.

Norton, B. (2010) Language and identity. In N. H. Hornberger & S. L. McKay (eds) *Sociolinguistics and Language Education.* Bristol: Multilingual Matters, 349–369.

Norton, B. & McKinney, C. (2011) An identity approach to second language acquisition. In D. Atkinson (ed) *Alternative Approaches to Second Language Acquisition.* New York: Routledge, 73–94.

Norton Peirce, B. (1995) Social identity, investment, and language learning. *TESOL Quarterly* 31 (3), 409–430. doi: 10.2307/3587803.

Ochs, E. (1986) Introduction. In B. Schieffelin & E. Ochs (eds) *Language Socialization Across Cultures.* Cambridge: Cambridge University Press, 1–13.

Prior, M. T. (2011) "I'm two pieces inside of me": Negotiating belonging through narratives of linguistic and ethnic hybridity. In C. Higgins (ed) *Identity Formation in Globalizing Contexts: Language Learning in the New Millennium.* Berlin: De Gruyter Mouton, 27–47.

Rossman, G. B. & Wilson, B. L. (1985) Numbers and words: Combining quantitative and qualitative methods in a single large-scale evaluation study. *Evaluation Review* 9 (5), 627–643. doi: 10.1177/0193841X8500900505.

Schieffelin, B. & Ochs, E. (1986) *Language Socialization Across Cultures.* Cambridge: Cambridge University Press.

Zappa-Hollman, S. (2007) *The Academic Literacy Socialization of Mexican Exchange Students at a Canadian University.* Unpublished doctoral dissertation, University of British Columbia, Vancouver, Canada.

Zappa-Hollman, S. & Duff, P. A. (2015) Academic English socialization through individual networks of practice. *TESOL Quarterly* 49 (2), 333–368. doi: 10.1002/tesq.188.

Zuengler, J. & Miller, E. R. (2006) Cognitive and sociocultural perspectives: Two parallel SLA worlds? *TESOL Quarterly* 40 (1), 35–58. doi: 10.2307/40264510.

Vít Dovalil

German as a foreign and a minority language in the light of the interests of social actors: The case of the Czech Republic

Abstract The chapter aims to analyze the position of German in the Czech Republic in the light of the interests pursued by various social actors. This issue is interpreted as a process as well as a result of language management which is carried out in metalinguistic discourses. Referring to Language Management Theory, the success of a management process oriented toward the achievement of specific interests depends primarily on socio-economic preconditions. These either determine the possibilities for improving the position of German in the Czech Republic, or, conversely, they explain why this improvement fails to occur. Both quantitative data and individual social actors' management activities are presented. The interests of selected social actors and their attempts to shape specific social networks to enhance power are in the foreground. Unequal power relations among actors are hierarchized according to Zhao's (2011) classification. Difficulties in protecting German as a minority language are interconnected with problems in teaching German primarily as a foreign language.

Keywords Language Management Theory, organized management, social actor, interests, German as a minority language, German as a foreign language, Czech Republic

1 Introduction

Institutions participating in the discourses on the support of multilingualism (not only) in the Czech Republic share the opinion that the competences of the majority of the Czech population in foreign languages—including German—is not satisfactory (Dovalil 2018: 277). The most recent Report of the Czech School Inspection, which was issued in March 2018, analyzes the development of language competences at primary and secondary schools in the school year 2016/17. It concludes that although some improvement may have been observed, the level of competences in foreign languages is not balanced. Generally speaking, the knowledge of German is lower than the knowledge of English. German tends to be chosen by weaker pupils. Besides this fact, German as the first foreign language is a rather rare phenomenon and this language is preferred in the regions with more a problematic social and educational situation (in the regions of Karlovy Vary and Ústí nad Labem). This goes hand in hand with the specific character of these towns—as a very popular spa and tourist center in the former case, and as an industrial center in the latter, both towns being located near the border with Germany. The motivation to learn German is nevertheless lower than in the case of English as well (CSI 2018: 9–11 and 36–37; see also CSI 2010). The conclusion of the recent report states "numerous opportunities" to improve the material as well as personnel conditions for foreign languages (CSI 2018: 37).

This rather unsatisfactory situation concerning the level of competences in foreign languages also holds for the current situation in most parts of Europe overall, as is stated, e.g., in one of the recent proposals for a Council Recommendation, the purpose of which is to improve the teaching and learning foreign languages in the whole EU:

> The only European Survey on Language Competences (ESLC) that has been carried out so far revealed a low level of competence in foreign languages. Only 42% of tested pupils reached the level of 'independent user' in the first foreign language, and merely a quarter of pupils did so in the second foreign language. This means that after several years of studying at school, the majority of young Europeans are not able to have a simple conversation in the foreign languages they have learned. An additional source of concern is that a considerable percentage of pupils—14% for the first language and 20% for the second—do not even reach the 'basic user' level. (COM (2018) 272 final)[1]

Concerning the macro level, there are practically no social actors participating in public discourses who would be satisfied with the level of competence in foreign languages and who would argue against the necessity to support teaching foreign languages. Hence, this broadly shared interest—as exemplified by the aforementioned quotation—underlies, and can be transformed into, a general (normative) expectation, the content of which can be expressed by the simple formulation that European as well as Czech citizens should possess higher competences in foreign languages in order to be able to communicate with other people more easily and effectively.

It follows, logically, that representatives of such institutions as Council of Europe, European Council, European Commission, or the Ministry of Education of the Czech Republic note apparent deviations from these expectations concerning the level of foreign language knowledge and evaluate them negatively. Social actors who share this negative evaluation proclaim that specific adjustments have to be designed to improve this relatively dismal situation.

1 The ESLC was conducted in 2011, and its findings were published in June 2012. More recent data are not available. The level of an independent language user as mentioned in the citation corresponds to the B-level of the Common European Framework of Reference, whereas the level of a basic user to the A-level. Low competences are projected—among other things—into hampered "meaningful exchanges between public administrations and individuals across borders" as well as into competitive disadvantages for both businesses and job seekers (COM (2017) 534 final, paragraph 3.6). See also COM (2018) 272 final, paragraphs 5 and 8 thereof, and EC & Eurydice (2017: 14–16).

If some criteria should be identified against which the implementation of these goals could be measured, then Grin's concept of the policy-to-outcome-path can be referred to. Grin (2003: 43–48) argues with three pillars as basic conditions for language use: capacities, opportunities and desire (or, at least willingness) to use the language.

Capacities are understood as an adequate degree of linguistic competence, which is typically raised by means of institutionalized education. Improvement, or deterioration in this qualitative parameter is measurable by means of tests; specific levels of these competences are defined by the Common European Framework of Reference for Languages: Learning, Teaching, Assessment (CEFR). Once the condition of sufficient capacities is fulfilled, the second factor—opportunities to use the respective language—needs to be pursued. This parameter is quantitative in nature and can be measured in terms of time as, e.g., total numbers of hours, during which a foreign language has been used. It is a relatively private matter and depends on sociocultural, or socioeconomic circumstances. However, provided a state is interested in increasing competences in foreign languages, it should take care of creating such opportunities for its citizens, or remove the respective obstacles. Grin relates this problem to minority languages, which could be exemplified by German in the Czech Republic:

> [G]enuine language vitality goes well beyond strictly private use, and encompasses the public use of a language. This is where the state often has a crucial role to play through its language policies. By creating opportunities for people to use their language outside of the strictly private sphere, authorities contribute to the supply of a linguistic environment. (Grin 2003: 43)

The lack of opportunities to use a language obviously contributes to significant decline in the speaker's capacities (knowledge). The third pillar, desire/willingness to use the language, is empirically observable in language choices. This desire to use a specific language manifests itself when an individual language has to be chosen. As a result of the speaker's attitude, one of such languages is preferred to the other by being used in real interactions.

Given these facts and criteria, the following framework research question is to be analyzed in this chapter: Which social actors behave toward German how, under which circumstances, and with which consequences?

2 Metalinguistic behavior toward German in the Czech Republic

The behavior of social actors who strive to strengthen the position of German in the Czech Republic is presented and analyzed on the basis of language management theory (Jernudd & Neustupný 1987; Fairbrother, Nekvapil & Sloboda 2018; Dovalil 2010, 2018; Dovalil & Šichová 2017; see also the website URL language management). In compliance with this theoretical framework, the following points of analysis are in the foreground:

1. The *subject* of the language management is the position of, as well as the competence in, German in the Czech Republic both in terms of German as a foreign language and German as a minority language. Although both statuses are relevant as the subject of promotion, the former status is more prevalent and better known in public than the latter. However, these statuses are mixed in some parts of the public discourse.
2. In terms of the kind of language management, *organized management* is primarily analyzed: several institutions' management acts are explored, which are trans-interactional in nature and contain ideological as well as theoretical elements (Nekvapil 2016: 15). As the processes of interconnecting such acts are traced, emerging networks of social actors trying to enforce the common interests more effectively are analyzed. They trigger the processes at the macro level, but they need to reach the micro level if they are to be considered implemented. Unequal power relations among the actors can be seen.
3. Based on the phases of the language management process, the analysis begins with the efforts of the social actors to persuade others about the fact that the position of German is too weak. This interest corresponds to the strategy to make other actors note a language problem (discursive creation of a language problem) and to make them evaluate this situation negatively. Depending on accessible data, this evaluation of the noted deviations from the actors' expectations and convenient adjustment designs are in the foreground. Difficulties accompanying their implementation are discussed as well. Special attention is devoted to the concerted efforts aimed at the removal of a discriminatory passage from the Framework Educational Program for Primary Education (hereinafter as Framework Program, or FEPPE), which prefers English as the first foreign language to all other foreign languages. Thus, the legislative framework and potential infringement upon international law are also taken into account. This rather defensive position does not entail that German should play a specific role in the Czech educational system.
4. As for the levels of language management, sociocultural/socioeconomic management represents the crucial point. In accordance with the logic of the theory, this first level of the management processes is decisive to strengthen the position of German in the Czech Republic. The category of success is interpreted within the interests pursued by the respective social actor. The central interest of the supporters consists in spreading and improvement of the command of German, which reflects linguistic management in the narrow sense at the third level of language management. What is specific in relation to German in the Czech Republic in the sociocultural sense is the fact that this language features a double status, being not only a foreign, but also a minority language. This clear-cut double status distinguishes German from other languages.[2] When

2 Polish is also a language of a neighboring country, and it is protected and taught as a minority language, but not as a foreign language in the Czech school system. Other

efforts aiming at improving the proficiency in German are undertaken, it is revealed that the status of German as a minority language could be advantageous for language management conducted in favor of German as a foreign language and vice versa.

The empirical part of the research draws upon the data reflecting the current situation of German and other foreign languages in the Czech Republic as well as the activities of various social actors as they have been carried out over the past two decades. Data for this chapter are gained from, and correspond to, various forms of metalinguistic behavior (discourses) of selected social actors from which these actors' interests can be derived (Dovalil 2010, 2018).

Social actors as such are identifiable through, and their behavior is observable in numerous discursive activities (Fenton-Smith & Gurney 2016: 74). Even though the identification of the actors is somewhat easier in the case of institutions representing the macro level (when compared with the micro level), they cannot be captured in their whole completeness anyway. Therefore, certain selection has to be carried out. Social actors enter the discourse by means of texts which are produced both in spoken and in written language. These thematically relevant texts were collected and analyzed as parts of trans-interactional sequences. If possible, immediate intertextual ties are identified, e.g., direct reactions of one social actor to the behavior of another one. The time perspective is maintained. This methodological procedure admits that impartiality, or objectivity in the traditional sense is not always attainable, which applies to every attempt to reconstruct discourses reflecting differing interests of social actors with unequal power positions.

Similarly to the identification of the actors themselves, the power relations are also to be derived from the discursive acts (Fenton-Smith & Gurney 2016: 74, 77). One of the transparent ways of placing the respective social actor into a hierarchy draws upon its authorities as they are defined in laws. However, informal aspects of (soft) power are not neglected.

The discourse on foreign languages allows us to identify the following social actors which have become involved in influencing the position of German in the Czech Republic: the Government Council for National Minorities (GCNM), two German minority organizations (*Landesversammlung der deutschen Vereine in der Tschechischen Republik* – Assembly of German Associations in the Czech Republic, hereinafter *Landesversammlung*, and *Verband der Deutschen und der Freunde*

---

minority languages such as Vietnamese, Hungarian or Bulgarian are not offered as foreign languages systematically either. Although Russian is a minority language as well as a foreign language in the Czech Republic, it is—unlike German—neither a language of a neighboring country, nor a language protected by the European Charter for Regional or Minority Languages. On the other hand, traditional foreign languages like French, Spanish, and Italian are offered in the educational system, but they do not have the status of minority languages in the Czech Republic.

deutscher Kultur in der Tschechischen Republik – The Union of Germans and Friends of German Culture in the Czech Republic, hereinafter *Kulturverband*), the Goethe Institute in Prague, the Embassies of Germany and Austria, the German-Czech Chamber of Industry and Commerce (hereinafter as Chamber), the Union of German Philologists in the Czech Republic (*Germanistenverband der Tschechischen Republik* in German, hereinafter as Union of German Philologists), and the Ministry of Education, Youth and Sports, including its affiliated organizations (hereinafter simplified as the Ministry of Education). These social actors are presented through their discursive activities in the following sections. Their differentiation in terms of power is based on Zhao's (2011: 910–912) classification in four types, which has been empirically elaborated on by Fenton-Smith & Gurney (2016) recently:

1. Actors with power are highly placed officials and/or people holding public offices. Their power as well as the power of the institutions represented by these people is derived from authorities as they are laid down in legal acts. These actors are the typical representatives of the macro-level language management. In this research, the Ministry of Education, the minister him/herself, and other employees authorized to act on behalf of this institution can be referred to.
2. Actors with expertise are exemplified by linguists or other professional people who occasionally become involved in language management processes. Here, representatives of the Union of German Philologists as well as experts working for the GCNM can be mentioned.
3. Actors with influence are primarily defined by the membership of social elites in them. This feature also applies to "a wide range of the people who have social influence because of their knowledge/skills [...] or just the public nature of their careers" (Zhao 2011: 910). Even though these actors do not possess any direct decision-making capacities, they may significantly contribute to convincing other actors (Fenton-Smith & Gurney 2016: 82). Projected into the discourse on German in the Czech context, representatives of the German-Czech Chamber of Industry and Commerce, both embassies, or of the Goethe-Institute may be included.
4. Actors with interest are defined *ex negativo* as actors possessing "neither power nor the personal prestige bestowed on the former three groups" (Zhao 2011: 910). They are situated at the micro level, getting involved rather passively in language management processes. Being also categorized as "latent actors," they are affected by decisions made by more powerful actors, but they may become more active at specific moments (Bandelow 2015: 312).[3] Members of the German minority organizations, foreign language teachers as well as individual pupils learning foreign languages belong to this least powerful group of actors.

3 Both Bandelow (2015), and Zhao (2011) confirm independently that these people's behavior has been explored only little so far.

3 The current situation of German and other foreign languages in the Czech Republic

From the quantitative point of view, the situation of foreign languages in the Czech Republic has been dominated by English approximately since the second half of the 1990s. The data of the Czech Ministry of Education indicate that whereas around 370,000 pupils were learning both English and German in the school year 1997/98 at primary schools, the distance between these two most popular foreign languages increased to half a million by the school year 2010/11. This difference exceeded 600,000 in the school year 2017/18. Thus, 4.4 times more pupils are currently learning English (785,000 pupils in total) than German (176,000 pupils in total) at Czech primary schools. Russian with 52,000 learners comes after German, being followed by Spanish (6,491 pupils) and French (6,145) in 2018.

No matter how apparent the distance between English and German has become in the course of the last two decades, German is one of the languages for which a slight increase in interest has been seen since the school year 2013/14, when a second mandatory foreign language was introduced. The current number of pupils learning German corresponds to that as of 2005:

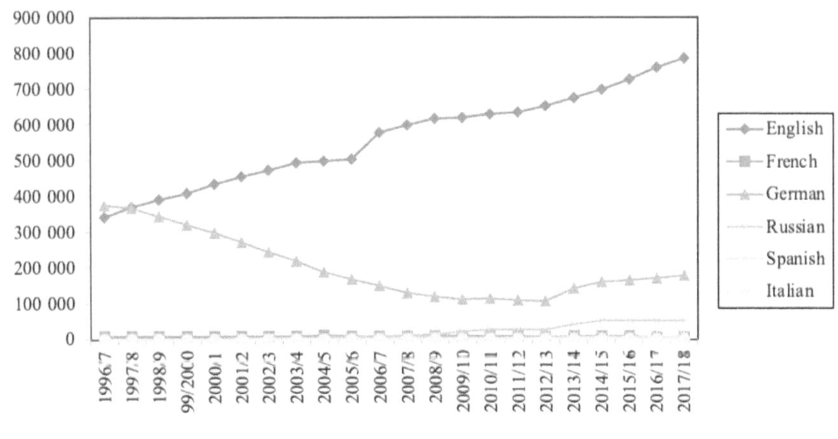

Figure 1: Numbers of pupils learning foreign languages at primary schools
Source: Ministry of Education of the Czech Republic (communication from August 2018)

The proportion of the German language related to the total number of pupils learning foreign languages has shrunk substantially from a half to less than one fifth since 1998.[4] Whereas the interest in foreign languages was dominated together

4 Looking back over the 1990s, Cink (1999: 29) stated in 1998 that German had held the first position since 1990 and had been the most frequently chosen foreign language

by English and German back then, Russian has become more visible recently. The comparison of these proportions reflecting the situation in 1998, 2008, and in 2018 is shown in the following table:

Table 1: Proportions of foreign languages at Czech primary schools in selected school years (%)

Language/school year	**1997/98**	**2007/08**	**2017/18**
English	49.7	80.4	76.5
French	1	0.9	0.6
German	49.1	17.2	17.2
Russian	0.1	1.2	5
Spanish	< 0.1	0.2	0.6
Italian	0	< 0.1	< 0.1

Source: Ministry of Education of the Czech Republic (communication from August 2018)

The situation at secondary schools reflects the lower total number of pupils attending this type of school. The distance between English and German amounting to approximately 220,000 pupils has remained stable since the school year 2013/14. The position of German at secondary schools became stabilized at around 160,000 pupils in 2014. Due to the demographic development of the age group of the pupils at secondary schools, it is not only the total number of those who were learning German that continued to decrease in the past decade. Correspondingly, the total number of English learners has dropped from over 436,000 to 380,000 pupils since 2010/11, as is shown in the following Figure 2:

with 52% proportion at that time. However, English's proportion had increased from 35% as of 1990/91 to 45% six years later.

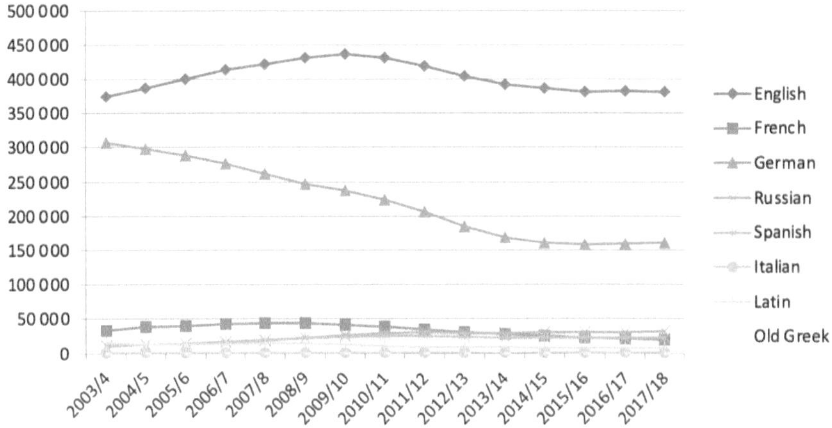

Figure 2: Numbers of pupils learning foreign languages at secondary schools
Source: Ministry of Education of the Czech Republic (communication from August 2018)

The segment of specialized post-secondary schools was introduced into the Czech educational system in 1996. The total number of students in these schools has been decreasing for more than a decade, which seems to reflect a specific crisis of this type of schools. It is the only segment in which the interest in German has also been continually decreasing since 2004. Unlike the secondary schools, no indication of stabilization can be observed yet. In 2018, the total number of German learners at the post-secondary schools dropped to one fifth when compared to the school year 2003/04 (from almost 15,000 pupils to hardly 3,200). The decrease in interest can also be seen in the case of English, but this tendency is much less steep (from 17,600 pupils in 2014 to 12,300 in 2018):

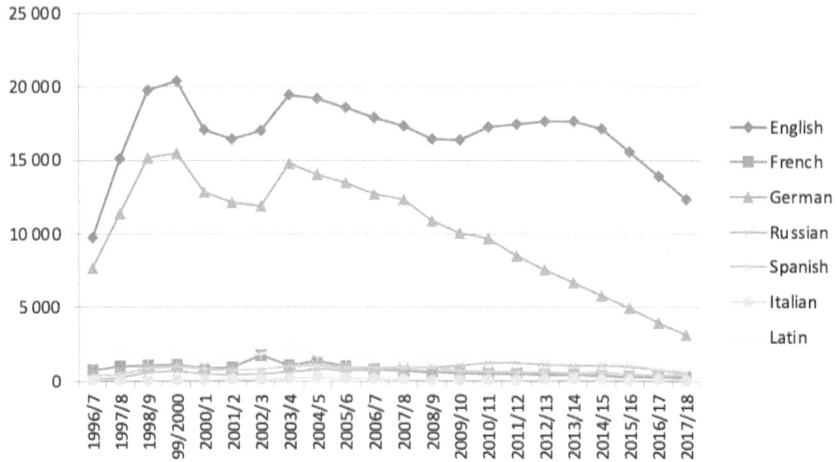

Figure 3: Specialized post-secondary schools
Source: Ministry of Education of the Czech Republic (communication from August 2018)

4 Social actors and their interests

The previous sections have provided an overview of the social actors, their power relations and the statistics from a general perspective. The following sections are devoted to individual social actors which participate in the discourse on German in the Czech Republic and realize their interests in it. The first part deals with organizations of the German minority and with conceptual inconsistencies in the status of German as a minority vs. foreign language. Then, language management acts conducted by the most powerful actor are analyzed, followed by the activities of actors with expertise and actors with influence.

4.1 German minority organizations and the Government Council for National Minorities as actors with interest and expertise

If we focus on the socio-cultural context of German, more specific information should be provided. As stated in Section 2 above, German has not only the status of a foreign language (along with English, French and some others as presented in the quantitative overview), but it has the status of minority language as well. This double status of German has gained higher relevance especially since the Czech Republic ratified the European Charter for Regional or Minority Languages (hereinafter as ECRML), which came into force in March 2007 in this country.

Since the German minority does not have any political party of its own, the activities of both German minority organizations concentrate on rather non-political aspects of social life of their members—culture, maintaining national traditions, celebrating national holidays, pilgrimages etc. Both organizations claim the maintenance of German language and culture as one of their explicit interests.[5] The chairpersons of both organizations are members of the GCNM.

This council is one of the advisory bodies of the Czech government. It is composed of 32 members, who represent several ministries (including the Ministry of Education), the ombudsman, the Association of the Regions of the Czech Republic as well as fourteen national minorities. It is established on the basis of the Act on the Rights of National Minorities 273/2001 Co. as subsequently amended.[6] The main scope of activities of this council is the preparation of materials concerning the national minorities for the government. It also oversees the obligations following for the Czech Republic from international treaties which have to do with the rights of national minorities.

Unlike for Polish, there is not any public minority school system with German as a language of instruction in the Czech Republic. Notwithstanding, people interested in German may potentially profit from private activities provided by German or Austrian educational institutions in the cities (Prague, Brno) as well as in the borderlands (in Znojmo, Liberec, and elsewhere). According to the census conducted in 2011, fewer than 19,000 Czech citizens claimed their German nationality. The remaining German-speaking minority was assimilated in the post-war period and its settlement is too dispersed to create compact areas. Moreover, many Germans abandoned the German language as a result of the process of post-war controlled assimilation. Hence, apart from families or other private contexts, the only systematic way of acquiring German is to choose this language as a first—if possible—foreign language in schools within the public educational system.[7]

However, conceptual inconsistencies concerning the status of German as a minority or foreign language can be observed in the public discourse. Examples can be quoted even from reports issued by GCNM. Thus, "Primary School of Czech-German Understanding" and "Thomas Mann Secondary School" are mentioned in the Report on the Situation of National Minorities in 2017 (as well as

5 The older organization, the *Kulturverband*, was founded in June 1969. It has around 1,300 members. The *Landesversammlung* with more than 7,000 members came into existence in 1991. For more details see the websites URL Kulturverband and URL Landesversammlung.

6 The status of the council is available at the website URL GCNM.

7 For more details concerning the development since the 1990s see Novotný (2015: 31–34), Nekvapil (2000), Neustupný & Nekvapil (2006), and Ammon (2015: 328–334). The most recent data are summarized in the Report on the situation of national minorities in the Czech Republic in 2017 and in the Report on the situation of national minorities in the Czech Republic in 2018 (see GCNM 2018 and 2019 respectively).

in 2018) in chapter 8.1 headed "Education in languages of the respective national minority – 8.1.1 German minority" as schools with German as a language of instruction (GCNM 2018: 28 as well as GCNM 2019a: 21 respectively). From the conceptual point of view interestingly enough, these schools "nabízí *pro české i německé děti* vzdělání a výchovu v 1.–5. ročníku s němčinou jako *jazyk cizí nebo mateřský*" [offer to *Czech as well as German children* education with German as *a foreign language or as a mother tongue* in the first through the fifth grade] (GCNM 2018: 28, italics mine).[8] Thus, the status of German as a *minority* and a *foreign* language are mixed. This confusion is confirmed on the same page by the total number of pupils who learned German at Czech primary and secondary schools in 2017: 331,224 pupils in total are stated, whereas fewer than 19,000 citizens claimed German nationality, as mentioned above. For German as a mother tongue in the context of German as a *minority* language, surprisingly enough, this Report (GCNM 2018) mentions as a success that a second mandatory *foreign* language was introduced in September 2013. However, this fact applies to the educational system in the whole Czech Republic and has little to do with the title of the chapter which is supposed to describe the situation of the German minority itself. Unlike in the older Report covering the situation in 2017, the Report on the situation in 2018 does not contain any numbers of pupils who learned German. Only a list of twelve schools remained in which some school subjects were permitted to be taught in German as a *foreign* language. The other passages are not adapted, they are just left out. Clear information about German as a *minority* language is missing. It is symptomatic of this issue that the Ministry of Education does not fund any programs promoting the education in German as a *minority* language (GCNM 2019a: 121–122). The subsidies amounted to 0 Czech crowns in 2018 (GCNM 2019a: 123).[9]

Similarly, a draft of the Fifth Periodical Report concerning the fulfillment of the Framework Convention for the Protection of National Minorities, which was issued in March 2019, contains almost the same passages in sections related to German. Most information in section headed "German minority schools" concern German as a foreign language again. The schools listed in this section are the ones in which some school subjects "are permitted to be taught in a foreign language," which is German in this case (GCNM 2019b: 57). The very loose relation to German as a minority language is underpinned by a table containing the list of universities

8 All translations in this chapter are mine. The same formulation is reprinted in the newer Report on the situation of national minorities in the Czech Republic in 2018 (GCNM 2019: 21). In the context of the missing public German minority school system, it is necessary to add that the statistics do not distinguish these two kinds of acquisition of German. Children of German or Austrian citizens who work (temporarily) in the Czech Republic are not differentiated either (*expatriates*).

9 This situation is not new. See Cink's (1999: 36) critical remark concerning "the inadequate promotion of German as a mother tongue" in cases of numerically weak German-speaking minorities.

at which German Studies are accredited.[10] The Goethe Institute's cooperation with the Ministry of Education also has to do primarily with German as a *foreign* language, and not with German as a *minority* language. This mistaken status of German can be traced back for several years in these reports.

This conceptual confusion also holds for the Fourth Periodical Report (ECMRL), another document issued by GCNM. Section I. 3. 1., which is devoted to German as a *minority* language, starts with a statement that German language "may be taught at primary schools as a first *foreign* language [...]. As of September 30, 2016, 7,582 pupils in total were educated in German as their first *foreign* language" (GCNM 2017a: 24).[11] Furthermore, several primary and secondary schools are listed in which "some subjects" are reported to have been taught in German. Strikingly enough, it is not possible to find out how many children with German as a mother tongue learn German in the public school system of the Czech Republic.

Difficulties in protecting German as a minority language were noted and evaluated negatively by the Council of Europe in December 2015. Its Committee of Ministers recommends, among other things, that the authorities of the Czech Republic

> [...] 3. adopt a structured policy for the protection and promotion of German [...], and create favorable conditions for [its] use in public life; 4. take resolute steps to make available teaching in or of German as a minority language in cooperation with the speakers. (CoE 2015: 1)

Another aspect specifying the sociocultural context of German in the Czech Republic has to do with geographical closeness to, and strong business ties with, economically strong neighbors (Germany and Austria). German minority organizations as well as numerous local organizations devote systematic attention to Czech-German cross-border activities in that they organize trans-frontier exchanges and mediate contacts between Czech and German institutions. At the macro level, the most important social actors in this field are the Czech-German Fund for the Future and Tandem – Center of Coordination of Czech-German Youth

---

10 This draft is likely to be changed, before the official version is published (personal communication with the member of the secretary of the GCNM Renata Weinerová from March 31, 2019).

11 The content of this quotation according to which more than 7,500 pupils "were educated in German" is not clear enough in this context. Does it mean that German was used as a regular language of instruction, which would correspond to the status of the minority language in the school system where the majority language (Czech) is taught as another mandatory school subject? Or rather, does it mean that these pupils were learning German as the first foreign language, and consequently English as the second, Czech being their mother tongue? And do these pupils claim the German nationality, or rather the Czech one? We can assume that the authors of this passage are likely to have used these concepts without deeper consideration. However, this quotation may reflect these experts' awareness of the extent of language assimilation of the German minority in the Czech Republic.

Exchange. These organizations' activities apply both to German as a minority, and as a foreign language (more information is available at the websites URL Czech-German Fund for the Future and URL Center of Coordination of Czech-German Youth Exchange).

4.2 Ministry of Education as an actor with power

Efforts to support German as well as other foreign languages in the Czech Republic are determined by legal norms, which are set by the most powerful national actors—parliament, government and—most specifically—by the Ministry of Education. Apart from legal norms at the national level, international law has also to be abided by. Management acts by these institutions which correspond to sources of law are enforceable by courts. The most relevant Czech source of law setting down the possibilities for which interests can be achieved (and how) in this field is the School Act 561/2004 Co. as subsequently amended.

Before this act—with the exceptions of some sections—came into force on January 1, 2005, the issue of preferring English as the first mandatory foreign language as well as determining English as a mandatory part of the secondary school-leaving exam had been discussed. The Ministry of Education had declared this interest as a priority in its Long-Term Plan of Education and Development of the Educational System of the Czech Republic. This extensive and detailed document was issued in connection with the preparation of the new School Act in March 2002. In a chapter devoted to quality improvement of foreign language teaching, the ministry defined the following adjustment plans:

> Návrh nového rámcového vzdělávacího programu pro základní vzdělávání počítá se zahájením výuky prvního cizího jazyka od 3. ročníku s průměrnou dotací 3 hodiny týdně [...] přednostně by měla být žákům nabídnuta výuka angličtiny; návrh [...] rovněž počítá jako s jednou z možných alternativ řešení zahájit výuku druhého cizího jazyka od 7. ročníku s průměrnou dotací 2 vyučovacích hodin týdně. Nabídnuty by měly být němčina, francouzština, španělština, italština a ruština; angličtina bude druhým povinným jazykem pro ty, kteří nezvolili angličtinu jako svůj první (hlavní) cizí jazyk. (Long-Term Plan of Education 2002: 21–22)

> [The proposal of a new framework educational program for primary education counts on the introduction of the first foreign language from the third grade on in an extent of three lessons a week [...] it is English that should be offered to the pupils primarily; the proposal [...] also counts on one of the possible alternatives to the solution to introduce a second foreign language teaching from the seventh grade on in an extent of two lessons a week. German, French, Spanish, Italian, and Russian should be offered; English shall be the second mandatory foreign language for those who have not chosen English as their first (main) foreign language.]

Nevertheless, the final version of the School Act did not lay down any specific foreign language as the first mandatory foreign language in the end. Concerning the secondary school-leaving exam, section 78 of the School Act merely mentions "a foreign language" in which pupils have to take this exam.

The language choices are restricted by the condition that this language has to be taught at the school which the pupils attend. Another restriction follows from section 7, paragraph 1 of Regulation 177/2009 issued by the Ministry of Education, according to which the secondary school-leaving exams are allowed to be taken in English, French, German, Spanish, or Russian only (in the order listed in the regulation).

The specific educational goals defined in the School Act are to be achieved by means of the Framework Educational Programs related to the pre-school, primary, secondary, and further education. In this crucial document, details concerning the first and second foreign language teaching are contained. The primary education, during which pupils have to start learning both the first as well as the second foreign language, is the most relevant period for their choices (Dovalil 2018: 290–291; Dovalil & Engelhardt 2012). In this respect, the impact of the school curricula on these decision-making processes is enormous. It reflects the fact that

> [l]argely reliant on the discourses of compulsory obligation, the site of language education is thought to be the domain that is most susceptible to planning [...] where teachers as professional practitioners are the policy product implementers and the students the passive recipients of the package. (Zhao 2011: 914)

Due to this, social actors participating in these decisions pursue their interests to effectively influence such decisions during this period. The decisions made in this phase of education usually have far-reaching consequences for later occupation, career and business opportunities of the respective person. Just for this reason, a part of language management acts of various social actors concentrates on the FEPPE (MŠMT 2017).

4.2.1 Discourses on the first and second foreign language within the Ministry of Education and its affiliated organizations

The FEPPE is one of the central documents regulating the overt language policy for schools. Its first version was approved in connection with the arising new School Act in December 2004 and came into force on February 1, 2005. Although the FEPPE has undergone several reforms since that time, the crucial passage in section 7.2 regulating the foreign language choices has been changed only insignificantly so far. The change affected mere modal verbs of one sentence: Instead of the wording "English *must be offered* to the pupils primarily" as formulated in the original version, nowadays "English *should be offered* primarily," which corresponds to the wording of the original proposal in the Long-Term Plan of Education from March 2002 after all.

Moreover, according to section 7.2 of the Framework Program, the following formulation has remained unchanged from the very beginning of its legal force:

> [...] přednostně by měla být žákům nabídnuta výuka anglického jazyka; pokud žák (jeho zákonný zástupce) zvolí jiný cizí jazyk než anglický, musí škola prokazatelně upozornit zákonné zástupce žáka na skutečnost, že ve vzdělávacím systému nemusí být zajištěna návaznost ve vzdělávání zvoleného cizího jazyka při přechodu žáka na jinou základní nebo střední školu. (MŠMT 2017: 143)[12]
>
> [English should be offered to the pupils primarily; when the pupil (his/her legal representative) chooses a foreign language other than English, the school has to demonstrably familiarize the legal representatives of the pupil with the fact that the educational system does not necessarily provide continuity of the chosen language when the pupil changes to another primary or secondary school.]

This passage has been criticized from several perspectives so far. The Fourth Periodical Report (ECRML) referred to the objections raised against this clause by supporters of German as a minority language within GCNM in the fall 2015. The essence of this critique consisted in the fact that this paragraph discriminates against all languages other than English, if these languages should be chosen as the first foreign language (GCNM 2017a: 24). This would potentially break international law (Art. 7, paragraph 2 of ECMRL, Art. 14 of the Framework Convention, and Art. 25 of the bilateral Czech-German Treaty) as far as the rights of members of the German minority are concerned. The reason is that they may feel effectively discouraged from learning German at least as the first foreign language, having no positive perspective of uninterrupted German classes.[13]

In reaction to the interest of the German minority to "remove the discriminatory clause from the Framework Program," the Ministry of Education missed the target by informing the GCNM that

> Ustanovení je v rámcovém vzdělávacím programu od roku 2005, a to z toho důvodu, že při přestupu na jinou školu může být problém se zajištěním výuky jiného cizího jazyka. Počítá se s revizí rámcového vzdělávacího programu zhruba v horizontu dvou

---

12 This passage corresponds to the wording of the most recent version of FEPPE as of June 2017, as well as to the previous versions from 2013 and 2016.

13 According to Art. 7, paragraph 2 of ECRML "[t]he Parties undertake *to eliminate*, if they have not yet done so, any unjustified distinction, exclusion, *restriction or preference relating to the use* of a regional or minority language and intended *to discourage or endanger the maintenance or development of it.* The adoption of special *measures in favor of regional or minority languages aimed at promoting equality* between the users of these languages and the rest of the population or which take due account of their specific conditions is not considered to be an act of discrimination against the users of more widely-used languages" (italics mine).

Framework Convention for the Protection of National Minorities states in its Art. 14, paragraph 2 that "[...] the Parties shall endeavor to ensure, as far as possible and within the framework of their education systems, that persons belonging to those minorities have *adequate opportunities for being taught the minority language or for receiving instruction in this language*" (italics mine).

> let. Ministerstvo samozřejmě může zvážit vznesenou připomínku v úpravě příslušných formulací vztahujících se k výuce prvního cizího jazyka. (GCNM 2017a: 24–25)
>
> [This passage has been a part of the Framework Program since 2005, because problems with ensuring foreign language teaching could arise when pupils change schools. A revision of the Framework Program will be taken into consideration in approximately two years. The ministry may obviously reconsider the objection if the formulation concerning the first foreign language teaching should change.]

Overall, this passage has been objected to twice in the GCNM so far. In the first case, a representative of the Ministry of Education in the Council rejected the objections on October 14, 2015:

> Formulace v rámcovém vzdělávacím program vychází z prokazatelného dlouhodobého *zájmu zákonných zástupců* dětí o výuku anglického jazyka a zároveň zohledňuje fakt, že anglický jazyk je dnes pro EU lingua franca. [...] Co se týče druhé části citace [...] ta je v programech obsažena s cílem chránit *zájem žáka* při případném přestupu na jinou školu [...]. Formulace zcela jasně dokazuje, že lze zvolit za první cizí jazyk jiný než anglický. Nelze tedy souhlasit s tvrzením, že jsou cizí jazyky vůči jazyku anglickému diskriminovány. (GCNM 2015: 6–7, italics mine)
>
> [The formulation of the point [7.2] in FEPPE is based on the long-term *interest of the legal representatives* of the pupils in English and reflects the fact that English is a lingua franca in the EU. [...] As for the second part of the quotation [...] its goal is to protect the *interests of the pupils* who want to change to another school [...]. The formulation shows clearly that it is possible to choose a first foreign language other than English. Hence, these other foreign languages are in no way discriminated against English.]

It turned out that the substance of the concept of discrimination was interpreted by this actor with power in its own way. Consequently, the ministry was not willing either to discuss this passage, or even to change it.[14]

This quite evasive attitude of the Ministry of Education dovetailed with its references to the dominance of English that had become the priority at all stages of the educational system since 2005. Rather than promoting German, it tried to vindicate its reluctance to negotiate this issue with other social actors as well as the lack of activities in favor of German. Paradoxically enough, this quotation can be used as justification of reasons why pupils should not (have or want to) learn German. Instead of promoting the pupils' interests to learn this language (as well as possible), these pupils need to be "protected" from such goals, if they changed to another school. Needless to say, this "protection" does not apply to any other

14 Further remarks criticizing this issue in terms of discrimination can also be found in Kreisslová & Novotný (2018: 134–135).

school subjects (sciences, history, geography etc.). The individual rights and needs of members of the German minority were disregarded.

This incentive was repeated on February 16, 2017. The original objections, which had been presented in 2015, were extended by a reference to the Czech-German Treaty.[15] Similarly to the previous situation, the ministry did not note any deviation from the expectations, which could be derived from the ECMRL, the Czech-German Treaty as well as the Recommendations of the Council of Europe from December 2015, and rejected any negotiations. The "protection" argument was repeated again: "[...] ustanovení je v rámcovém vzdělávacím programu od roku 2005, a to z toho důvodu, že při přestupu na jinou školu může být problém se zajištěním výuky jiného cizího jazyka" [The formulation has been a part of FEPPE since 2005, because problems in ensuring the classes of the other foreign language may arise when pupils want to change to another school] (GCNM 2017b: 6–7). The status of German as a minority language and the real protection of its members' rights remained ignored.

The lack of continuity of learning a foreign language other than English may cause frustration and may discourage many pupils from choosing German (French or Russian) as their first foreign language (Dovalil 2018: 298–302). This holds even more specifically for pupils in the German minority who do not have any possibilities of being educated in German as a language of instruction and who are demotivated by this situation (Kreisslová & Novotný 2018: 134–136). Passage 7.2 of the Framework Program is inconsistent with the necessity of continual language learning, which represents one of the factors positively influencing successful language acquisition. Correspondingly, (not only) recent documents issued by the European Commission take this indispensable biographical continuity explicitly into account:

> Biographical continuity means not only that educational institutions should follow each other in a vertical perspective, for example from pre-primary to primary to secondary education, but also that there should be cooperation between different educational environments where a child participates in each particular phase. (COM (2018) 272 final: 19)

4.2.2 Difficulties in introducing the second mandatory foreign language

As already mentioned in the statistical overview, the decision to introduce a second mandatory foreign language came into force on September 1, 2013. Sladkovská &

15 Art. 25, paragraph 2 of the Czech-German Treaty on Good Neighborliness and Friendly Cooperation from 1992 lays down that "[smluvní strany] *vynaloží veškeré úsilí, aby rozšířily* výuku jazyka druhé země na školách a jiných vzdělávacích institucích" [the Parties *shall make every effort to spread the teaching* of the language of the other country in schools as well as in other educational institutions] (italics mine).

Šmídová (2010: 2), representing the Research Institute on Education back then, an organization affiliated with the Ministry of Education, point out that the original intention to introduce the second mandatory foreign language, which was motivated by the purpose to comply with the European language policy *mother tongue + two*, was going to be implemented as early as 2005. However, this decision was postponed by six years initially. The authors interconnect this fact with ongoing discussions about several unresolved parts of the Framework Program at that time.

The most decisive argument against the introduction of a second foreign language as a mandatory school subject appeared to be the assumption that two foreign languages would have overloaded weaker pupils. For this reason, the second foreign language received the status of elective subject in 2005. This compromise was believed to enable to find a solution by 2011 (Sladkovská & Šmídová 2010: 2). As a part of their analysis, the authors refer to the dominant position of English, which they explain quantitatively by the introduction of the first mandatory foreign language in the third grade (Sladkovská & Šmídová 2010: 7).

Simultaneously, they also refer to the decrease in the numbers of pupils learning German. They interconnect the necessity to try to implement the European principle *mother tongue + two* with the infrastructure for teaching German existing so far. Besides that, they also mention the factor of neighborhood with German-speaking countries as well as the tradition of teaching this language in the Czech Republic. Consequently, they conclude that "[...] jsou zde jasné argumenty, proč by výuka němčiny měla být na českých školách nabízena a vyučována v plnohodnotné roli cizího jazyka" [there are clear arguments, why German should be taught and offered at Czech schools as a fully-fledged foreign language] (Sladkovská & Šmídová 2010: 9).[16]

In spite of these arguments in favor of German, removing the obstacles from the Framework Program which had been significantly complicating the possibility of choosing this language as the first foreign language for several years was not considered. Similarly, possibilities for strengthening German as a foreign language by its status as a minority language were also disregarded.

With reference to a survey conducted in 1687 primary schools throughout the Czech Republic in May 2010, i.e., three years before the second mandatory foreign language was introduced, they indicate several advantages of this intended change: better foreign language competences resulting, e.g., into better opportunities to find employment, advantages for the border regions (which favors particularly German), and higher attractiveness of the respective schools for future pupils and parents (Sladkovská & Šmídová 2010: 12).

On the other hand, the same two main problems were mentioned as in 2005—overloading the weaker pupils as well as the difficulties in ensuring the foreign language classes. But unlike in 2005, when these assumptions were just stated,

16 This formulation also shows a very defensive position of those who would be willing to support German.

the authors put together some counter-arguments. They point out that learning foreign languages, mathematics, or sciences are comparably difficult, and that weaker pupils may have problems in finding employment, in which case at least some second foreign language skills could be very helpful for them in the end (Sladkovská & Šmídová 2010: 12). Overall, the conclusion of this analysis was unequivocal: the second foreign language was to become a mandatory school subject from the school year 2012/13 on. It was to be taught in the seventh, eighth and in the ninth grades, with two lessons a week.

Despite this clear-cut recommendation, this adjustment plan was implemented not only yet another year later than originally postponed, but even in a more limited extent, i.e., only from the eighth grade on (Dovalil 2018: 291–292).

One more strategic document concerning foreign language teaching, the preparation of which began prior to 2005, should be pointed out—National Plan for Foreign Language Teaching (MŠMT 2005). Although it also reflected the principle *mother tongue + two*, English was supposed to become the first mandatory foreign language (MŠMT 2005: 6). German was mentioned twice, in both cases along with Polish as a language of the neighboring countries. German was not supposed to be allowed to be chosen as the first foreign language on an equal footing with English. This document was in force between 2005 and 2008, but has not been replaced by any newer strategy since then.[17] In the course of this period, the interest in German suffered a steep drop especially at primary schools and came close to its lowest values ever as can be seen in Section 3 above.

4.3 Actor with expertise

The Union of German Philologists is one of the social actors with expertise for which the interest in promoting German is of capital importance. This organization with around eighty members unites scholars of German philology working at universities (linguists, literary scientists as well as experts in didactics). It was founded in 1999.[18] Its presidium has regularly discussed this topic in connection with the applicants for German Studies at the universities in the Czech Republic from the very beginning. Decreasing level of the command of German on the part of the applicants as well as their total numbers were regularly observed. Causes of this development were sought. More importantly, several members of this Union possessing expert knowledge in the didactics of German as a foreign language have been participating in the work of expert boards of the Ministry of Education since the 1990s, including the preparatory works on FEPPE as well as its

17 In terms of Language Management Theory, its content is presented and analyzed in details in Dovalil (2010).

18 For more details see the website URL Union of German Philologists of the Czech Republic. Referring to its documents, this organization is abbreviated as UGP in this subchapter.

changes. However, their expertise has not always been influential enough under all circumstances.

In 2004, a new chairwoman and presidium were elected. Based on the plenary session of the Union of German Philologists in October 2006, the new chairwoman took the initiative and addressed the Ministry of Education in a series of letters, the first of which was sent on March 19, 2007. Noting the deviations from the expectations as well as negative evaluation of the situation were in the foreground.

In this letter, the presidium wanted to draw minister Dana Kuchtová's attention to this problem and to get more involved in shaping the conception of foreign language teaching back then. The main interest consisted in maintaining the extent of teaching German at primary as well as secondary schools. Apart from the inconvenience to concentrate on English only at the expense of other foreign languages, the presidium argued with economic aspects as well as with the longstanding tradition of teaching German:

> Pozice německého jazyka by proto měla být v koncepci výuky cizích jazyků na základních školách posílena. Je-li naším cílem úspěšné uplatnění žáků v praxi, musíme mít na paměti, že německy mluvící země jsou našimi nejvýznamnějšími hospodářskými a obchodními partnery, kteří jsou ve všech regionech České republiky zastoupeni řadou firem a kteří v současné době otevírají svůj pracovní trh pro odborníky nejrůznějších stupňů vzdělání i specializací. Schopnost komunikovat v němčině zvyšuje pracovní konkurenceschopnost absolventů našich škol. Výuka německého jazyka má přitom u nás dlouhou tradici, o jejíž udržování a rozšiřování se snaží řada kvalifikovaných učitelů. (UGP 2007: Conception of foreign language teaching – request for appointment, March 19, 2007)
>
> [Therefore, the position of German in the conception should be strengthened at primary schools. If the successful employment of our pupils is our goal we have to bear in mind that German-speaking countries are our most important economic partners who are represented in all regions through many companies, which open the labor market for experts of various degrees of education and specializations. German skills increase the competitiveness of our school-leavers and university graduates. At the same time, teaching German has a long tradition in our country. Many qualified teachers strive for keeping and extending this tradition.]

The presidium concluded with a request for a meeting with the minister and presented its interest to discuss its suggestions to design specific adjustments related to teaching German in the future. Although this appointment took place in April 2007, no tangible conclusions in favor of German were achieved which could have been implemented, partially due to the fact that a new minister was appointed several months later.

The situation repeated itself one year later. The next plenary session of the Union of German Philologists, taking place in May 2008, charged the presidium to continue the dialogue with the Ministry of Education to join forces to solve this serious and alarming problem (UGP 2008: The situation of teaching German at primary and secondary schools—request for appointment, June 9, 2008). The presidium pointed out the cultural and historical traditions of German in Central Europe. Despite these efforts, the FEPPE's preference of English over all other foreign languages as the first foreign language was not changed.

As the figures shown in Section 3 illustrate the tendencies, the numbers of pupils interested in German did not stop dropping in 2008. Another new minister of education, Josef Dobeš, was informed about the situation by the Union of German Philologists after its plenary session in September 2010. In its letter from September 17, 2010, the Union took a stand on a new stage of the discussions about introducing English as the first mandatory foreign language as well as mandatory secondary school-leaving exam in this language. In its statement, the Union of German Philologists was aware of the importance of English explicitly. At the same time, it argued against further strengthening the position of English in the Czech educational system. Unlike other foreign languages, the demand for English would not weaken, rather, it would grow. Moreover,

> Česká republika by se zavedením angličtiny jako povinného prvního cizího jazyka a současným odsunutím zavedení výuky povinného druhého cizího jazyka ještě více než dosud vzdálila od principu evropské jazykové politiky označovaného jako 1+2 (tj. ovládání mateřského jazyka a vyvážená výuka dvou jazyků dalších), který dbá i na aktivní podporu výuky jazyků sousedních zemí, tj. v případě České republiky němčiny. (UGP 2010: Statement of the Union, September 17, 2010)

> [By simultaneous introducing English as the first mandatory foreign language and postponing the introduction of a second mandatory foreign language, the Czech Republic would recede from the principle of the European language policy designated as 1+2 (i.e., command of the mother tongue and balanced acquisition of two more foreign languages), which heeds active promotion of teaching the neighboring countries' languages, including German in the case of the Czech Republic.]

The Union presented its persuasion that its remarks and comments would be taken seriously, and offered its experts who would help to implement the principle *mother tongue + two* more efficiently. As for the status of English, we can add that this language has been introduced neither as a first mandatory foreign language, nor as a part of the mandatory secondary school-leaving exam so far.

Representatives of the Union participated in numerous negotiations with the representatives of the Ministry of Education in which the introduction of the second mandatory foreign language was discussed. This decision was made in January 2013 and came into force on September 1, 2013. Besides the arguments presented by Sladkovská & Šmídová (2010) in section 4.2.2, and along with other predominantly didactic reasons, it was pointed out that English and German are both Germanic languages, which opens various possibilities of taking advantage of the pupils' competences in English for learning German. Adjustments identifying strategies which would make learning German (L3) after English (L2) easier were designed. The representatives could refer to running research projects.[19]

Another aspect, which was noted and perceived as unfavorable in 2014, had to do with the quality of teaching German. It concerned the education of teachers and their qualification as required by section 12 of the Pedagogical Workers Act 563/2004 Co. One of the problems was identified in narrowing down the expert component of foreign language teachers' qualification. The Union of German Philologists pointed out that foreign language teachers should acquire not only high communicative competence, but also linguistic and literary expert knowledge:

> Hluboká znalost a reflexe systému jazyka jsou základním předpokladem pro to, aby byl učitel schopen jednotlivé jevy žákům vysvětlit. Znalost literatury je nepostradatelná nejen pro chápání kulturního prostředí dané jazykové oblasti a jazyka samotného, ale i dalších charakteristik jazykového společenství (historie, ideologie, sociálního prostředí apod.). (UGP 2014: Statement of the Union, October 8, 2014)

> [Profound knowledge and reflection of the language system are basic preconditions for a teacher to be able to explain individual phenomena to the pupils. Knowledge of literature is indispensable not only for understanding cultural milieus of the respective language area and the language itself, but also other features of the language community (its history, ideology, social setting etc.).]

The Union did not agree to the reduction of the expert qualification to a language exam at the level C1 according to CEFR. It referred to the fact that it was not clear which institutions' exams should be accepted. The Union's interest in guaranteeing equal qualification of teachers at primary and secondary schools with those working at language schools which were entitled to grant state exams was interconnected with difficulties of graduates from master programs in German Studies in getting adequate jobs in the educational system and with their motivation to study German at the universities. In conclusion of this letter, the chairwoman asked the minister, Marcel Chládek, for a meeting and an opportunity to elaborate on more detailed arguments. Regardless of the above mentioned reasons, the Pedagogical Workers Act has not been amended, which means that foreign language teachers working for language schools do not have to graduate from master programs focused on the respective foreign language.

19 See, e.g., homepage of the project "Multilingualism at Czech schools: learning and teaching German after English" https://www.muni.cz/vyzkum/projekty/13604?page=5. Accessed April 4, 2019. This three-year-project was realized between 2011 and 2013. Numerous publications concerning various aspects of teaching and learning German as a foreign language after English are listed there.

4.4 Actors with influence

There are some institutions which can be understood as actors with influence in this context: the German-Czech Chamber of Industry and Commerce (hereinafter also as Chamber), the Goethe-Institute, and the Embassies of Austria and Germany. The Chamber, which was founded in 1993, supports the economic collaboration between German and Czech companies and their business activities both in the Czech Republic, and in Germany.[20] It also provides companies with various services when they enter the market in the respective country. Its representatives often take part in meetings which are organized by the Goethe Institute and aim at the explicit promotion of German. In this context, the Chamber issues reports, taken over by public media, from which the demand for German among German-speaking employers follows (Dovalil 2018: 289). Generally speaking, availability of people with good knowledge of German is in the economic interest of all actors. It reduces the unemployment rate on the Czech labor market, and it enables the German companies to grow. One aspect of this economic interest consists in the higher salaries of such employees, which is, however, only a side effect of the economic interests of the investors in German-speaking employees in the Czech Republic.

According to a survey conducted by the Chamber in 2010, the results of which were presented in 2011, almost 93% of German employers took a good command of German by (potential) Czech employees for very important or at least important. At the same time, the Chamber reported that German-speaking Czech employees were not very well available. Only 15% of the companies evaluated the situation as "good," whereas 38% as "bad." For 41% of the companies, the situation was "satisfactory," but for 6% entirely "unsatisfactory." In terms of the tendencies of the development, the companies did not see any changes (45%), or they saw even some deterioration (18%). "Some improvement" was communicated by 27% of the companies.

Newer results based on a later comparable survey were presented in 2015.[21] Compared to the situation in 2011, the importance of the good command of German dropped from 93% to 88%, whereas the importance of English for German companies rose slightly from 86% to 89%. The availability of potential employees with good command of German was evaluated as good by 12% of the companies and as satisfactory by 40%. The percentage of the evaluation as unsatisfactory remained the same (6%), whereas the percentage of those who took the availability for bad increased slightly to 42%. Overall, the situation did not undergo any substantial

20 For more details see the website URL German-Czech Chamber of Industry and Commerce.

21 A press conference of the Chamber on January 15, 2015, in which the German as well as the Austrian ambassador took part. The data for this survey were collected during the second half of the year 2014. 275 companies were addressed.

changes, and no signs of improvement could be observed. Similarly to the Union of German Philologists' evaluation, the Chamber also evaluates the situation concerning German in the Czech Republic relatively negatively. However, although the knowledge of German is definitely advantageous when one looks for a job in a German or Austrian company, this does not necessarily mean that the lack of this knowledge would be a serious disadvantage. These companies continue operating quite well in the Czech Republic anyway.

Not only economic, but also cultural and specific language-related interests underlie the activities of the Goethe-Institute. The most visible management act, which corresponds to a global adjustment design in favor of German, has become known as the ŠPRECHTÍME campaign.[22] This campaign was unveiled in September 2011 in order to enhance the attractiveness and prestige of German and to point out the advantage following from the competences in this language. German is presented as a language bringing an added value if compared with English which is viewed as obvious.[23] Embassies of both German-speaking neighboring countries took part in the preparatory work and continue to support it financially. The campaign has been addressing not only schools, but also the public sphere from the very beginning. Thus, it helps make Czech population note that learning German might pay off (Dovalil 2018: 293–294; see also Filipová 2016). Gradually, the campaign got more focused on students of technical disciplines. Since 2014, special actions designated as "Day with German" have been organized in various regions of the Czech Republic.

On the level of a declaration, the Ministry of Education also claimed allegiance to this campaign. The former minister Kateřina Valachová welcomed the decision of both embassies as well as other German, Austrian or Czech institutions to start this campaign in order to open new opportunities and to help overcome communication barriers between Czechs and their neighbors. In this way, she supported the efforts to strengthen the prestige of German in the Czech Republic.[24]

One important remark concerning the time context of the beginning of the campaign needs to be added. In September 2011, the Czech Republic had been an EU member state for seven years. However, the free movement of Czech citizens on the labor market in Germany and Austria had been permitted for mere four months back then (since May 1, 2011). This fact appears to be a strong paradox, because Germany and Austria decided to co-finance the Šprechtíme campaign on the one hand, but had been inhibiting the natural demand for German by the restriction of the free movement for Czech employees on the other. These political acts were

22 See the website URL ŠPRECHTÍME.

23 This is one of the features of the Czech media discourse on foreign languages anyway (Dovalil 2018: 288–289).

24 Kateřina Valachová served as Minister of Education from 2015 to 2017. Her statement concerning this campaign is presented on http://www.sprechtime-databaze.cz/about/. Accessed on April 4, 2019.

apparently inconsistent with each other.[25] These circumstances generate a question to what extent it would have been more efficient for German from a long-term perspective to allow the Czech citizens to work in Austria and Germany than to co-finance the campaign.

4.5 Interconnecting activities in favor of German

Attempts to interconnect the activities in favor of German could be traced through various management acts, although no explicit and systematic plans to coordinate "a coalition for German" had been made before. Despite the fact that the processes as they are described in this section are primarily seen from the perspective of the Union of German Philologists, other perspectives are not neglected.

Representatives of this Union have always been conscious of the fact that they should address other institutions and find out their attitudes toward German. In this way, partners were supposed to be identified who could potentially help to intensify the efforts to make the problem more visible. Noting, rather negative evaluation of the situation, and designing adjustments were supposed to be taken into account.

Economic interests related to the level of the knowledge of German underlie the activities conducted by the German-Czech Chamber of Industry and Commerce. The above mentioned press conference aiming at the presentation of the results of its survey was coordinated with the German and Austrian embassies. Representatives of the Goethe-Institute also participated in this press conference. Apart from the data related to the underused potential of German for Czech employees, the Šprechtíme campaign, organized by the Goethe-Institute, was commented on. Austrian ambassador pointed out significant advantages of German for career and job opportunities. As stated by the representatives of the Chamber, more than 6,000 German and Austrian companies created over 150,000 jobs in the Czech Republic. The sector of science and technical innovations is included. Hence, the great demand for employees does not meet the adequate supply, which slows down the economic growth of the whole country in the end.

Regular communication also takes place between the embassies and the Union of German Philologists. Representatives of the Union are invited on the occasion of various anniversaries, which makes discussions about this issue possible.[26] In spite of the clear interest of both embassies in improving the knowledge of German in the Czech Republic, the representatives of the embassies are aware of

25 As for English, neither Great Britain, nor Ireland introduced restrictions of this kind in May 2004.

26 The most recent meeting of the representatives of the Union with the German ambassador in Prague took place on July 11, 2018, the last meeting with the Austrian ambassador on November 7, 2018. Unfortunately, a complete list of such meetings is not available.

the political background and many historical interconnections, which make direct, or even offensive actions in favor of German delicate. As the representatives of the embassies emphasized it during a meeting in July 2012 (Austrian Embassy) or in March 2012 (German Studies Students' conference Pragestt at the Faculty of Arts in Prague), this very political issue would have to be worked through by the Czech side itself, because imposing German on the Czech population was unthinkable.[27] The historical burden as a part of the sociocultural management still impedes at least a part of management activities in favor of German. Therefore, the promotion of German in terms of promoting partnership was said to have always been in the foreground.[28]

One member of the presidium of the Union of German Philologists participates in the activities of the GCNM. Through this simultaneous membership, both bodies can be mutually informed, which is particularly valuable in terms of the information flow from the German minority to the Union and vice versa. Based on these contacts, one of the vice-presidents of the Council for National Minorities arranged a meeting with representatives of the Ministry of Education and a representative of the Union of German Philologists, which took place at the ministry in January 2019. Possibilities for removing the passage 7.2 from the Framework Program as a part of its next revision related to better protection of the German minority were discussed. This protection was interconnected with easier identification of schools which would be willing to guarantee teaching German as the first foreign language and to cooperate with other schools in which continuity of teaching this language would be assured. This adjustment design was based on the assumption that easier availability of such information about where German (as a foreign language) is taught continually would support stronger interests in German on the part of members of this minority as well. They would not have to feel discouraged from acquiring this language.[29]

27 My personal communication with the then Austrian ambassador in Prague Ferdinand Trauttmansdorff and with one of the then representatives of the German embassy Thomas Motack. Both confirmed that their embassies (had) communicated with the Ministry of Education and consulted the situation of German in the Czech Republic. These consultations depended in no way on the cooperation with the Union of German Philologists.

28 This aspect of language "partnership" is discussed by Krumm (1999: 42–45). He also places emphasis on the strategy according to which the promotion of German has to be based on cooperation on both sides and to reflect the concept of helping the partner to help himself ("Hilfe zur Selbsthilfe" in German original, Krumm 1999: 47).

29 However, one of the representatives of the Ministry of Education referred to the potential danger which would consist in removing the second mandatory foreign language from the Framework Program (instead of strengthening it). Such a step would obviously exacerbate the situation of German (personal communication with the Secretary of the Ministry of Education Jindřich Fryč in January 2019).

No matter how much information may be shared among the participating social actors, their activities have not been coordinated yet. Similarly, the general interest in increasing the competence in German is likely to be too vague and would need to be specified in clearer goals.

5 Conclusion

The basic interests underlying the management acts as they are carried out by the respective social actors can be summarized as follows: the Union of German Philologists, an actor with expertise, expresses its existential interest in supporting German, because one whole academic discipline—the German Studies, i.e., activities of experts in German linguistics, literary science as well as didactics—depends on (very) good level of competences in German on the part of at least some groups of the Czech population. Similarly existential in nature are the interests of the organizations of German minority. Though their leaders also act in some cases as people with expertise, most members of this minority belong to the less influential people with interest. Primarily economic interests are observed in the case of German-Czech Chamber of Industry and Commerce. In spite of economic advantageousness of German skills, the behavior of a part of the Czech population reveals that the real economic incentive to learn German seems to be smaller than it is usually claimed in public discourses conducted by this social actor. Culture-related as well as economic interests are important for the embassies and the Goethe Institute. German courses supplied by the Goethe Institute must meet the adequate demand, if, e.g., long-term activities in culture are supposed to be financed. For the Ministry of Education, no comparable interest can be derived from its activities.

The analysis shows that the organized language management in favor of German in the Czech Republic is generated by shared deviations from several social actors' expectations (largely actors with expertise and actors with influence), which consist in better and much more widespread command of German in this country. Activities carried out by the institutions from the macro level are in the foreground. The expectations are based on socio-economic arguments, according to which it pays off to be able to speak German in terms of career and employment. However, these deviations are not shared by many individuals on the micro level, which hinders the management process at early stages. Thus, the promotion of *noting the problem* within the Šprechtíme campaign has not brought any substantial impact. The deviations from the expectations are noted and evaluated apparently negatively by the Union of German Philologists, German minority organizations, Goethe Institute, the German-Czech Chamber of Industry and Commerce as well as by the embassies of both German-speaking neighbors of the Czech Republic. Clear interests in as high level of the knowledge of German as possible are presented in numerous discourses which underlie the adjustment designs.

One part of these adjustments has to do with looking for partners, which appears to help to achieve one of the clearly identifiable goals—removal of the discriminatory clause from the Framework Program which makes the choice of

German as the first foreign language in the Czech school system quite difficult and inconvenient. If teaching German is not ensured continually, then pupils interested in German may feel discouraged from choosing this language as their first foreign language, which may have adverse impacts on the maintenance of German within the German minority in the end. This is an attempt to manage one of the sociocultural circumstances more favorably for German, first. The GCNM and the Assembly of German Associations in the Czech Republic were identified as suitable partners, because several references to potential inconsistencies with international law appear apparent. Hence, the status of German as a minority language could help improve the situation of German as a foreign language. This sociocultural management is followed by the communicative management, which goes hand in hand with looking for opportunities to use German in such social networks, in which the demand for German reproduces itself. The labor market is such a segment.

A somewhat less clear position can be observed in the case of the Ministry of Education. This social actor also shares the basically negative evaluation of competences in foreign languages as outlined above, but unlike those actors, no specific interest in German is present. Rather, a distinct preference for English continues. Attempts to make the ministry remove, or change the wording of, the discriminatory clause in section 7.2 of the Framework Program, which would enable to choose German as the first foreign language more easily, have not been successful so far. On the other hand, after the delay from 2005, a second foreign language was introduced as a mandatory school subject in 2013, which has had a favorable impact on German since that time. The ministry does not reflect the status of German as a minority language thoroughly and, basically, evades the criticism raised by the Council of Europe in this point. Symptomatically, the ministry does not fund any program for teaching German as a minority language. As shown in its reactions to objections presented within the GCNM, it keeps insisting on restrictions of the choices of the first foreign language instead, as they have been laid down in the Framework Program from the very beginning. Hence, this Framework Program rather reduces the opportunities as well as the desire and willingness to learn and to use German (the second and the third pillar of Grin's policy-to-outcome-path).[30] On the other hand, some declarations explicitly oriented

30 Concerning this issue, I take advantage of the last possibility of updating some important details. Ultimately, in a revised version of the Framework Program as of January 2021 (coming into force on September 1, 2021), the ministry relinquished the discriminatory clause from section 7.2 as it is discussed above in part 4.2.1 (MŠMT 2021: 149). However, this section continues to discriminate between *a foreign language* (meaning de facto a *first* foreign language) and *another foreign language*, which preserves hierarchical relations. The languages categorized as *another foreign language* are listed quite explicitly: German, French, Spanish, Italian, Russian, Slovak, Polish, or yet another foreign language. Schools must offer English at least as *another foreign language* to pupils who did not choose it as a foreign (= their first

in favor of German can also be found, e.g., the support of the Šprechtíme campaign. However, such non-binding declarations are inconsistent with the legally binding legislative framework and do not correspond to the practices carried out so far.

The other part of the adjustments concerns the didactics and teaching German in terms of the linguistic management in the narrow sense (third level). In this point, the ministry has always acted more cooperatively. It cooperates with the Goethe Institute as well as with several experts from the Union of German Philologists. However, as long as the management activities concentrating on this third level has been impeded by quite unfavorable socio-cultural management at the very first level for two decades, the situation has not improved.

Regardless of the fact that implementation of this extensive organized language management could not be analyzed in this chapter in detail, the continuing dissatisfaction with the situation on the part of most of the analyzed organizations makes the interpretation plausible that previous cycles of the German-related management processes have rather failed so far. This is at least partially explainable by reference to the initiation of the processes on the macro level against the will of the micro level. This means that—from the global point of view—the management process has finished in the phase of negative evaluation. This fact confirms the hierarchization of social actors in terms of their power, because the actors with expertise as well as those with influence are less powerful than the Ministry of Education, which is classified as the central actor with power.

Although some partial adjustment designs have already been implemented (the most visible of them being the introduction of the second mandatory foreign language), some others have not. In a very general respect, a specific adjustment design could potentially consist in involving even more powerful social actors—such as courts—in the solution to language problems. As the problematic point 7.2 of the Framework Program appears to have been inconsistent, e.g., with Article 7, Paragraph 2 of the European Charter for Regional or Minority Languages it could have been checked by a court, because legal regulations such as the Framework Program, whose legal force is lower than law, must obviously comply with national laws and—even more—with international treaties (ECRM or the Czech-German bilateral treaty). A judgment in a legal dispute would help clarify to what extent pupils claiming German nationality and being interested in German are entitled to feel discouraged from choosing this language at least as their first foreign language when no school system with German as a language of instruction exists. This judgment would enrich the current discourse and would take a prominent position in it in terms of its power. It would have to be abided by all other social actors, including the Ministry of Education.

---

foreign) language. It is not clear to what extent this simple revision will impact foreign language teaching. This change has not been publicized yet and may remain unknown for the general public. Nevertheless, one formal obstacle impeding the choice of German as the first foreign language no longer exists.

Related to Zhao's (2011) hierarchization in terms of power, a superordinate category could be added, or some specification within the group of actors with power could be carried out when the position of courts is considered. The differentiation of the position of the people with expertise depends on contexts and on their discursive acts. Once they act as individuals their position corresponds to that of the people with interest, operating more actively as latent actors at specific moments (Bandelow 2015: 312). Only their affiliation with institutions (not necessarily solely the Union of German Philologists, but also with the respective university or faculty) bestows the second highest status on them.

Several examples of discrepancies and inconsistencies within various social actors' efforts to strengthen German are exemplified: Although both Germany, and Austria supported the Czech Republic's accession to the EU in May 2004, they did not allow Czech citizens to move freely in their labor markets and insisted on this restriction for as long as possible. Similarly, the Czech (oslovak) government made the Treaty on Good Neighborliness and Friendly Cooperation with Germany, according to which German as well as German Studies were supposed to be supported in the Czech Republic, without satisfying the expectations of these actors.

Acknowledgments

This work was supported by the European Regional Development Fund-Project "Creativity and Adaptability as Conditions of the Success of Europe in an Interrelated World" (No. CZ.02.1.01/0.0/0.0/16_019/0000734) and by the Charles University project Progres 4, Language in the shifting of time, space, and culture. Thanks are due to the editors of the volume for their valuable comments on various versions of this chapter. Thanks are also due to members of the presidium of the Union of German Philologists, the chairwoman Lenka Vaňková as well as Hana Andrášová and Věra Janíková for sending me valuable data.

References

Ammon, U. (2015) *Die Stellung der deutschen Sprache in der Welt* [The Position of the German Language in the World]. Berlin, Munich & Boston: Walter de Gruyter.

Bandelow, N. C. (2015) Advocacy coalition framework. In G. Wenzelburger & R. Zohlnhöfer (eds) *Handbuch Policy-Forschung* [Handbook Policy Research]. Wiesbaden: Springer, 305–324.

Cink, P. (1999) D-A-CH: Sprachförderung und Zusammenarbeit aus mitteleuropäischer Perspektive [Germany-Austria-Switzerland: Language promotion and cooperation from Central-European perspective]. In H.-J. Krumm (ed) *Sprachen – Brücken über Grenzen. Deutsch als Fremdsprache in Mittel- und*

Osteuropa [Languages – Bridges over Borders. German as a Foreign Language in Central and Eastern Europe]. Vienna: Eviva, 26–38.

CoE (2015): Recommendation 5 of the Committee of Ministers on the application of the European Charter for Regional or Minority Languages by the Czech Republic. On WWW at https://www.coe.int/t/dg4/education/minlang/Report/Recommendations/CzechCMRec3_en.pdf. Accessed April 4, 2019.

COM (2017) 534 final: Communication from the Commission to the Council and the European Parliament. Boosting growth and cohesion in EU border regions. EC Brussel, September 20, 2017. On WWW at https://eur-lex.europa.eu/legal-content/en/TXT/?uri=CELEX%3A52017DC0534. Accessed April 4, 2019.

COM (2018) 272 final: Commission staff working document accompanying the document proposal for a Council recommendation on a comprehensive approach to the teaching and learning of languages. EC Brussels, May 22, 2018. On WWW at https://eur-lex.europa.eu/legal-content/EN/TXT/HTML/?uri=CELEX:52018SC0174&from=EN. Accessed April 5, 2019.

CSI (2010) Tematická zpráva – Souhrnné poznatky o podpoře a rozvoji výuky cizích jazyků v předškolním, základním a středním vzdělávání v období let 2006–2009 [Thematic report – Summarized findings on the support and development of foreign language teaching in the pre-school, primary and secondary education between 2006 and 2009]. On WWW at http://www.csicr.cz/cz/85027-podpora-a-rozvoj-vyuky-cizichjazyku. Accessed April 4, 2019.

CSI (2018) Rozvoj jazykové gramotnosti v základních a středních školách ve školním roce 2016/2017 [Development of language literacy in primary and secondary schools in the school year 2016/2017]. On WWW at https://www.csicr.cz/getattachment/0806b65c-19c4-40e4-b8c0-abd335308886/TZ-Rozvoj-jazykove-gramotnosti-v-ZS-a-SS-2016-2017.pdf. Accessed April 4, 2019.

Dovalil, V. (2010) Sind zwei Fremdsprachen in der Tschechischen Republik realistisch? Zu den aktuellen Problemen der tschechischen Spracherwerbsplanung [Are two foreign languages in the Czech Republic realistic? On the current problems of the Czech acquisition planning]. In U. Ammon, J. Darquennes & S. Wright (eds) *Sociolinguistica* 24 (Foreign Languages in Schools of the European Union). Berlin & New York: Walter de Gruyter, 43–60.

Dovalil, V. (2018) Qual der Wahl, or spoiled for choice? English and German as the subject of decision-making processes in the Czech Republic. In T. Sherman & J. Nekvapil (eds) *English in Business and Commerce: Interactions and Policies* (= English in Europe 5). Berlin & Boston: Mouton de Gruyter, 276–309.

Dovalil, V. & Engelhardt, O. (2012) *Die gegenwärtige Situation des Deutschen in der Tschechischen Republik: Qualitative Forschung an Schulen* [The Contemporary Situation of German in the Czech Republic: Qualitative Research at Schools]. An Unpublished Research Report. Praha: Česko-německý fond budoucnosti/Czech-German Fund for the Future.

Dovalil, V. & Šichová, K. (2017) *Sprach(en)politik, Sprachplanung und Sprachmanagement* [Language Policy, Language Planning and Language Management]. Heidelberg: Universitätsverlag Winter.

EC & Eurydice (2017) *Key Data on Teaching Languages at School in Europe.* On WWW at https://op.europa.eu/en/publication-detail/-/publication/73ac5ebd-473e-11e7-aea8-01aa75ed71a1/language-en/format-PDF. Accessed April 4, 2019.

Fairbrother, L., Nekvapil, J. & Sloboda, M. (2018) Methodology in language management research. In L. Fairbrother, J. Nekvapil & M. Sloboda (eds) *The Language Management Approach: A Focus on Research Methodology.* Berlin: Peter Lang, 15–39.

Fenton-Smith, B. & Gurney, L. (2016) Actors and agency in academic language policy and planning. *Current Issues in Language Planning* 17 (1), 72–87.

Filipová, M. (2016) *Šprechtíme – Eine Kampagne zur Förderung der deutschen Sprache und Kultur in der Tschechischen Republik* [Šprechtíme – A Campaign Promoting the German Language and Culture in the Czech Republic]. Jena: Friedrich-Schiller-Universität. Unpublished Master Thesis.

Grin, F. (2003) *Language Policy Evaluation and the European Charter for Regional or Minority Languages.* Basingstoke: Palgrave.

Jernudd, B. H. & Neustupný, J. V. (1987) Language planning: For whom? In L. Laforge (ed) *Actes du Colloque international sur l'aménagement linguistique / Proceedings of the International Colloquium on Language Planning.* Québec: Les Presses de L'Université Laval, 69–84.

Kreisslová, S. & Novotný, L. (2018) Between language revitalization and assimilation: On the language situation of the German minority in the Czech Republic. *Journal of Nationalism, Memory & Language Politics* 12 (1), 121–139.

Krumm, H.-J. (1999) Die deutsche Sprache – eine Brückensprache für Mittel- und Osteuropa? [German language – a bridging language for Central and Eastern Europe?] In H.-J. Krumm (ed) *Sprachen – Brücken über Grenzen. Deutsch als Fremdsprache in Mittel- und Osteuropa* [Languages – Bridges over Borders. German as a Foreign Language in Central and Eastern Europe]. Vienna: Eviva, 39–51.

MŠMT (2005) *Národní plán výuky cizích jazyků* [National Plan for Foreign Language Teaching]. On WWW at http://www.syka.cz/files/narodni_plan_vyuky_ciz_jaz.pdf. Accessed April 4, 2019.

MŠMT (2017) *Rámcový vzdělávací program pro základní vzdělávání* [Framework Educational Program for Primary Education]. On WWW at http://www.msmt.cz/file/43792/. Accessed April 4, 2019.

MŠMT (2021) *Rámcový vzdělávací program pro základní vzdělávání* [Framework Educational Program for Primary Education]. On WWW at http://www.nuv.cz/file/4982/. Accessed February 25, 2021.

Nekvapil, J. (2000) On non-self-evident relationships between language and identity: How Germans do not speak German, and Czechs do not speak Czech. *Multilingua* 19 (1/2), 37–53.

Nekvapil, J. (2016) Language management theory as one approach in language policy and planning. *Current Issues in Language Planning* 17 (1), 11–22.

Neustupný, J. V. & Nekvapil, J. (2006) Language management in the Czech Republic. In R. B. Baldauf & R. Kaplan (eds) *Language Planning and Policy in Europe.* Vol. 2: *The Czech Republic, The European Union and Northern Ireland.* Clevedon, Buffalo & Toronto: Multilingual Matters, 16–201.

Novotný, L. (2015) German language and German minority. *Annual of Language & Politics and Politics of Identity* IX, 23–42.

Sladkovská, K. & Šmídová, T. (2010) *Souhrnná analýza k postavení dalšího cizího jazyka u nás a v Evropě* [Summarized Analysis of the Position of the Additional Foreign Language in Czechia and in Europe]. Prague: VÚP.

Zhao, S. (2011) Actors in language planning. In E. Hinkel (ed) *Handbook of Research in Second Language Teaching and Learning.* Vol. 2. New York & London: Routledge, 905–923.

Other documents and reports

Common European Framework of Reference for Languages: Learning, Teaching, Assessment. On WWW at https://www.coe.int/en/web/common-european-framework-reference-languages. Accessed April 4, 2019.

Dlouhodobý záměr vzdělávání a rozvoje výchovně vzdělávací soustavy České republiky (pro oblast předškolního, základního, středního vyššího odborného a dalšího vzdělávání), březen 2002 [Long-Term Plan of Education and Development of the Educational System of the Czech Republic (for Pre-School, Primary, Secondary and Further Education), March 2002]. Praha: MŠMT.

European Charter for Regional or Minority Languages. On WWW at https://rm.coe.int/CoERMPublicCommonSearchServices/DisplayDCTMContent?documentId=0900001680695175. Accessed April 4, 2019.

Framework Convention for the Protection of National Minorities. On WWW at https://rm.coe.int/CoERMPublicCommonSearchServices/DisplayDCTMContent?documentId=09000016800c10cf. Accessed April 4, 2019.

GCNM (2015) *Zápis z jednání Rady vlády pro národnostní menšiny 14. října 2015* [Protocol from the Meeting of the Government Council for National Minorities, October 14, 2015]. Praha: Úřad vlády ČR.

GCNM (2017a) *Čtvrtá periodická zpráva o plnění závazků vyplývajících z Evropské charty regionálních či menšinových jazyků v České republice* [The Fourth Periodical Report on Fulfilment of Obligations Following from the European Charter of Regional or Minority Languages in the Czech Republic]. Praha: Úřad vlády ČR.

GCNM (2017b) *Zápis z jednání Rady vlády pro národnostní menšiny 16. února 2017* [Protocol from the Meeting of the Government Council for National Minorities, February 16, 2017]. Praha: Úřad vlády ČR.

GCNM (2018) *Zpráva o situaci národnostních menšin v České republice za rok 2017* [Report on the Situation of National Minorities in the Czech Republic in 2017]. Praha: Úřad vlády ČR.

GCNM (2019a) *Zpráva o situaci národnostních menšin v České republice za rok 2018* [Report on the Situation of National Minorities in the Czech Republic in 2018]. Praha: Úřad vlády ČR.

GCNM (2019b) *Pátá periodická zpráva o plnění zásad stanovených Rámcovou úmluvou o ochraně národnostních menšin podle článku 25 odstavce 2 této Úmluvy. Pracovní verze, březen 2019* [The Fifth Periodical Report on Fulfilment of Principles Laid Down by the Framework Convention for the Protection of National Minorities. Draft, March 2019]. Praha: Úřad vlády ČR.

German-Czech Chamber of Industry and Commerce (2011) *Průzkum Česko-německé obchodní a průmyslové komory: Využívání cizích jazyků ve firmách* [Survey of the German-Czech Chamber of Industry and Commerce: Employing Foreign Languages in Companies]. Praha: DTIHK.

German-Czech Chamber of Industry and Commerce (2015) *Průzkum Česko-německé obchodní a průmyslové komory: Využívání cizích jazyků ve firmách* [Survey of the German-Czech Chamber of Industry and Commerce: Employing Foreign Languages in Companies]. Praha: DTIHK.

Union of German Philologists (2007) Letter "Conception of foreign language teaching – request for appointment," March 19, 2007.

Union of German Philologists (2008) Letter "Situation of teaching German at primary and secondary schools – request for appointment," June 9, 2008.

Union of German Philologists (2010) Letter "Statement of the Union of German Philologists of the Czech Republic on the planned changes in foreign language teaching in the Czech Republic," September 17, 2010.

Union of German Philologists (2014) Letter "Statement of the Union of German Philologists of the Czech Republic on the current changes in the education of foreign language teachers," October 8, 2014.

Websites

Center of Coordination of Czech-German Youth Exchange (Tandem) URL: www.tandem-org.cz

Czech-German Fund for the Future URL: www.fondbudoucnosti.cz

European Survey on Language Competences URL: http://ec.europa.eu/dgs/education_culture/repository/languages/library/studies/executive-summary-eslc_en.pdf

German-Czech Chamber of Industry and Commerce URL: https://tschechien.ahk.de/

Government Council for National Minorities (GCNM) URL: https://www.vlada.cz/assets/ppov/rnm/Statut_narodnostni_mensiny_2018.pdf

Kulturverband URL: http://www.kulturverband.org/?page_id=20&lang=de

Landesversammlung der deutschen Vereine in der Tschechischen Republik URL: http://www.landesversammlung.cz/de/

Language Management URL: languagemanagemen.ff.cuni.cz

ŠPRECHTÍME URL: homepage http://www.goethe.de/ins/cz/prj/jug/spr/udp/de8128950.htm

Union of German Philologists of the Czech Republic URL: www.svazgermanistu.cz

Chikako Ketcham

Non-Japanese business people's use of Japanese language in their workplace in Japan

Abstract In the midst of concerns about the declining birthrate and aging population, foreign human resources have been increasing in Japan. Yet, communication with Japanese business people (JBP) in the workplace has become an issue when employing and retaining foreign personnel in Japanese companies. Although some Japanese companies that have taken the helm in the global market have implemented language policies that have changed the official language of their companies to English, the effectiveness of the language use in the workplace remains unclear. This chapter, aiming at examining the Japanese language use of non-Japanese business people (NJBP) from their perspective, presents the findings from interviews with six NJBP working in different linguistic environments in Japan, such as Japanese companies that predominantly use Japanese language, Japanese companies that have changed their official language to English, and multinational foreign capital companies. The focus of the analysis were the NJBP's interests behind their language use. The results show that NJBP use Japanese language depending on their own interests regardless of the corporate language policies or Japanese sociocultural norms. Furthermore, the study reveals that the language adjustment of the NJBP influences the power relations between JBP and NJBP.

Keywords language management in the workplace, non-Japanese business people, power relations, business efficiency, communication in the workplace

1 Introduction

It is widely acknowledged that, amid the globalizing economy, it is of the utmost urgency for Japanese companies to secure competent non-Japanese human resources as businesses face the challenges of an aging population coupled with a birthrate in decline. According to Ministry of Internal Affairs and Communication (2019), the working age population (15–64 years old) in Japan as of October 2019 was 75,072,000, a decrease of 379,000 from the previous year. The working-age population peaked in 1995 and had declined by 12.5% by 2019. In October 2019, the working-age population's share of the total was 59.5%, the lowest since comparable 1950, and this decrease is expected to accelerate further. On the other hand, the number of foreign workers as of October 2019 was 1,658,804, a 13.6% increase from the previous year, the highest on record since the notification of foreign employment status became mandatory in 2007 (Ministry of Health, Labor and Welfare 2019).[1] In the intensified competition to hire competent human resources due to a worldwide labor shortage, the retention of non-Japanese business people (NJBP)[2] in Japanese companies is very low. Moreover, Japanese corporations are clearly less popular than other foreign capital corporations in Japan among foreign university graduates from Japanese universities (Ministry of Economy, Trade and Industry 2016). To improve the low retention rate of NJBP in Japanese companies, the Japanese government has called for the transformation of the current Japanese human resource management, where performance-based evaluations are not transparent and compensation is largely seniority-based.

However, according to a large-scale survey targeted at the management of Japanese companies conducted by the Ministry of Health, Labor and Welfare to study the actual state of accepting NJBP in Japanese companies, the highest percentage of respondents, 29.5%, answered that they had problems with NJBP's Japanese language skills, followed by 19.5% who answered that they had concerns about NJBP's communication with Japanese employees (Ministry of Health, Labor and Welfare 2015). Successful communication relies on the mutual efforts of both parties. In Japanese companies, however, the NJBP who are unable to adapt to the communication norms held by Japanese business people (JBP) are considered to be the subject of the amendments. Furthermore, even though the Japanese companies are concerned with the Japanese language proficiency of their non-Japanese employees, there are few companies that support NJBP by offering adequate Japanese language training (Ministry of Health, Labor and Welfare 2015).

Meanwhile, since 2010, Japanese companies cultivating global markets have been clueing into the economic trends in expanding the scope of procurement of raw materials, labor, and financing as well as accelerating the speed of doing so. Some of the major Japanese companies have been shifting the corporate language from Japanese to English for business efficiency. While there is controversy over the pros and cons of adopting English as a corporate language in Japanese multinational companies, it is allegedly good news for NJBP, and especially for those whose communication ability in Japanese language could be problematic (Norisada 2012). Some Japanese companies which adopt English as their corporate language (CECLs) are enhancing their English language training programs to improve the employees' TOEIC scores among their own ranks. CECLs measure employees'

---

1 Ministry of Internal Affairs and Communication (2021) showed the confirmed data as of June 2021. The working-age population in Japan was 74,096,000. The working-age population's share of the total was 59.1%. Ministry of Health, Labor and Welfare (2021) announced the number of foreign workers as of 2020 was 1,724,328, a 4% increase from the previous year. The increase was limited due to the immigration control under the COVID19 pandemic.

2 In Japanese human resource management, foreign workers are categorized as 'non-Japanese.' This article defines foreign white-collar employees with full time employment as NJBP.

TOEIC scores as a criterion to assess the improvement of their global business efficiency. Economic expansion influences companies' language policies. However, corporate language policy is a mere principle for information sharing in English, and does not always reflect actual language use, which is in fact very often the result of the negotiation of the concerned parties.

While the world faces a wave of globalization, there are countries that are trying to reduce immigrants, prioritizing the local language skill over core business competency as a means of employment migration exclusion (Canagarajah 2017). On the other hand, in order to address the problem of a declining population, Japan is entering a period of increasing the number of foreign people and hiring more foreign talents in business. These two attitudes toward foreigners seem to be pulling in opposite directions, but both share the common interest of securing the necessary number of immigrants for their own countries. Japan was initially unwilling to accept foreigners other than tertiary educated 'highly skilled foreign personnel,' but as of April 2019 it started accepting overseas workers undertaking simple labor under an amendment to Japan's Immigration Control Act. The Japanese government has announced that it has no plans to implement further immigration measures in Japan, but it is becoming increasingly possible for foreign workers except for those who are low-skilled laborers, to obtain permanent residency (Nakamura 2020).

Hence, in order to live and work together in Japanese workplaces, it is essential to develop effective and collaborative language policy by studying not only the host country's perceptions, but also NJBP's perceptions of the language use. To this end, this article aims to examine the NJBP's interests in using Japanese language in the workplace. If communication problems with NJBP exist in workplaces, it is essential to study how NJBP use and manage language(s) (cf. Neustupný 1995).

2 Communicationat work

The Japanese government and companies in Japan have been trying to increase the number of NJBP in the past three decades. This section reviews the past research studying how Japanese language has been used at work in contact situations. Firstly, we review the historical setting confirming the power of economic trends behind the increase of the number of NJBP in Japanese companies. Secondly, we move into the literature review investigating the Japanese language use of NJBP at workplaces where Japanese language was predominantly used in contact situations. Lastly, we consider the findings regarding the language use of NJBP in multilingual workplace environment, including CECLs, foreign capital multinational companies, and Japanese companies located outside of Japan.

2.1 Increase in foreign workers behind Japan's economic trend

From the late 1980s to the early 1990s, due to the growing labor shortage in the corporate sector under the bubble economy of Japan, the number of foreign workers increased in line with the increasing internationalization of Japan's economy and society. The appreciation of the yen and the widening of economic disparities with neighboring Asian countries had increased the benefits of labor migration across national borders. On the other hand, a large number of illegal aliens working in the field of unskilled labor became a problematic issue in Japan.

The Japanese government revised the Immigration Law adding the 'Technical Intern Training Program' in 1993 for an official aim to train technical skills to foreign trainees during the training period. However, in fact, out of those Technical Trainees, 40% were international students from developing countries working as part-timers and technical interns, many of whom had been forced to engage in illegal and stressful work (Nishinippon Shimbun 2018). Thus, the training program has been provided not for the foreign trainees but as a means for the Japanese economy to compensate for the most recent shortage of simple labor.

Since 2010, facing the growing competitions in global markets, the interests of Japanese companies to procure talented employees who can successfully work in the market have increased. In order to attract competent workers from overseas, the Japanese government amended Japan's immigration law. In 2015, a new residence status, 'Highly Skilled Specialist,' was introduced to expand the range of working type from 'Management,' which was previously defined as tied to foreign capital companies, to 'Management and Administrations' which are not tied to foreign capital. Hence, a foreign employee has just recently come to be considered 'officially' as a 'Highly Skilled Specialist' in a management or administration position in Japanese companies.

It has been common for NJBP to hold managerial positions in foreign capital companies, but in Japanese companies, NJBP have been treated as specialists who generally need the supervision of Japanese management. In the analysis done by the Cabinet Office of the Japanese government (2019), NJBP in Japanese companies have not been regarded as human resources who can replace JBP, but as complementary resources, and have been accepted when there is a need to perform tasks that make use of foreign people's unique skills.

In the future, the amendment of the 'Management and Administrations' in Japanese capital companies is expected to increase career opportunities for NJBP to gain managerial power in Japanese companies.

2.2 Communication in Japanese monolingual workplaces

With an increasing number of NJBP holding positions such as specialists, engineers, and managers after the mid-1990s, quantitative surveys on Japanese language usage by NJBP have taken into account the level of their Japanese language proficiency. Those surveys had targeted both JBP and NJBP to examine how NJBP use Japanese language in communication with JBP within their workplaces. Sei (1998) conducted a quantitative survey among seventy-seven NJBP who had advanced Japanese language skills and used mostly Japanese language in their workplaces and sixty-five JBP who had been communicating with NJBP in Japanese in forty-three companies (thirty-four Japanese capital companies and nine foreign capital companies) in Japan. The results revealed that both JBP and NJBP had been finding many barriers in the Japanese language skills of the NJBP. The JBP considered the main barrier to be in the NJBP's lack of ability to use the Japanese language appropriately depending on situational context. On the other hand, the NJBP had great psychological difficulties in dealing with the prejudices of the JBP who insisted all the problems in communication were caused by NJBP. The most difficult communication for the NJBP was 'stating their own opinions to JBP.' As a result, Sei (1998) asserted the importance of improvement in the working environment of Japanese companies to accept Japanese speaking NJBP. Using a quantitative survey targeting hundred NJBP who used Japanese language in both Japanese and foreign capital companies, Kondo (2007) revealed the psychological difficulty of Asian business people working in Japanese companies where JBP imposed Japanese sociocultural norms on the Asian business people. In the workplaces where Japanese is predominantly spoken, NJBP experienced difficulty in sociocultural or sociolinguistic aspects of the Japanese language, such as, stating their own opinions to JBP, using the appropriate honorific forms, and in listening to JBP's opinions without expressing counterarguments. Along with the increase of NJBP in Japanese companies, a qualitative case study examined Chinese business people's attitudes towards conflicts with JBP in Japanese companies. Tachikawa (2013) conducted semi-structured interviews targeting four Chinese business people asking about their strategies how they dealt with intercultural conflicts that arose in the workplace. The results suggested 'avoidance' and 'accommodation' were the most commonly used as effective strategies, influenced by workplace factors such as the lower positions of the Chinese business people as a subordinate or a linguistic/cultural minority.

Meanwhile, the Cabinet Office (2019) summarized current research data done by public sectors and showed that the biggest problem of employment of NJBP is 'Japanese language proficiency of NJBP' followed by 'inappropriate communication skills of the NJBP with JBP.' The results of study are the same as those of Sei (1998) introduced above. Thus, the issue of intercultural communication between NJBP and JBP has remained unresolved in Japanese companies for at least twenty years.

2.3 Language use in multilingual workplaces

Studies on Japanese language usage by both NJBP and JBP in a branch/subsidiary of Japanese companies located outside Japan have been conducted since 2000s when Japanese companies started transferring their production sites. Aibara (2009, 2012) shows that due to the lack of English proficiency, Japanese expatriates using the Japanese language in their workplaces in Hong Kong avoided expressing their dissatisfaction with the Japanese proficiency of their Chinese subordinates in order to encourage them to continue using Japanese when speaking with them. Kubota (2013), studying the language use of both Japanese expatriates and Chinese employees in the Japanese subsidiaries in China, reports that Japanese subsidiaries were supporting Japanese language training for Chinese employees who have worked for the company for a long time in order to secure excellent Japanese speakers in their companies, since skilled multilingual Chinese business people tend to move to Euro-American companies. The above-mentioned papers suggest that outside of Japan, the low English proficiency of JBP influenced the language adjustment of JBP towards NJBP as well as the power relations between NJBP and JBP.

Until the 2010s, in the vast majority of Japanese companies, Japanese was the common language used in the workplace and so there were few papers studying Japanese language use within the multilingual environments of Japanese companies. Morita (2018) points out that CECLs were studied only from the viewpoint of Japanese human resources management and English education. Norisada (2012) criticizes the papers studying CECLs for focusing only on the controversy over economic efficiency and the influence of English language education of JBP. The efficiency of English as a lingua franca in Japanese companies depends on the employees' English proficiency and the actual use of English at work. However, Kubota (2016) and Amelina (2010) suggest that the efficiency is questioned when a majority of employees are from non-native English-speaking countries, or when a type of work or an industry doesn't require English language competence.

On the other hand, studies on NJBP who work in the Japanese branches of European capital companies, culturally and linguistically diverse workplaces, indicate that NJBP's language choice depends on the topics of communication and power relations between the opposing parties even though a multinational corporation may lay down an explicit official language policy (Fairbrother 2015a, 2015b). Fairbrother (2015c, 2018) conducted semi-structured and interaction interviews with three multilingual employees working in subsidiaries of the separate three European capital multinational companies to examine the language practice of the employees in the workplace. The results point out that the employees' practices were seen not only in use of language varieties such as hybrid or pidginized languages but also in 'multiform' practices applied to sociolinguistic and sociocultural practices, which were influenced by the hierarchical power structure of the workplace. In multinational companies, contention about language is not just about the issue of language choice, but also about how language is used (Fairbrother 2015c, 2018).

"Interests are aspirations for a certain state of affairs that is favorable to the subject. Power operates on interests. Power is the capacity to implement one's interests" (Neustupný 2002: 3). This statement aptly applies to institutional discourse which is controlled by power holders (Fairclough 1989). Fairclough focused on the critical language study raising the awareness of 'language in its social context,' stating that "nobody who has an interest in modern society, and certainly nobody who has an interest in relationships of power in modern society, can afford to ignore language" (1989: 3). When we study the communication of NJBP within the workplaces, it is important to investigate the hidden power behind the communication.

Since the 1990s, globalism has encouraged the development of multilingual business environments in Japan, increasing the number of CECLs in the interest of economic efficiency. However, studies show that choice of language in CECLs depends upon the interests of the interlocutors (Bargiela-Chiappini & Nickerson 2003). For example, Amelina (2010), who studied multilingual practices of highly qualified eighteen transmigrant professionals during their stay in Germany, points out certain types of motivation behind the professionals' language choice such as network building, personal relationship maintenance, career development, and conflict management. The highly qualified professionals use not only English language as a special purpose register as the linguistic repertoires of internationally working professionals, but also their own mother tongue for network building, and the host language for an instrument against power imposition and exclusion from the host country (Amelina 2010).

In summary, the studies on employees' language management outside of Japanese companies go beyond the choice of language and examine language strategies which applied to new power relations. However, the prior studies focusing on the NJBP's use of the Japanese language limited their scope to the Japanese linguistic environment, and few of them studied more complex linguistic environments, such as those involving multiple languages at CECLs, or of multilinguals in multinational companies in Japan. It is therefore necessary to expand the scope when studying how NJBP use language and languages at workplaces in Japan. In addition, in Japanese workplaces where JBP are the majority, it is crucial to examine the adjustment of the interactions from the NJBP's viewpoint to better understand their interests as well as the underlying power relations. As Nekvapil and Sherman (2009) claim, if an individual reiterates certain management strategies in daily interactions and such strategies are generalized among individuals on the micro level, it could be a starting point for organized language management of the company on the macro level, which provides a frame for language management and its implementation within the company in general.

3 Method

The data used in this study was collected between February and August 2016 and in March 2019. The data collected in 2016 consist of interviews with eleven foreign business people in total. Each interview was approximately 90 minutes long and combined the methods of a semi-structured and an interaction interview (Neustupný 2003). The aim of the interviews was to find out about the ways in which the interviewees communicate in Japanese language at work and the interests that they were following when in the course of their language management. The interviews were divided into four stages: first, the purpose of the research was explained to obtain the understanding and cooperation of the interviewee; second, the interviewee was asked to report the events in a short period of time (15–30 minutes) of the day; third, the interviewee was asked to describe details of the interaction such as what purpose, to whom, what type of situation, or how they felt after the interaction. Finally, the interviewer elicited the behavior and awareness of the interviewee after the interaction, and provided the hypothesis held by the interviewer to the interviewee to ascertain the interviewee's responses. The interviews were mainly conducted by interaction interview. And only when the interviewees had referred to some past event did the interview switch to a semi-structured one to ask about past events. The interaction interview aims at capturing an act of interaction as much in its original form as possible and can provide in-depth insights into the actor's perceptions (Muraoka 2002). In order to obtain as accurate information as possible, the interviewees were asked to report events or interaction that occurred on the same day of the interview.

The six participants whose cases are discussed in this study were selected as representing NJBP using Japanese language in their workplaces in Japan. All the six NJBP have high to intermediate Japanese language proficiency. Prior to the interviews, the interviewer, a tester for oral proficiency interview by the American Council on the Teaching of Foreign Languages, assessed the NJBP's Japanese proficiency levels as shown in Table 1. The interviews with the NJBP were conducted in Japanese, except for AM2 who spoke mainly in English. As of August 2016, the working period of each NJBP in the company varied from 2.5 years to 4 years. Out of the six NJBP, five NJBP were working in multilingual working environments including CECLs and one business person was working at a Japanese capital company where Japanese language is the only language being used among the employees within the company. After the interview, the information on the NJBP's companies such as a company policy understood by the employees as the corporate philosophy was collected from the company's information site to study the corporate culture in which the NJBP were working.

Follow-up surveys were conducted in March 2019 by email to update the career status of interviewed NJBP. Out of six interviewees, three continued developing their careers in the same companies, as shown in Table 1. The other three left Japan. One of them (TM5) was working in the same company's head office in the US. The other two quit the Japanese company and returned to their home countries. The follow-up survey also asked the three NJBP who decided to remain in Japan what they considered to be the successful factors for their career in Japan.

Table 1: Participant profile as of August 2016 and March 2019

Interviewee	VF1	AM2	IM3	CF4	TM5	CF6
Gender	Female	Male	Male	Female	Male	Female
Nationality	Vietnamese	American	Indian	Chinese	Taiwanese	Chinese
1st Language	Vietnamese	English	Malayalam	Mandarin	English	Mandarin
J-Proficiency[a]	A-high	I-mid	A-mid	A-mid	A-mid	A-mid
Period[b]	4 years	3 years	4 years	3 years	4 years	2.5 years
Environment[c]	CECL	CECL	CECL	Mono	Multi	CECL
Capital[d]	Japanese	Japanese	Japanese	Japanese	American	Japanese
Employment[e]	Same	America	Same	Same	America	China

a Japanese language proficiency: A-high (Advanced-high); A-mid (Advanced-middle); I-mid (Intermediate-middle)
b Period of employment as of 2016
c Linguistic environment of the workplace: CECL (multilingual using English as a 'common language' and Japanese language); Mono (monolingual); Multi (multilingual)
d Capital of the company: Japanese (Japanese capital company); American (American capital company)
e Place of employment as of 2019: Same (employed by the same company as in 2016 and staying in Japan), America, China

The collected data was analyzed based on Language Management Theory (LMT) (Jernudd & Neustupný 1987). The target of LMT is to scrutinize one's behaviors towards language and particularly the processes underlying how one can conceptualize language and interactional problems and how one tries to remove them. The interactions of NJBP at workplaces in Japan mostly occur in contact situations between speakers from different cultures which studies using LMT often concern themselves with. LMT focuses on the norms of the actors, which are the prerequisite for the process of language management to occur. When there is a deviation from the norm, the actor noted it as a deviation, evaluated it negatively, and then a plan is made for adjusting the evaluated deviation (problem). Finally, as the next process, the adjustment is implemented. The LMT is an essential theory to investigate an interaction of a non-Japanese business person in contact situations such as what kinds of events or issues they perceived as a problem, how they behaved to remove the problem, and how they evaluated the adjustment.

In order to analyze the language management of NJBP in the workplace, events and incidents that NJBP noted as deviations from their norms were extracted from the transcribed data for closer study. Then the process of language management by NJBP—how they noted and evaluated problems, formulated adjustments, and implemented them—was examined in each case. The extracted data that NJBP noted as deviations were categorized based on a framework of behavior classification in contact situations (Neustupný 1995) into sociocultural, sociolinguistic (communicative), and grammatical (linguistic) behaviors. Focusing on language variations such as a language choice or a way of speaking categorized as the sociolinguistic behavior (communicative management), the extracted data were examined to see how NJBP made their adjustment by noting a deviation, under what circumstances, and to whom the adjustment was implemented, and by what expected norms and motivating interests the adjustment was influenced.

Nekvapil (2009) states that one of the merits of LMT is its continuous interest in the interplay of simple and organized management as a 'language management cycle.' When interlocutors do not solve problems by themselves, they turn to professionals to solve the bigger problems. In these cases, several features need consideration in the context of organized management, such as social networks, company policy, or government policy, etc. In addition to the extracted data, each of the NJBP's companies' information, such as corporate policy, number of NJBP in the department of the NJBP, was studied to check the consistency of power relations between NJBP and the company the NJBP worked for.

Moreover, the extracted data was analyzed to see why and how NJBP evaluated their language management after implementing the adjustment. Kimura (2014) emphasized the importance of process after an implementation of the adjustment in language management as a cyclical process. If a problem is not removed, the language management will be repeatedly practiced within a language management cycle for long time. Therefore, the analysis focuses on the reason of the adjustment as a motivating interest of the NJBP when they use Japanese language, as well as the evaluation of the adjustment post-implementation.

The following two research questions will be discussed. First, what are the interests that compel NJBP to implement the adjustment in Japanese language, whom do they serve and why? Second, what kind of power relations underpin the interests of NJBP to implement the adjustment in Japanese?

4 NJBP's interests in using Japanese

The language adjustments of NJBP were observed in three domains of interest: (1) utilizing their Japanese language skills for time efficiency and other work-related goals; (2) developing open communication; and (3) fostering informal in-group solidarity. This section will also discuss the power relations operating behind NJBP's interests in their language use.

4.1 Time-efficiency and other work-related goals

In monolingual Japanese companies, using Japanese in the business setting is standard among employees, regardless of their nationality (Morita 2018). Hence, there are few opportunities for tertiary skilled NJBP to be highly evaluated by the companies. On the contrary, Japanese language proficiency of NJBP is assessed by the monolingual Japanese companies as an incomplete level for accomplishing the business task. In other words, the Japanese language proficiency of the NJBP is measured in terms of how far it is inferior to the standard level of native speakers of Japanese (Ministry of Health, Labor and Welfare 2015). Meanwhile, in CECLs, three NJBP that were interviewed for this study admitted to switching from English to Japanese to achieve their business goals when speaking with JBP in short business meetings where time efficiency was their top priority.

The excerpt presented in Example 1 describes an informal negotiation between NJBP and JBP in CECL over language competency of JBP. As a planner of sales promotions, VF1 routinely holds half-hour-long meetings about four times a day to sell promotional ideas to other departments. If her plan is adopted by her in-house clients, her performance will be evaluated as an achievement. In the meetings, she needs to negotiate with Japanese managers from other departments who are the decision-makers on her proposals. When the senior JBP started speaking English in the meeting, VF1's language management was not in line with the company's language policy which stipulates English as corporate language.

Example 1

すごい向こうから英語で喋ってくれたんですけど、ま、ちゃんとした英語じゃなくて、なんか片言だったら、ちょっといらいらするというか。何言いたいか分からないときは、日本語でやってくれた方がいいんじゃないのかなと思います。「日本語でいいですよ。」とか。あんまりミーティングの時間、長くないじゃないですか。その気を遣う時間とか、余裕がないです。向こうは多分、「あ、そうですかね。日本語でもいいですか。」とか、なんかすごく嬉しそうに言ってくれて。その後は日本語でやってくれました。 (VF1)

[He spoke to me in English, but, hm, not proper English. Well, if their English is bad, I get, like, irritated. When I don't understand what they want to say, I think it may be better for them to use Japanese. So I said something like, "In Japanese is fine." The meeting is not that long, right? I don't have time to consider his feelings or something. He said quite happily something like, "Oh, is that so? You don't mind doing it in Japanese?" After that we spoke Japanese.]

VF1 noted the English skills of the JBP, whose job rank was some levels higher, as a deviation from her communicative norm of an efficient exchange of information and made a negative evaluation. Then she planned an adjustment to switch the meeting language from English to Japanese. After successfully implementing the plan, she re-evaluated her interaction positively, describing that the Japanese manager seemed happy about it. The process of her language management reveals a power shift being generated in the CECL workplace. Despite the advantageous position over the non-native-Japanese-speaking employee, the Japanese manager follows the lead of the lower-ranked non-Japanese employee to hold the meeting in Japanese, against the corporate language rule. The power imposition of a Japanese native speaker over a non-native Japanese speaker does not exist here. Instead, a foreign worker with high Japanese language proficiency is taking the initiative over a Japanese native speaker in Japanese to serve her interests. In a short meeting, VF1 chose Japanese to get her business done succinctly. Moreover, another dimension of power seems to back up her decision. The company in which VF1 works has been officially announcing corporate concepts for ways to work successfully. One of the concepts reflects the policy of the company which prioritizes time efficiency and emphasizes the speed of actions. For example, it urges the employees to "Accomplish in one month what it takes other companies a year to do, because we can only win by being many times faster than our competitors." VF1's language practice seems to be affected by the corporate ideology to prioritize time efficiency, which suggests, on the one hand, that NJBP may seek to increase opportunities to utilize their advanced Japanese language skills, and on the other hand, that JBP may lose opportunities to improve their English skills. Consequently, it may increase the language skill divide. In response to the question from the interviewer as to whether she feels that speaking with JBP in Japanese robs the JBP of opportunities to practice English in CECL, VF1 made a comment about the JBP who accepted the language switch.

Example 2

多分、その人たちも、何回もそういうミーティング、参加したことありますので。私たちじゃなくて、他の部署の人に、同じことあると思いますので、逆に違和感とかないですね。多分、全員、違和感とかない。(VF1)

[They have probably also participated in such meetings many times, not with us, but with other [foreign staff] in other departments, so I think, as they have similar experiences, on the contrary, they do not feel discomfort or whatever. Probably no employees feel any discomfort about it.]

VF1 justified her language management as common practice, even suggesting that all employees feel that speaking Japanese with JBP is the right solution, since everyone acknowledged the JBP's low proficiency of English would prevent JBP from accomplishing their professional tasks and would shake JBP's authority. VF1 used Japanese in her meeting with the Japanese manager for the sake of her own business goal as well as because of the manager's low English proficiency.

The following excerpt explains the interest of a non-Japanese business person who is a native English speaker. It paints a similar picture to the examples presented above, whereby his language management operates for the sake of similar interests in a daily business meeting. In AM2's department, he is the only foreigner out of twelve employees. His department was holding daily meetings to exchange information about twelve employees' schedules and work progress. At the morning meeting on the same day of the interview, the facilitator, a Japanese supervisor, was conducting the meeting in a mixture of Japanese and English as usual. But when AM2 took his turn to explain his schedule and information, he started speaking in Japanese from the beginning. In response to the question from the interviewer as to whether it is easier for AM2 to communicate in English with his Japanese colleagues rather than in Japanese, AM2 replied as shown below.

Example 3

Well, some people, for example, in my group, cannot speak English very well at all. And for those people, I think I should speak Japanese, because I need to communicate with them. And even the people who cannot speak English very well, we end up speaking in Japanese, an, just because it's easier to communicate yeah. (AM2)

AM2 noted his Japanese colleagues' low English proficiency as a deviation, because he could not communicate with them, designed the adjustment to switch the meeting language from English to Japanese, and implemented his adjustment even though his Japanese boss and colleagues were speaking English during the meeting. AM2 described his Japanese boss and colleagues as 'some people' to generalize AM2's language management to switch to Japanese in daily meetings. He also added his language switch to Japanese with other JBP outside of his department as a common practice.

The folowing example details an interaction between an Indian manager and a Japanese subordinate in the department meeting at CECL. IM3 has sixteen multinational subordinates and among those, one Japanese subordinate does not have sufficient English proficiency for communicating. IM3 described the situation when he had implemented the language switch into Japanese only for this Japanese subordinate against the company language policy to hold meetings in English.

Example 4

顔っていうか、あの人が理解してないみたいな、分かるので大体。みんなが、こうやってる人達と、すっごく画面だけ見ている人達とか。画面は英語で書いてあるから、日本人も英語は一応読めるんですけど。私、言ってること、ま、アクセントから問題があるかもしれないけど、言ってることが分かってないのかなと思うので、一応、聞いてみました。「分かりましたか。」って聞いて。皆の前で言えないかもしれないから、「なんとなく分かりました。」って言ったら、その「なんとなく」でも、私、もう1回、日本語で説明したんです。あの，私として、その人が理解してもらいたいので、言語として、どっちでもいいかなと思います。(IM3)

[Through his facial expression, I kind of gathered he didn't understand. There were people who were doing this, and there were people who were just looking at the screen. English was displayed on the screen, so Japanese people can at least read English. But I thought he–maybe because of my English accent–did not understand what I was saying, so, I asked him just in case, "Did you understand?" He answered, "I more or less understood." He might have not been able to answer the question in front of everyone, so even though his response was 'more or less,' I explained it again in Japanese. Well, as far as I am concerned, I want him to understand, so I feel like it doesn't really matter which language I use.]

IM3 noted a deviation from a Japanese subordinate who only looked at the monitor screen without looking at him when he was conducting a visual presentation in English. He noted the subordinate's lack of eye contact as a deviation, assuming his speech in English was not understood by the Japanese subordinate. IM3 evaluated the eye movement of his subordinate negatively, and designed the adjustment to ask his Japanese subordinate at the end of the English presentation whether he understood. After implementing his adjustment, he noted the response of the JBP as another deviation, and evaluated it negatively, assuming the JBP did not completely understand what he had said. Then, he designed the adjustment to reiterate what he had said in Japanese. For the purpose of managing his department to achieve the business goal, he implemented his own language management for his Japanese subordinate by breaking the official meeting rule. IM3 used Japanese language in his own interest in managing his Japanese subordinate, who was ten years older than him. Through his use of Japanese language, he has gained power to manage his multinational department as well as developed his professional career as an IT manager in a Japanese capital company. As of April 2019, IM3 has been assigned a higher position in the same company to manage many more multinational employees.

Corporate culture, which prioritizes time efficiency and goal achievement, gives power to NJBP to take leadership and switch the meeting language to Japanese to compensate for the low English proficiency of JBP. The power of the 'common' language rule of CECLs has been weakened due to the fact that employees choose Japanese over English for the sake of better business efficiency. It also confirms that language choices in the workplace are not done by static top-down power dominance of participants, but are dynamically spurred on by notions of efficiency, productivity, and corporate interests (Nekvapil & Sherman 2009).

4.2 Developing open communication

Previous research has shown that when working in the Japanese workplace using mostly Japanese, Japanese sociocultural norms prevent NJBP from stating their own opinions to senior JBP freely. In Japanese native situations, communication strategies for maintaining good relationships suggest the speaker's avoidance of confrontation of the conversational opponent in line with Japanese sociocultural norms (Noda 2004). And NJBP who were working in monolingual Japanese workplaces needed to follow the communication strategies to maintain good relationships. My interview data, however, revealed various communication strategies adjusted by NJBP who were working not only in multilingual foreign based companies or CECL, but also in monolingual Japanese companies to build close relationships with JBP without being tied to Japanese sociocultural norms.

A year after joining a monolingual Japanese company, CF4 implemented a language adjustment to solve a communication problem in her workplace. She noted her lack of friendly open communication with her Japanese colleagues even after one year with the company as a deviation, and evaluated her relations with Japanese colleagues negatively. She then planned to design adjustment to interact with her Japanese colleagues outside business hours. She has implemented the adjustment to communicate with them in informal settings repeatedly and evaluated her adjustment positively. After implementing the adjustment, she claimed to have gained confidence in herself to express her professional opinions even against her Japanese superiors, as well as gained her pragmatic competence to make better sales results than before.

Example 5

最初は、自分、多分考え方も、あの、全然、あのまだ中国的な考え方とか、全然日本の考え方じゃなくて。なんで、あの、昼も、仕事と一緒に、なきゃいけないのか。あとは、行ったら何を喋るんですかって、抵抗感あって、行かなかったです。それで1年間がずっと続いて、やばいと認識してまして。やっぱ、会話がないと、どうしても距離は縮めないです。[...]行き始めると、毎回行ってます、ほぼほぼ。日本の会社に入って初めて分かったのが、お昼と夜の飲み会は、ちょっと言い過ぎなかもしれないんですけれど、仕事と同じ重要ということが分かりました。そこで、あの、相手と自分の関係を見ているとかの、多いと思います。それから、多分、自信がつけて、はっきり言えるようになっているところもあると思います。(CF4)

[At first, I, maybe I still had that, a Chinese way of thinking, not at all a Japanese way of thinking. I thought, why should I spend even lunchtime with work colleagues? Even if I went out for lunch with them, I wondered what we would even talk about and so I was reluctant and didn't go. The situation continued like that for a year and finally I realized that it can't go on like that. Because, after all, without conversation, you can't really get closer. [...] Since I started eating out with them, I've been going out with them every time, almost. It's only occurred to me after I started working for a Japanese company, but socializing at lunchtime and having drinks after work, well, it may sound like an overstatement a bit, but I understood that they are as important as work. Through these, well, I think I'm often watching my relationships with other people. Since then, maybe, I think I gained confidence and learnt to express [my opinions] clearly.]

During the interview, CF4 described an interaction with her superior about a sales discount rate to her Chinese clients. CF4 had opposed the decisions made by her superior and convinced him. As the first salesperson who is in charge of growing Chinese market, she openly disclosed her counter-opinions to her Japanese superior with confidence. She thought she understood the demand of Chinese clients better than he did. When she spoke Japanese, she did not avoid confrontation with her conversational partner along with the Japanese sociocultural norm, but followed her Chinese norm that dictates using explicit speech style. In response to the questions in the follow-up survey conducted in 2019, CF4 explained that her assertive speaking style of communication, in which she wasn't afraid of friction with her boss, helped with her career development in the company. As of the spring of 2019, she was an overseas assistant sales manager in charge of a broad area of overseas markets with both Japanese and non-Japanese subordinates. In the monolingual Japanese workplace, CF4 was interested in developing her professional career and had built an open relationship with her Japanese colleagues through her assertive speaking style, which was different from her Japanese counterparts. On the other hand, she was using her native language, Mandarin, to deal with Chinese clients and had achieved better sales results than the Japanese sales employees of her company. Within the company, she was using Japanese language as part of her language repertoire to build open relationships and had proved her competence. As a multilingual speaker who can utilize her language repertoire, CF4 has influenced power relations between JBP and NJBP.

The second example using Japanese language to develop open communication was seen in a multilingual environment at an American capital multinational IT consulting company. TM5 used Japanese language as a communication tool without being tied to Japanese sociocultural norms. The corporate culture of his company was quite casual without making strict language rules. All the meeting rooms were equipped with colorfully designed furniture to enhance the free speech of employees in a relaxed atmosphere. TM5 used Japanese language when he spoke with Japanese clients as well as his Japanese superior whose English proficiency was not sufficient to communicate in English. TM5 was an account executive to provide IT solutions to major Japanese companies. His main responsibilities were to work as an intermediary between his client companies and his in-house IT specialist such as asking clients' demands, delivering the demands to an IT specialist to create the solutions, and providing the solution to the clients. TM5 described a negotiation in an in-house meeting with a Lebanese IT engineer and his Japanese superior being held on the same day as the interview. TM5 organized the meeting to discuss a solution to be provided to a client he was in charge of. He asked his Japanese superior who had sales career in a Japanese market to join the meeting to support him whenever he could not answer questions from the IT engineer.

Example 6

えっと二人とも年上でした。フラットじゃなかったんですけれども、ま、会社、基本が、けっこうフラットな感じなので。私の上司があまり英語、喋れないので、3人、日本語で。まあ、私は敬語を使ってたんですけど。上司は、ほとんど喋らなかったんですけども[...]もうひとりは、レバノン人です。ま、日本語、ペラペラですけど。外国人の方なので、もうちょっと、プログレッシブな感じの会話でした。「これが、もうちょっと情報も分からないと、こっち側、戦略できないので。理想的には、事前にもうちょっとインフォメーション欲しい。」とか強く言って。で、私が「ちょっと、そちらは分からないので、次回のミーティングで一緒に行けばと思います。そのミーティングで、あの、詳細を一緒に聞きましょう。」って話になって。[...]そうですね、ま、リラックスではないですけれども、けっこうプログレッシブな感じのコミュニケーションでした。(TM5)

[Well, they were both older than me. It wasn't flat, but the company was basically pretty flat. My boss can't speak English very well, so the three of us spoke Japanese. I was using the honorific form of Japanese. My boss didn't speak much, though. [...] And the other one was Lebanese. Well, his Japanese is fluent. Because he was a foreigner, the conversation felt a bit more progressive. He requested strongly "If we don't have a bit more information, we won't be able to make a strategy. Ideally, I need like a little more information beforehand." Then, I said something like, "I don't know much more, so how about we go to the next meeting [with the clients] together? We'll ask for the details together." [...] Well, it wasn't relaxing, but it was a pretty progressive communication.]

This interaction interview took place the day before TM5 left for a week-long vacation. TM5 was tasked with listening to the client's requests in detail and passing them on to an engineer in the company, but due to the fact that he could not work the following week, he noted the request from the engineer to bring information prior to the meeting with the client as a deviation, and designed the adjustment to react assertively in Japanese language. TM5 used Japanese language as a means to hold a meeting including his Japanese superior. But in fact, during the meeting, TM5 spoke mainly with the Lebanese engineer, adjusting his speaking style in an aggressive manner to negotiate with him. Thus, in his multilingual company, TM5 used various speaking styles of Japanese language to develop professional open communication not bound to Japanese sociocultural or sociolinguistic norms.

Moreover, TM5 shed light on the use of honorific forms of the Japanese language. In interactions in Japanese language that take place in workplaces, the choice of Japanese honorific and plain (non-honorific) forms is governed by sociolinguistic variables and sociocultural norms where hierarchical differentials and power relations are clearly manifested. TM5 implemented his adjustment to use honorific forms to speak with his Japanese superior in his less hierarchical workplace.

Another comment by TM5 concerning a Japanese honorific form suggests his linguistic norm for speaking with JBP. He described a dialogue between two Japanese colleagues which he had observed in a casual in-house meeting. TM5 noted that a Japanese colleague of his used a speech style lacking in honorific forms toward the elder colleague as a deviation from his Japanese linguistic norm, and evaluated the young colleague's Japanese speech style negatively.

Example 7

私は言ってないですけど、ちょっと失礼かなと思ったんです、正直、残念ながら。27歳のほうが33歳の人に、「これは考えた方がいいんじゃない？」って感じで言ったら、隣のみんなが、「ううっ、大丈夫かな。」って感じになったんですね。[...]外国人が日本に来て、英語とか使ってて、敬語を使わなくても問題ないと思います。日本人ってラベルがつけられたら、まあ、あの、イメージが悪くなったり。(TM5)

[I didn't say anything, but frankly I thought he was a bit rude, unfortunately. When the 27-year-old said to the 33-year-old. "Don't you think you should rethink this?" everyone around felt. "Well, is that okay?" [...] I think there is no problem if foreigners who come to Japan are speaking English or Japanese without using honorifics. But when labelled a native Japanese speaker, well, that person's image gets tarnished.]

For TM5, honorific form of Japanese language does not mean a manifestation of a hierarchical power but a speech style to be used with elder/superior Japanese. In Japanese monolingual workplaces, JBP frequently assess the communication skills of NJBP through the usage of Japanese honorific forms based on the Japanese linguistic, sociolinguistic, and sociocultural norms. Conversely, in a less hierarchical multinational American capital company, this assessment aspect of usage of Japanese honorific form was different. A non-Japanese business person assessed his Japanese colleague's Japanese speaking style towards older Japanese colleagues negatively from Japanese linguistic norms. But this assessment was implemented only in the case of Japanese native situations, not contact situations.

4.3 Fostering informal in-group solidarity

This study has shown examples that NJBP are using various Japanese speaking styles according to their own interests. The interlocutors with whom NJBP use Japanese language are not limited to JBP, but also include NJBP who are culturally and linguistically diverse. NJBP utilize Japanese as a lingua franca to adjust the power relations to foster an informal in-group solidarity. This section shows examples of two NJBP working in multilingual workplaces.

CF6 speaks English, Chinese, and Japanese at the CECL where she works. In her business hours, she uses Japanese to deal with domestic Japanese clients. But when she interacts with her colleagues during lunch breaks, she chooses languages according to her companions. She described her informal interaction with her colleagues during the lunch break on the same day as the interview. She spoke Japanese with two Chinese, one American, and one Japanese colleague. When the interviewer asked CF6 why she spoke Japanese even though her Japanese colleague could speak English fluently, she answered the following.

Example 8

外国籍の同僚と一緒にランチする時、英語で喋ってます。中国人の同僚とだけ話す時は中国語、日本人がいると日本語。一応、働いている中で、周りもほとんど日本語使っていますので、あの英語圏の方、うまく喋れなくても、なんとなく分かります。多分、日本人に対しては日本語で話した方がいいかなと思います。(CF6)

[I speak English when I have lunch with foreign colleagues, Chinese when talking with only Chinese colleagues, and Japanese when there is a Japanese person present. As people around me use mostly Japanese language at work, even those, who are from English-speaking countries and do not speak Japanese fluently, can more or less understand Japanese. I think that it is better to talk to Japanese people in Japanese.]

In her informal socializing, CF6 uses Japanese language with her Japanese colleagues regardless of their English proficiency. CF6 is interested in using Japanese language with her Japanese colleagues as a lingua franca to perfect her competence in a host country's language, as well as to protect her non-Japanese networks by speaking English with her non-Japanese friends. Ironically, in CECLs, NJBP use Japanese language as a lingua franca with JBP, but outside of the surveillance of CECLs, they speak English as a lingua franca excluding JBP.

Meanwhile, Kubota (2016) has suggested that English used as a lingua franca does not always function well with people from non-English dominant countries. The interview with CF6 showed the example that a Chinese employee did not use English language to communicate with her Korean employee. In informal settings, CF6 did not use English, but Japanese to communicate with Korean colleagues as an alternative language to English. When explaining why she used Japanese with her Korean colleagues in informal settings, CF6 said she often felt it difficult to make friends with Korean nationals in her informal English-speaking network. Thus, she spoke Japanese as a lingua franca. Yet, Japanese used as a lingua franca also does not always function well with people from cultures that use honorifics and those that do not. When CF6 was using Japanese language with her Korean colleague, she noted a comment of the Korean colleague as a deviation, and evaluated it negatively. The following excerpt describes her adjustment to exclude her Korean colleague from her informal in-group network. When a non-Japanese business person from another department left the company, CF6 wrote a short message to an older Korean colleague who was working with that person in the same department.

Example 9

韓国人の先輩がいる部署の外国人が辞めると聞いて、その人に、「あの人は、どこに行くの？」って、メッセで聞いたら、「私が先輩なのに、なんで敬語使わないの？」って返してきて、びっくりして、「え？」って。別にオーストラリア人とか、インドネシア人は、そこまで気にしてないです。[...]返事しませんでした。彼は1コ上ぐらいです。その人と廊下で会いましたけど、無視して。それから話してません。(CF6)

[When I heard that a foreigner in the department where I have an older Korean colleague was quitting, I asked him in a short message, "Where is the person going?" and he replied, "I'm your senior, why don't you use honorific language?" and I was so surprised, "What?" I thought. I don't think Australian or Indonesian colleagues are that bothered. [...] I didn't respond. He was about a year older than me. After that, I saw him in the hallway but ignored him. Since then, I've never spoken to him.]

In her informal Japanese communication, CF6 did not use the Japanese honorific forms from her communicative norms. Having assumed her Korean colleague shared the informal communicative norm just like other NJBP, CF6 contacted him in Japanese. Contrary to her expectation, the Korean colleague evaluated her non-honorific forms of Japanese negatively, pointing out the lack of politeness towards her senior. CF6 noted that as a deviation from her communicative norms in informal networking, and implemented her adjustment not to respond to his comment and ignored him. She uses language as a means to form her different in-groups and foster the informal in-group solidarity.

It is important to consider the fact that many NJBP have traveled widely in their careers and have experience with multiple cultures as well as with some general business culture norms. When these differences have to be negotiated ethically within the in-group, there is the example that NJBP use Japanese, a language of the host country, as a lingua franca, to foster their multinational informal in-group solidarity. VF1 has kept her in-group community with four multinational colleagues by having lunch together every week since she joined the company. Inside her community, she uses Japanese with her friends regardless of nationality. During the interview, she explained about her long-lasting socializing lunch meeting with her multinational colleagues.

Example 10

すごい気持ちが伝わるから色々相談します。ひとりはタイ人です。その先輩と私は外国人どうしですけど、日本語で喋ってるんですよ、英語じゃなくて。日本語はスゴイ丁寧じゃないですか。だから、人、落ち着くと言うか。[...]先輩も自分の言いたいこと全部私に言うから、私も全部言ったら、多分喧嘩になるんじゃないですか。他の日本人の先輩だったら、多分、なんか黙ってくれると言うか、言わなくなります。でも、その外国人の先輩とだったら、私が、あまり言わなくなります。(VF1)

[I'm very comfortable talking about various topics with them. One friend is Thai. This older colleague and I are both foreigners, but we use Japanese, not English, when talking together. I think the Japanese language is so polite. People feel calm when they speak Japanese. [...] My older [Thai] colleague tells me everything she wants, so if I also told her everything, it would probably lead to a quarrel, right? With my Japanese seniors, if I were to complain about something to them, they would probably hold back their opinions, or just say nothing. But with this Thai colleague, if she complains to me about something, I don't say much.]

VF1 spoke Japanese as a lingua franca to adjust power relations with her multinational friends. She said her Japanese speaking style depended on her interlocutor. When she speaks with Japanese friends, she feels like expressing her opinion aggressively with maintaining mutual relations with her Japanese friends who listen to her opinion quietly. Whereas when she speaks with her foreign friends, she plays a role of listener to make good relations. As Fan pointed out adjustment behaviors used by native Japanese speakers for collaborative conversations can be seen even in Japanese conversation among non-native Japanese speakers as well (Fan 1999). A non-Japanese business person speaks Japanese as a lingua franca to foster her in-group solidarity. VF1 speaks Japanese not only for the Japanese, but also for herself to live with people from different cultures in a society. As of April 2019, VF1 was married to a Japanese and enjoying her career in the same company while expanding her networking.

4 Conclusion

NJBP use Japanese language to communicate with both JBP and NBP as motivated by their own interests in their daily interactions, through which new power relations seem to be generated in the workplace. Some of the NJBP's language management described in interviews seemed to be practiced by the NJBP repeatedly in their daily life. Looking at NJBP's strategic use of Japanese language at work, we see several underlying interests behind their language management.

Firstly, one common interest involves a desire to increase efficiency of communication and accomplish work-related goals by speaking Japanese with JBP. Some NJBP are actively using Japanese to compensate for JBP's lack of English skills. This tactic of NJBP to impose their Japanese proficiency on JBP is capable of bringing about a shift of power relations taking away the power of JBP as native Japanese speakers. Moreover, a company policy of CECLs which enhances business efficiency has led NJBP to use Japanese language in daily interaction against the language policy of CECLs. CECLs tend to assess the achievement of their own language policy by the fact of the increase of their employees' TOEIC scores. However, in order to develop efficient and sustainable language policy in the future, it may be essential for CECLs to scrutinize how the employees use languages in their daily interactions in the workplace.

Secondly, NJBP spoke in Japanese, one part of their language repertoires, in the interest of developing open communication with their business counterparts. Some NJBP implemented language adjustment to state explicit counter opinions against their Japanese superiors rather than to conform to the preference for avoiding confrontation based on the sociocultural and sociolinguistic norms of JBP. NJBP's interest in developing open communication to establish good relations with their business counterparts makes NJBP use various speaking styles in Japanese. The follow-up survey showed the fact that NJBP who continued to develop their careers in Japanese companies have not necessarily been making adjustments in accordance with Japanese pragmatic norms dictating that speakers hide their own discomfort to avoid any confrontation. Furthermore, NJBP's use of Japanese honorific forms are not always tied with Japanese sociocultural norms but used from the pragmatic norms of NJBP. Japanese language textbooks explain the usage of honorific forms in the context of power difference along with suggestions for using an indirect speech style to protect the face of power holder. However, a use of Japanese honorific forms in accordance with power relations shown in the Japanese language textbooks is not always in line with the pragmatic norms of NJBP at contact situations in multilingual environments.

Lastly, NJBP use Japanese as a lingua franca in the interest of fostering their in-group community's maintenance of good relations in the multinational in-groups to which they belong in Japan.

NJBP use Japanese language at work in a wide variety of Japanese language styles in accordance with their pragmatic norms, which are not always aligned with those of Japanese sociolinguistic norms or Japanese sociocultural norms.

And, such various styles of Japanese language seem to be empowering NJBP to influence power relations in Japanese companies.

Japan is one of the first countries in the world to face a rapid decline in population. Japan's working age population will be rapidly declining in the coming twenty years, with the largest decline occurring in the age group of between 35 and 44 years old. The average number of years of work experience for this age group is about fifteen, which in most cases corresponds to middle managerial positions (Nakamura 2020). In human resource management, Japanese companies have been weighing team responsibility focusing on training middle managerial positioned employees to gain organizational management skills. When a number of multinational employees will be in middle managerial positions in Japanese companies, how will Japanese companies manage their multinational organizations? Japanese government and companies need to draw a picture to build strong organizations as well as to establish Japanese language policies in the workplace aimed at not only the management of workplace efficiency, but also at developing collaborative organizations. As this chapter suggests, NJBP are using Japanese language in various speaking styles for their own interests. As we think about the future of Japan, we can learn a lot from the present interactions of the NJBP, who will be a part of Japanese society in the future.

This study has focused on NJBP's interests analyzing NJBP's adjustments in Japanese language based on LMT. However, to enrich the research on Japanese language use in the workplace, the other side of the interactions, the experiences of JBP, also need to be studied to gain a clearer picture of communication in the workplace in Japan.

References

Aibara, S. (2009) Bijinesu sesshokubamen ni okeru Nihongo bogowasha to gakushūsha ni shōjiru mondai: Kaigai de Nihongo o shiyō suru Nihongo bogowasha no shiten o saguru [Problems that arise in business discourse between native and non-native speakers of Japanese]. *Matani ronshū* 3, 49–77.

Aibara, S. (2012) Bijinesu sesshokubamen ni okeru Nihongo bogowasha no mondai ishiki [Problem awareness regarding Japanese native speakers in business discourse]. *Waseda Nihongo kyōikugaku* [Waseda Studies in Japanese Language Education] 11, 109–133.

Amelina, M. (2010) Do other languages than English matter? International career development of highly-qualified professionals. In B. Meyer & B. Apfelbaum (eds) *Multilingualism at Work: From Policies to Practices in Public, Medical and Business Settings.* Amsterdam: John Benjamins, 235–252.

Bargiela-Chiappini, F. & Nickerson, C. (2003) Intercultural business communication: A rich field of studies. *Journal of Intercultural Studies* 24 (1), 3–15.

Cabinet Office (2019) Kigyō no gaikokujin koyō ni kansuru bunseki: Torikumi to kadai ni tsuite [Analysis of foreign employment in companies: Initiatives and issues]. *Seisakukadai bunseki shirīzu* [Policy Issue Analysis Series] 18. On WWW at https://www5.cao.go.jp/keizai3/2019/09seisakukadai18-6.pdf. Accessed September 26, 2021.

Canagarajah, S. (2017) *Translingual Practices and Neoliberal Policies: Attitudes and Strategies of African Skilled Migrants in Anglophone Workplaces.* Berlin: Springer. doi: 10.1007/978-3-319-41243-6_1.

Fairbrother, L. (2015a) The management of language and power in intercultural contact situations in Japan. *International Journal of the Sociology of Language* 232, 59–78.

Fairbrother, L. (2015b) Language management in the Japanese workplace. In W. V. Davies & E. Ziegler (eds) *Language Planning and Microlinguistics: From Policy to Interaction and vice versa.* London: Palgrave Macmillan, 186–203. On WWW at https://doi.org/10.1057/9781137361240. Accessed March 8, 2021.

Fairbrother, L. (2015c) The 'multiform' linguistic, sociolinguistic and sociocultural practices of plurilingual employees in European multinationals in Japan. *The Japanese Journal of Language in Society* 18 (1), 162–175.

Fairbrother, L. (2018) The management of everyday English interactions in the Japanese branches of European multinationals. In T. Sherman & J. Nekvapil (eds) *English in Business and Commerce: Interactions and Policies.* Berlin: De Gruyter Mouton, 149–171.

Fairclough, N. (1989) *Language and Power.* New York: Longman.

Fan, S. K. (1999) Hibogowasha dōshi no Nihongo kaiwa ni okeru gengo mondai [Language problems in Japanese conversations between non-native speakers]. *The Japanese Journal of Language in Society* 2 (1), 37–48.

Jernudd, B. H. & Neustupný, J. V. (1987) Language planning: For whom? In L. Laforge (ed) *Actes du Colloque international sur l'aménagement linguistique / Proceedings of the International Colloquium on Language Planning.* Québec: Les Presses de l'Université Laval, 69–84.

Kimura, G. C. (2014) Language management as a cyclical process: A case study on prohibiting Sorbian in the workplace. *Slovo a slovesnost* 75 (4), 255–270.

Kondo, A. (2007) *Nihonjin to gaikokujin no bijinesu komyunikēshon ni kansuru jisshō kenkyū* [Empirical Study on Business and Communication between Japanese and Foreigners]. Tokyo: Hitsuji shobō.

Kubota, R. (2013) 'Language is only a tool': Japanese expatriates working in China and implications for language teaching. *Multilingual Education* 3 (4). doi:10.1186/2191-5059-3-4. On WWW at http://www.multilingual-education.com/content/3/1/4. Accessed March 8, 2021.

Kubota, R. (2016) Neoliberal paradoxes of language learning: Xenophobia and international communication. *Journal of Multilingual and Multicultural Development* 37 (5), 467–480. doi: 10.1080/01434632.2015.1071825.

Ministry of Economy, Trade and Industry (2016) *Heisei 27 nendo Ajia sangyōkiban kyōka tō jigyō hōkokusho: 'Uchinaru kokusaika' o susumeru tame no chōsa kenkyū* [Report on Project for Strengthening the Industrial Base of Asia in FY2015: Study on Enhancing 'Internal Globalization']. On WWW at https://warp.da.ndl.go.jp/info:ndljp/pid/10317643/www.meti.go.jp/meti_lib/report/2016fy/001029.pdf. Accessed September 26, 2021.

Ministry of Health, Labor and Welfare (2015) *Gaikokujin rōdōsha no ukeire ni kansuru jittai chōsa* [Survey on the Actual Conditions of Acceptance of Foreign Workers]. Kōsei rōdōshō shokugyō anteikyoku [Employment security bureau].

Ministry of Health, Labor and Welfare (2019) *'Gaikokujin koyō jōkyō' no todokede jōkyō matome (October 2019)* [Status of Reporting on the Employment of Foreign Workers by Employers]. On WWW at https://www.mhlw.go.jp/stf/newpage_09109.html. Accessed March 8, 2021.

Ministry of Health, Labor and Welfare (2021) *'Gaikokujin koyō jōkyō' no todokede jōkyō matome (October 2021)* [Status of Reporting on the Employment of Foreign Workers by Employers]. On WWW at https://www.mhlw.go.jp/stf/newpage_16279.html. Accessed December 17, 2021.

Ministry of Internal Affairs and Communication (2019) *Population Census 2019*. Statistics Bureau of Japan. On WWW at https://www.stat.go.jp/data/jinsui/2019np/pdf/gaiyou.pdf. Accessed September 26, 2021.

Ministry of Internal Affairs and Communication (2021) *Tōkei heddo rain 12 gatsugō* [Statistic Headline. December issue]. Statistics Bureau of Japan. On WWW at https://www.stat.go.jp/info/headline/pdf/202112.pdf#page=3. Accessed December 17, 2021.

Morita, L. (2018) Does doing things the Japanese way attract highly-skilled migrants? *Cogent Social Sciences* 4, Article 1430725. On WWW at doi.org/10.1080/23311886.2018.1430725. Accessed March 8, 2021.

Muraoka, H. (2002) Shitsumonchōsa: Intabyū to ankēto [Question surveys: Interviews and questionnaires]. In J. V. Neustupný & S. Miyazaki (eds) *Gengo Kenkyū no Hōhō* [Methods in Language Research]. Tokyo: Kuroshio shuppan, 125–142.

Nakamura, J. (2020) Gaikokujin rōdō (Tokushū Heisei no rōdōshijō) [Foreign labor (Special issue on labor market in the Heisei era)]. *The Japan Institute of Labour* 62 (4), 30–33.

Nekvapil, J. (2009) The integrative potential of language management theory. In J. Nekvapil & T. Sherman (eds) *Language Management in Contact Situations: Perspectives from Three Continents.* Frankfurt on the Main: Peter Lang, 1–11.

Nekvapil, J. & Sherman, T. (2009) Pre-interaction management in multinational companies in Central Europe. *Current Issues in Language Planning* 10 (2), 181–198.

Neustupný, J. V. (1995) *Atarashii Nihongo kyōiku no tameni* [Towards a New Japanese Language Education]. Tokyo: Taishūkan Shoten.

Neustupný, J. V. (2002) Language and power into the 21st century. A paper for the *International Conference on Language and Empowerment*, Malaysian Association of Modern Languages, Kuala Lumpur, Malaysia, April 11–13, 2002. On WWW at http://languagemanagement.ff.cuni.cz/bibliography. Accessed October 2, 2021.

Neustupný, J. V. (2003) Japanese students in Prague: Problems of communication and interaction. *International Journal of the Sociology of Language* 162, 125–143.

Nishinippon Shimbun (2018) Shin'imin jidai [New-immigrant era]. On WWW at http://nishinippon.co.jp/feature/new_immigration_age/article/418041/. Accessed March 8, 2021.

Noda, M. (2004) Hidden disagreement: Relation maintenance in the Japanese discourse of disagreement. In P. Szatrowski (ed) *Hidden and Open Conflict in Japanese Conversational Interaction*. Tokyo: Kuroshio shuppan, 95–123.

Norisada, T. (2012) Eigo no shanaikyōgo o kangaeru [Thoughts on English as an adopted official language]. *Kansaigakuin daigaku shōgakuronkyū* [Journal of Business Administration of Kwansei Gakuin University] 59 (4), 1–32.

Sei, R. (1998) Gaikokujin shain to Nihonjin shain: Nihongo ni yoru komyunikēshon o habamu mono [Foreign staff and Japanese staff: Barriers in business communication in Japanese]. *Ibunka Communication* [Intercultural Communication] 10, 57–73.

Tachikawa, M. (2013) Bijinesu komyunikēshon ni okeru ibunkakan konfurikuto e no taiō: Chūgokujin bijinesupāson no tairitsu kanri hōshiki kara [Intercultural conflict resolution in business communication: A study of conflict management styles in Chinese business people]. *Journal of Japanese Language Teaching* 155, 189–197.

Epilogue

Björn Jernudd

Some remarks on power in simple and organized language management

Abstract In this chapter, I will present a series of individual remarks regarding the relationship between power and language management. The first set of remarks will concern simple management, i.e., the management that occurs in individuals' discourse, face to face, and the second set relates to organized management. Throughout these remarks, I use 'power' to refer to the obligation created by a speaker to adjust a language expression in discourse, or the prescription regarding an individual's discourse implemented by an agency or another institution.

Keywords power, discourse, simple language management, organized language management

1 Introduction

This chapter consists of a set of remarks on power and language management, first in relation to simple management, i.e., the management that occurs in individuals' discourse, face to face, and then in relation to organized management (for a more extensive discussion of simple *vs.* organized management, see Nekvapil 2006: 96). In line with one of the themes of this volume, the main question I pose is that how power is exercised *on* discourse. In doing this, I will make reference to and consider the relationships between various sociolinguistic and communication theories and the language management process.

2 Simple language management and power

2.1 Power and communication accommodation theory

Noting differences in discourse interaction between oneself and others, evaluating and considering whether to adjust our utterances, possibly adjusting to our communication partners, possibly mutually, are accommodation behaviors (on accommodation theory, as presented by Howard Giles and others (Giles & St. Clair 1979) in the 1970s, cf. Yan & Imamura 2017). It could be argued that any accommodation, either mutual or not, is at least in part motivated by the interactants' perception of the power differential between them. In mundane interactions, talk commences, participants note features of each other's speech, evaluations occur, and accommodations (i.e., adjustments) follow. Status, stance and identity are thus negotiated and 'happy communication' is accomplished. Communication accommodation theory (CAT) , however, points to a much more specific set of accommodation behaviors in light of power as a contextual factor in discourse management. The power potential between interlocutors is mutually signaled when, for example, "people in subordinate positions would converge to those in superordinate positions" (Giles & Ogay 2007: 297); and "divergence will occur the more group members feel their status in the intergroup hierarchy [in any society] is illegitimate and unfair" (Giles & Ogay 2007: 299). Power differentials are reflected in mutual adjustments by speakers to their interlocutors within the ongoing interaction, yet there is no explicit exercise of power. A vector of power may, however, be identified in speech when people, in CAT terms, over-, under- or contra-accommodate. To take but one example of over-accommodation, younger people (e.g., caretakers) may over-accommodate in communication with the elderly, even making adjustments of otherwise normal adult speech in the direction of baby talk. Such speech behavior on the part of caretakers is not merely patronizing, but even suggestive of inappropriately directive speech and controlling of the relationship (Coupland, Coupland, Giles & Henwood 1988: 9–10, 32).

2.2 Two cases of power as hegemony

2.2.1 Hegemonic battle: Which language to use?

A very curious case of obvious interest in maintaining communication, yet upsetting that goal in doing so, is reported by Tamah Sherman (2009: 92, 93). Participants in an encounter battle over which language to use in a given interaction: who will be victorious and force his or her interlocutor to his or her own variety selection. The very uselessness of this kind of battle (rather than facilitating ongoing communication) suggests that power is exercised, putting one's interlocutor in a situation where he or she must break off communication, create a standoff by using his or own selected variety, or submit to using the other selected variety. Sherman (2009: 78) attributes such behavior to 'a different set of norms for hosting, a hegemonic set'; and, yes, hegemony is realized as an exercise of power.

2.2.2 Hegemony by contempt

Evaluating a particular variety as 'dialect' or 'jargon' or 'worthless gibberish,' uncivilized, or irrelevant to current civil society, is an example of hegemony by contempt. The precise circumstances for such negative evaluation of a variety vary, as does the severity of proscription in discourse. The variety becomes invisible in the public context. Pervasive projection of contempt seriously damages its speakers' own interest in managing and even using their languages. Examples abound in the sociolinguistic, anthropological and language rights literature of first peoples' wholesale oppression by colonizers, often with this outcome (see for example de Varennes 2016).

2.2.3 *Dominance in speaking*

The discourse relationship between females and males, in the US and some European societies, is a much-discussed issue in the literature on power and language. Zimmerman & West (1975: 125) in their classic text, state that: "just as male dominance is exhibited through male control of macro-institutions in society, it is also exhibited through male control of at least a part of micro-institutions." In a review article, Kunsmann elaborates (2013: section 5.1): "As we have seen, one of the controlling mechanisms in micro-institutions is related to the strategy of interrupting. As men are interrupting more often than women, male dominance can be established in conversations. Thus, turns are claimed, topics are initiated and maintained by men or abandoned by women."

Devices by which men exercise power successfully in dyadic or group situations in which women participate are by controlling the right to speak, notably by interruption. Dominance in discourse through such speech behavior is not, of course, a feature limited to gendered male-female interaction, nor is this the only feature used to establish dominance. Kunsmann continues (also 5.1): "questions may also be used as controlling mechanisms... questions require answers in many conversational situations. When questions in form of facilitative rather than polite or modal tag-questions, therefore, are combined with a specific statement they can be used to maintain or to control the direction of the conversation."

Happily, women's fight for gender equality is winning the day, both in speech and in endeavors. Kunsmann recognizes how the "controlling mechanisms" listed in the quote above applies generally in anyone's speech: "As women use this type of question more often than men, female dominance can be established."

2.2.4 *A knowledge differential between communication partners*

2.2.4.1 *Does better knowledge confer power in discourse?*

Power by virtue of differential knowledge in a role-relationship has been a topic of interest in discourse linguistics for some time. For example, Tannen discusses the question of power in discourse (1987: 4) in this way: "Thus doctors, lawyers, and teachers, in examining rooms, courts, and classrooms (respectively, of course) are doing business-as-usual on their home turf, while their clients pass through the system, often confused and always ignorant of the intricacies of the system. This suggests a problem inherent in understanding power in discourse." Tannen addresses the problem in the continuation of the above quote and with reference to another author: "As McDermott says it, 'meaning is really in the situation,' and most of what people understand in interaction can't be located in the words spoken."

"If knowledge is to be taken as a form of power," writes Fairbrother (2009: 135), then using language that expresses that knowledge is an exercise of power. It may seem reasonable to suggest that a speaker with knowledge 'has' power in relation to an interlocutor. This power would emanate from performing one's role as *knowledgeable*, as an expert in relation to an interlocutor, about the topic at hand, by using role-specific professional language, whether innocently or unwittingly performing that role appropriately. However, one may think of knowledge as a source of power in a different manner. A speaker's use of role-specific expressions may solicit the interlocutor's next turn request for an adjustment in the very weak sense of seeking clarification of what an expression means. In such an exchange of turns, the first speaker does not oblige the adjustment of the second speaker's speech. It would be a contradiction of the role relationship and of the very purpose of the interaction to interpret such a request by the second speaker as submitting to power. Or the second speaker may remain passive, possibly evaluating the professional speech as inadequate for the resolution of the issue at hand. Worse, the first speaker may deflect or not meet the request for adjustment by the second speaker. This is unfortunate, but I do not see how the perception of power in the role-relationship in question has changed; I do see how the second speaker ends up less informed, perhaps confused, and possibly ready to consult with another expert. Most of us leave things as they are when we talk, as we just want to get on with the transaction.

Much is being made of the 'power' role held in particular by a physician vis-à-vis the patient. Wherein lies the power here? I recognize my physician's greater knowledge and therefore authority and greater power over conditions relating to my illness, not over me, and with intent to cure me. I would not be there otherwise. Several of us are complicit in creating this interaction. The physician may be her sweetest and most apologetic self in our interaction and I will still submit to her authority. As a patient I respect the physician's sought-after knowledge and diagnosis and treatment, including, even, being ordered about.

The interaction attributes power by virtue of knowledge, of the role into which the physician is cast and supported by an institutional environment of the 'clinic' or the 'hospital.' The physician in the clinical environment has a very well-defined kind of power and it exists externally to discourse.

2.2.4.2 Is pre-adjustment by knowledgeable interlocutors an exponent of power in discourse?

The knowledge differential which is inherent in the expert-to-lay role-relationship has consequences for formulating discourse when one speaker makes the assumption that the other speaker is not his or her equal in disentangling the finer points of his or her expert discourse (cf. Fairbrother 2009; Sherman 2009). The first speaker may note and preemptively avoid such expressions as s/he evaluates to possibly be beyond his or her interlocutor's immediate comprehension. The first speaker accommodates to the second speaker by substituting any range of expressions, as adjustments, that keep the second speaker in the know, and that engage him or her as an active participant in moving the issue forward to a successful, actionable finish: whether taking the right prescription at the right time or installing the right kind of glass in the door to the veranda.

There is also the reciprocal of a knowledgeable speaker's adjustment to another's lack of specialist language. Nemoto (2009: 239) reports on participants' "I don't know what to say properly" and "my clumsy speech." This is self-exclusion, of avoiding speaking and participating altogether, because of feeling "clumsy" and "overwhelmed;" and evaluating one's own potential of speaking as in-advance-inadequate. If we name the listener who evaluates him or herself as a self-determined inadequate participant, then his or her interlocutor does not exercise power in this interaction—the first speaker pre-adjusts on the basis of his or her own perceived future inadequacy.

2.2.4.3 Questions as power in discourse?

As broad a behavior as some question-answer sequences has been linked to exercise of power. I have already referred to the use of facilitative questions above in male-female interaction (in some societies). Sociocultural and legal power may inhere in how a first turn speaker evaluates a second turn speaker's response in question-answer adjacency pairs in particular settings. Yoshimitsu (2009: 221) and Marriott (2009: 171) bring up interviewing, a question-answer exchange, as one such setting. However, is an interviewee's accommodation towards an interviewer's line of enquiry evidence of power imposition by the interviewer? Yes, one leads, the other responds, but the latter's agreed role is not to question. The situation is characterized by the interviewing situation's constraints, but it is not one of the exercise of power. In fact, it would be most disconcerting for an interviewer to learn that s/he has led the interviewee in a particular direction, or forced answers, precisely something that must not happen in interview situations.

3 Organized language management and power

3.1 States and language determination

The clear intent of exercise of power over speech communities occurs in a state as states implement *national* (*official*, labels are not important) language policies by regulation of situations of appropriate use of designated variety (or varieties). Power resides in a political authority. European history offers examples. (Re-)organizing states in Europe into nation-states, accompanied by an ideology of nationalism, broke up, subordinated or oppressed a multitude of small and unto-themselves-operating and -identifying communities, touting the preferred value of a national language, the one unifying, standard language. Industrialization hand in hand with radically transformed land use and a centralizing bureaucracy reinforced social and communicational change. A multitude of policies were implemented to nurture participation in this complex transformational socio-economic process, under a political umbrella of the ideology of nationalism.

As new states emerged during the middle of the previous century, equivalent processes unfolded when the state determined and funded development of a designated language. An example is Dewan Bahasa dan Pustaka (the Malaysian Language and Literacy Agency) to develop Bahasa Malaysia (on this agency, see also below.) I quote a mission statement for the Dewan formulated by its director (1957–1969) Tun Syed Nasir bin Ismail and as rendered in English translation by the Dewan:

> It is clear that language is not just an important factor in the national cultural constitution of a nation but it is also important in the nurturing of religious precepts. And it is equally clear to us who live in this independent nation that differences arising from the diversity of religions and cultures can be resolved with language as a tool towards national unity. (CITRA 2003, 2004: xiii)

The process through which members of society rallied around the national-language-in-creation, Bahasa Malaysia, remains unclear. The International Research Project on Language Planning Processes yielded some insights (Rubin, Jernudd, DasGupta, Fishman & Ferguson 1977). Prescribed usages must have been mandated in producing texts in government offices and companies, and of course in education. The Dewan took on projects to formulate norms for specialized areas of work, published broadly, and ran courses. It stands to reason that trainees and specialists would fall in line: through notings and subsequent adjustment to prescribed norms by reference to guidelines and prior texts, followed by routinization.

Agencies (of organized language management) are under orders to produce new language and make the population use it, but how individuals eventually appear to have adjusted accordingly remains subject to investigation. New usages consolidate when individuals make up a captive audience, such as bank tellers or civil servants or teachers, who are expected to follow normative guidelines; or when new entrants to writing follow norms of written language through which they learn and that surround them. Power is exercised by obliging adjustments according to prescribed norms.

Silencing someone by *pro*scribing the use of one language and *pre*scribing the use of another is the limiting case of exercising power by an organized language management authority. Lest we forget, there is no ambiguity about the direct exercise of power when schools were used to erase Otherness in many states, e.g., in Sweden (for nation-state policy directed at the Saamí in Sweden, see Elenius 2016), and in the US. In the US, young members of the first nations were removed from their native communities and placed in schools to undergo, by today's evaluation, forced assimilation. A certain Richard Henry Pratt had convinced the Bureau of Indian Affairs to open the Carlisle Indian School in Carlisle, Pennsylvania: "Transfer the savage-born infant to the surroundings of civilization and he will grow to possess a civilized language and habit," he wrote; more succinctly put, "Kill the Indian, Save the Man" (Yu 2009). These are violently discriminatory actions because they sought to erase Otherness (Swenson 2017).

3.2 States and language development

Besides managing variety selection, organized language management also controls a wide variety of kinds of language expression, such as terminologies, naming, spelling, unto which power is realized, e.g., by sanctions directed at inadequate usage or by mandated implementation. The agency charged with developing Malaysia's national language, Bahasa Malaysia, offers a paradigmatic example of the mission of such agencies at present. Its specific objectives have probably changed somewhat over the decades, but I reproduce here one version from 2003:

1. To develop and enrich the national language in all fields including science and technology.
2. To promote literary talent especially in the national language.
3. To print or publish or assist in the printing or publication of books, magazines, pamphlets and other forms of literature in the national language as well as in other languages.
4. To standardize the spelling and pronunciation of and to coin appropriate terminologies in the national language.
5. To encourage the correct use of the national language.
6. To encourage the extensive use of the national language for all purposes in accordance with the existing laws. (CITRA 2003, 2004: 9)

3.3 Implementation of public discourse thru schools

The state implements organized language management thru schools, to prepare individuals for specialized roles in society. Communication in bureaucracies, enterprises, in a most all-encompassing range of speaking and writing situations outside of narrowly private encounters, require language performance according to norms. I will refer to this set of norms as public discourse. Teleman, a Swedish historian of language cultivation, does not mince words: "Skolan är alltså en av de institutioner som staten betjänar sig av för att säkra samhällets fortbestånd" [The school is thus one of those institutions that the state puts to use to secure continuity of society] (Teleman 1979: 106).

Parents and peers control much of a maturing child's language environment. The growing individual will also soon be expected to adjust his or her own language to the language management demands by child care institutions and schools. The child will take for granted care-givers' and then teachers' invitations to adjustment in discourse and in education, being essentially socially powerless, while being controlled. Public discourse constitutes and maintains the societal order, and the young are socialized into its language[s] (and society) foremost by schooling (see Hirsch, Jr. 2016), by being taught content while at the same time acquiring constitutive vocabulary and phraseology, including the ability to organize one's discourse, i.e., of disposition and formulation. In his book *Språkrätt*, Teleman (1979) unveils how schooling manages language use by the young. *Språk* is *language*, and as for *rätt*, I give it two interpretations, as

- on the one hand, *'has a right'*
- on the other *'is correct.'*

There is a relationship between the two interpretations, because individuals in contemporary societies:

- have a right to education (thus, to language education)
- in order to acquire norms of language use, and
- to perform adequately according to those norms.

Different types of language management issues arise in this educational process. Teleman classifies these as follows:

(1) Normkonflikt [norm conflict]
(2) Normlucka [norm gap]
(3) Maskineriet strejkar [the machinery doesn't work]

3.3.1 Norm conflict

Paraphrasing Teleman, *norm conflict* (1979: 120) typically occurs—and the context here is school—when the pupil follows private norms but teachers demand that the pupil generates discourse according to public norms. Obvious examples are spelling deviations from codified orthographic norms due to the pupil's divergent phonology. Syntactic and especially stylistic differentials between pupils' written efforts and public norms pose considerable challenges to pedagogy while spelling deviations due to a mismatch between spelling and the pupil's pronunciation can be readily explained. One can only hope that teachers do not misuse their corrective power but instead offer insight into why adjustments would be advisable, however arbitrary they may seem to the person still in school. Otherwise, the pupil may feel that s/he cannot generate adequate, i.e., approved, discourse, thus avoids expressing her/himself. The pupil ends up writing about something else, not writing at all, or tries anyway (for copious examples in Danish and Swedish, see Teleman 1979: 121–128).

3.3.2 Norm gaps

Norm gaps (Teleman 1979: 129) to a lesser extent concern vocabulary, other than of course not having acquired some words, but also phraseology, idioms, idiomatic phrases, text structure, and much else. As to gaps in vocabulary, the pupil cannot express content adequately, and therefore generates a meagre or just plain inadequate expression (for examples in Danish and Swedish, see Teleman 1979: 129–136).

3.3.3 *Machinery doesn't work*

The *machinery doesn't work* (Teleman 1979: 136) happens when the pupil cannot apply norms which he or she is aware should be applied. The pupil tries but loses control one way or the other of formulating him or herself, whether in speaking or writing. This example may serve: "ville se efter vem som hämtade det var;" my translation 'wanted to find out who collected it was.' Two possible formulations got mixed up (Teleman 1979: 136).

3.4 Implementation of norms beyond school

From babyhood, an individual is exposed to more or less rigorous norms for language use. Parenthetically, most people are not aware of the organized language management agencies that produce public language norms. Norm-giving and -authorizing agencies abound, language advisory services may not abound, but surely surround us in daily life.

Individuals turn to these agencies to request evaluations and adjustments, overwhelmingly to find consolation in what they accept as 'correct,' thus there is no question of sanction having to be exerted. Yet sanctions are subtle little devils when it comes to using 'correct' language. These agencies' output carries the authority of the norm, made visible by deviations, and the benefits of managing these deviations accrue differentially across the speaking and writing population (Beneš, Prošek, Smejkalová & Štěpánová 2018; Jernudd 2018). As an individual commits to an adjustment, the norm authority's power is consummated. And so it goes. We witness a process of circular cumulative causation (Myrdal 1968, III).

The Prague School pioneered an understanding of standard language. I need not go into its motivations and character, other than to also refer to three stylistic characteristics that Teleman attributes to public language: its impersonality, its standardization, and its complexity; all three closely motivated by the functioning of the kind of society that public language serves (Teleman 1979: 66 ff.). That kind of society is one in which: "The writing classes manage and develop public language. This means that those classes exercise power over the use of [public] language" (Teleman 1979: 69, translation mine). Once an adult, the individual unremarkably submits to language management demands. Few contest the adult's submission to the power of social institutions, to norms upheld by the same. Thus society is constantly (re)constituted. A necessary good, if not good it is the harsh reality, despite implications of inequality and exclusion (cf. Karlberg 2005).

3.5 Power by constraints on discourse

There is also imposition. The Trump administration in the US issued directives (Eilperin & Sun 2017) that list and negatively evaluate expressions to be avoided in use in several government documents. For example, "employees at the Department of Health and Human Services were told to avoid certain words—including "vulnerable," "entitlement" and "diversity"—when preparing requests for next year's budget." Such editing brings to mind the Newspeak scenario (Orwell 1949). Power is exercised by obliging noting a language expression listed by authority and—aware of its negative evaluation by a government agency as recipient of any text being formulated with it—adjusting to its recommended replacement, or reformulating. I am reminded of the early years of replacing male-referencing vocabulary, say, *fireman* to *firefighter,* in the interest of advocating gender equality (DeFrancis 1994). This much gentler process of noting mobilizes gender awareness and an expectation that (in this case: the Honolulu local government) documents are edited to conform. The requirement of using particular vocabulary items in particular documents within local government may demand compliance—although the sanction in such a case would probably be limited to a rewrite.

Quite severe, however, is the recent enactment of a law in Poland that prescribes avoidance of expressions, thus implementing censorship of use of specific phrases, as one component of a broader prohibition, "banning people from accusing Poland of Holocaust atrocities." The Polish government prohibits language "referring to concentration camps as 'Polish death camps' " (Noack 2018).

4 Concluding comment

Errare humanum est. Whether we interpret this in the Pope's meaning that forgiveness, then, is divine, or perhaps even in Seneca's meaning that, then, persisting is diabolical, the simple truth is that talk channels every interpersonal relationship. Interpersonal dominance, power if you like, will also so be channeled and sought to be accomplished by managing one's own speech and possibly interfering in another's speech. Language Management Theory models and strives at understanding in depth how speech is generated and managed—this chapter's topic of power in discourse included.

Interestingly, institutional power to oblige adjustment and eventually routinization of choice of variety is limited because talk must be overheard to be sanctioned, that is to say, to be noted by a particular other as the negatively evaluated variety in use. That simply cannot be done on a 24-hour basis. Writing, however, is visible and therefore accessible to control. We shall keep talking as we please, yet we remain constrained by the necessity to navigate institutional requirements.

References

Beneš, M., Prošek, M., Smejkalová, K. & Štěpánová, V. (2018) Interaction between language users and a language consulting centre: Challenges for language management theory and research. In L. Fairbrother, J. Nekvapil & M. Sloboda (eds) *The Language Management Approach: A Focus on Research Methodology.* Berlin: Peter Lang, 119–140.

CITRA (2003, 2004) Kuala Lumpur: Dewan Bahasa dan Pustaka, Institute of Language and Literature.

Coupland, N., Coupland, J., Giles, H. & Henwood, K. (1988) Accommodating the elderly: Invoking and extending a theory. *Language in Society* 17 (1), 1–41.

DeFrancis, J. (1994) On degendering English. *Biography* 17 (3), 296–300.

de Varennes, F. (2016) Language, rights and opportunities: The role of language in the inclusion and exclusion of indigenous peoples. *International Journal on Minority and Group Rights* 23 (3), 281–305.

Eilperin, J. & Sun, L. H. (2017) Trump administration targets certain words and the bureaucracy pushes back. *The Washington Post,* December 20, 2017. On WWW at https://www.washingtonpost.com/national/health-science/trump-administration-targets-certain-words-and-the-bureaucracy-pushes-back/2017/12/21. Accessed April 2, 2020.

Elenius, L. (2016) Stiftsledningen och minoritetspolitiken [Church district management and minority politics]. In D. Lindmark & O. Sundström (eds) *De historiska relationerna mellan Svenska kyrkan och samerna: en vetenskaplig antologi* [The Historical Relations between the Swedish Church and the Sámi People: A Scientific Anthology]. Skellefteå: Artos, 469–515.

Fairbrother, L. (2009) Native speakers' application of contact norms in intercultural contact situations with English-speaking, Chinese-speaking and Portuguese-speaking non-native speakers of Japanese. In J. Nekvapil & T. Sherman (eds) *Language Management in Contact Situations: Perspectives from Three Continents.* Frankfurt on the Main: Peter Lang, 123–150.

Giles, H. & Ogay, T. (2007) Communication accommodation theory. In B. B. Whaley & W. Samter (eds) *Explaining Communication: Contemporary Theories and Exemplars.* Mahwah: Lawrence Erlbaum, 293–310.

Giles, H. & St. Clair, R. N. (eds) (1979) *Language and Social Psychology.* Oxford: Blackwell.

Hirsch, Jr., E. D. (2016) *Why Knowledge Matters: Rescuing Our Children from Failed Educational Theories.* Cambridge: Harvard Education Press.

Jernudd, B. (2018) Questions submitted to two language cultivation agencies in Sweden. In L. Fairbrother, J. Nekvapil & M. Sloboda (eds) *The Language Management Approach: A Focus on Research Methodology.* Berlin: Peter Lang, 101–117.

Karlberg, M. (2005) The power of discourse and the discourse of power: Pursuing peace through discourse intervention. *International Journal of Peace Studies* 10 (1), 1–25.

Kunsmann, P. (2013) Gender, status and power in discourse behavior of men and women. *Linguistik Online* 5 (1). doi: https://doi.org/10.13092/lo.5.1017. Accessed July 9, 2019.

Marriott, H. (2009) Japanese speakers' management of transference behaviour in an Australian context. In J. Nekvapil & T. Sherman (eds) *Language Management in Contact Situations: Perspectives from Three Continents.* Frankfurt on the Main: Peter Lang, 169–184.

Myrdal, G. (1968) *Asian Drama: An Inquiry into the Poverty of Nations.* Vol. 3. New York: The Twentieth Century Fund.

Nekvapil, J. (2006) From language planning to language management. *Sociolinguistica* 20, 92–104.

Nemoto, H. (2009) Negotiation of norms in academic contact situations. In J. Nekvapil & T. Sherman (eds) *Language Management in Contact Situations: Perspectives from Three Continents.* Frankfurt on the Main: Peter Lang, 225–243.

Noack, R. (2018) Polish president signs Holocaust bill, drawing rare U.S. rebuke. *The Washington Post*, February 6, 2018. On WWW at https://www.washingtonpost.com/news/worldviews/wp/2018/02/06/polish-president-to-sign-holocaust-bill-despite-international-concerns/. Accessed February 6, 2018.

Orwell, G. (1949) *Nineteen Eighty-Four: A Novel.* New York: Harcourt, Brace and Co.

Rubin, J., Jernudd, B. H., DasGupta, J., Fishman, J. A. & Ferguson, Ch. A. (eds) (1977) *Language Planning Processes.* The Hague, Paris & New York: Mouton.

Sherman, T. (2009) Managing hegemony: Native English speakers in the Czech Republic. In J. Nekvapil & T. Sherman (eds) *Language Management in Contact Situations: Perspectives from Three Continents.* Frankfurt on the Main: Peter Lang, 75–96.

Swenson, K. (2017) 'Long time coming': Army returns remains of Arapaho children who died at assimilation school. *The Washington Post,* August 9, 2017. On WWW at https://www.washingtonpost.com/news/morning-mix/wp/2017/08/09/a-long-time-coming-army-returns-remains-of-arapaho-children-who-died-at-assimilation-school-in-1800. Accessed August 27, 2017.

Tannen, D. (1987) Remarks on discourse and power. In L. Kedar (ed) *Power Through Discourse.* Norwood: Ablex, 3–10.

Teleman, U. (1979) *Språkrätt* [Right to Language]. Lund: Liberläromedel.

Yoshimitsu, K. (2009) Management of study differentials by Japanese students at an Australian university. In J. Nekvapil & T. Sherman (eds) *Language Management in Contact Situations: Perspectives from Three Continents.* Frankfurt on the Main: Peter Lang, 207–224.

Yu, J. (2009) *Kill the Indian, Save the Man.* On WWW at http://pabook2.libraries.psu.edu/palitmap/CarlisleIndianSchool.html. Accessed August 27, 2017.

Zhang, Y. B. & Imamura, M. (2017) *Communication Accommodation Theory and Intergroup Communication.* Online Publication Date: July 2017. On WWW at http://communication.oxfordre.com/view/10.1093/acrefore/. Accessed April 1, 2020.

Zimmerman, D. H. & West, C. (1975) Sex roles, interruptions and silences in conversation. In B. Thorne, & N. Henley (eds) *Language and Sex: Difference and Dominance.* Rowley, MA: Newbury House, 105–129.

Index

Prague Papers on Language, Society and Interaction
Prager Arbeiten zur Sprache, Gesellschaft und Interaktion

Edited by/Herausgegeben von Jiří Nekvapil, Tamah Sherman and Petr Kaderka

Vol. 1 Nekvapil, Jiří / Sherman, Tamah (eds): Language Management in Contact Situations. Perspectives from Three Continents. 2009.

Vol. 2 Wilson, James: Moravians in Prague. A Sociolinguistic Study of Dialect Contact in the Czech Republic. 2010.

Vol. 3 Barát, Erzsébet / Studer, Patrick / Nekvapil, Jiří (eds): Ideological Conceptualizations of Language. Discourses of Linguistic Diversity. 2013.

Vol. 4 Marián Sloboda / Petteri Laihonen / Anastassia Zabrodskaja (eds): Sociolinguistic Transition in Former Eastern Bloc Countries. Two Decades after the Regime Change. 2016.

Vol. 5 Lisa Fairbrother / Jiří Nekvapil / Marián Sloboda (eds.): The Language Management Approach. A Focus on Research Methodology. 2017.

Vol. 6 Marek Nekula / Tamah Sherman / Halina Zawiszová (eds.): Interests and Power in Language Management. 2022.

www.peterlang.com

www.ingramcontent.com/pod-product-compliance
Ingram Content Group UK Ltd.
Pitfield, Milton Keynes, MK11 3LW, UK
UKHW041825100926
8556IPUK00002B/21

9 783631 860618